Nuclear Waste: Socioeconomic Dimensions of Long-Term Storage

Also of Interest

* *Accident at Three Mile Island: The Human Dimensions*, edited by David L. Sills, C. P. Wolf, and Vivien B. Shelanski

The Nuclear Impact: A Case Study of the Plowshare Program to Produce Natural Gas by Underground Nuclear Simulation in the Rocky Mountains, Frank Kreith and Catherine B. Wrenn

The ELF Odyssey: National Security Versus Environmental Protection, Lowell L. Klessig and Victor L. Strite

The Political Economy of Arms Reduction: Reversing Economic Decay, edited by Lloyd J. Dumas

* *Dear Survivors*, John Burton

* *Science, Politics, and Controversy: Civilian Nuclear Power in the United States, 1946-1974*, Steven L. Del Sesto

The Socioeconomic Impact of Resource Development: Methods for Assessment, F. Larry Leistritz and Steven H. Murdock

Risk in the Technological Society, edited by Christoph Hohenemser and Jeanne X. Kasperson

Health Risks of Energy Technologies, edited by Curtis C. Travis and Elizabeth L. Etnier

Cancer Risk: Assessing and Reducing the Dangers in Our Society, Office of Technology Assessment

* Available in hardcover and paperback.

Westview Special Studies in Science, Technology, and Public Policy/Society

Nuclear Waste: Socioeconomic Dimensions
of Long-Term Storage
edited by Steve H. Murdock, F. Larry Leistritz,
and Rita R. Hamm

Critical in solving the nuclear waste problem are such issues as the techniques needed to equitably select waste repository sites; the implications for economies, populations, public services, social structures, and future generations in siting areas; the best means for mitigating short- and long-term public and private impact of repositories; and the type of citizen involvement that best ensures the full participation of national, state, and local interest groups in the siting process. The contributors to this book examine these and related issues, offering the perspectives of sociology, economics, philosophy, and political science and representing the differing views of various regions of the nation.

STEVE H. MURDOCK is associate professor and head of the Department of Rural Sociology, as well as associate professor of sociology, at Texas A&M University. F. LARRY LEISTRITZ is professor of agricultural economics at North Dakota State University. Dr. Murdock and Dr. Leistritz are authors of *Socioeconomic Impact of Resource Development: Methods for Assessment* (Westview, 1981) and *Energy Development in the Western United States: Impact on Rural Areas* (1979). RITA R. HAMM is a research associate in the Department of Rural Sociology at Texas A&M University. She is coauthor of the manuals *Socioeconomic Analysis of Repository Siting (SEARS): Guide to Data Base Preparation* and *Socioeconomic Analysis of Repository Siting (SEARS): Users Manual*.

Nuclear Waste: Socioeconomic Dimensions of Long-Term Storage

edited by Steve H. Murdock,
F. Larry Leistritz, and Rita R. Hamm

Westview Press / Boulder, Colorado

Westview Special Studies in Science, Technology, and Public Policy/Society

Published in 1983 in the United States of America by
Westview Press
5500 Central Avenue
Boulder, Colorado 80301
Frederick A. Praeger, President and Publisher

Library of Congress Catalog Card Number 83-60130
ISBN 0-86531-447-0

Composition for this book was provided by the editors
Printed and bound in the United States of America

Contents

List of Tables and Figures xiii
List of Contributors xv
Foreword *by Russell Youmans* xvii
Acknowledgments xxi

Introduction

An Overview of the Dimensions of Nuclear
Waste Management and Repository Siting
Steve H. Murdock, F. Larry Leistritz, and
Rita R. Hamm

Rita R. Hamm   1

The Nuclear Waste Problem   1
Scope of the Effort   4
Issues in Waste Management and Repository
   Siting   5
Organization and Content of the Work   12
Conclusion   15

DIMENSIONS OF THE NUCLEAR WASTE PROBLEM

1 Geologic and Engineering Dimensions of
   Nuclear Waste Storage
   Earl R. Hoskins and James E. Russell

   Earl R. Hoskins and James E. Russell   19

Nuclear Wastes: The Magnitude of the
   Problem   19
Alternative Storage or Disposal Systems   22
Alternative Storage Media   32
Conceptual Design of a Nuclear Waste
   Repository in Salt   34
Problems and Unresolved Issues   37
Summary   38

vii

2   Ethical Considerations Surrounding Nuclear
    Waste Repository Siting and Mitigation
    Ted F. Peters   41

    Issues of Uncertainty and Equity of Risk   . . .   42
    Issues of Equity   44
    The Issue of Intergenerational Responsibility .   50
    Implementation Ethics   53
    Conclusion   54

3   Federal, State, and Local Socioeconomic
    Management Dimensions in Nuclear Waste Disposal
    James R. Finley   57

    The Mined Geologic Repository Program   57
    National Waste Terminal Storage Program   58
    Repository Siting Process   58
    Management of Socioeconomic Impacts   62
    Socioeconomic Program Tasks   66

4   Legal Constraints to Repository Siting
    William C. Metz   73

    Basic Legal Framework   74
    Legal Site Precluders   83
    Legal Site Conditionals   85
    Other Legal Constraints   87
    Conclusion   89

5   Intricacies of the Nuclear Waste Problem
    Steve H. Murdock, Rita R. Hamm, and
    F. Larry Leistritz   91

    Population Dimensions   93
    Environmental Dimensions   94
    Technological Dimensions   95
    Organizational Dimensions   96
    Interfaces   98
    Conclusion   99

IMPACTS OF NUCLEAR WASTE STORAGE AND REPOSITORY SITING

6   The Socioeconomic Impacts of Repositories
    John K. Thomas, Rita R. Hamm, and
    Steve H. Murdock 103

    Factors Affecting an Assessment of
      Socioeconomic Impacts   103
    Overview of Socioeconomic Impacts   109
    The Socioeconomic Assessment Process   115

Conclusion 117

7 Assessing the Economic and Fiscal Effects
   of Repository Siting
   Robert A. Chase, F. Larry Leistritz, and
   John M. Halstead 119

   Economic and Fiscal Effects of Repository
      Development 120
   Methods for Assessing Economic and Fiscal
      Effects 128
   Conclusions 133

8 Assessing the Demographic and Public
   Service Impacts of Repository Siting
   Steve H. Murdock and Rita R. Hamm 135

   Demographic and Public Service Impacts 136
   Assessing Demographic and Public Service
      Impacts 143
   Conclusions 156

9 Assessing the Social Effects of Repository
   Siting
   John K. Thomas, Don E. Albrecht, and
   Steve H. Murdock 157

   Social Effects of Repository Siting 157
   Special Social Effects of Repositories 162
   Social Assessment Methods 163
   Integration of Research Methods 174

MITIGATION OF THE IMPACTS OF NUCLEAR WASTE
STORAGE AND REPOSITORY SITING

10 Resolving Problems in Repository Siting:
   A Review of Issues and Mitigation Measures
   John M. Halstead and F. Larry Leistritz 179

   Dimensions of Impact Mitigation 182
   Impact Assistance Legislation 189
   State and Industry Mitigation 192
   Summary 199

11 Planning for Impact Management: A
   Systems Perspective
   F. Larry Leistritz, John M. Halstead,
   Robert A. Chase, and Steve H. Murdock 201

Rationale for Impact Management Programs . . . 202
An Impact Management Framework 204
Impact Management--A Systems Framework 206
Program Implementation 219
Conclusions and Implications 221

12 Additional Considerations for Repository
    Impact Mitigation
    John M. Halstead and F. Larry Leistritz 223

    Addressing Fiscal Realities 224
    Addressing the Unique Effects of Repository
      Siting 226
    Conclusions and Implications 229

LOCAL COMMUNITY RESPONSE AND PARTICIPATION IN
NUCLEAR WASTE REPOSITORY SITING

13 Community Response to Large-Scale Federal
    Projects: The Case of the MX
    Stan L. Albrecht 233

    The MX System 234
    Community Mobilization 236
    Parallels with Nuclear Repository Siting . . . 243
    Conclusions 248

14 Community Development in Nuclear Waste
    Isolation
    Donald E. Voth and Billy E. Herrington 251

    Alternative Roles for Community Development . . 252
    Steps in the Community Development Process . . 254
    Community Development Alternatives for
      Nuclear Repository Siting 256
    Comparison of the Two Alternatives 260
    Summary 264

15 Citizen Participation in Nuclear Waste
    Repository Siting
    Robert E. Howell, Marvin E. Olsen,
    Darryll Olsen, and Georgia Yuan 267

    Public Participation in Large-Scale
      Developments 271
    A Theoretical Basis for Citizen
      Participation 277
    A Citizen Participation Program for
      Repository Siting 279
    Conclusion 287

Summary and Conclusions

**Socioeconomic Factors Affecting the Future of
Nuclear Waste Management and Repository Siting**
Steve H. Murdock, F. Larry Leistritz, and
Rita R. Hamm 291

    Summary 291
    Conclusions 296

References 307
Index 337

Tables and Figures

Tables

3.1 Site Suitability Criteria 61
3.2 Socioeconomic Program Tasks
     and Major Issues Raised by
     the Public 65
4.1 Summary of State Legislation on HLW 76
6.1 High-Level Nuclear Waste Repository
     Employment Requirements 106
6.2 Possible Standard Socioeconomic Impacts
     of Repository Siting 111
6.3 Possible Special Socioeconomic Impacts
     of Repository Siting 113
7.1 Energy Facility Employment
     Characteristics 121
8.1 Expected Workforce Requirements and
     Projected Project-Related Inmigration
     for Uranium and Plutonium Recycle Waste
     Repositories by Geographic Region and
     Geologic Media for Selected Years 139
8.2 Expected Public Service Requirements
     Associated with Inmigrant Populations
     for Uranium and Plutonium Waste
     Repositories in Salt Formations by
     Geographic Region for Selected
     Years and Services 144
9.1 Dimensions and Indicators of Social
     Impacts 170
10.1 Nuclear Waste Repository Impacts and
      Parallel Facilities' Impacts 181
10.2 Chronology of Federal Legislation
      Addressing Resource Development and
      Socioeconomic Mitigation 190
11.1 Measures to Reduce Inmigration 209
11.2 Methods of Financing Impact Mitigation . . . 213
11.3 Major Compensation Mechanisms 217
11.4 Chronological Sequence of Key Impact
      Management Activities 220

13.1   Attitudes Toward Deploying MX in Utah
       and Nevada by Respondent Categories 237
14.1   Community Development Approaches 252

Figures

1.1   Nuclear Fuel Cycle 21
3.1   NWTS Program Management Structure 59
3.2   Repository Siting Schedule 63
14.1 Causal Schema for Community
      Development 255

Contributors

Don E. Albrecht, Research Scientist, Department of Rural Sociology, Texas A&M University, College Station, Texas 77843

Stan L. Albrecht, Professor of Sociology, Department of Sociology, Brigham Young University, Provo, Utah 84701

Robert A. Chase, Research Associate, Department of Agricultural Economics, North Dakota State University, Fargo, North Dakota 58105

James R. Finley, Socioeconomic Project Manager, Office of Nuclear Waste Isolation, Impact Analysis Office, Battelle Project Management Division, 505 King Avenue, Columbus, Ohio 43201

John M. Halstead, Research Associate, Department of Agricultural Economics, North Dakota State University, Fargo, North Dakota 58105

Rita R. Hamm, Research Associate, Department of Rural Sociology and Energy Extension Instructor, Center for Energy and Mineral Resources, Texas A&M University, College Station, Texas 77843

Billy E. Herrington, Research Associate, Department of Agricultural Economics and Rural Sociology, University of Arkansas, Fayetteville, Arkansas 72701

Earl R. Hoskins, Brockett Professor of Geophysics, Geology, and Geography and Professor of Mining Engineering, Texas A&M University, College Station, Texas 77843

Robert E. Howell, Extension Sociologist and Chairman of the Department of Rural Sociology, Washington State University, Pullman, Washington 99164

F. Larry Leistritz, Professor of Agricultural Economics, Department of Agricultural Economics, North Dakota State University, Fargo, North Dakota 58105

William C. Metz, Manager, Energy Development Impact Analysis, Brookhaven National Laboratory, Building 475, Upton, New York 11973

Steve H. Murdock, Associate Professor and Head, Department of Rural Sociology and Assistant Director, Center for Energy and Mineral Resources, Texas A&M University, College Station, Texas 77843

Darryll Olsen, Research Associate, Department of Rural Sociology, Washington State University, Pullman, Washington 99164

Marvin E. Olsen, Professor of Sociology, Department of Sociology, Washington State University, Pullman, Washington 99164

Ted F. Peters, Associate Professor of Systematic Theology, Pacific Lutheran Seminary and The Graduate Theological Union, Berkeley, California 94703

James E. Russell, Brockett Professor of Mining Engineering and Professor of Geophysics, Department of Petroleum Engineering, Texas A&M University, College Station, Texas 77843

John K. Thomas, Research Scientist, Department of Rural Sociology, Texas A&M University, College Station, Texas 77843

Donald E. Voth, Professor of Rural Sociology, Department of Agricultural Economics and Rural Sociology, University of Arkansas, Fayetteville, Arkansas 72701

Georgia Yuan, Research Associate, Department of Rural Sociology, Washington State University, Pullman, Washington 99164

Foreword

This book examines the socioeconomic implications of nuclear waste management and repository siting primarily for rural areas in the United States, although broader, societal wide issues are also examined. The research on which it is based was not undertaken to encourage or discourage the nuclear industry in the United States, but rather to attempt to find solutions to a problem that must be addressed. Unquestionably, a method of waste isolation must be developed to protect the population and the environment since high-level nuclear wastes exist and will continue to be generated for at least the next two or three decades.

It seems most unlikely that a nuclear waste isolation site would be established in a metropolitan area--but where are the likely sites? Nuclear waste isolation will occur in rural areas. Because the rural areas of the American West and South are generally more sparsely populated than the rest of the nation, these are the likely places to look for hazardous waste sites. Given the national distribution of energy and other resources, many other large-scale projects will also likely occur in these regions.

Several of the issues addressed in this book are uniquely nuclear in nature. But much of this work would be helpful in assessing the many other types of large, long-term development projects occurring in rural areas. In this regard, this volume applies to energy, mining, water, and defense projects that dominate life in many rural communities across the nation.

The changes likely to occur in a rural area as a result of a repository are ones of high public interest-- at least locally. The type of facility discussed here is a very visible activity in a rural area. During the construction phase of such a facility, this activity may dominate all other events in the surrounding rural area. Employment during the operational phase will make the facility a major local employer--frequently the largest single employer in the area. The same magnitude of activity in even a small metropolitan area would not be nearly so visible, and so the rural nature of such issues also makes them local public issues.

Given a high level of public interest, questions arise as to who is going to make decisions about siting, who will influence these decisions, and about the type and quality of the information that should be used in making these decisions. This volume will help communities involved in the site determination process.

The siting issue is an important one for both local areas and the nation. Can a community veto a decision to site hazardous wastes nearby? Can we find a site that will satisfy national needs and yet not sacrifice local autonomy and the quality of local rural life? This book helps bring the issues surrounding nuclear waste management and repository siting more clearly into focus, and will hopefully help create awareness of the need for local issues to be resolved with the long-term interests of the community taken into account.

Because repositories will likely be placed in rural areas, the Department of Energy and their management team from the Office of Nuclear Waste Isolation at Battelle Laboratories looked to USDA and eventually to the land grant university system to identify research and extension personnel who were knowledgeable about the socioeconomic impacts of large-scale projects in rural areas and about the nature of and means to resolve economic, social, and political problems in rural areas. The land grant system provided flexibility in selecting researchers with specific socioeconomic interests that relate to large rural projects, regardless of their location in the nation. Thus, the Western Rural Development Center (WRDC) in conjunction with personnel from Texas A&M University and North Dakota State University helped in identifying appropriate university researchers across the nation to examine the socioeconomic dimensions of nuclear waste management and repository siting within a comprehensive DOE-sponsored project entitled the Socioeconomic Analysis of Repository Siting. This project, though headquartered at WRDC, is thus the result of a national research effort involving research and extension people in the Southern and North Central as well as the Western region of the United States. Several of the chapters in this book are derived in part from work completed directly for this project and nearly all of the authors are indebted to this project for initiating their involvement in the analyses of waste management and repository siting issues.

It is our hope that rural residents, researchers, local, state, and Federal decision makers, and other readers of this book will find it useful for gaining a greater understanding of the socioeconomic dimensions of nuclear waste management and repository siting and helpful in addressing issues related to many types of

major projects and their impacts on rural communities
throughout the United States.

Russell Youmans, Director
Western Rural Development Center
Corvallis, Oregon

Acknowledgments

In completing this work, the support and encouragement of several entities have been indispensable. The Department of Rural Sociology, the Texas Agricultural Experiment Station, and the Center for Energy and Mineral Resources at Texas A&M University and the Department of Agricultural Economics and the North Dakota Agricultural Experiment Station at North Dakota State University have provided extensive support and receive our sincere appreciation. We also express our appreciation to the Office of Nuclear Waste Isolation, the U.S. Department of Energy, and the U.S. Department of Agriculture for initiating our involvement in nuclear waste research issues.

We wish to thank the many persons who assisted in the preparation of the manuscript. Thus, the clerical and drafting assistance of Rosemary Friedrick, Lou Detherage, Kelly Creighton, Lori Cullen, Becky Dethlefsen, Ona Richards , RaeLynn Shattuck, and Michael Reinhard is gratefully acknowledged. We also wish to thank Patricia Bramwell for directing much of the manuscript preparation. We extend very special appreciation to Lynnette Spurrier who tirelessly typed the entire manuscript. Her dedication and competence made completion of the manuscript possible. We also wish to extend appreciation to our publisher, Lynne Rienner, for her assistance.

We also extend our appreciation to numerous colleagues who reviewed and suggested revisions that have clearly improved the manuscript. In particular, we wish to thank James Copp, Howard Ladewig, Donald Senechal, Banoo Parpia, Karen Maki, Thomas Stevens, Brenda Ekstrom, Arlen Leholm, and Eldon Schriner.

Finally, we wish to thank the contributing authors for their willingness to revise their chapters to comply with the overall themes and guidelines of the work.

Steve H. Murdock
F. Larry Leistritz
Rita R. Hamm

Acknowledgments

Introduction

An Overview of the Dimensions of Nuclear Waste Management and Repository Siting

Steve H. Murdock
F. Larry Leistritz
Rita R. Hamm

THE NUCLEAR WASTE PROBLEM

High-level nuclear waste management is a growing national concern with a long history of technical, social, and political controversy. As of 1980 there were roughly 77.4 million gallons of highly radioactive liquid wastes, 6,700 metric tons of spent nuclear reactor fuel, and 152 million tons of radioactive tailings left over from uranium mining and processing (U.S. Department of Energy, 1981b), and recent analyses (Office of Technology Assessment, 1982) indicate that over 72,000 metric tons of spent fuel will be produced by the nation's 74 operational nuclear plants and the 85 additional plants presently under construction by the year 2000. In addition, if a solution to the waste problem is not found, some plants may be forced to cease operation in the early to mid-1990s. Even if nuclear power generation was to cease immediately, the issues surrounding the management of high-level nuclear wastes would have to be addressed and decisions concerning their disposal or storage would have to be made.

The issues surrounding waste management are not new. High-level wastes have been produced as a result of weapons testing for over thirty years and from commercial nuclear power production for over twenty years. In fact, the most widely favored technical procedure for waste storage--mined geologic repositories (U.S. Department of Energy, 1980b)--was recommended as a means of waste storage over twenty-five years ago (National Academy of Sciences, 1957). Thus, despite years of concern and extensive analysis, an acceptable solution to the waste problem has not been obtained, and the Federal government has been unable to develop a comprehensive waste management policy with a broad base of support.

What is increasingly apparent, however, is that although many experts believe that there appear to be "no fundamental technical questions about the ability to design, construct and operate storage facilities" (Office of Technology Assessment, 1982: 22), and that

1

uncertainties concerning disposal are decreasing?

> . . . there is more to nuclear waste management
> than solving technical problems. The process
> by which decisions are arrived at and the
> degree of trust and mutual regard between
> levels of government and between citizens and
> their governments count just as much in
> determining the outcomes of struggles over
> nuclear waste . . . (League of Women Voters,
> 1980: 44).

For such management to succeed, experts also believe that
it is essential

> . . . to handle the broad policy and strategic
> issues as well as the social, political and
> institutional issues that concern states and
> local communities and other groups. It is the
> failure to address these kinds of issues, not
> just the strictly technical ones, that has
> undermined much of the credibility of the waste
> management program (Office of Technology
> Assessment, 1982: 32).

In other words, social science issues (broadly defined)
may be as, or even more, critical than technical concerns
in the development of successful high-level nuclear waste
management and repository siting policies.

The social science dimensions that bear on the
issues of waste disposal or storage are multifaceted and
complex, however. They include such dimensions as the
psychological and social psychological questions related
to the fears and anxieties likely to be created in local
residents who reside in close proximity to repository
sites; political questions about the role of various
levels of government and the potential role of Federal
and states rights in repository siting; economic
questions related to repository development, mitigation
and the local construction and operational impacts of
repository development; and demographic questions
concerning the potential effects of repository
development on population growth or decline. They also
include social and institutional questions about the
ability of society to create the institutional structure
necessary to insure the long-term management of a
repository and questions concerning the equity issues
likely to be raised by residents of regions selected to
receive repository sites and by various groups within
local siting areas. These and numerous other questions
require resolution if wastes are to be managed
effectively and equitably.

It is clear then that some of the most crucial
issues in high-level nuclear waste management raise

complex social science questions. There is thus an obvious need to describe, clarify and suggest solutions to some of the social science questions that affect waste management and repository siting.

Given the obvious significance of such social science issues for waste management, it is somewhat surprising that they have received such limited attention in the published literature. Although these issues have received relatively extensive attention in governmental and research center reports (Maynard et al., 1976; Greene and Hunter, 1978; Lindell et al., 1978; Hebert et al., 1978; Brenner, 1979; Cluett et al., 1979; Garvey, 1979; Rankin and Nealey, 1981; Murdock and Leistritz, 1981) and the literature on general nuclear questions, particularly as it relates to attitudes toward nuclear power, is extensive (Melber et al., 1977; Farhar et al., 1979; Rankin et al., 1982; Resources for the Future, 1980; Mitchell, 1979), little discussion of the specific social science issues related to nuclear waste management and repository siting has appeared in published form. In fact, this literature is not generally available commercially.

In addition, of the works that are available, most provide discussions concentrated on the societal-wide issues related to nuclear waste management (Hebert et al., 1978). Most efforts to date have thus failed to adequately examine yet an additional level of concern-- what a repository is likely to mean to those residents living near the repository site. How a repository site will affect such residents, how these residents can affect the siting process and what steps are available for mitigating local siting area impacts have not been adequately addressed.

Finally, much of the existing literature on nuclear waste, particularly that available from the Federal government, tends to reflect a limited number of points of view. Given the number of different perspectives that exist on nuclear waste and the wide range of alternatives available for addressing nuclear waste issues, works presenting a large number of diverse options and policy alternatives seem desirable, but few such works exist.

In sum, few publications that discuss the general social science issues related to nuclear waste, and that provide a diversity of perspectives on how such issues can be addressed, are available. In fact, none have examined such issues as they relate to local siting areas. Clearly, there is a need for additional efforts that examine both the general dimensions of nuclear waste management and the implications of repository siting for communities near potential repository sites.

SCOPE OF THE EFFORT

This volume addresses the need for additional discussions of the social science issues related to waste management and repository siting by first providing a general introduction to the technical, ethical, and socioeconomic as well as the management and legal dimensions of the nuclear waste problem (chapters 1 through 5) and then by focusing on three of the many social science areas of concern related to the implications of nuclear waste repository siting for local communities near repository sites. The three areas examined include the potential socioeconomic impacts of nuclear waste siting on communities near the repository site (chapters 6 through 9), the alternatives for and potential means of mitigating and managing the socioeconomic impacts of repository siting (chapters 10 through 12), and the role of citizen participation and community development in the repository siting process (chapters 13 through 15). Throughout the work, the intent is to provide a diversity of perspectives. It is left largely to the reader to evaluate the relative utility of the approaches presented.

This book, then, is an attempt to provide a single-source reference that presents a broad-based overview of the socioeconomic issues and dimensions of the nuclear waste problem with particular emphasis on repository siting. Its intended audience includes social scientists interested in the analysis of the impacts of high-level nuclear technology, private and public utility officials, state and local decision makers attempting to legislate and plan for the management of such wastes, and knowledgeable members of the public who wish to obtain an overview of the socioeconomic dimensions of the waste storage problem. The discussion in and the audiences for the work are broad, but its content is limited in several ways.

A major limitation of the effort relates to the substantive emphases of the work. It examines only some of the key social science issues related to siting. Specifically, its focus is on the economic, demographic, public service, fiscal, and social dimensions of the impacts, mitigation and public participation concerns related to nuclear waste management and repository siting. The psychological, political, philosophical, and similar concerns that are equally important are given only limited attention. It is, of course, impossible to adequately discuss all of the social science issues related to repository siting in a single work. Those chosen for emphases admittedly reflect the editors' and authors' areas of professional expertise and interest. They are clearly important areas of concern, but no claim is made that they represent all of the significant social science issues related to repository siting.

A second limitation results from the fact that after the general discussion in chapters 1 through 5, the work focuses its attention nearly totally on local siting area issues in the United States rather than on impacts, mitigation, or participation issues at the regional, national, or international levels. The discussion takes a localistic focus, and since most siting areas are likely to be rural, low density areas, the focus is on the likely effects of repository siting on rural communities. The discussion is thus largely limited (at least in the last three sections of the work) to local repository siting issues in rural areas of the nation.

Finally, the work may also be limited by the biases of its authors. That is, this book contains some chapters that are drawn from extensively revised versions of works originally completed as a result of contract work completed for USDA and DOE (see the Foreword). We believe these auspices have not affected the works in this book, but the auspices for these works must be acknowledged. In addition, nearly all of the authors are scholars from land-grant universities which are mandated to enhance and improve rural areas and ways of life through research and extension activities. As a result, a bias toward rural concerns and the preservation of rural areas is evident in several chapters. We believe overall, however, that the chapters in the work are not overly influenced by such factors and that the discussion is, in fact, better informed because of the experiences and backgrounds of the editors and authors.

ISSUES IN WASTE MANAGEMENT AND REPOSITORY SITING

Even with the limitations noted above, the focus and intent of this book are broad, involving discussions of numerous nonsocial science, as well as social science, dimensions of waste management and repository siting. The general dimensions examined include socioeconomic, technical, ethical and philosophical, legal, and political and management-related issues. The purpose of this section is to provide an introduction to the concerns and issues in each of these dimensions that are discussed in detail in the remaining chapters of the book. The intent is thus to provide a context for understanding the remainder of the text and to make the interrelated complexities of waste management and repository siting evident.

The Technical Issues

The technical dimensions of waste management and storage involve numerous complex issues. Among the most significant are those surrounding the types of wastes that should be stored or disposed of, the types of media that can best be used as storage media, how such wastes can be contained and transported safely to designated storage or disposal sites, and the best means of repository construction and management (U.S. Department of Energy, 1980b). High level nuclear wastes vary in form and in the periods over which they remain radioactive. These different forms of high level wastes are generally referred to as high-level wastes, transuranic wastes, and spent fuel from reactor operations. These wastes must be stored or disposed of, but whether reprocessing should be reinstituted and, if so, in what form, how long present and even expanded temporary storage can continue to house existing wastes, and wastes likely to be produced in the near future, are yet unresolved questions.

Further questions have been raised concerning the best media for storing wastes. Options examined include subseabed disposal, very deep hole disposal, rockmelting disposal, island disposal, ice sheet disposal, deep well injection disposal, space disposal, and mined geologic disposal. Mined geological disposal in bedded salts or salt domes is the most advanced and thoroughly analyzed form of disposal, but advocates of each of the other disposal forms and of the use of basalt, granite, tuff and shale media also exist.

There are yet additional questions related to the packaging and transportation of wastes. It is generally agreed that the wastes will require some treatment prior to packaging and that the packaging must be capable of acting as a barrier to radioactive nuclide mobilization and release into the geologic system, must allow for safe handling, and must preserve the ability to retrieve the waste safely throughout the repository demonstration period, but questions concerning the selection of the best substances (for example, metals, ceramics, glasses, and so on) to be used in manufacturing waste cannisters remain. The transportation dimensions are even more complex. Such transport is most likely to occur by rail, but the safeguards essential for the areas surrounding likely transportation routes and the probabilities and consequences of potential accidents in transit continue to be debated (Schilling et al., 1979).

Finally, some questions remain about repository design and construction. Should the design include a potential reprocessing facility with the repository? What will be the operational life of a repository? Should the construction schedule be lengthened or shortened? These and similar questions are yet unresolved.

The technical issues are, as noted earlier, closer to resolution than those in the social science area. They are not totally resolved, however, and a basic understanding of them remains a major requirement for examining the nuclear waste issue.

Legal, Political, and Management Issues

Many of the technical issues are inseparable from the legal, political and management issues of waste management. The siting of a nuclear repository requires not only that technical issues be resolved, but that solutions to such issues be obtained and implemented and a repository site or sites be selected. The key questions related to these dimensions include:

- What level of government and what entities at each level should make the repository siting decision?

- What should be the role of states and local areas in the siting process?

- How can the long-term management of repositories by insured?

- What legislation will be necessary to: (1) insure that a repository can be sited; (2) enable site area residents to be properly compensated for the potential costs and risks of repositories; and (3) establish a repository management structure that is adequately insulated from the political fluctuations that might prevent its adequate maintenance and monitoring?

The issues related to these dimensions are clearly complex. The conflicts between Federal and state governments over waste siting have existed for decades (Smith, 1979) and continue to be problematic. States often complain that Federal agencies fail to provide them with adequate knowledge of repository analyses and of potential siting decisions. Federal agencies are constrained by Congress, and congressional members are forced to attempt to resolve an issue that is perceived as having few desirable consequences, that requires a facility that few areas wish to host, and which raises continuing concerns about potential regional sacrifices for national gain.

Equally problematic, state involvement does not always insure adequate involvement of those residents in the potential siting area communities. Federal programs such as those that have involved the State Planning Council and the Consultation and Concurrence and Consultation and Cooperation Programs have often constrained Federal agencies to contacts with local groups designated by state agency officials. Yet, state agency officials have often failed to adequately involve local citizens. Mutual distrust and mutual suspicion have thus often characterized Federal-state, Federal-local and state-local relations related to repository siting, and Federal and state bureaucracies have often found themselves at odds with their political constituencies because of waste management issues (Hebert et al., 1978).

Even if such political difficulties and the political context were less complex, the management issues related to repositories would be difficult to address. What type of entity can be created that will ensure safe management of nuclear wastes for the thousands of years for which such management may be necessary is unclear. Such a structure, though nearly impossible to envision, seems essential. Even for the short-term management of the facility (30 to 50 years), it is not clear who should own and manage the facility-- the Federal government, a private concern, or a newly created independent quasigovernmental entity. It is equally difficult to determine what roles state and local governments should play in repository management. Should they participate directly or indirectly in management decisions, serve only as monitors of project activities, or play no active role?

In sum, then, the legal, political and management issues in high-level nuclear waste management are among the most complex of those related to repository siting and management. They are unlikely to be resolved easily or quickly but their resolution must occur before repository siting can be completed and the construction of a repository be initiated in the United States.

Ethical and Philosophical Dimensions

Although other large-scale developments with both national and local implications (power plants, dams, military bases, etc.) have ethical and philosophical dimensions, waste storage facilities have particularly strong ethical implications. Because of questions related to their safety and to the very long periods of time over which they will affect society, and because repository siting involves equity issues requiring that one generation decide that one region of the nation must bear the risks for the entire nation for generations to come, nuclear waste issues are imbued with particularly significant ethical poignance. Such major issues as those involving the just resolution of regional and generational questions of risk and uncertainty, geographical equity, intergenerational responsibility and the ethics involved in the siting decisions related to repositories must be addressed. Many of these issues may be unresolvable, but failure to understand them is tantamount to a failure to understand the complexity of the nuclear waste issue in the United States.

Socioeconomic Dimensions

The last major sets of factors which we have selected to use for categorizing dimensions of the nuclear waste issue are the social and economic. It is these dimensions that are the major focus of this book, and they affect and are affected by nearly all of the other technical, political, managerial, and ethical dimensions described above.

There is no one correct means of categorizing the social and economic dimensions of high-level nuclear waste repository siting and management (see Hebert et al., 1978; Cluett et al., 1979; Brenner et al., 1979 for others), but we have chosen to examine three broad categories of these dimensions which we believe are central to understanding management and siting issues. These are:

. the economic, demographic, public service, fiscal, and social (socioeconomic) impacts of repository siting on communities near the repository sites

. the mitigation of socioeconomic and other impacts of repository siting

. the public participation and community development issues in repository siting and management

We have, then, chosen to focus on those socioeconomic issues likely to affect rural residents as a result of a repository being sited near their communities, on how these residents can participate in the siting and management process, and on what alternatives are available to mitigate the consequences of such developments for siting areas. Each of these three areas requires the consideration of numerous components.

Impacts. The siting of high-level nuclear waste repositories may result in numerous impacts on areas near such sites. These impacts may be conveniently placed into two broad conceptual categories--standard impacts and special impacts (Murdock and Leistritz, 1981). Standard impacts are those likely to result from any large-scale development which results in a relatively large (compared to the local area's baseline) population increase in an area. These are impacts that would also likely occur if any large-scale project such as a power plant, an industrial firm, or similar facility involving an equal number of new employees were to be located in an area. The special impacts or effects of a repository result from the fact that it is a facility handling radioactive materials which are perceived and thus reacted to in a manner quite different than those for other types of large scale developments.

There are numerous types of standard and special impacts but one convenient categorization scheme (Murdock and Leistritz, 1979) places such impacts into five categories--economic, demographic, public service, fiscal, and social. Economic impacts include such standard effects as those on employment, income, business activity and special effects such as those on land values and uses likely to be affected by repository siting. Demographic effects refer to those changes that occur in population size, distribution and composition as a result of repository siting. These might include both standard trends such as the population increases that normally accompany a large development or special effects such as outmigration of residents due to repository safety concerns. Community service impacts include those related to the level, quality, and distribution of community services. Again, these impacts may include both standard impacts such as the increases in demands likely to result for police, fire, and similar services due to population increases, and special effects such as the demands for special services and service planning (for example, training in the treatment of radiation exposure or emergency preparedness planning) as a result of repository siting.

Fiscal impacts include such standard effects as the need to increase funding to pay for services during development and the standard jurisdictional and timing dimensions such demands entail. They also include such special fiscal concerns as how a Federal tax-exempt repository can pay for the service demands and special impacts (for example, fear and anxiety) of a repository. Finally, social impacts include effects on the social structure, attitudes, values, perceptions, and quality of life in rural areas. Standard social impacts often include increased formalization of social organizations and altered levels of resident satisfaction with their community as it undergoes rapid growth. Special social effects include such effects as those on residents' levels of fear and anxiety for their own safety and that of future generations. Thus, the potential impacts of repositories are numerous and varied and knowledge of what these impacts are likely to be and how they can be assessed and measured must be part of the knowledge base acquired by anyone interested in repository siting and nuclear waste issues.

Mitigation. The mitigation of the impacts of repositories involves equally complex issues. Although many large-scale developments have utilized impact management plans (Halstead et al., 1982), special issues arise in regard to repositories as a result of the potential length of time over which mitigation measures might be appropriate, and the fact that the potential recipients of such mitigation might include several generations of residents.

In general, mitigation measures are beneficial to developers, local communities, and to society at large to the extent that they result in the more efficient, equitable, and expeditious construction of essential projects. Impact management broadly defined (chapter 10) requires that a comprehensive yet flexible approach involving all interested parties and careful planning based on an integrated assessment, management, and monitoring system be used.

Mitigation usually involves measures to minimize demands on local systems, to enhance the capacity of local systems, to compensate individuals, or to provide incentives to local interests. A complex range of alternatives has been used to mitigate the impacts of other large-scale projects but which mitigation alternatives may be most appropriate for repository siting is still subject to debate. Even more difficult is the question of who should be compensated. Although some interests should clearly be compensated (for example, landowners, local governments), other parties, such as residents some distance from the site or future generations of local residents, may be less clearly deserving of compensation.

Whatever mitigation approach is used, it is clear that a long-term monitoring program is likely to be required for repositories, but its components require careful delineation. What should be monitored and for what periods thus remain as issues of contention.

The mitigation of repository impacts thus involves a multifaceted set of considerations related to all stages of repository siting, construction, operation, and postoperational periods. The careful analysis of such factors is thus essential for understanding the socioeconomic dimensions of repository and waste management.

Public Participation and Community Development. Public participation and community development issues play a major role in any large-scale project likely to have significant impacts on communities surrounding a development site. They are particularly significant when large-scale Federal projects with undesirable characteristics are involved. Repositories are clearly such projects, and the issues surrounding public participation and community development in the repository siting and management process are complex. They include such diverse concerns as how best to insure that all local parties are involved in the repository siting process, the alternative means possible for such involvement, and the development of mechanisms to insure a proper mix of Federal, state, and local inputs into the resolution of siting issues. As with many of the issues related to impact mitigation, there is no one set of solutions that is best for all communities and all interests in communities, and an understanding of alternatives for each dimension of public participation is central to understanding the nuclear waste problem.

In sum, nuclear waste management and repository siting involve complex issues. To understand these issues, it is essential to have a basic understanding of the technical, ethical, political and management as well as the socioeconomic dimensions of the waste problem and of repository siting. These dimensions each involve complex issues that have yet to be fully resolved but each is likely to affect and be affected by each of the others. The socioeconomic dimensions of the nuclear waste problem are numerous but of particular concern are those related to communities near potential repository sites and thus likely to be impacted by repository siting, construction, and operation. The socioeconomic impacts, public participation and community development, and mitigation issues as they affect such communities are of central concern, and it is clear that the dimensions of these issues, as well as numerous others must be better understood if the problems of nuclear waste management and repository siting are to be adequately addressed. This volume as outlined below hopefully provides both a general understanding of the technical, ethical, management, and legal issues of waste management and makes a concerted step towards increasing our understanding of the socioeconomic dimensions of nuclear waste management and repository siting.

ORGANIZATION AND CONTENT OF THE WORK

In addition to this introduction, the book is organized into four major sections and a conclusion. The major sections contain chapters on:

- the dimensions of the nuclear waste problem

- the impacts of nuclear waste storage and repository siting

- mitigation of the impacts of nuclear waste storage and repository siting

- local community response and participation in nuclear repository siting

Dimensions of the Nuclear Waste Problem

- Section I of the work delineates the various dimensions bearing on the nuclear waste problem.

Chapter 1 by Hoskins and Russell provides a description of the geologic and engineering dimensions of nuclear waste storage. This chapter is essential to anyone who wishes to understand the socioeconomic dimensions of nuclear waste because many of the socioeconomic factors affecting nuclear waste are limited by the geologic and engineering restrictions that must be placed on the handling and storage of nuclear materials.

The second chapter by Ted Peters examines alternative philosophical and ethical perspectives on nuclear waste and waste storage. This is a unique chapter in that it vividly portrays the basic paradigms and precepts that underlie the fundamental issues of man's legacy to future generations and alternative viewpoints on the levels of responsibility that each generation bears for the welfare of the next generation.

Chapter 3 by James Finley provides an overview of the present governmental policies and management issues in waste management, examines current government programs for interfacing the interests of various levels of government, and describes the current programs and plans for siting and managing nuclear waste storage facilities.

The fourth chapter by William Metz outlines the legal constraints that might potentially be used by state, local, and/or special interest groups to delay or stop the siting of a high-level nuclear waste repository. Nuclear, environmental, and other forms of legislation are succinctly described and their implications for repository siting examined.

The fifth and final chapter in this section by Murdock, Hamm, and Leistritz provides an examination of the interrelationships among the numerous socioeconomic issues bearing on the waste storage problem. Social, economic, political, psychological, institutional, and unique or special aspects of the waste problem are briefly introduced and the intricacies and interrelations among these issues are briefly described.

Impacts of Nuclear Waste Storage and Repository Siting

. Section II changes the focus of the work from the broad dimensions bearing on the nuclear waste problem to the conceptual and methodological issues surrounding the assessment of the socioeconomic impacts of a storage repository. The focus of this section is on describing the means available for insuring that adequate information on each of the major socioeconomic dimensions of the siting process are made available to local, state, and Federal decision makers.

Chapter 6 by Thomas, Hamm, and Murdock provides an overview of the socioeconomic dimensions that must be assessed in the siting process from both a legislative and conceptual perspective. The chapter briefly overviews both the major types of socioeconomic impacts and the methods for assessing such impacts.

The seventh chapter by Chase, Leistritz, and Halstead describes the major economic and fiscal impacts likely to affect repository sites and describes means for assessing these impacts. The uncertain effects of repositories on economic growth in a siting area and the uncertain fiscal implications of such sites are examined in detail in this chapter.

Chapter 8 by Murdock and Hamm examines the impacts likely to occur in the populations and public services of impacted areas and alternatives for assessing these impacts. Of critical concern and importance in this chapter is the description of the potential effects of repositories on population loss as well as growth and the unique service needs likely to be created by repository siting.

The last chapter in this section, chapter 9, by Thomas, Albrecht, and Murdock provides a description and discussion of the social impacts of a repository and the procedures for assessing such impacts.

Mitigation of the Impacts of Nuclear Waste Storage and Repository Siting

- Section III examines alternatives for the mitigation of the impacts of repository siting. It addresses the likely need for various types of short-term and long-term compensation for repository siting areas and alternative forms and types of mitigation approaches and programs.

Chapter 10 by Halstead and Leistritz presents case study examples of the strategies that have been used for mitigating the impacts of large-scale projects and describes the likely relevance of each strategy for repositories. This chapter provides an excellent overview of mitigation alternatives used in a variety of projects throughout North America.

The eleventh chapter by Leistritz, Halstead, Chase, and Murdock describes the basic elements of the impact management process. Key dimensions of the assessment, project management, and monitoring phases of mitigation are described.

Chapter 12 discusses particularly acute difficulties in mitigation planning for repositories. Halstead and Leistritz discuss those mitigation issues unique to repositories, and some of the alternative legislative and management arrangements necessary to address such issues.

Local Community Response and Participation
in Nuclear Waste Repository Siting

. The final section of the book--Section IV--
examines the critical issue of local site-area
community and citizen involvement in the
repository siting process. This section
examines how communities may respond to
alternative siting processes and alternative
forms and types of community involvement.

The chapter by Albrecht (chapter 13) in this section
departs slightly from the nuclear theme of the work in
that it presents a case study of community responses to a
nonnuclear facility. It makes a vital contribution,
however, because no nuclear repository has yet been sited
and knowledge of the likely management and siting
dimensions of such a repository may be gained by
analyzing those of other large-scale facilities such as
the MX system. In addition, this chapter presents a
superb real-life example of the need for citizen and
community involvement, and the likely consequences of
failing to obtain that involvement, in siting a major
facility.
Chapters 14 by Voth and Herrington and 15 by Howell,
Olsen, Olsen, and Yuan describe the needs and potential
forms for community development and citizen participation
in repository siting. Each of these chapters provides a
broad overview of alternative forms for community
development and citizen participation in large-scale
projects and discusses likely alternatives of utility in
repository siting.

Summary and Conclusions

The concluding section of the work attempts both to
summarize the work and to look at the future
socioeconomic aspects of nuclear waste and waste
repository siting. It attempts to ascertain the most
critical issues in nuclear waste storage and to suggest
the needed directions that research and policy
formulation must take if they are to address these
issues.

CONCLUSION

The dimensions of nuclear waste management and
siting examined in this volume span a variety of
technical, philosophical, political, and socioeconomic
issues. Although emphasis is placed on the socioeconomic
issues and single issues are examined in separate
chapters, it is evident that actual waste management and
repository siting decisions will be made in a context in

which these and other dimensions will interactively
determine the actual courses of action selected. Any one
volume, then, can only hope to provide limited insights
into the complexity of issues that will affect waste
management and repository siting. Hopefully, this volume
will provide at least some understanding of the
complexity of the dimensions surrounding nuclear waste
management and repository siting. It is to the task of
describing these dimensions that we now turn our
attention.

Dimensions of the
Nuclear Waste Problem

1
Geologic and Engineering Dimensions of Nuclear Waste Storage

Earl R. Hoskins
James E. Russell

This chapter examines the geologic and engineering dimensions of nuclear waste storage. The waste characteristics, existing and projected quantities of radioactive materials that need to be stored, various disposal or storage strategies or alternatives, geologic media under consideration, and repository construction techniques and problems are discussed. The subject has been exhaustively studied for over twenty-five years. In 1957, a committee of the Division of Earth Sciences of the National Academy of Sciences-Natural Research Council published a report, entitled **The Disposal of Radioactive Wastes on Land** (National Academy of Sciences, 1957). Since then, research results have accumulated rapidly. The authors of this chapter have between them more than twenty feet of bookshelves of various studies made since 1957, all devoted to this subject, and that is certainly not a complete record. Perhaps the most complete recent summary is the **Final Environmental Impact Statement, Management of Commercially Generated Radioactive Waste** (U.S. Department of Energy, 1980a). Much of this chapter is summarized from that report. We will concentrate our discussion on commercially generated radioactive wastes because national defense program wastes are managed as a separate program. The characteristics of these Defense Department generated radioactive materials are somewhat different from the commercial wastes; however, in a generic sense, the defense wastes pose similar hazards, and they will probably be stored and managed similarly to the commercial wastes. The discussion presented can thus be seen as generally applicable to the overall nuclear waste storage problem.

NUCLEAR WASTES: THE MAGNITUDE OF THE PROBLEM

Radioactive waste products are classified into four major categories, reflecting their origin and potential hazard. These four categories are: (1) high-level wastes, (2) transuranic wastes, (3) low-level wastes, and

(4) uranium mill tailings.

The commercial nuclear fuel cycle and the type of waste generated at each step is shown diagramatically in figure 1.1. The recycle route is shown as a dashed line since there are no active reprocessing plants for spent fuel from commercial power reactors in the U.S. at this time.

High-level wastes are the by-products of nuclear reactors. They are both thermally hot and highly radioactive. Initially, these by-products are locked up in the "spent reactor fuel rods." These spent fuel rods are removed from nuclear power reactors when they have been used until they can no longer efficiently contribute to the nuclear chain reaction. High-level wastes are characterized by their high energy radiation. In concept, spent fuel can be reprocessed to separate the high-level wastes from the remaining fissile material in the rods and this repurified fuel can then be reformed and recycled through the reactors. If the spent fuel rods are reprocessed, a much smaller volume of high-level wastes will need to be transported and stored as well as providing for a much more efficient utilization of the natural resource. However, the question of whether or not to reprocess fuel rods is a difficult policy issue as bomb-grade plutonium is produced during reprocessing, and the security of the inventory at the reprocessing plants becomes an extremely important matter.

Transuranic wastes consist of compounds of the elements that are heavier than uranium. They are produced primarily by reprocessing and are characterized by medium energy radiation and slow decay rates. Both transuranic and high-level radioactive wastes require isolation from the biosphere as they constitute significant long-term hazards.

Low-level radioactive wastes include rags, papers, filters, and resins from commercial, medical, and university nuclear facilities. They are dilute; that is, they contain small amounts of radioactive material which is contaminating the carrier. They do not require extensive shielding and they do not generate large quantities of heat. Low-level wastes pose a relatively low potential hazard and are safely disposed of by controlled shallow burial at suitable locations.

Mill tailings are the leftover wastes from uranium mining and milling consisting of very large volumes of rock and soil that contain the residual natural radioactivity left after most (more than 90%) of the uranium has been extracted from the ore. Tailings are not a major radiological hazard except when incorporated into buildings as aggregate in mortar and concrete.

At the beginninng of 1981, there were about 6,700 metric tons of spent fuel assemblies from commercial nuclear power plants in temporary storage. These spent

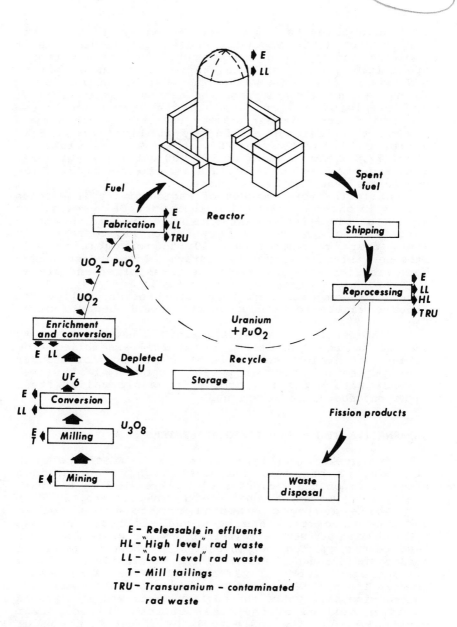

E – Releasable in effluents
HL – "High level" rad waste
LL – "Low level" rad waste
T – Mill tailings
TRU – Transuranium – contaminated
rad waste

Figure 1.1

Nuclear Fuel Cycle

fuel assemblies have a volume of nearly 104,000 cubic feet. Each 1,000 megawatt nuclear power plant unit produces about 33 tons or 390 cubic feet of additional spent fuel assemblies each year. The total amount of additional radioactive waste that must be handled in the future depends directly upon the number of reactors that are completed and operated in the future and these projections are, at best, highly uncertain at this time. A recent Department of Energy publication (1981b) estimates that by the year 2000, there will be a total of about 72,000 metric tons or 950,000 cubic feet of spent fuel assemblies that will have to be stored (or reprocessed and the wastes stored).

While the total amount of radioactivity in defense wastes is about equal to that in commercial wastes, the volume of the defense wastes is much greater because a large part of it is in a very dilute liquid form. In 1980, there were more than 10 million cubic feet of defense wastes in temporary storage. Liquid wastes must be solidified before they can be transported and placed in permanent storage facilities and by the year 2000 we expect to have over 1 million cubic feet of solidified defense wastes to handle and store (U.S. Department of Energy, 1982).

High-level nuclear wastes are all now in temporary surface storage facilities. Spent fuel assemblies from commercial nuclear power plants are being stored under twenty-feet of water in pools at power plant sites. Defense wastes are now stored in double-walled steel tanks on federal reservations.

ALTERNATIVE STORAGE OR DISPOSAL SYSTEMS

Storage of nuclear wastes in mined caverns underground has been the most highly recommended alternative of the various studies performed in the past twenty-five years (National Academy of Sciences, 1957).

While geologic disposal or storage in mined underground caverns has been and still is the most favored concept, several alternatives for waste isolation have been suggested and investigated, however (National Academy of Sciences, 1957). These alternatives include: (1) geologic disposal, (2) extraterrestrial disposal, wherein the nuclear wastes would be shot into space, (3) seabed disposal, where the nuclear waste would be placed in holes drilled at the ocean bottom, (4) ice sheet disposal, where the waste would be placed in the polar ice caps, (5) waste disposal in a matrix of drilled holes rather than mined caverns, (6) deep well injection, where liquid wastes are forced through a pipe into a deep geologic formation, (7) the rock melting concept, which makes use of the large amount of thermal energy from the radioactive waste to heat the host rock to its melting point wherein the molten rock mixes with the radioactive waste and finally crystallizes as the energy release decays with time, (8) the transmutation concept, and (9) the no-action alternative. All of the alternative disposal methods proposed so far are considered to be either inherently less safe or to have more unresolved technical problems compared to underground storage (Alternative 1). Briefly, the characteristics of the geologic and other disposal alternatives are as follows (for further detail, see U.S. Department of Energy, 1980a; and Russell, 1977).

Geologic Disposal Concept

Geologic disposal of radioactive wastes is the disposal of radioactive wastes in conventionally mined repositories deep within the geologic formations of the earth. It includes the concept of the use of multiple barriers to provide a series of independent checks to the release of radionuclides to the biosphere.

The multiple barriers that could contain nuclear waste in deep-mined repositories fall into two categories: (1) geologic or natural barriers and (2) engineered barriers. Geologic barriers are expected to provide isolation of the waste for at least 10,000 years after the waste is emplaced in a repository and probably will provide isolation for millenia thereafter. Engineered barriers are those designed to assure total containment of the waste within the disposal package for an initial period during which most of the intermediate-lived fission products decay. This time period might be as long as 1,000 years in which case the radiation levels and heat generation rates of the total waste would drop by factors of approximately 1,000 and 100, respectively. Engineered barriers must be designed to withstand the severe radiation and thermal conditions initially present.

The two most important components of the geologic barrier to be considered in choosing a nuclear waste site are the host rock itself and the geologic surroundings. A properly chosen host rock will have physical and chemical properties that contribute to repository performance. The depth and lateral extent of the host rock mass also contribute to the isolation capability of the repository. Tectonic stability and a noncommunicating hydrologic regime would ideally be combined with these rock properties to maintain long-term repository strength and isolation integrity. The geologic barriers must be selected so as to provide a stable long-term environment for the waste that is not likely to be disturbed by natural events or human activities.

The six principal factors relevant to the qualification of any potential site are:

1. Properties of the host rock. The physical, chemical, and thermal properties of the host rock determine the rock's capability to isolate and contain the waste and reduce unwanted interactions between the rock and waste. These possible interactions include radiation effects on the rock and chemical and physicochemical interactions. Important rock characteristics include strength, permeability, thermal conductivity and expansion, and radiation resistance.

2. Depth of repository below the land surface. Presently it is assumed that a range of from 600 to 1,000 meters of earth material will exist between the repository and the land surface. This will provide a barrier between the waste and the biosphere and protect the repository from human activities. Dimensions of the host rock are also considered so that the repository will be buffered by rock material laterally and below as well as above it.

3. Tectonic stability of the repository area and region. Proper consideration of this important factor will reduce the likelihood of deformation or disruption of the host rock and thus increase the probability of repository integrity.

4. Hydrologic regime (that is, surface-water and ground-water considerations). This is important because the existence of connected water channels could provide potential pathways for waste transport away from the repository.

5. Resource potential of the repository site and area. A low natural resource potential is desirable to avoid loss of any economic resource due to the repository's existence and to reduce the likelihood of future exploration activities for resource recovery.

6. The multibarrier safety feature. This combines the redundant isolation features provided by the rock properties, the geologic setting, and engineered barriers to give overall added confidence that the waste will remain isolated.

Engineered barriers in the disposal system consist of the waste form, the waste package, and the seals. The following recent discussion of engineered barriers is taken from Klingsberg and Duguid (1980).

Waste Form. The waste form is a component of the waste package but is discussed separately because of its independent development. The function of the waste form is to provide a barrier to the release of radionuclides. Because the most likely transport mechanism to the biosphere is by solution in moving ground water, minimal leaching characteristics of the waste form are of prime importance. For spent fuel, the properties of the cladding must also be considered because it will provide an additional barrier to exposure of the fuel to water. The cladding also contains fission product gases released from the spent fuel (for example, tritium, xenon, and iodine) and hinders their entry into free spaces within the canister. Other properties of the waste form that must be considered include inertness, thermal properties, resistance to mechanical shock, phase stability, gas generation, and compatibility with other components of the waste package.

Waste Package. The waste package is defined to include everything that is placed in the repository waste emplacement hole--the waste form, filler, canister, overpack, sleeve, and backfill. Each of these components is intended to provide protection in addition to that supplied by the host rock and its surrounding strata. These waste package components provide:

1. containment of fission products for extended periods

2. lowering of release rate of radionuclides to the host rock

3. minimizing access of water to the waste form

One may envision how this multibarrier waste package will perform by considering the case of ground water moving through the natural system toward the waste package. Water first would encounter the emplacement hole backfill, which would be chosen for its sorptive properties, its relative impermeability to water, its ability to combine with water to make a new mineral form, or its ability to buffer the water to minimize corrosion of the canister (that is, control pH, Eh, and water composition).

Water passing through the backfill would encounter a sleeve, an overpack, or both, made of corrosion-resistant materials. The canister which contains the waste is the next physical barrier. Use of a solid filler inside the canister could provide an additional resistance to water inflow. If all these sequential resistances to water inflow were to fail, the waste form itself would be a major barrier to release of radionuclides because of its low solubility.

If some nuclides are eventually mobilized by ground

water, they would have to travel out through the same waste package barriers. The filler and backfill would function as sorptive barriers to retard the movement of radionuclides. Thus, the waste package can reduce the rate at which radionuclides enter the natural system. The combined chemical and physical delay of nuclide release would result in a substantial decay of the radioactivity before the nuclides could enter the natural system, where there will be additional delay (and consequent decay) because of sorption along the ground-water flow path.

Repository Seals. In developing a repository, exploratory boreholes and repository shafts will have to be made into the host rock. In addition, a proposed repository site may already have some boreholes or wells from previous exploratory or resource-recovery activities. These holes are potential paths by which ground water can flow to the repository.

The sealing requirements for the repository include:

1. All boreholes into the repository must be adequately sealed and the seals should maintain their integrity throughout, and as far beyond, the thermal period as is reasonably achievable.

2. Boreholes must be prudently sited and used. To the extent possible, exploration and development requiring boreholes through or near a proposed repository site will use previously existing holes to minimize the total number of holes requiring sealing. Similarly, new holes will be used for as many purposes as possible and will be located (when possible) to coincide with proposed repository shaft or pillar locations. Wherever possible, boreholes will be located outside the immediate repository location.

3. Existing boreholes must be located and sealed.

4. Shafts and boreholes must be carefully constructed. Final sealing will be considered in the selection of shaft designs and excavation techniques. This consideration of shaft/borehole construction will include the extent of existing fractures in the surrounding rock as well as fractures caused by the excavation technique. If extensive fractures are created, it might become necessary to grout them. Excavation techniques that cause extensive fracturing will be modified or avoided if possible. In addition, techniques used to seal aquifers during shaft construction

should not reduce the effectiveness of later final shaft sealing.

Successful sealing of penetrations associated with underground weapons tests has been achieved at the Nevada Test Site. These seals have withstood not only high temperatures and pressures but also strong transient ground motions without losing their integrity. However, accumulated experience must be supplemented by additional research and development, because repository seals must retain their integrity for much longer periods of time than those considered in previous applications.

Space Disposal Concept

Space disposal has been suggested as a unique option for permanently removing high-level nuclear wastes from the earth's environment. In the reference concept, high-level waste is formed into a ceramic-metal matrix, and packaged in special flight containers for insertion into a solar orbit, where it would be expected to remain for at least one million years. The National Aeronautics and Space Administration (NASA) has studied several space disposal options since the early 1970s (National Aeronautics and Space Administration, 1974). The concept involves the use of a special space shuttle that would carry the waste package to a low-earth orbit where a transfer vehicle would separate from the shuttle and place the waste package and another propulsion stage into an earth escape trajectory. The transfer vehicle would return to the shuttle while the remaining rocket stage inserts the waste into a solar orbit.

Space disposal is of interest because, once the waste is placed in orbit, its potential for environmental impacts and human health effects is judged to be nonexistent. However, the risk of launch pad accidents and low earth orbit failures have not been determined.

The space disposal option appears feasible for only a small proportion of selected long-lived radionuclides such as ^{129}I, or even for the total amount of reprocessed high-level waste that will be produced. Space disposal of unreprocessed fuel rods and other high volume wastes does not appear economically feasible or practical because of the large number of flights involved.

Subseabed Disposal Concept

It has been suggested that wastes could be isolated from the biosphere by emplacement in sedimentary deposits beneath the bottom of the deep sea (thousands of meters below the surface), which have been deposited over millions of years. The deposits have been shown by laboratory experiments to have sorptive capacity for many radionuclides that might leach from breached waste packages. The water column is not considered a barrier, however, it will inhibit human intrusion and can contribute to dilution by dispersal of radionuclides that might escape the sediments.

One subseabed disposal system incorporates the emplacement of appropriately treated waste or spent reactor fuel in free-fall needle-shaped "penetrometers" that, when dropped through the ocean, would penetrate about 50 to 100 meters into the sediments. A ship designed for waste transport and placement would transport waste from a port facility to the disposal site and would be equipped to emplace the waste containers in the sediment.

Subseabed disposal is an attractive alternative disposal technique because technically it appears feasible that, at least for high-level waste and spent fuel, the waste can be placed in areas having relatively high assurance of stability. If at some point in time all of the barriers failed, the great dilution and the slow movement should retard the return of radionuclides to the human environment in biologically important concentrations. The research needed to technically permit subseabed disposal to go forward has been projected not to be as costly or time consuming as some other alternatives (U.S. Department of Energy, 1980a). On the other hand, the subseabed concept has the disadvantage of the need for special port facilities and for additional transportation steps in comparison to mined repositories on the continent.

As noted, subseabed disposal is believed to be technologically feasible; however, international and domestic legal problems to its implementation would require favorable resolution. Whether subseabed disposal can provide isolation of wastes equal to that of deep geologic repositories has not been fully assessed. Because of volume considerations, subseabed disposal does not appear practical for transuranic (TRU) wastes and some other method would be required for their disposal.

Ice Sheet Disposal Concept

Disposal in continental ice sheets has been suggested as a means of isolating high-level radioactive waste. Past studies have specifically addressed the emplacement of waste in either Antarctica or Greenland (U.S. Department of Energy, 1980a). The alleged advantages of ice sheet disposal, which are disposal in a cold, remote area and in a medium that would isolate the wastes from man for many thousands of years, cannot be proven on the basis of current knowledge (U.S. Department of Energy, 1980a).

Proposals for ice sheet disposal of high-level wastes and/or spent fuel suggest three emplacement concepts:

- Passive slow descent--waste is emplaced in a shallow hole and the waste canister melts its own way to the bottom of the ice sheet.

- Anchored emplacement--similar to passive slow descent but an anchored cable limits the descent depth and allows retrieval of the canister and prevents movement to the bottom of the sheet.

- Surface storage--storage facility supported above the ice sheet surface with eventual slow melting into the sheet.

Ice sheet disposal, regardless of the emplacement concept, would have the advantages of remoteness, low temperatures, and the isolating effects of the ice. On the other hand, transportation and operational costs would be high, ice dynamics are uncertain, and adverse global climatic effects as a result of the melting of portions of the ice are a remote possibility. The Antarctic Treaty now precludes waste disposal in the Antarctic ice sheet. The availability of the Greenland ice sheet for waste disposal would depend upon acceptance by Denmark and the local government of the island itself.

A great deal of research appears to be needed before the potential of ice sheet disposal is determined. Even though the apparent bowl-shaped ice cap of Greenland would result in the wastes melting to the bottom of the bowl where they might remain permanently, the consequences of release of radioactive decay heat to the ice are uncertain. Because of weather extremes and environmental conditions on the ice sheets, difficulties are also predicted for transportation of the wastes to the site, waste emplacement, and site characterization (U.S. Department of Energy, 1980a).

Very Deep Hole Waste Disposal Concept

A very deep hole concept has been suggested that involves the placement of nuclear waste in holes in geologic formations as much as 10,000 meters (6 miles) underground. Potential rock types for a repository of this kind include crystalline and sedimentary rocks located in areas of tectonic and seismic stability.

Spent fuel or high-level waste canisters could be disposed of in very deep holes. However, it is not economically feasible to dispose of high-volume wastes (for example, TRU) in this manner and thus another alternative, such as deep geologic repositories, is also required if spent fuel is reprocessed. There is some question whether or not drilling of holes to the depths suggested and in the sizes required can be achieved.

The principal advantage of the very deep hole

concept is that certain (but not all) wastes can be placed farther from the biosphere, in a location where it is believed that circulating ground water is unlikely to communicate with the biosphere.

Well Injection Disposal Concepts

Two methods of well injection have been suggested: deep-well liquid injection and shale/grout injection.

Deep-well liquid injection involves pumping acidic liquid waste to depths of 1,000 to 5,000 meters (3,300 to 16,000 feet) into porous or fractured strata that are suitably isolated from the biosphere by relatively impermeable overlying strata. The waste is expected to remain in liquid form and may thus progressively disperse and diffuse throughout the host rock. Unless limits of movement are well defined, this mobility within the porous host media formation would be of concern because of its eventual release to the biosphere.

For the shale/grout injection alternative, the shale is fractured by high-pressure injection and then the waste, mixed with cement and clays, is injected into the fractured shale formations at depths of 300 to 500 meters (1,000 to 1,600 feet) and allowed to solidify in place in a set of thin solid disks. Shale has very low permeability and predictably good sorption properties. The formations selected for injection would be those in which the wastes would be expected to remain within the host shale bed. This requirement is expected to limit the injection depths to the range stated above.

This alternative is applicable only to reprocessing wastes or to spent fuel that has been processed to liquid or slurry form. Therefore, well injection is not sufficient to dispose of all wastes generated, and a suitable additional technique would be required.

Rock Melt Waste Disposal Concept

The rock melt concept for radioactive waste disposal calls for the direct placement of liquids or slurries of high-level wastes or dissolved spent fuel, with the possible addition of small quantities of other wastes, into underground cavities. After the water has evaporated, the heat from radioactive decay would melt the surrounding rock. The melted rock has been postulated to form a complex waste form by reaction with the high-level waste. In about 1,000 years, the waste-rock mixture would resolidify, trapping the radioactive material in what is believed to be a relatively insoluble matrix deep underground. Since solidification takes about 1,000 years, the waste is most mobile during the period of greatest fission product hazard.

Not believed to be suitable for rock melt disposal are wastes from reprocessing activities such as hulls, end fittings, and TRU wastes remaining after dissolution. Because of the inability to accommodate these wastes, some other disposal method would have to be used in conjunction with the rock melt disposal concept.

Transmutation Concept

In the reference transmutation concept, spent fuel would be reprocessed to recover uranium and plutonium (or processed to obtain a liquid high-level waste stream in the case where uranium and plutonium are not to be recycled). The remaining high-level waste stream is partitioned into an actinide waste stream and a fission product stream. The fission product stream is concentrated, solidified, and sent to a mined geologic repository for disposal. The waste actinide stream is combined with uranium or uranium and plutonium, fabricated into fuel rods, and reinserted into a reactor. In the reactor, about 5 to 7 percent of the recycled waste actinides are transmuted to stable or short-lived isotopes, which are separated out during the next recycle step for disposal in the repository. Numerous recycles would result in nearly complete transmutation of the waste actinides; however, additional waste streams are generated with every recycle. Transmutation, however, provides no reduction in the quantities of long-lived fission product radionuclides such as ^{99}Ic and ^{129}I in the fission product stream that is sent to geologic disposal.

No-Action Alternative

The no-action alternative would leave spent fuel or reprocessing wastes at the sites generating the waste or possibly at other surface or near-surface storage facilities for an indefinite time. In this alternative, existing storage is known to be temporary, and no consideration has been given to the need for additional temporary storage when facilities in use have exceeded their design lifetime. There seems to be no question but that at some point in time, wastes will require disposal and that considerable time and effort will be required to settle upon an adequate means of disposal. It seems clear that development of acceptable means of disposal of wastes is sufficiently complex and of sufficiently broad national importance that coordination of research and development, construction, operation, and regulation at the Federal level is required and that the no-action alternative is unacceptable. Indeed, adoption of a no-action alternative by the Department of Energy could be construed as not permissible under the responsibility mandated to the Department by law. Neither would a no-action alternative be in accord with the President's message of February 12, 1980, when he stated that ". . .

resolving . . . civilian waste management problems shall not be deferred to future generations" (U.S. Department of Energy, 1980a: 1.21).

Thus, although numerous alternatives exist for waste storage, at present, the disposal of radioactive wastes in conventionally mined underground caverns thus appears to be the best choice in terms of both technical feasibility and inherent overall project safety.

ALTERNATIVE STORAGE MEDIA

Given that the most likely, first to be used, method of radioactive waste storage and/or disposal will be mined underground caverns, the next problem becomes one of site selection. At this time (1982), the Department of Energy is in the process of qualifying various rock types as potential repository hosts. Rock types currently under investigation include: (1) rock salt deposits (both thick bedded sequences and salt domes), (2) crystalline rocks such as granites and gneisses, (3) volcanic rocks such as basalts and tuffs, and to a much lesser extent, (4) sedimentary rocks such as shale and limestone.

Salt is being studied because of its dryness (that is, it occurs without circulating fresh water), its relatively high thermal conductivity, its ability to flow and "reheal" itself when under stress at high temperatures, its relative abundance in the U.S., and its occurrence in tectonically stable basins. Salt was the rock type recommended for a nuclear waste disposal facility in the very first studies (National Academy of Sciences, 1957), and therefore its characteristics as a disposal media have been more thoroughly investigated than any other rock types. Crystalline rocks such as granite have potential because they are strong and durable, resistant to stress, and, if unfractured, they have low permeability and porosity. Both Sweden and Canada are investigating crystalline rocks as potential repository sites and the U.S. Department of Energy has run a series of in situ tests in granite on the Nevada Test Site. Basalt has desirable strength and thermal expansion properties. The DOE had developed an in situ experimental site in basalt near Hanford, Washington. Tuff at the Nevada Test Site is being studied because of its strength, high sorptive qualities, and location adjacent to other sorptive rocks (Johnstone and Wolfsberg, 1980).

Site-selection investigations of a particular rock type consist of three phases: regional reconnaissance, study area investigation, and confirmation of the site (Russell, 1977). A particular area or formation may be eliminated from further consideration at any step. The regional reconnaissance study of a particular formation determines if areas exist in a region where the rock unit being considered: (1) has at least the minimum thickness necessary for a storage facility, (2) does not exceed the maximum depth for optimum emplacement, (3) is not within the range of regional tectonics and seismicity that exceeds allowable limits, (4) has favorable hydrologic characteristics, and (5) contains negligible quantities of valuable mineral resources, such as oil and gas. All available data on structure, stratigraphy, depth, thickness, hydrology, mineralogy, petrology, natural resources, and surface characteristics are collected and reviewed during the reconnaissance study. County-size regions are identified and selected for geologic study areas.

The second phase, study area investigation, includes more detailed study of the characteristics listed above in the county-size regions that were identified by the above descriptions. Additional core logs and geophysical surveys may be necessary during this phase to adequately define the geology and hydrology of an area.

The third phase, confirmation of the site, will include a very detailed geological and hydrological evaluation of a localized area. Extensive coring and logging will be necessary to determine the mineralogy, stratigraphy, and hydrology of the rock unit. At this time, in situ engineering studies of mechanical and thermal behavior of the rock mass will be made. Fluid and ion migration studies in the particular rock unit will also be made.

The suitability of salt deposits for a radioactive waste disposal site has been extensively investigated in both field and laboratory experiments since the issuance of the National Academy Report in 1957. This report states that salt deposits are the most promising method of disposal of high level waste at the present time, and that the great advantage is that water cannot pass through salt. Also, any fractures are self healing. Thus, abandoned salt mines or cavities are, in essence, long enduring tanks. Salt properties investigated in the laboratory include thermal properties such as thermal conductivity, heat capacity, and thermal expansion coefficients; structural and mechanical properties such as stress-strain relationships and creep behavior; trapped moisture effects; and radiation effects on salt crystal structure and brine inclusion.

The most definitive field study to date was Project Salt Vault, which was conducted by Oak Ridge National Laboratory in the late 1960s at a salt mine at Lyons, Kansas. The Project Salt Vault experiment included a specially mined experimental area where electric heaters and simulated radioactive waste were placed in the salt. The area was extensively instrumented, and the data collected during that experiment provide a definitive data base on which to base designs in salt. The Salt

Vault experiment is described in the final report on the project (Bradshaw and McClain, 1971).

Project Salt Vault provided considerable information to verify the suitability of salt formations for geologic disposal of radioactive waste. Unfortunately, the Lyons, Kansas site was not acceptable for a terminal storage facility because of the presence of unplugged boreholes and a nearby solution mining activity. As a result, a search for another suitable site was instigated, and a site was identified in the Permian Basin thirty miles east of Carlsbad, New Mexico where Sandia Laboratories is presently developing a Waste Isolation Pilot Plant (WIPP) for deep geologic disposal of low-level and intermediate-level radioactive waste from the defense program. The WIPP Project is not intended to serve as a storage or disposal site for commercially generated radioactive wastes.

CONCEPTUAL DESIGN OF A NUCLEAR WASTE REPOSITORY IN SALT

Several conceptual designs for high-level waste repositories have been prepared for sites in salt domes (for example, Parsons, Brinckerhoff, Quade, and Douglas, Inc., 1976). These are not specific to any particular site because no such site has yet been selected, but the conceptual design is useful because it describes the type of facility which is likely to be developed.

The conceptual repository consists of a relatively conventional room-and-pillar mine at a depth from 800 to 3,000 feet which provides space for high-level waste, intermediate-level and cladding waste, and low-level waste. Vertical shafts provide a means of moving the solidified waste in specially designed containers from the surface to the subsurface storage area. The reference facility has four shafts: a men-and-materials shaft, a ventilation shaft, a low-level waste shaft, and a high-level and intermediate-level waste shaft.

High-level and intermediate-level wastes must be handled remotely through a specially designed transporter vehicle. The transporter will move the waste to the disposal rooms, where it will be lowered into a hole in the floor and the hole closed with a concrete plug for radiation protection. In the case of low-level waste in 55-gallon drums, the containers will be lowered through the shaft and then stacked in the disposal rooms similar to a warehousing operation.

The repository described has an excavation area that will underlie 2,000 acres. DOE will acquire surface and subsurface title to this land. Surface facilities for receiving the waste and the support buildings will occupy approximately 200 acres, which will be the only surface evidence of the repository. The remainder of the 2,000 acres will be leased for selective surface usage.

Surrounding the 2,000-acre area overlying the excavation will be a controlled area two miles in diameter for which DOE will have to acquire subsurface title. Control of this buffer zone is necessary to insure that no commercial mining or drilling operations compromise the safety and integrity of the disposal area. Surface activities in the buffer area may be unrestricted. All the facilities at the repository must be designed to standards that will allow the facility to be licensed by the Nuclear Regulatory Commission (NRC). Surface facilities will be designed to survive natural disasters. Radiation monitoring devices will be maintained in operations inside the repository, on the surface, and outside the area to monitor for leaks. Charges to user utilities for the disposal services will be high enough to provide funds for the long-term radiation monitoring of the area after decommissioning (U.S. Department of Energy, 1982).

The mine design will be conservative because of the unique character of the materials being buried. Special care will have to be taken to provide for long-term safe reentry into the facilities. Thermal effects produced by heat-generating radioactive waste include thermal stability of the host formation, structural integrity of the mine during operation, structural integrity of the formation, brine migration in the case of a repository in salt, chemical reactions in the host rock, and fill around the canister, temperature rise in nearby aquifers, temperature increase beyond the disposal area, and temperature increase at the earth's surface. The thermally driven effects most directly related to underground design and construction problems involve rock mechanics.

The two major objectives of rock mechanics are to predict: (1) the structural behavior of a repository during the construction, operation, and retrievability phases and (2) the large-scale rock deformations and stresses resulting from the repository over very long periods of time. Rock mechanics data provide input to the site-selection process regarding acceptable rock types and the allowable depth and thickness of formations. Rock mechanics studies determine: (1) allowable thermal loading densities based on deformational and strength characteristics of rock under alternative temperatures and pressures, (2) acceptable room geometry and orientation, (3) retrievability based on room and emplacement hole closure rates, and (4) local and large-scale consequences of backfilling rooms. The thermal expansion of a large volume of rock by the heat-generating waste will provide a temporary surface uplift while creep in mine pillars will cause a final subsidence above the repository. These effects can influence the environment at the surface, and they are presently under study.

Rock mechanics studies presently underway to analyze such dimensions are split into three basic areas: laboratory studies, numerical modeling studies, and field studies. Since it is impossible to run tests on the very long-term (tens of thousands of years) effects of heat-generating wastes on rocks, it is necessary to rely heavily on numerical simulation studies to predict their response. The laboratory rock mechanics studies provide rock property data for input to the numerical modeling studies. In addition, bench-scale tests in the laboratory provide validation of numerical modeling predictive capability. The field studies provide the in-situ properties of rock masses and in-situ rock stresses. In addition, the field studies provide additional validation of the predictions of the numerical modeling studies for the short-term case. The numerical modeling studies predict both the near-field and far-field response of the rock mass to a repository.

The technology for excavating and constructing a repository at a well-selected site is in hand and should present no unmanageable difficulties (McClain and Russell, 1980). One factor, however, that has a great influence on the design, economics, operational and long-term safety of geological waste isolation is the thermal power output of the nuclear wastes that will be transferred into the host rock mass. The thermal power generated in a repository can be controlled by aging wastes on the surface before emplacement, diluting reprocessing wastes, and increasing the spacing between emplacement holes.

Currently, no large-scale, long-term experience is available on the effect of thermal stresses on the mining of salt underground. The question of appropriate thermal loadings for salt is discussed in detail in Russell (1979). Basically, the effects of the heat production on the wastes (which decay with time) are considered on three different scales. First, the temperature field that develops in the immediate vicinity of an emplaced canister is considered. Factors considered at this scale include: (1) the stability of the emplacement hole--that is, will it creep shut and prevent easy retrievability of the waste canister during the retrieval period; (2) the brine migration, which is a function of both the temperature gradient and the absolute temperature of the salt; single-phase brine inclusions tend to move up the thermal gradient toward the heat source while mixed-phase inclusions tend to move away from the heat source; and (3) the corrosion of the canister material, which will be accelerated by brine migration into the emplacement holes. Corrosion of the waste canisters can prevent easy retrieval of the canisters and can also result in the production of hydrogen gas which may pose an operational hazard.

The second level of detail considered in determining

thermal loading is the room scale (sometimes called the near-field region). At this scale, the primary concern is the overall structural stability of the repository rooms. Consequently, the temperature fields that will develop in the pillars are of interest, as is whether or not this temperature will cause creep to accelerate to the point where unacceptable room closures will be experienced and whether either will make the repository unsafe during the operational phase or will make remining necessary before canisters could be retrieved, if retrieval should be necessary. The Project Salt Vault experiment (Bradshaw and McClain, 1971) provides some data on the deformations to be expected in the storage rooms and pillars. Recently, computerized simulations using laboratory-determined properties of rock salt have been able to reasonably calculate the deformations that were observed during the Project Salt Vault experiment (Wahi et al., 1977; Ratigan and Callahan, 1978).

The third level of detail for thermal and rock mechanics considerations is the repository scale, or regional scale. Since a large amount of thermal energy will be emparted into the salt rock mass, the rock mass temperature will rise, and thermal expansion will occur. This thermal expansion will result in a gentle doming of the land surface over the repository. The thermal expansion of the large mass of rock, with the resulting upward movement, could conceivably fracture impermeable barriers that prevented the dissolution of the salt by circulating fresh water from overlying aquifers. In addition, the time-dependent upward movement of the ground mass in the localized area of the repository could cause changes in surface drainage and erosion patterns, which could have some environmental impact. Consequently, the large-scale ground movements, in particular their transient nature, are being modeled numerically to gain a better understanding of the phenomena involved. Also, a coupling is being made of the thermal field with the hydrologic field and the deformation/displacement field in the rock mass overlying a repository, which must ultimately be considered on a site-specific basis.

The thermal loading, in terms of kilowatts per acre of a particular waste type and age, is a site-specific problem. At this conceptual stage, only recommendations that appear to form a reasonable basis for proceeding with the designs can be made. These recommendations are presented in Russell (1979).

PROBLEMS AND UNRESOLVED ISSUES

There are four main periods in the life of a mined nuclear waste repository (Klingsberg and Duguid, 1980).

1. Construction: This is the period during which the installation is being excavated and outfitted. In-situ testing will be performed, and the site will be confirmed or rejected at this time. Only the usual underground construction and mining hazards exist during this period.

2. Operation: During this period radioactive waste is placed in the repository. At this time, it should be possible to retrieve the waste without great difficulty. The potential problems during the operational period include: the general hazards in transporting and handling the radioactive waste packages, the verification of the structural design, ventilation of the installation and any unsuspected potential underground water inrushes.

3. Thermal: This is the first thousand years after the repository has been filled and sealed. It is during this period that the decay of fission products in the high-level waste produces high temperatures in the canister and their surroundings as well as intensive radioactivity. Depending upon how closely the cavities are spaced in the repository and the rock type chosen, rock temperatures could locally exceed $100^{\circ}C$ (boiling point of water). Most of the laboratory and field studies on the various rock types and the majority of the numerical modeling and design studies that have been done have concentrated on the stability of the repository during this period.

4. Post-Thermal: This is the period during which no further significant heat production takes place but radiation from long-lived isotopes continues at unacceptably high levels. If the repository survives the thermal period intact, its structural integrity should not be challenged during the post-thermal period except by externally induced calamities, such as giant meteorite impacts, major nearby earthquakes, dramatic changes in sea level or inadvertent or deliberate intervention by people.

SUMMARY

We have in the United States a large inventory of

radioactive wastes of various types and levels of hazard. We expect this inventory to grow, not just with the continued development and use of nuclear power reactors, but also with the continued development and use of radioactive materials in national defense, medicine, industry, and research. These existing radioactive wastes are presently being stored in temporary surface facilities. The radioactive wastes do pose a long-term (greater than 1,000 years) hazard to human health, if they are not adequately isolated.

Numerous alternative permanent storage and/or disposal strategies have been proposed and studied. One of the least desirable and most potentially hazardous courses of action that can be taken at this time (from a technical point of view) is to do nothing and continue to store the existing radioactive wastes and any future additions to the inventory in temporary surface facilities. The "best" alternative (again from a technical perspective) developed after about 25 years of study is containment of these wastes in mined caverns, deep underground.

There are still uncertainties in site selection criteria, in the design of the underground openings (particularly in regard to their long-term stability at elevated temperatures) and in the prediction of both cultural and natural hazards and their effects on the repository over a very long (greater than 1,000 years) time frame. Yet, the design problems are within the current state-of-the-art, once a particular site has been chosen. While it is not possible to accurately predict or totally eliminate the effects of natural disasters over long periods of time, it is possible to minimize the negative effects of these impacts by careful site selection. The site selection process itself thus emerges as the major difficulty in repository siting. Again, the technical site selection and site qualification problems that exist appear to be solvable within the current state-of-the-art. Site selection for a radioactive waste facility, however, involves more than just technical issues, and it is these nontechnical issues that are the subject of most of the rest of this book.

2
Ethical Considerations Surrounding Nuclear Waste Repository Siting and Mitigation

Ted F. Peters

The storage of high-level nuclear wastes involves a number of ethical and moral issues as well as technical and engineering dimensions. The potential long-term health and safety effects of the nuclear materials stored in repositories, the extremely long periods of time over which such materials may be dangerous, and the equity implications of the siting of a repository in any given area are unlike the issues involved in other large-scale projects. They involve, in fact, major philosophical issues basic to human perspectives on social relationships and on insuring the future of mankind. They are issues likely to lie at the core of the debate over repository siting and to form the basis for societal-wide concern about the repository siting process. An understanding of the basic philosophical issues likely to affect, either directly or indirectly, the nuclear repository siting process is thus essential to an evaluation of the socioeconomic dimensions of nuclear waste storage.

The purpose of this chapter is to provide an overview of four key philosophical and ethical issues related to the siting of high-level nuclear waste repositories which reflect the dominant complex of values in our American culture here labeled the "ethic of equity." The four issues are (1) uncertainty and risk; (2) equity; (3) intergenerational responsibility; and (4) implementation ethics.

In examining the four issues, it is assumed that there are two basic criteria for determining the satisfactoriness or unsatisfactoriness of a waste management proposal: safety and permanence. "My paramount objective in managing nuclear wastes," President Jimmy Carter told Congress on February 12, 1980, "is to protect the health and safety of all Americans both now and in the future." By "safety" we mean protection of the biosphere from radioactive contamination; that is, keeping the level of radiation exposure as low as reasonably achievable (ALARA).[1] By "permanence" we mean that future generations will enjoy the same safety protections we wish for ourselves. Whether or not isolation of toxic waste can be made safe and permanent provides a framework through which we can view the ethical ramifications of siting and mitigation.

The approach taken in this chapter might be called microethics or <u>public ethics</u>. Conventional social ethics or ethical theory in general is concerned with broad ideals, with the establishment and justification of philosophical principles for ordering the whole of human community. In contrast, the goal of public ethics is much more modest. The task of public ethics is to: (1) articulate and clarify the various (even conflicting) public values relevant to a problem; (2) identify and evaluate policy options according to the dominant value complex of a society; and (3) rank alternatives in some order of ethical preferability. We will apply this method to high-level nuclear waste repository siting and mitigation. The broader social, ethical issue of whether or not the U.S. should employ domestic or military nuclear power will not be addressed.[2]

ISSUES OF UNCERTAINTY AND EQUITY OF RISK

Uncertainty

Although uncertainty and risk are not ethical issues in themselves, they are factors which influence and qualify each concern regarding the nuclear fuel cycle. These two terms, risk and uncertainty, do not mean the same thing. Risk has to do with exposure to the chance of injury or death, whereas uncertainty has to do with a lack of conclusive knowledge regarding the nature or degree of the risk. The issue raised by uncertainty is whether or not we should proceed until more is known. The issue raised by risk is one of equity versus inequity.

There are at least three areas of widespread uncertainty that will have a bearing on our ethical concerns (Hebert et al., 1978: 11). The first is uncertainty regarding the health effects of low levels of radiation received in low doses over long periods of time. The second concerns the adequacy of technology to prevent toxic wastes from escaping to the biosphere before decaying to a harmless state, and the third uncertainty has to do with the role played by human fallibility and malevolence. The questions these three uncertainties raise are the following: given these uncertainties should we proceed with terminal storage or follow a no-action policy? Given the criteria of safety and permanence, what are the options?

The first option is no-action. This would mean that high level wastes (HLWs) would remain in their present reactor site and away from reactor (AFR) locations. As time goes by, the quantity of stored wastes would increase. The advantage of this option is that we would be buying time, awaiting technological breakthroughs that might provide greater certainty regarding the ability of the program to provide permanent protection for the biosphere. There is also a disadvantage. The temporary nature of the present above ground storage facilities makes them relatively more susceptible to deterioration, natural cataclysm, and sabotage. In short, while waiting for certain permanence, we might be sacrificing safety.[3]

The second option is to proceed despite the uncertainties. This would, in theory, provide greater safety than the present, temporary storage policy. It has the further advantage that hope for technological breakthroughs on the part of future generations may partially obviate our doubts regarding the ability of the present generation to establish permanent protection.

Risk

Risk can be defined simply as probable loss. But there are two common ways to think about risk, one technical and one more existential. Technically speaking, risk is the probability that an event with adverse effects will occur multiplied by the degree of expected adversity. The technical community calculates risks numerically and compares them quantitatively by using hazard indices. On this basis, due to the low probability factor, calculated risks in nuclear waste management are quite low when compared to risks more commonly confronted (for example, automobile accidents, being struck by lightening, and so on) (Hebert et al., 1978: 14).

In contrast to the technical community, the general public seems to have a tendency to focus on the degree of magnitude, almost ignoring probability. That is, the public presumes the validity of Murphy's Law: if something can go wrong, it will go wrong. From the perspective of the actual or potential victim of contamination, low statistical probability is of little comfort. It is the high magnitude that is so frightening.

The fear is existential, not mathematical, and the psychological effect of this fear is not likely to be relieved by appeals to mathematically calculated low probabilities of exposure to radiation. If this preconscious association of nuclear radiation with the risk of terrifying disease, disfigurement, and death is really at work in our society, then some of the great emotional heat generated by proposals regarding nuclear policy and programs can be understood (Pahner, 1976).

ISSUES OF EQUITY

Equity and Ethics

Equity in common parlance refers to the quality of being fair or impartial in matters of justice. Impartiality is a way of honoring equality and establishing equity, and what the DOE is engaged in now is the establishment of the rules of the equity game as they apply to nuclear waste repository siting. This almost preconscious and prereflective operative ethic of impartiality is rooted in a much more noble and well thought out complex of public values. It is the set of values articulated clearly during the eighteenth century enlightenment and the American Revolution. Because these values have themselves shaped Western culture, they are so much a part of our tradition and present consciousness that they play the role of axiom and norm. The complex of things highly valued includes equality, dignity, freedom, rational knowledge, and justice.

By dignity we mean what Immanuel Kant did when he said that a person should always be treated as an end, not a means. Applied to the present situation, dignity requires that industrial production and technological advance be guided by human ends and purposes.

By freedom we mean primarily autonomy of the individual. In the eighteenth century, the revolution sought liberty in two forms: freedom from ecclesiastical authority in telling us how to think and freedom from the king in telling us what to do. Both forms of liberty depend upon rational knowledge. We believe that truth is important only when it is arrived at by the individual's own reasoning powers. And, further, we need rational and knowledgeable individuals to make up the electorate if our democracy is going to work. Hence, we put high value on education, freedom of speech, and the right to know about facts that influence our lives.

This brings us to the concept of justice. In his widely read **A Theory of Justice**, Harvard professor John Rawls advances an understanding of "justice as fairness." Two fundamental principles, arranged in serial order so that the second is dependent upon the first, stand at the heart of his theory of justice.

1. Each person is to have an equal right to the most extensive basic liberty compatible with a similar liberty for others.

2. Social and economic inequalities are to be arranged so that they are both (a) reasonably expected to be to everyone's advantage, and (b) attached to positions and offices open to all (Rawls, 1971: 60).

For Rawls, equality and equity prescind from these two principles. By equality he means "the features of human beings in virtue of which they are to be treated in accordance with the principles of justice."[4] (We have been calling this equity in order to distinguish it sharply from equality of natural endowment, economic power, social status, and so on).

One aspect of Rawls' theory is of particular interest to us as we ask about nuclear waste disposal siting. It is the difference principle:

> All social values--liberty and opportunity, income and wealth, and the bases of self-respect--are to be distributed equally unless an unequal distribution of any, or all, of these values is to everyone's advantage. Injustice, then, is simply inequalities that are not to the benefit of all (Rawls, 1971: 62).

This difference principle implies two important things. First, undeserved inequalities call for redress (i.e., somehow they should be compensated) (Rawls, 1971: 100). Second, inequality--in our case inequality of risk--can be justified if it works out to everyone's benefit, even to the indirect benefit of the risk-taker. Mitigation, which seeks to equalize risk and benefit for some individuals on behalf of the needs of the entire society, is an example of Rawls' notion of reciprocity, the "principle of mutual benefit" (Rawls, 1971: 102).

By equity of risk we do not mean everyone's risk is equal; rather, everyone's treatment before the law is equal. Equity has to do with procedure. It means, at minimum, a fair and impartial adjudicating of risk matters. And where some individuals are subjected to greater risk than others, and when this subjection is done deliberately to benefit the whole group, the equity principle implies mitigation in the form of increased benefit or compensation for those shouldering increased risk.

The issue of equity of risk makes its appearance primarily when confronting the question of geographical location for the terminal storage facility. It makes its appearance secondarily on the question of intergenerational ethics. In both cases the actual ethical concerns may be obscured by nuclear age psychology (that is, by the perhaps unrealistic fear caused by current images of radioactive effects upon human health). This raises an additional issue then for implementation ethics: to what extent are U.S. government and industry officials morally responsible for sympathetically working through and calming the fears of the affected populace?

Each of these risk-equity issues--geographic equity,

intergenerational responsibility and implementation
ethics--is discussed in the following pages.

The Issue of Geographic Equity

Can the whole society ask only a small community--a
community which may or may not benefit directly from a
nuclear reactor--to bear the greatest risk by hosting the
waste disposal site? It appears that if only a few high
level waste disposal sites are selected, claims of
geographical inequality will be raised. The residents of
a state hosting the repository will be put at risk from
radioactive contaminants generated in other states. This
will be an extension of procedures presently in force for
low level waste burial and high level storage. What
forms of compensation will there be for those who live
near a waste repository? What mechanisms of redress will
go into effect for those individuals who may actually
suffer genetic or health damage? These questions about
involuntary and undue increase in risk arise in regard to
the residents who will remain in the waste disposal site
area.

Accidents of Geography. Just as we have accidents
of birth, we have accidents of geography. Some
individuals are naturally endowed with high intelligence
or strong physical constitution, while others are born
mentally retarded or physically weak. Justice as
fairness does not require that we equalize these natural
inequalities; it requires that we provide appropriate
opportunity and fairness of social procedure. The just
society seeks to coordinate all the natural inequalities
into a cooperative fraternity so that everyone benefits.
What about accidents of geography? Some individuals
may be born on and inherit a plot of mother earth in
North Dakota that is later discovered to be pregnant with
petroleum; but North Dakota winters can reach 40 degrees
below zero and there is much snow to shovel. Others grow
up in the Detroit area learning manufacturing skills with
the invitation to work on an automobile assembly line,
but an economic slump brings long hours waiting in
unemployment lines. We take it for granted that our
geographical location is determinative (that is, it opens
some doors and closes others). It grants its own
combination of benefits and risks.
How then should we think about salt domes? What
about the people residing near Richton, Mississippi, or
Vacherie, Louisiana? In a sense they are endowed with a
natural resource that in principle can serve to benefit
us all. Just as the whole nation needs the automobiles
produced in Detroit's backyard or the electrical power
generated by a Columbia River dam, so also the whole
nation may need the particular geological formation that
exists in the backyards of only a few select communities.

Can we consider a salt dome repository containing HLW as just one more accident of geography? We might be tempted to say "yes" and then draw the implication that dome area residents should receive no special treatment. Certainly autoworkers in Detroit receive no special treatment by virtue of their geographical location. They must be satisfied with their respective risks and benefits. Should repository residents be treated (or nontreated) the same way?

To argue that they should be treated the same way and given no special redress (even granting truth to the perception that risk to health is increased) rests upon what we might call the naturalistic fallacy. The naturalistic position presupposes that the way things are naturally supplies us with the criterion for establishing what is good (or at least what is satisfactory) and hence, what ought to be.[5] The appeal to the natural state of affairs, however, has not in fact been treated as satisfactory with regard to certain other matters. Rivers are not left to run their course; governments and corporations dam them up. If a proposed dam causes population dislocation, the dislocated are compensated. Damaging weather in the form of drought or tornado in agricultural areas often results in disaster relief and low interest loans for rebuilding. Even Chrysler Corporation in Detroit has received financial aid during a business slump. Thus, it would be inconsistent to deny redress to salt dome area residents by appealing to the natural risk factors due solely to accidents of geography.

On the other hand, this same set of observations can be used to support the notion that it is just to have the repositories located in somebody's backyard. First, HLWs now exist. Whether stored AFR or finally disposed of, they must be located somewhere. To place them nowhere is not an option. Second, some locations are more appropriate than others. Due to the seriousness of health and safety factors, the most appropriate host geological formations are demanded. As in the case of dam construction, justice can similarly be done if the inequalities of risk resulting from repository siting meet two criteria: (1) they can be reasonably expected to result in everyone's advantage, and (2) those individuals and communities incurring particularly adverse impacts are offered a means of redress and are duly compensated. These two criteria satisfy the complex of public values earlier adumbrated.

We need to consider one more point regarding accidents of geography, namely, benefits. One can inherit benefits as well as risks. The issue of geographical equity is sometimes formulated: those people residing near a waste repository will bear a risk greater than the benefit they gain from nuclear power, and in some cases they may derive no benefit at all from nuclear power. Some propose to remedy inequality by locating nuclear power plants and repositories together in nuclear parks so local residents receive both benefits and risks together. But this reasoning is fallacious. (Locating them together may be a good idea but other technical or fiscal reasons should be mustered.) Such reasoning presupposes that benefit means strictly the home use of electricity drawn directly from the reactor. This is too narrow an understanding of benefits. The benefits from nuclear power generation are quite diffuse. In addition to residential use, reactor power fuels industries which may send their products all across the country if not the world. Because the nation's energy supply comes from diverse sources—coal, gas, petroleum, solar conversion, hydropower, and so on—nuclear reactors represent only one gear in the larger energy transmission system. The various systems are linked, interrelated, overlapping, and mutually reinforcing. The whole nation benefits from the whole energy program. It is difficult and even unnecessary to try to discern just who individually is benefitting directly or indirectly from a given nuclear power generation plant.

Confronting Geographical Inequality. The issue of unequal distribution of risk must be confronted. A plan for establishing a so-called equal distribution of risk would be nonsense, however. The cost of disposal in mined geologic repositories plus the very special conditions required of the host site means we could not geographically distribute repositories so as to equalize exactly the risk among the entire citizenry, nor could we even among those selected elements of the citizenry who profit most directly from the generation of such wastes. And when it comes to spreading something to achieve equality, it is not risk to health and safety that we ordinarily wish to spread. What we should spread at most is economic liability so as to be prepared to compensate those residing in the high risk zones.

The criterion of safety would imply that we ought not increase risk just to attain equal distribution. If by minimizing risk we end up with some individuals facing greater risk than others, the inequality can be justified only (1) by determining that increased risk to the few results in increased benefit for the whole of society and (2) by compensating those bearing the greater risk. The ethical burden of geographical inequality falls primarily on the shoulders of point two, mitigation. It is in the presuppositions and assumptions brought to the mitigation process that we locate the ethical issues.

Ethical Options. The parties to any mitigation process will include repository area residents, U.S. government officials, nuclear industry representatives, and legal counselors. What are the ethical options?

There are options other than the system of public ethics which we have just examined.

The first option is that of self-sacrificing love. This ethic places humility and service higher on the ladder of values than equality. Equality is not repudiated, just subordinated. Rather than dub other people as equals, it exalts them. Applied to the repository residents facing the prospect of geographical inequality, such an ethic of self-sacrificing love could possibly motivate some to volunteer to put a repository into their own backyard in order to reduce risk to others. Because of its radical character, the ethic of self-sacrificing is extremely rare. It is not part of our public ethics. We cannot count on very many U.S. communities embracing it. And if they did, it would be unfair (or inequitable) to permit them to do so without appropriate compensation.

A second option is utilitarian hedonism. Hedonism is that scheme in which happiness is defined as pleasure (the satisfaction of desire) and that pleasure, and only pleasure, is intrinsically good, while pain is bad. Utilitarianism as a form of hedonism is popularly known as: "the greatest happiness of the greatest number."[6] This principle is ambiguous, however, because it is not clear as to whether the emphasis is to be placed on the greatest happiness or on the greatest number (Sahakian, 1974).

Utilitarianism teaches further that the rightness of actions is to be determined by their consequences. If a given action actually functions to maximize the quality of happiness or to spread happiness to more people, then it is judged as right. Extreme utilitarianism teaches that moral rules are only rules of thumb and that they can be broken whenever doing so presents the opportunity for producing greater happiness for more people (Smart, 1967: 171-183).

By applying utilitarianism to the issue of geographical equity, the principle of equity itself may be abrogated if the resulting action would increase the satisfaction of desire. Increasing the risk to safety for some U.S. residents could be justified if the net good consequences for some people exceeded the bad consequences for others (that is, if the benefits exceeded the costs). One might even quantify the factors and produce a cost-benefit formula. However, the weakness in this approach is that it fails to provide moral criteria for determining who gets the costs and who gets the benefits. Its ambiguity on this point could be employed to justify the imposition of severe risk upon a minority as long as the action maximized benefits to the social aggregate or even to a select wealthy few. It would in addition relativize the criterion of safety, because a sacrifice in safety could be considered a cost outweighed by a benefit of still higher prosperity.

A third option is our ethic of equity (that is, justice as fairness). One form of ethical law is the golden rule: do unto others as you would have them do unto you. In some fashion or other, the golden rule may make its appearance during disposal site mitigation procedures. Community residents will undoubtedly say, "Well, if it's so safe, why don't you put it in your own backyard!" Those in charge of siting these materials, if they want to be ethical, will have to affirm in all honesty that they are not asking others to shoulder responsibilities they themselves are unwilling to shoulder. The program recommendation should be translatable into a universal law: we are not asking the residents near the disposal site to do anything we ourselves would not be willing to do if we were in their situation.

In interpreting this universal law, the distinction made earlier between equality and equity applies. Equity requires impartiality and fairness in procedure. It does not require that everyone share the identical risk. Mitigation is the tool whereby we achieve equity, not equality. Because of the complex of values which constitute the ethic of equity, we may draw at least three operative corollaries from this universal law. First, the repositories should be made as safe as possible; that is, at least as safe as the designers and managers would require if they themselves were to live in the vicinity. Second, a means of redress should be open so that residents may choose to move out of the area and resettle elsewhere at no financial loss to them. Third, those who choose to remain should be compensated in reasonable proportion to the adverse effects of social, economic, cultural, and quality of life impacts.

Compensation and Bribes. The ethic of equity would further discriminate between compensation and bribes. Justified would be compensation (to the degree that it could be accurately calculated) as payment for actual damages or loss incurred as a result of repository siting. Not justified ethically would be overpayment or bribes that amount to windfall profits based solely on accidents of geography. The difference between these two, however, will be very difficult to determine.[7] The disruption of a community's quality of life could not be quantified and measured simply in terms of dollar repayments. Because of this, the ethic of equity might suggest that any known error tip toward the side of overpayment or reward rather than risk inequity.

THE ISSUE OF INTERGENERATIONAL RESPONSIBILITY

With regard to the discussion among philosophers and ethicists that is most relevant to HLW management, overwhelming attention has focused on one particular issue: the impact of nuclear waste disposal on future generations. The concern over the impact of radioactive waste upon future generations is predicated upon our technical inability (or at least our uncertainty regarding such inability) to meet one of the two criteria for satisfactory waste disposal: that is, permanence. The issue involves the questions of: how can we morally justify the bequeathal on the part of the present generation of risks and responsibilities that might gravely endanger the health and safety of future generations? How morally appropriate is it for one group to satisfy its own consumptive desires for a few decades and then exact payment from countless as yet to be born civilizations for hundreds of thousands of years? Note that this formulation makes a certain technological assumption, namely, it is now not possible to guarantee permanence on the basis of present disposal technolgy. This is the uncertainty assumption. A change in the uncertainty assumption would result in a change in the formulation of the issue.

In addition to uncertainty, there is risk. Time of radioactive decay is one factor in determining the degree of risk; however, risk has to do with the possibility of exposure and its concomitant adverse physical effects. Even with the most optimistic technical estimates regarding the future behavior of buried nuclear waste, some vigilance will be required of our descendents in order to maintain their own safety. At minimum, they will have to read the instructions on a monument marking an unattended waste repository warning against drilling into it. At maximum, they may be required to run expensive institutions to monitor and service the repositories in order to protect their own safety and well-being. How much vigilance the present generation can require of them is an ethical question.

If uncertainties remain regarding isolation of toxic materials, we might have to consider a disposition that is reversible. Plans are already being made to maintain retrievability of spent fuel rods for a half century pending decisions regarding reprocessing. But more might be called for here. Perhaps it should be retrievable by a future generation with comparable or superior technology in the event that that generation produces a better form of waste management or if it needs access to the HLW to prevent the life-threatening migration of nuclides (Lovins and Price, 1975: 34). In suggesting this principle of retrievability, however, we increase the possibility of site sabotage and nuclear vandalism.

The Option of Discounting the Future

Economist Kenneth Boulding has introduced us to terms such as time-discounting and discounting the future. In doing so he acknowledges a human tendency to avoid taking responsibility for posterity (that is, the further into the future we look the less we believe it affects our current responsibility) (1972: 239).

The practice of discounting the future can be supported with ethical reasoning. The first argument on behalf of discounting the future is based upon uncertainty. We cannot be certain today just what future effects our HLW repositories might have; we cannot even be certain that anyone will be alive in the distant terrestrial future; and if they are alive, we do not know what their technological capabilities will be. Therefore, we should proceed with plans to maximize benefits for ourselves in the near future. Uncertainties regarding not yet existent progeny should not be a determining factor in present decision making on HLW management.

The second argument prescinds from the first. We will call it the hope argument. The hope argument contends that one ought to choose the option which holds the greatest hope, even if it also holds the greatest risk. This argument has the advantage of facing realistically the uncertainty assumption. Although it might appear to compromise the criterion of permanence, it would do so with the expectation that something still better may result. Its chief disadvantage (at least in terms of the equity ethic) is that it may invite laxity regarding the responsibility of the present generation to seek that breakthrough. By implication, it might subordinate the rights of the as yet unborn to the rights of those currently alive.

The third argument in behalf of present desires over future obligations presupposes indefinite continued growth in prosperity. It assumes that future generations will be better off than present or past generations. Why should we sacrifice on behalf of our richer descendents? We should not be obligated to impose sacrifices on poorer contemporaries to benefit richer successors. In other words, this argument presupposes no obligatons to future generations.

There is another option apart from our ethic of equity. Some justification for discounting the future can be drawn from a mindset quite prevalent in contemporary North American society. We may call it the ethic of self-realization. According to this scheme, the highest good or moral ideal consists in realizing, actualizing, or fulfilling one's true nature or self. Its roots go back to classical eudaemonism (from the ancient Greek word for "happiness"), the ideology of satisfying one's appetites, and more recently draws from the work of psychologist Abraham Maslow and his "hierarchy of needs" thesis.

If self-realizationism follows a radically individualistic track, then it will have only minimal concern for members of future civilizations we will never live to see. It would seek happiness at the top of the hierarchy of needs, at the level of intellectual or psychological fulfillment, not at the primary level of food, shelter, and safety. This requires affluence. Affluence requires energy. Advocates of self-realization could be persuaded to accept the trade-offs required by the nuclear power industry if they could be guaranteed benefits in the form of more of the good life. Mitigation will require considerable cultural if not financial compensation for self-realizationists.

The Option of Intergenerational Equity Ethics

With regard to intergenerational responsibilities associated with high-level waste management, five elements seem apparent: (1) whether or not nuclear power generation in general proceeds, high-level waste exists now and something needs to be done about it; (2) the potential hazard to human health and environmental safety will remain for hundreds if not thousands of years; (3) the ethic of equity common to our culture presupposes that we share some sort of moral community with generations as yet unborn; (4) there are at minimum moral constraints against the present generation taking neglective action that would result in harm to future generations; and (5) there may be positive obligations of one sort or another which we today must exercise on behalf of our progeny.

IMPLEMENTATION ETHICS

What does the discussion above indicate about the implementation of repository policies? Three things. First, it requires at minimum the best application of technology and management we can offer to reduce the degree of risk to as low a level as is achievable. This may be called executive or implementation ethics.

We must use our best design. In addition, no quality gap should be permitted between design and implementation. The best technology ought not be compromised due to fiscal thrift or managerial corner cutting.

Second, we owe our progeny knowledge of the hazard. The withholding of knowledge seems to violate the ethical sensibilities of post-enlightenment Western people. It would be consistent with the ethic of equity to use multiple forms of communication with future generations, least of which would be an on-site warning monument. The availability of a complete description of repository holdings would maximize the options of future generations. We are obligated to take all measures possible to help insure the site against nuclear vandalism or sabotage, but complete ignorance of its existence does not seem to be an ethical means for achieving this insurance.

If an honest assessment of our technological capability leaves a significant number of uncertainties remaining, then a third requirement might be called for. Mitigation may require site management expense sharing and accident indemnification. The present benefactor of nuclear power should consider investing a portion of the accrued wealth in an endowment fund, gathered from a repository deposit tax. Some of the interest could be drawn for maintenance expenses, with the remainder being compounded to create an accident insurance fund. Should there be a continuity of financial institutions over a long period with a minimum of expensive repository emergencies, the eventual dispersal of accrued wealth could be seen as a fortuitous contribution by the present generation to the welfare of the future.

An Implementation Ethic

In sum, it would be advisable to cultivate and reinforce a moral climate that honors safety, thoroughness, and careful judgement. This is asking for more than quality design engineering. It is asking for the deliberate encouragement of a safety ethic among all those involved in nuclear waste management.

CONCLUSION

This chapter provides an overview of ethical considerations surrounding the siting and mitigation of nuclear waste repositories. The ethical premises discussed are those of the dominant American culture, and these values are applied to four major repository-related issues: uncertainty and risks, geographic equity, intergenerational ethics and implemenation ethics. The questions raised are those which need to be addressed as potential repository sites are selected and communities in various states become involved in repository plans. Indeed, they are issues which not only Federal, state, and local government officials and the citizens of the affected communties must resolve, but which the public-at-large must also resolve, given that universal criteria of safety and permanence and the complex of American values which include equality, dignity, freedom, rational knowledge, and justice.

NOTES

1. The Swedish Stipulation Act of April 1977 requires that the final disposition of highly radioactive

waste be effected with "absolute safety." When pressed as to how "absolute safety" should be interpreted, a committee of Parliament said that a "draconian" interpretation of safety requirements is not intended. The term "draconian" ordinarily means excessively severe, inhuman. The Swedish Radiation Protection Agency has adopted a guideline of a maximum radiation exposure dose rate of 10 millirems per year around nuclear power plants. No specific dose rate has as yet been assigned to final disposal sites (Johansson and Steen, 1981: 22f, 35, 67f, 181). Hence, we employ here the qualifier ALARA (as low as reasonably achievable). See the work of Maxey (1978: 130).

2. This is an extremely important issue, to be sure. However, even if there were to be a decision to invoke an immediate moratorium on all fission processes that radically altered our social and economic order, the present concern of public ethics would remain. High level nuclear wastes already exist in significantly large quantities. Something must be done about them. Even if production of high-level nuclear waste were to cease tommorrow, we would still be confronted with the task of disposing of already existing waste. Therefore, we may deal with the question of HLW disposal as an issue of public ethics because the basic ethical concerns are likely to remain constant regardless of how the larger question of nuclear power generation is resolved.

3. "The no-action alternative is undesirable because of the temporary nature of present storage of wastes, the need to construct additional facilities for extended storage as present facilities reach their design lifetime, and because the no-action alternative is contrary to the presidential proclamation and could be construed as contrary to the mandate given DOE by law" U.S. Department of Energy, 1980b: 1.31.

4. Rawls uses moral capacity rather than imputed dignity to justify human equality. But that is not important to our concern in this paper. What is important is his difference principle (1971: 504).

5. By "naturalistic fallacy" I am referring to the age old attempt to derive an "ought" from what "is," something the philosopher David Hume said one ought not do. My motive in using the term here is not to argue for a philosophical foundation to ethics; it is rather to alert the reader to the possible fallacious justification for leaving nature in its present state; that is, for avoiding taking technological action. In recent philosophical discussion the term "naturalistic fallacy" recalls G. E. Moore's polemic against naturalistic and metaphysical systems of ethics, wherein he contends that (1) the **good** cannot be defined in terms of natural qualities and, furthermore, (2) the **good** is the fact indefinable. To define it in any terms other than itself is to commit a fallacy (1968: 10-13, 73, 77). W.K.

Frankena (1967: 50-63) has also argued that the
naturalistic fallacy does not have the status of a
logical fallacy. It rather represents a position taken
on whether or not one can define the good. Again, the
point I am making here is much more modest in scope,
namely, our moral action cannot be guided simply by the
condition of the present state of nature.

6. It seems that this principle of utility was
first stated in this form by Francis Hutcheson (1725)
that action is best which procures the greatest happiness
for the greatest numbers. Utilitarianism's most famous
proponents were Jeremy Bentham (1748-1832) and John
Stuart Mill (1806-1873).

7. Carnes et al. use the term "incentives" to
include three functionally different categories: (1) to
mitigate potential risks or adverse impacts which occur
during construction and normal operation of the facility;
(2) to **compensate** individuals for actual damages in the
event of an abnormal occurrence; and (3) to **reward** the
host community for assuming the costs and risks
associated with resolving a nonlocal problem (1981: 115).
This glossary successfully blurs the distinction between
compensation and bribe. A case could possibly be made,
however, that it is just and equitable that a community
be so rewarded.

3
Federal, State, and Local Socioeconomic Management Dimensions in Nuclear Waste Disposal

James R. Finley

The United States Department of Energy (DOE) has the lead role in managing the nation's high-level nuclear wastes. This chapter presents an overview of the DOE management program with particular emphasis upon the socioeconomic management component. This component examines the socioeconomic effects arising from the siting, construction, and operation of nuclear waste repositories. The overall management structure of DOE and general considerations in repository siting are discussed first, followed by a detailed discussion of the management structure and the goals, scope, and components of the socioeconomic management program.

THE MINED GEOLOGIC REPOSITORY PROGRAM

Mined geologic repositories have been selected as the means of disposing of the nation's high-level radioactive wastes. **The Final Environmental Impact Statement: Management of Commercially Generated Radioactive Wastes** (U.S. Department of Energy, 1980a) evaluated alternative methods of disposal and concluded that emplacement of radioactive wastes in deep geologic formations would result in minimal and acceptable environmental consequences. Subsequently, DOE published a decision to proceed with the program of research and development leading to the siting and development of geological repositories (U.S. Department of Energy, 1981c).
In making this decision, the protection of the health and safety of the populace was of primary concern to DOE. The repositories to be sited thus will be engineered to provide maximum safety to populations in close proximity to repository sites (see chapter 1 for a description of the technical features of a repository).

NATIONAL WASTE TERMINAL STORAGE PROGRAM

The Department of Energy established the National Waste Terminal Storage (NWTS) Program to insure that nuclear waste management problems will not be deferred to future generations. The NWTS program identifies potential repository sites and develops technologies and methods required to design, license, construct, operate, and decommission repositories.

Four related projects function within NWTS. The Office of Nuclear Waste Isolation (ONWI) is responsible for developing generic technology common to geologic repositories and for exploration of non-DOE lands. The Basalt Waste Isolation Project (BWIP) investigates basalt formations underlying DOE's Hanford site. The Nevada Nuclear Waste Storage Investigations (NNWSI) is looking at different types of rock (mainly tuff which is a volcanic ash) at the DOE Nevada Test Site. The feasibility of subseabed disposal, an alternative to mined geologic disposal, is being studied by the Subseabed Disposal Program.

The Department of Energy's Office of Waste Isolation is responsible for overall direction of the NWTS program. This office provides direction and guidance on technical programs and has responsiblity for budgetary allocations. Organization of the management structure is displayed in figure 3.1. The Department of Energy, with lead responsibility for waste management, coordinates Federal interagency relationships in waste management, maintains working relationships with the regulatory agencies (that is, the Environmental Protection Agency and the Nuclear Regulatory Commission), and develops ties and working relationships with the states.

REPOSITORY SITING PROCESS[1]

In keeping with the primary concern of DOE, protection of the public health and safety is the primary objective of the selection of the candidate sites for a nuclear waste repository. Site selection requirements, criteria, principles, and procedures have been developed to insure that the primary objective is met.

Site Functional Requirements

Functional requirements of the candidate sites for a repository apply to the repository operation function and to the containment and isolation function. For operations, a site must provide: (1) an adequate volume of rock for underground mining and waste emplacement, (2) a host rock in which underground areas can be safely mined, (3) suitable surface features for above ground facilities, (4) a hydrologic environment compatible with

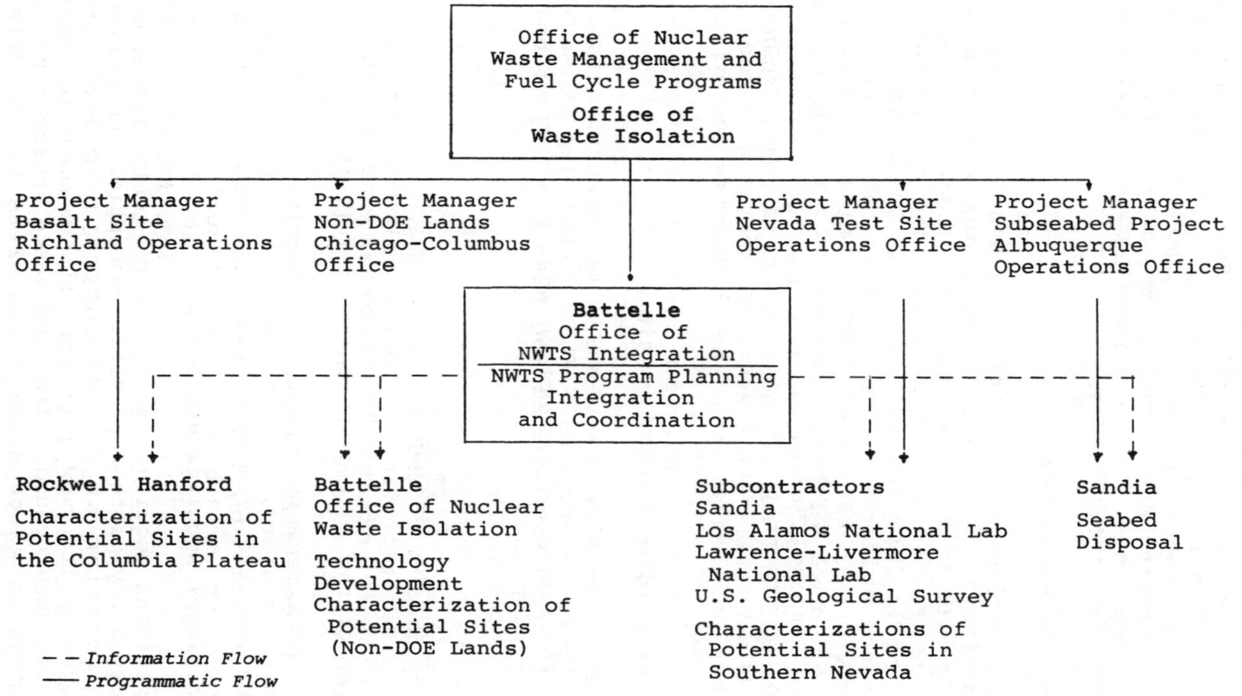

```
          ┌─────────────────────┐
          │ Office of Nuclear   │
          │ Waste Management and│
          │ Fuel Cycle Programs │
          │                     │
          │    Office of        │
          │  Waste Isolation    │
          └─────────────────────┘
```

Project Manager
Basalt Site
Richland Operations
Office

Project Manager
Non-DOE Lands
Chicago-Columbus
Office

Project Manager
Nevada Test Site
Operations Office

Project Manager
Subseabed Project
Albuquerque
Operations Office

```
          ┌─────────────────────┐
          │     Battelle        │
          │    Office of        │
          │  NWTS Integration   │
          ├─────────────────────┤
          │ NWTS Program Planning│
          │   Integration       │
          │  and Coordination   │
          └─────────────────────┘
```

Rockwell Hanford

Characterization of
Potential Sites in
the Columbia Plateau

Battelle
Office of Nuclear
Waste Isolation

Technology
Development
Characterization of
Potential Sites
(Non-DOE Lands)

Subcontractors
Sandia
Los Alamos National Lab
Lawrence-Livermore
 National Lab
U.S. Geological Survey

Characterizations of
Potential Sites in
Southern Nevada

Sandia

Seabed
Disposal

− − Information Flow
─── Programmatic Flow

Figure 3.1

NWTS Program Management Structure

the construction and sealing of shafts, and (5) a location at which environmental and socioeconomic impacts from repository construction and operation would not render the site unacceptable. For containment and isolation, the site must provide natural barriers to contain the wastes, isolate the wastes from man, and assist in keeping man away from the wastes; that is, it must be deep enough to discourage human intrusion (U.S. Department of Energy, 1982a).

Site Performance Criteria

Site performance criteria have also been developed. These criteria are those conditions that enable a candidate site to meet the functional requirements and to address environmental and socioeconomic considerations (Office of Nuclear Waste Isolation, 1981). These site performance criteria, summarized in table 3.1, can be categorized into two sets. One set (Criteria 1 through 8) is concerned with public health and safety. The second set (Criteria 9 and 10) contributes to environmental and socioeconomic acceptability. However, all of the criteria are taken into account in the search for repository sites and the determination of site suitability.

Principles Guiding Repository Siting

DOE has developed several principles to guide the repository siting process. These principles, discussed in detail in the **National Siting Plan** (U.S. Department of Energy, 1982a), are:

1. public involvement
2. quality of information
3. compliance with NRC procedures
4. consideration of the potential impacts of proposed actions in accordance with the National Environmental Policy Act (NEPA)

Stepwise Procedure for Siting

The principles, functional requirements, and site performance criteria have been formulated by DOE because perfect, flawless sites for repositories do not exist in nature. At the same time, many sites exist which could be shown to be suitable for waste disposal. DOE and its contractors intend to concentrate their resources on investigating the more favorable sites. In order to do so, a method of screening sites has been developed to assist in narrowing the focus to three or more alternative sites from which one or more sites may be selected for development.

The screening process consists of four basic steps

Table 3.1

Site Suitability Criteria

Criteria	Subcriteria
1. Site geology	Minimum depth Thickness and lateral extent of host rock
2. Geohydrology	Geohydrological regime Hydrological regime/shaft construction Subsurface rock dissolution
3. Geochemistry	Geochemical interactions

4. Geological character-
   istics
	Subsurface setting
	Host rock characteristics
	Induced stresses and host
	   rock response
	Engineering feasibility

5. Tectonic environment	Tectonic elements Major regional faults Near faults Quaternary igneous activity Uplift or subsidence rates Ground motion
6. Human intrusion	Resources Exploration history Ownership control
7. Surface characteristics	Surficial hydrologic system Surface topographic features Meteorological conditions Nearby hazards
8. Demography	Human proximity Transportation risk

9. Environmental
   protection
	Environmental impact
	Land use conflicts
	Normal and extreme environ-
	   mental conditions

10. Social, political,
    and economic impacts
	Social impact
	Access and utility
	   requirements

which lead to a detailed characterization of specific sites. The site functional requirements, performance criteria, and principles outlined above set the standards for assessment during each step. The basic steps are:

1. national surveys to determine regions containing host rock, geohydrologic environments, and ecological and socioeconomic conditions amenable to repository development

2. regional surveys to evaluate and identify, through literature reviews, any smaller-sized areas

3. area surveys to screen for locations

4. locations, which are usually tens of square miles, are studied to identify a site or sites for detailed site studies

Consultation with state and local officials and dissemination of public information occurs at each step, as appropriate. As each screening decision is made, there is a review and consultation with involved states.

Repository Development Schedule

The first repository for disposal of high-level nuclear waste is scheduled to be in operation around the year 2000. Between now and that date, there are several key activities that must be accomplished. These include the digging of exploratory shafts at three potential repository sites, design and construction of a test and evaluation (T&E) facility which will provide necessary experience in waste disposal techniques, the filing for and receipt of a license to construct a repository from the NRC, and repository construction. The overall NWTS repository schedule is displayed in figure 3.2.

MANAGEMENT OF SOCIOECONOMIC IMPACTS[2]

To manage socioeconomic impacts resulting from the siting, construction, operation, and decommissioning of a nuclear waste repository, The Office of Nuclear Waste Isolation (ONWI) has established a socioeconomic group. This group manages the subcontract activity and develops recommendations for impact mitigation. The ONWI Socioeconomic Program is discussed below.

63

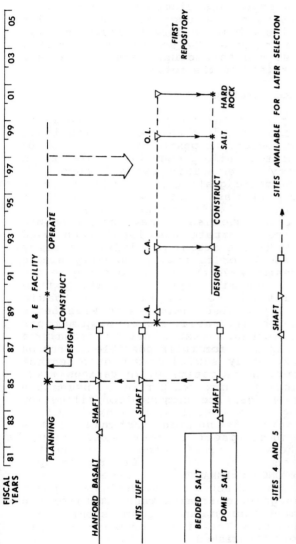

Figure 3.2

Repository Siting Schedule

Issues Addressed by the Socioeconomic Program

The Socioeconomic Program is designed to address waste isolation issues of a socioeconomic nature. A brief summary of the major socioeconomic issues which have been raised by the public to date is shown in table 3.2. This table also indicates the socioeconomic program tasks which are designed to address these issues and others which may be raised in the future.

Objectives, Goals, and Strategies

The major objective of the socioeconomic program is to address social, economic, and related institutional issues so that mined geologic repositories can be sited, constructed, and operated while preserving highly valued aspects of community life. This overall objective supports NWTS' programmatic goals to: (1) address major social and economic issues associated with radioactive waste isolation in a timely manner, (2) attain interaction with affected parties to make socioeconomic activities responsive to state and local needs and preferences, so that, to the extent possible, necessary agreements may be made prior to final repository siting decisions, and (3) design ways and means to mitigate any adverse social and economic impacts resulting from repository construction and operation. The basic strategy for addressing socioeconomic issues will be to analyze issues raised by the public and develop methods of resolving these issues. Issues determined to be significant will be assessed for their possible impact on the ONWI program. Mechanisms will be designed so that socioeconomic impacts can be mitigated in various ways, including consultation with affected parties, information dissemination and exchange, and compensation/mitigation programs.
An integral part of the basic strategy is a community development process that will ensure incorporation of the views of affected and interested states and localities in the program. Other principle components include provisions for assessing the socioeconomic impacts at affected sites, designing impact mitigation, and designing institutions to monitor the effectiveness of impact mitigation.

Scope of Socioeconomic Program

A range of activities is planned to achieve the socioeconomic program objectives. Key activities are to: (1) coordinate and integrate the socioeconomic efforts of DOE, ONWI, and the states, (2) analyze socioeconomic issues and impact assessments, (3) meet NEPA and other regulatory criteria that may require evaluation and mitigation of adverse social and economic impacts, (4)

Table 3.2

Socioeconomic Program Tasks and
Major Issues Raised by the Public

Socioeconomic Program Tasks	Major Issues Raised by the Public
Socioeconomic Impacts and Assessments	• What are the socioeconomic impacts involved in siting a repository? . How will land values in the vicinity of a repository be affected? . How will a repository affect the quality of life in a community? . What effect will the population influx have on community services? . Will fear and anxiety cause people to move out of a community? . Will a cost-of-living increase result and how will it affect those on fixed incomes? . Will the repository create a boomtown situation? . What will happen to the community once the site is closed? . Will there be an equitable distribution of risks and impacts? . Will those who live near a waste facility bear greater risks than others? . Is the present generation transferring inordinate risks to future generations?
Community Development Approach to Impact Mitigation	• Will socioeconomic impacts be mitigated? . How will social disruption and economic problems be dealt with? . How can community growth and development occur in an orderly and timely fashion? Will technical assistance be provided for community growth? . Will there be adequate front-end financing provided by the federal government for socio-economic impact mitigation? . Can fear and anxiety over radiation contamination be alleviated? . What is the role of the public in waste management decision making?
Monitoring and Organizational Analysis	• What institutions will be responsible for operating the repository? . When will the transfer of waste ownership occur? . What organization or institution will own the waste? . How will socioeconomic impacts and mitigation efforts be monitored? . How long will DOE monitor the repository site?

provide a systematic assessment of the tangible and intangible benefits and costs to a community that could result from repository development and operation, (5) design strategies to mitigate adverse social and economic impacts and methods to implement such strategies, (6) assist repository site communities in assessing their development needs and organizing for impact management, and (7) provide socioeconomic input to and review of various documents produced throughout the NWTS program.

Approach to Implementing the Program

Innovative methods, including new legislation for mitigating socioeconomic impacts, may be required for the implementation of the nuclear waste isolation program. There are two classes of impacts that must be addressed. One class consists of standard or conventional impacts that would be associated with any large-scale construction or mining activity. Another class includes special or nonconventional impacts, such as public perceptions of health and safety risks associated with nuclear waste isolation.

The program will be implemented through a combination of DOE actions and guidance, supported by ONWI staff and subcontractor activities.

SOCIOECONOMIC PROGRAM TASKS

Major tasks of the socioeconomic program are designed to address and resolve issues raised by Federal, state, and local agencies and the public and to meet legal and regulatory requirements. The major task areas include efforts to: (1) develop socioeconomic impact methodologies and provide impact assessments, (2) design and implement a community development approach to impact mitigation, and (3) conduct institutional and organizational analyses related to the monitoring and management of a repository system.

Socioeconomic Impacts and Assessments

The nuclear repository siting process requires consideration of a large number of potentially significant socioeconomic impacts. The impacts will result primarily from the relatively large scale of the project contrasted to the size of nearby communities. The siting, construction, and operation of repositories will involve many standard effects similar in nature to those of other large developments. Some of the impacts include: (1) economic effects such as increased local employment, (2) demographic effects, for example, increased population growth, (3) fiscal impacts such as changes in property values and reassessments, (4) increased demands for community services, and (5) social impacts such as perceived changes in the quality of life. Nuclear waste repositories may also have effects that are unique or special; that is, those related to public perceptions of health and safety aspects of waste transportation and isolation. Examples of such special effects would be public perceptions of health and safety risks from the storage of radioactive materials and the possible psychological stress of residents near a repository site. The standard and special impacts both at localities along transportation routes and at repository sites will be addressed in the program.

There are two kinds of assessment activities. One is to select, refine, and develop impact assessment methodologies; the other is to conduct the assessments. These activities are supported by special studies in which the range of inquiry can be broad, as in a literature review or a scoping study, or it can be limited to a very specific subject, such as the question of how to assess special effects.

Methods to assess socioeconomic impacts are being formulated to provide a consistent basis for comparing impacts across the NWTS units. Current efforts in this area include selection, development, refinement, and validation of methods for assessing economic, demographic, public service, fiscal, social, and special impacts of repositories. A SocioEconomic Analysis of Repository Siting Model (SEARS) is being developed which will permit comparative assessments to be made of the impacts a repository would have on alternative sites. As the methods and procedures are refined to meet the needs of the program, they will be verified to ascertain their validity and reliability. Upon verification, they will be utilized in impact assessments.

Impact assessment occurs at various phases throughout the ONWI siting program, but emphasis is placed on community-level analysis, early shaft construction, test and evaluation, facility authorization, and final repository site selection. Environmental decision or recommendation documents will be produced for each phase. The socioeconomic impact analysis will become more detailed as the program moves to the location in detailed site characterization stages. Because most socioeconomic impacts are site-specific, socioeconomic variables can be expected to play an increasingly important role in the decision process during later phases of the siting process. Procedures now being developed will be used to guide site characterization efforts in data collection and in the analysis of socioeconomic impacts. These efforts will contribute to the socioeconomic component of environmental assessments, environmental impact statements, other environmental documents, and decision/recommendation documents which permit the site selection program to move forward.

Community Development Approach to Impact Mitigation

The socioeconomic impacts of a repository can be mitigated using a wide spectrum of mechanisms. The socioeconomic program is designed to define the range of mitigation measures that might be used, conduct analyses of the merits of the alternatives, and make recommendations to and obtain approval from DOE on specific courses of action to be followed in mitigation. Also the program is geared to assist DOE in implementing the approved mitigation strategy.

Mitigation is defined by the Council on Environmental Quality (CEQ) as actions to avoid, minimize, reduce, eliminate, or compensate for adverse impacts. An integrated and coordinated socioeconomic mitigation strategy is being developed to meet the requirements of the broad CEQ definition of mitigation.

The socioeconomic program approach to mitigation includes three components: (1) a community development approach to impact management, (2) direct mitigation through compensation and the provision of incentives, and (3) involvement of affected parties in planning and implementation. Each of the three components depends upon the others, and adequate and acceptable mitigation, as publicly perceived, can be achieved only by interaction with affected localities through the public participation and involvement of citizens.

Because the impacts of large-scale developments can depend in part on local action or inaction, a developmental planning approach to community impact management is being pursued. This community development and planning approach will incorporate needs of the residents and preferences of state and local officials, and will be conducted in consultation with DOE.

A community planning document has been prepared to assist in local impact management (ONWI, 1981). The purposes of the document are to:

1. focus on the social and economic impacts that may be experienced in the communities affected by repositories

2. initiate discussions with the states and communities on methods to eliminate or reduce these impacts

3. propose mechanisms for providing financial and technical resources to the affected communities

This document will be a primary instrument used with the states and communities and will be periodically revised and updated. Since state and local conditions, customs, laws, and regulations vary, there may be state-specific additions to the document prepared later in the site selection process.

Several direct and immediate benefits are foreseen for localities near repository sites. These benefits would result primarily from externally generated resources coming into a community through repository workers' salaries and purchases of locally supplied goods and services. At the same time, a community may be adversely affected by increased demands for goods and services that cannot be immediately met, or for which there is no corresponding immediate means of financing. Compensation and incentive mechanisms to offset such shortcomings are being studied. Currently, the principle mechanisms for compensation where enabling legislation exists are:

1. payment-in-lieu-of-taxes on Federally acquired property, based on the condition in which it was acquired prior to Federal involvement

2. provision of monetary assistance to local educational agencies

The amount of such assistance and its timing are not expected to be sufficient to alleviate adverse impacts of repository construction and development; therefore, alternative arrangements will be analyzed.

Criteria are being established for evaluating alternative forms of compensation and siting incentives. Once the criteria are established and various alternatives evaluated, a set of mechanisms for mitigation through compensation payments and for incentives to siting a repository will be recommended to DOE. One alternative to be emphasized will be inclusion of such mitigation costs in the waste storage and disposal fees to be charged utilities. Legislation currently before the Congress of the United States would resolve the issue of mitigation, as the wording being considered for inclusion in the legislation would permit direct payments to affected states and localities.

Employment of local residents during the construction and operation phase of a large facility is one means of minimizing population influx and attendant pressures on local services. A vocational training program will be investigated, and if deemed appropriate, a program for training local residents for employment at the repository site will be designed.

Evaluation and Recommendation of Citizen Involvement Techniques. Legislation establishing DOE directs it to provide for, encourage, and assist public participation in the development and execution of national energy programs. As public concern over nuclear waste management has grown, public participation has become an integral and recognized part of the NWTS program.

Citizen participation can cultivate a greater understanding of the technical and social issues involved. Public officials can then better proceed with proposed actions. Also through the process of interaction, DOE, the states, and localities will have developed a better understanding of the probable impact of the repository upon many facets of community life.

The public participation process being developed for the socioeconomic program is concerned primarily with the regional and/or local effects associated with siting a repository, and is not involved in the decision process for the siting of a repository. Procedures being developed will facilitate Federal, state, and local interaction in efforts to develop mitigation through compensation payments, to achieve appropriate and acceptable siting incentives, and to provide input to the community development process.

Monitoring and Organizational Analysis Task

Socioeconomic aspects of monitoring and organizational issues in waste management are considered in this task. Studies will be conducted to provide DOE and NWTS project elements with information on organizational forms for socioeconomic monitoring and institutional considerations for the waste isolation operational systems.

Principle activities in monitoring and organizational analysis will be: (1) design of an organizational structure to monitor socioeconomic impacts, and (2) an enumeration and analysis of socioeconomic-related institutional considerations and their implications for the waste isolation program.

After impacts have been projected by socioeconomic assessments and mitigation procedures have been developed and implemented, a program to monitor the effectiveness of these procedures will be designed. The monitoring is necessary to determine whether trends indicating projected impacts actually occur, whether mitigation is functioning to alleviate those impacts, and whether the mitigation program needs to be revised to cover any unforeseen impacts. Federal, state, and local units will be involved in socioeconomic monitoring, with each level having explicit responsibilities. Determination of roles and functions for each affected level and jurisdiction will be negotiated through the process of consultation with each affected level of government. This activity will specify roles and functions in data collection, the schedule for data collection, analysis, and the way mitigation efforts are to be monitored. Design of the organizational structure for socioeconomic monitoring will permit efficient and effective utilization of mitigation resources.

Socioeconomic aspects of institutional considerations need to be resolved and a framework needs to be established for the expeditious development of a waste isolation system.

The socioeconomic program in ONWI includes consideration of socioeconomic aspects of institutional issues in waste management. Studies will be conducted to provide DOE and ONWI program elements information on matters such as interagency coordination, waste ownership, transfer of ownership, responsibility for the impacts of waste transport, and repository operation and control. The socioeconomic group also assists in studies to examine issues such as means to protect repositories from human intrusion and the social science perspectives in perpetuating knowledge of repository records and markers.

NOTES

1. The reader should consult the **National Siting Plan** (Public Draft) by NWTS for a comprehensive presentation of the repository siting process, upon which this section is based (U.S. Department of Energy, 1982a).

2. This section addresses the socioeconomic program of the Office of Nuclear Waste Isolation which is concerned with investigations of non-DOE lands. It does not address programs of the NNWSI or BWIP, although they may be similar in their approach.

4
Legal Constraints
to Repository Siting

William C. Metz

In considering the site selection process for high level radioactive waste (HLW) repositories, various legal constraints must be taken into account. These constraints, if not resolved, may delay the use of a potential site or result in its rejection. The purpose of this chapter is to provide an **overview** opinion of major potential legal constraints which may be encountered in the siting process. In some cases, the constraints represent a minority viewpoint. Approaches to overcoming certain constraints are presented where possible.

Users of the various legal constraints upon repository siting will have diverse goals, which may include stopping a repository by any means because of technical, safety, and moral concerns; changing the location of a repository for personal or scientific reasons; securing a degree of leverage over the design of, or benefits from, the repository; or gaining a right to be heard. In some instances, for a variety of reasons, all possible obstacles to the siting of a repository will be utilized through the adoption of a shotgun approach. Knowledge of the goals and rationales of those who may threaten or seek to oppose repository sitings can help to resolve some of the problems in advance, by using this knowledge to correct misconceptions or reach satisfactory compromises.

Legal considerations surrounding the siting of an HLW repository are best reviewed in terms of four categories: (1) the basic legal framework, which includes general legal issues related to repository siting and control over nuclear wastes, (2) legal site precluders, which include executive orders and Federal and state statutes that can eliminate certain areas from consideration as repository sites, (3) legal site conditionals, which include regulations, executive orders, and Federal and state statutes that could necessitate modifications of repository siting and construction plans, and (4) other legal constraints, which include Indian tribe rights, common law, and state constitutional environmental rights.

New legal obstacles might arise from previously dormant local, state, and Federal statutes or from innovative approaches and interpretations of existing statutes. Legal issues that may arise over a proposed site will vary greatly depending on whether the site is to be situated on Federally-owned or private land (which has to be Federally acquired).

BASIC LEGAL FRAMEWORK

The basic legal framework for HLW repository siting is provided by the U.S. Constitution and seven Federal statutes--the Atomic Energy Act of 1946 (60 Stat. 755), the Atomic Energy Act of 1954 (Public Law 93-703, 68 Stat. 919), the 1959 Amendments to the Atomic Energy Act (Public Law 86-373, 73 Stat. 688), the Energy Reorganization Act of 1974 (Public Law 93-438, 88 Stat. 1233), the 1978 Appropriations Act Rider (Public Law 95-691, 92 Stat. 2953), the National Environmental Policy Act (Public Law 91-190, 83 Stat. 852 [codified at 42 U.S.C. paras. 4321-4361 1970]), and the Administrative Procedures Act (5 U.S.C. paras. 500-576 [1980]). Although interpretations and definitions are continually evolving in the courts, the Constitution and these Acts are generally interpreted to: give the Federal Government control over the nuclear field; give the Federal Government the right to supersede state and local laws, take land, and site a repository in the name of national interests; create the authority for a repository; establish a policy of environmental protection; and provide decision-making guidelines. These statutes and a number of associated legal issues pertaining to the basic legal issues of repository siting are discussed separately and in greater detail below.

Congressional intent regarding Federal regulation of nuclear materials is expressed in six pieces of legislation. Under the 1946 Atomic Energy Act, the Federal government assumed absolute monopoly over all fissionable materials and related facilities. Later, in the 1954 Atomic Energy Act, the Federal Government opened nuclear energy to public development but vested itself with the exclusive power to license the possession, transfer, and use of "source," "special nuclear," and "by-product" materials. In 1959, to clarify the roles of the states and the Federal Government with regard to the control of these materials, Congress amended the 1954 Act to prohibit the Atomic Energy Commission (AEC) from delegating regulatory authority over nuclear waste disposal to the states. The Energy Reorganization Act of 1974 replaced the AEC with the Nuclear Regulatory Commission (NRC) and the Energy Research and Development Administration (ERDA) and vested licensing and regulatory authority over HLW storage with NRC. This authority was reaffirmed in the Department of Energy Organization Act of 1977, which specifically bars the DOE from exercising waste management regulatory authority currently assigned to NRC. Finally, in the 1978 Appropriations Act Rider, Congress directed that "any person, agency, or other entity proposing to develop a storage or disposal facility . . . for high-level radioactive wastes . . . shall notify the Commission" (Public Law 95-691, 92 Stat. 2953).

The legislative history of the statutes regulating nuclear power suggests that Congress intended the Federal Government to have absolute control over the management of HLW. Indeed, several recent court cases have seemingly affirmed Federal preemption of nuclear regulation. Nonetheless, a minority view holds that because of unclear Federal laws, regulatory gaps, and an apparent absence of Federal leadership, state and local governments retain some rights in HLW management, most importantly for the protection of public health and safety.

As a result of these Federal failures and gaps, many states and localities have enacted legislation regulating HLW or prohibiting its disposal within their boundaries (table 4.1). As of September 1982, approximately 160 state laws, initiatives, and resolutions and 250 local laws pertaining to HLW had been passed thoughout the country. Pending legislation is even more widespread. Six states have not yet enacted laws regulating nuclear HLW, but 5 of these have had legislation pending in various legislative sessions. The positions and inventiveness of the 50 state governments (governors, legislators, and attorney generals) vary and, depending upon internal public pressure and the possibility of having a site selected within its borders, a state could quickly adopt a legal position barring HLW.

Yet, the current majority opinion is that because of the commerce (Art. I., Sec. 8, cl. 3) and supremacy (Art. VI, cl. 2) clauses of the U.S. Constitution these state and local regulations could not withstand a constitutional challenge of Federal preemption. These two clauses were the basis for decisions in four recent court cases, **Northern States Power Co. v. Minnesota** [447 F. 2d 1143 (8th Cir 1971)], **Pacific Legal Foundation** v. **State Energy Resources and Development Commission** [472 F. Supp. 191 (S.D. Cal. 1979)], **Washington State Building Council** v. **Spellman** [518 F. Supp. 928 (E.D. Wash, 1981)], and **Illinois** v. **General Electric Co.** [No. 81-2768 and 81-2778 (7th Cir July 13, 1982)]. In the former case, the supremacy clause was invoked to deny the State of Minnesota the right to regulate the amount and quality of radioactive effluents discharged from a nuclear power plant. In the **Pacific Legal Foundation** case, the court struck down a California statute that, because of a

Table 4.1

Summary of State Legislation on HLW*

States that ban the import of HLW for terminal disposal:

Alabama	Michigan	Oregon
Louisiana	Montana	West Virginia
Maryland		

States with conditional HLW disposal laws:

Alaska	Iowa	North Carolina
Arizona	Kansas	North Dakota
Arkansas	Kentucky	Rhode Island
Colorado	Maine	South Dakota
Connecticut	Minnesota	Texas
Delaware	Mississippi	Utah
Florida	Nevada	Vermont
Georgia	New Hampshire	Virginia
**Hawaii	New Mexico	Wisconsin
Indiana	New York	

States that have imposed state requirements on HLW
transportation:

Arkansas	Maine	Ohio
California	Maryland	Oregon
Colorado	Massachusetts	Rhode Island
Connecticut	Michigan	South Carolina
Delaware	Minnesota	South Dakota
Florida	New Hampshire	Tennessee
Georgia	New Jersey	Vermont
Illinois	New Mexico	Virginia
Kansas	New York	Washington
Kentucky	North Carolina	Wisconsin
Louisiana		

States with no HLW legislation:

Idaho	Nebraska	Pennsylvania
Missouri	Oklahoma	Wyoming

---

*The table illustrates, by generalized category, laws pertaining to HLW enacted as of September 1982 and is based on information provided in the "State Nuclear Legislative Report," issued periodically by Ms. Sherry Haber, State Governmental Affairs Manager, Public Affairs and Information Program, Atomic Industrial Forum, Inc., and the "Information Report on State Legislation," issued periodically by the Office of State Programs, U.S. NRC.

**State Constitutional Amendment

perceived absence of an "express" or explicit congressional declaration to preempt state and local legislative intrusion in nuclear regulation, imposed a moratorium on nuclear power plant construction pending development of a waste disposal system. The court's finding in this case was that an "implied" congressional intent to preempt existed with the commerce clause, since obstacles to nuclear power plant development were held to affect the national interests through interfering with the interstate transmission of electricity. The **Washington State Building and Construction** case affirmed that states were granted some measure of authority over the disposal of radioactive wastes (specifically low-level) within their own borders, but the authority is not total. Washington's Initiative 383 which closed state borders to low-level radioactive waste originating from outside the state was found unconstitutional and pre-empted by the supremacy and commerce clauses. Illinois' Spent Fuel Act which prohibited the transport into and storage in the state of nuclear wastes originating from out-of-state facilities was found unconstitutional in the **Illinois** case by the U.S. Court of Appeals under the commerce and supremacy clauses. While it was recognized that the state may have a compelling interest in safeguarding its residents from the hazards of radioactivity, the court determined that the interest is unaffected by the origin of the radioactive material. Thus, the exercise of Federal authority to supersede incompatible state laws has been ruled legitimate several times.

However, these rulings of Federal preemption come at a time when the Supreme Court appears to be severely restricting the application of the preemption doctrine, finding that the historical police powers of the states (to promote economic stability and well-being, as well as the health and safety of citizens) under the Tenth Amendment of the Constitution are not to be superseded by a Federal act unless that is the clear and manifest purpose of Congress. Accordingly, states are continuing to question the existence of a national policy promoting nuclear development found by the courts under the "expressed" intent of the Atomic Energy Act and the Federal Government's right, implied by the commerce clause, to regulate electricity production and sale. Although Federal sovereignty under the supremacy clause permits implementation of national policy by superseding state-enacted obstacles ("taxation, regulation, or otherwise") regardless of whether a Federal law expressly preempts state action, a review of the legislative history of the Atomic Energy Act reveals only a congressional objective that nuclear energy be fostered and encouraged, with no apparent intent that all states be required to develop nuclear power (Meek, 1979). Further, there is no Federal constitutional authority for the protection of public health and safety, only an NRC licensing responsibility to protect against radiological hazards to public health and safety. Linking Federal preemption of state regulation of radiological hazards to the commerce clause when the hazards do not arise from the interstate transmission and sale of electricity is therefore tenuous and questionable (Jaksetic, 1979). Clearly, national policy regarding nuclear power and the extent of Federal rights to preempt states' Tenth Amendment police power rights require further definition through future court cases.

Because they have the authority to regulate nonradiological aspects of the nuclear industry, some states may attempt through careful "tailoring" of legislative initiatives to use financial, land use, safety, health, or environmental concerns as the rationale for delaying or halting an HLW repository. While the courts may refuse to accept such legislative tailoring, it has been contended that in the **Pacific Legal Foundation** case (see above) the court itself engaged in tailoring:

> While [the court] condemns nullification of exclusive federal regulation 'through careful tailoring of state legislative purposes,' the opinion engages in the same 'careful tailoring' in order to invalidate the statute. The court deleted the state's rationale of 'financial risk' and inserted 'radiological hazard' as the 'true' legislative intent. It is remarkable how the court rewrote history, dismissed the documented intent, and substituted its own conclusion regarding legislative purpose. Nor does the court explain why 'careful tailoring' is improper. In the absence of express preemption, there is no reason why a state may not cautiously tread the line of permissible local options (Bauman and Platt, 1979: 201).

One method of tailoring which ten states (seven states have enacted laws, two states adopted resolutions, and one state passed an initiative) have utilized is that of a ban on the disposal of HLW produced out of state. Their efforts could fail, as evidenced in a recent parallel **Philadelphia v. New Jersey** [437 U.S. 617 (1978)] refuse case where the commerce clause was cited as preempting a state ban on interstate refuse movement, unless some criterion other than the place of origin is used to distinguish one state's HLW from another's.

If an HLW repository is to be located on private land, the Federal Government may have to use its constitutional powers under the jurisdiction clause (Art. I, para. 8 cl. 17) or the eminent domain/condemnation authority of the supreme sovereign (Art. I) to acquire the site. Although most states have adopted statutes, some with their request for statehood, giving "automatic consent" to any Federal land acquisition, these statutes can be revoked or conditioned as an obstacle. In this event, the Federal Government could invoke the jurisdiction clause of the U.S. Constitution, the only constitutional mechanism which expressly provides for Federal acquisition of private lands. However, state challenges could arise over the question of whether an HLW repository falls within the clause's provisions for land acquisitions for the "Erection of Forts, Magazines, Arsenals, Dockyards, and other needful buildings" (Jaksetic, 1979). The Federal Government can also exercise the right of eminent domain to acquire private land for a repository. Although a state could challenge the action on the grounds that obtaining a repository site is not within the scope of congressional authority under Article I of the Constitution, the decision in the **Northern States Power** case of implied Federal preemption of state regulation of radiological hazards appears to lend support to the Federal Government's right to exercise the power of eminent domain for repository site acquisition (Jaksetic, 1979).

Opposition by states is not eliminated if Federal land is selected for a repository site. Over the past decade the Federal Government has exhibited a retrocession tendency, yielding some of its exclusive jurisdiction over Federal lands to the states. This trend may have to be reversed at a proposed site, probably by congressional action and with state-initiated political repercussions, in order to site an HLW repository on Federal land. The property clause of the Constitution forces Congress to pass legislation specifically overriding state laws under the supremacy clause, if a state does not consent to Federal jurisdiction over Federal land. In several states, efforts to acquire exclusive Federal jurisdiction can be expected to encounter opposition based on mining laws, mineral leasing acts, rights to extralateral mineral pursuit, and correlative rights.

The provisions of the Federal Land Policy and Management Act of 1976 (FLPMA) (43 U.S.C. paras. 1701-1782) pose an additional obstacle to siting a repository on Federal land. Under the FLPMA, land withdrawals from the public domain aggregating five thousand or more acres can be made for periods of not more than twenty years. Land withdrawals for the considerably longer periods required for a repository would therefore necessitate the passage of special legislation (Percival, 1980). Exclusive Federal control over a repository site may also conflict with other aspects of the FLPMA, which give local and state governments a measure of authority over the use of Federal lands.

Under the National Environmental Policy Act of 1969

(NEPA), all Federal agencies recommending major projects that may be expected to have a significant impact on the environment are required to "utilize a systematic, interdisciplinary approach which will ensure the integrated use of the natural and social sciences and the environmental design arts in planning and decisionmaking which may have an impact on man's environment" and "make available to states, counties, municipalities, institutions, and individuals, advice and information useful in restoring, maintaining, and enhancing the quality of the environment" [Section 102 (A)]. NEPA provisions are enforced through the courts, and "litigation has been voluminous" (Taylor, 1978: 376). NEPA offers easy access to litigation delays for those in opposition to a repository.

The construction of an HLW repository will undoubtedly be regarded as a major Federal project for which an environmental impact statement (EIS) will be required under Section 102 (2) (c) of NEPA. While the courts have recognized that NEPA is a "full disclosure law," only a few court decisions have raised the issue of the substantive sufficiency of an EIS. In order to avoid or reduce the possibility of a lengthy delay, the repository EIS should take into account the factors weighed in determining the substantive sufficiency of an EIS, these being:

> . . . the purpose underlying the impact statement requirement, the practicability and reasonableness of including additional data, the extent of compliance with the procedural requirements of 102 (2) (c), the immediacy or remoteness of the threatened environmental harm, the cost-benefit analysis actually conducted by the decisionmaking agency, objective good faith, and the existence of undiscussed possibilities for mitigation of harm (Taylor, 1978: 377).

The provisions of the Administrative Procedures Act (APA), which outline decision-making guidelines for Federal agencies, are applicable to all DOE and NRC proceedings, and are further reinforced for NRC by the Atomic Energy Act itself. The APA can provide a basis for delaying litigation and can become a significant obstacle to the siting of a repository, if the courts find a lack of rational basis or a disregard of relevant facts in a DOE or NRC decision. HLW repositories, by their very controversial nature, will be challenged. Courts applying the arbitrary, capricious, and unreasonable standard of review will undertake a "searching and careful" inquiry into the facts and make a "substantial inquiry" into the whole record (**Overton Park v. Volpe**, 1971) to ensure that decisions related to an

HLW repository are rational and that NRC has taken a "hard look" (**Dupont de Nemours v. Train,** 1976) at all relevant factors. Under the hard-look doctrine, "assumptions must be spelled out, inconsistencies explained, methodologies disclosed, contradictory evidence rebutted, record references solidly grounded, guesswork eliminated, and conclusions supported in a 'manner capable of judicial understanding'" (Rodgers, 1979). Under the Atomic Energy Act, citizens have a statutory right to be free from undue health and safety risks (**Ethyl v. EPA,** 1976). Because these Federal agency actions in siting a repository present some unknown health risks and "touch(es) on fundamental personal interests in life, health, and liberty" (**EDF v. Ruckelshaus**), the courts may adopt a more skeptical and probing approach than usual in reviewing DOE and NRC proceedings under the APA standard.

The transport of nuclear wastes is primarily a Federal rather than a state or local regulatory concern. This authority is granted in the commerce clause of the U.S. Constitution, the Atomic Energy Act which empowers the Federal Government to regulate nuclear wastes, the Energy Reorganization Act of 1974 which vests this authority with NRC, and the Hazardous Materials Transportation Act of 1974 (HMTA) (49 U.S.C. 1801 et seq. 1976) under which the Department of Transportation (DOT) is given statutory authority over hazardous materials transport. However, because NRC has elected not to regulate common and contract carriers of radioactive wastes and because highway traffic control, road maintenance, and the operation of intrastate carriers have long been subject to state regulation, state (31 states) and local governments have begun to impose controls on the transport of nuclear wastes through their jurisdictions.

Laws that regulate and restrict nuclear waste transport on "an equal or greater level of protection to the public than is afforded" [49 U.S.C. 1801 et seq. (1976)] are not preempted by the HMTA. But in requiring Federal approval of all state and local restrictions Congress intended in the HMTA that the Federal Government occupy the field of hazardous material transport, and state and local requirements that are inconsistent with the HMTA or with its implementation by the DOT would therefore be preempted. Accordingly, an outright ban on HLW transport, as was passed in Louisiana, can be preempted, but very stringent standards, such as those enacted by New York City [N.Y.C., N.Y., Health Code para. 175.11 (1979)], can be accepted as being consistent with legitimate state rights (Bauman and Platt, 1979).[1] Delays in a repository's operation could occur if DOT takes exception to state and local controls on the routing, provision of advance notification of shipments, or requirements for state police escorts or acquisition of permits. However, if the Federal Government takes title to HLW shipments before transporting them to a Federal repository, state and local regulations will not apply. For under the principle of intergovernmental immunity established in the celebrated case of **McCulloch v. State of Maryland** [17 U.S. (4 wheat) 316, 4L. Ed. 579(1819)], states are forbidden to interfere with or obstruct the activities of the Federal Government.

Although state and local legal impediments to the interstate transport of nuclear waste will not necessarily hinder repository siting, they could delay its operation. Efforts should therefore be made to resolve nuclear waste transport issues well before a repository's projected operation date.

Since an HLW repository will hold radioactive wastes that will be hazardous for tens of thousands of years, intergenerational issues will almost certainly arise in legal actions surrounding the planning and construction of the repository. That future generations are entitled to just treatment at the hands of their predecessors is a cornerstone of American thought and jurisprudence. The Constitution states that we "secure the Blessings of Liberty to ourselves and our Posterity" (U.S. Const. Preamble), and the fiduciary obligation of present generations to the unborn is expressed in NEPA as "the responsibilities of each generation as trustee of the environment for succeeding generations" [42 U.S.C. Sect. 4331 (b)(1)(1970)]. According to Jim Gardner, writing in **Environmental Law,** while the courts probably will not accept a case for an unborn litigant, "standing to assert constititutional jus tertii--the rights of third parties--has been recognized in the past (p. 50)." But, "in order to invoke the jurisdiction of a Federal court, a litigant would need to assert that a proposed action would cause 'distinct and palpable injury to himself' as well as to future generations (p. 50)." Also, "the claim of the surrogate litigant must fall within some exception to the 'prudential standing rule that normally bars litigants from asserting the rights or legal interests of others in order to obtain relief from injury to themselves (p. 50).'" The Supreme Court "has exhibited a pronounced antipathy to jus tertii claims in recent terms (p. 52)," but in Gardner's opinion it is uncertain how they would characterize the relationship between a well-known public interest litigant, such as the Sierra Club or the Natural Resources Defense Council, and future generations, the theoretically ideal plaintiffs. These plaintiffs, however, would probably be restricted to our immediate successors, two generations ahead. It is improbable that jus tertii claims can be made for generations tens of thousands of years in the future (Gardner, 1978).

LEGAL SITE PRECLUDERS

A number of Federal and state statutes and executive orders currently preclude or eliminate certain areas from consideration as repository sites. Principal among these are the Endangered Species Act (16 U.S.C. paras. 1531-1543), Executive Order 11990 for Protection of Wetlands [42 FR 26961 (May 25, 1977)], the Coastal Zone Management Act (16 U.S.C. paras. 1451-1464), and the Wilderness Act (16 U.S.C. paras. 1131-1136). Less important statutes that might preclude potential repository sites include the Wild and Scenic Rivers Act (16 U.S.C. paras 1271-1278) and various state laws pertaining to mineral rights. Federal precluding statutes can be amended or removed through new congressional action, and executive orders can be voided by a president.

Growing public concern over the nation's rapidly disappearing wildlife led to the enactment in 1966 of the Endangered Species Preservation Act and, in 1973, to the stricter Endangered Species Act. While the earlier Act covered only endangered species, the 1973 Act authorized the Fish and Wildlife Service also to list and protect threatened species. In addition, this later Act directed all other Federal agencies to develop projects for insuring that their own programs do not diversely affect endangered and threatened species, encouraged public participation in Federal listing and protection actions, and provided for the states to play a role in the Act's implementation. A modifying amendment was added in 1978 as a result of the Supreme Court decision in **TVA** v. **Hill** (the famous snail darter case) and in the midst of growing concern that Federal agencies were being too rigidly and sweepingly prohibited from all actions potentially jeopardizing the continued existence of any threatened or endangered species or adversely modifying its critical habitat. This amendment added an exemption procedure to be used in cases of insoluble conflict between the Endangered Species Act and Federal actions.

Under Executive Order 11990, Protection of Wetlands, implemented in 1977, the Federal Government is directed to prevent, to the extent possible, the destruction or adverse modification of Federally-owned wetlands. Both direct and indirect Federal support of new construction in these wetlands is to be avoided whenever a practical alternative exists. Thus, although the Secretary of the DOE could allow a repository to be constructed on Federally-owned wetlands, if it was determined that no practical alternative existed and if all reasonable measures were taken to minimize adverse environmental impacts, it is likely that such a decision would be challenged in the courts.

The Coastal Zone Management Act of 1972 is the result of national interest in the effective management, beneficial use, protection, and benign development of the lands and waters of our coastal zone. As amended, the Act encourages and assists states and local governments in exercising effectively their responsibilities in the coastal zone through management plans and grant programs for land acquisition. Any Federal agency that proposes to undertake a development project in the coastal zone must ensure that the project is, to the maximum extent practicable, consistent with approved state management plans. The repository siting process will have to take coastal zone management activities into account unless the Secretary of Commerce can show that the repository is necessary to national security.

Under the Wilderness Act of 1964, Congress sought to preserve land in its natural condition for present and future generations of American people. A National Wilderness Preservation System composed of Federally owned lands designated by Congress as "wilderness areas" is to be left unimpaired for future use and enjoyment. New lands can be added to the System through initiation by the President, the Department of Interior, or the Department of Agriculture and effectuation by Congressional Act. Any proposal to site an HLW repository in a wilderness area would probably evoke a public outcry and would certainly require an Act of Congress for implementation. Therefore, wilderness lands and their adjacencies are likely to be avoided.

In the Wild and Scenic Rivers Act, as amended, Congress declared that certain selected rivers of the nation are to be preserved in free-flowing condition and that they and their immediate environments are to be protected for the benefit of and enjoyment by present and future generations. While the Act primarily prohibits construction projects that would alter the flow of any stream designated as a wild and scenic river, the declaration of policy includes a statement expressing a general objective of also protecting water quality. This latter objective could well be invoked to challenge any proposal to site a repository near a wild and scenic river.

Under traditional property laws, the owner of the land surface can sell the rights to the underlying minerals, and in many states the sale, conveyance, grant, or transfer of subsurface mineral rights can be made whole or in piecemeal sections. Clearly, separate ownership of surface and mineral rights could present obstacles to the taking of private lands for a repository. Additional problems could arise if a repository were sited on land overlying gas or oil reservoirs. Rights to these fugitive minerals are traditionally governed by the "rule of capture," which allows surface owners to produce oil and gas from wells on their land holdings regardless of the ownership of the tracts which these fuels may have originally underlain. (one state, Utah, also permits, in certain situations, the extralateral pursuit of a mineral vein into subsurface estates not owned by the pursuer.) Such practices may preclude the siting of a repository in potential oil and gas deposit areas, since a producing well outside the repository boundaries could extract oil and gas located within the repository area. To be sure, state mineral laws could be overridden by Federal legislation, but it is unlikely that Congress would enact laws to facilitate the siting of a repository near valuable mineral resources. Indeed, it is the explicit policy of the DOE to avoid areas of potential mineral value because they would be attractive to future generations.

LEGAL SITE CONDITIONALS

A number of executive orders and Federal and state statutes, while they do not eliminate or disqualify any potential HLW repository sites, provide limited protection to certain areas and resources. They could cause conditions to be imposed on the approval of plans for a repository siting. Typically, these conditions would be satisfied by design and layout changes or other plan modifications directed at minimizing adverse impacts on the protected area or resource. Major Federal acts and orders in the "modifying" category are the National Historic Preservation Act (16 U.S.C. paras. 470-470+), Executive Order 11593 for Protection and Enhancement of the Cultural Environment [36 FR 8921 (May 15, 1971)], and the Safe Drinking Water Act (42 U.S.C. paras. 300f-300j-9). At the state and local levels, statutes pertaining to land use, pollution control, and energy facility siting can currently be used to regulate and modify Federal projects. In some instances, just the threat of local and state government legal action could result in concessions from the Federal Government seeking to avoid possible delays in a site's use.

The National Historic Preservation Act of 1966, as amended, was enacted to preserve the nation's historical and cultural heritage. Historical and cultural preservation was further promoted by Executive Order 11593 for the Protection and Enhancement of the Cultural Environment, effective May 1971. Under these statutes, the acquisition and preservation, restoration, and maintenance of Federally-owned sites, structures, and objects of historical, architectural, or archaeological significance have become Federal policy. Proposals for siting an HLW repository near significant cultural sites will require careful attention to impacts and positive modifications to minimize any adverse impacts, thereby reducing the potential for unnecessary delays.

The Safe Drinking Water Act of 1974 and its 1977 Amendments established a joint state and Environmental

Protection Agency program for the adoption and enforcement of laws regulating public drinking water systems. The Act requires state governments to exercise primary enforcement responsibility for drinking water regulations no less stringent than those promulgated by the Environmental Protection Agency. It also sets limits on the amount of radioactive materials that may be released to public drinking water systems irrespective of whether the material originates from sources under NRC jurisdiction. Thus, despite Federal preemption of the nuclear field by the Atomic Energy Act, state governments are congressionally authorized, indeed required, to prevent radioactive contamination of public drinking water supplies and to protect public health. The Safe Drinking Water Act will not necessarily preclude a site, but states could invoke it to request modifications of siting or construction plans.

State and local land use and pollution laws can affect the construction and operation of an HLW repository, since although they cannot prohibit activities on Federal lands, they can be used to regulate many aspects of these activities. Unless Congress supplies a "clear manifestation" of intent to supersede these laws, a repository could be delayed by the necessity of Federal challenges to hindering state and local laws.

Under Section 202 of the Federal Land Policy and Management Act (FLPMA), Congress provided for the resolution of conflicts between Federal and non-Federal land use plans by giving the Secretary of the Interior discretion to preempt state and local land use laws. Yet, it has been argued that Section 701 of the same Act preserves state and local government land-use controls, and certainly nothing in the FLPMA sets an express limit to "the public power of the respective States" or deprives any state or political subdividision of "any right it may have to exercise civil and criminal jurisdiction on the national resources lands" [43 U.S.C. section 1701 (1976)]. In the absence of clear congressional intent to preempt state and local land use laws, state and local governments have passed laws to regulate or influence the use of Federal lands, but not to preclude Federal use of the land. For example, by zoning the area around a potential or proposed site or by establishing restricted "floating" zones without specifying their locations, state and local governments could seek to bring about site modifications. In fact, in recognition of the potential power of land use controls, Colorado, Oregon, and Wyoming have recently enacted legislation to regulate activities on Federal lands (Percival, 1980).

Pollution control regulations currently provide state and local governments with additional means of influencing activities on Federal lands, since Federal facilities are subject to standards set by states pursuant to the Clean Air Act (42 U.S.C. para. 1857 et seq. as amended), the Federal Water Pollution Control Act (33 U.S.C. para. 1251 et req.), the Noise Control Act (42 U.S.C. paras. 4901-4918), and the Resource Conservation and Recovery Act [43 U.S.C. paras. 6901-6987 (1976)]. Although a state or local law must not be a disguised attempt to accomplish a purpose other than pollution control (**Ray v. Atlantic Richfield Co.**, 1978), states can impose stricter pollution regulations than the minimum standards set by these Acts even if they interfere with national policy (**State ex rel. Andrus v. Click**, 1976). In FLPMA, Congress expressed an intent that energy developments on Federal land not interfere with non-Federal efforts to control pollution. A clear congressional statement of intent to preempt any overbearing state and local pollution laws and regulations would be necessary to prevent challenges and delays. Of course, a careful study of state and local pollution laws that might apply to a potential site and the initiation of appropriate design modifications in advance could reduce the potential for legal delays.

OTHER LEGAL CONSTRAINTS

Several other legal constraints can also affect the siting of an HLW repository. Among these are the rights of Indian tribes, common law, and state constitutional environmental rights. A proposed repository site that is perceived by area Indian tribes to directly or indirectly affect Indian property or usage rights will encounter complex legal obstacles. Indian tribes are quasi-sovereign, independent governments that control their tribal property and other resource ownership rights under the protection of both their trustee, the United States Government, and the Constitution.

The Supreme Court has ruled that Indian property and usage rights, which are recognized in hundreds of treaties, statutes, executive orders, and judicial rulings, are constitutionally protected, with the United States Government having a full fiduciary obligation to hold Indian resources in trust for the perpetual and beneficial use of the Indian. State governments have no jurisdiction over an Indian tribe's exercise of its treaty rights, with the states of Arizona, New Mexico, Washington, and the Dakotas explicitly disclaiming jurisdiction; this is also true of rights to off-reservation resources (Council of Energy Resource Tribes).

Indian lands cannot be sold, condemned, or considered replaceable. Titles to rights-of-way are retained by Indian tribes. Leases for Indian lands must be approved both by the governing body of the tribe and a trustee, the Secretary of the Interior; Congress has limited leases to a maximum of ten years. Congress is the only body of the United States Government that can authorize actions that will significantly affect Indian property or other recognized Indian rights. Even if a tribe were to grant DOE the permanent acquisition of tribal land for a repository site, it would take an explicit act of Congress to extinguish Indian title, and judicial review would follow. If Congress abrogated a tribe's rights on its own initiative to facilitate the siting of a repository, the United States Government, as trustee, would come under judicial review for "conflict of interest" in breaching its judiciary obligations.

Many Indian tribes have possessory or usage rights in off-reservation areas which give a tribe the right to hunt, fish, gather food, or hold ceremonial activities in specific locations. Some tribes have water rights that prohibit certain off-reservation, upstream water usages or disturbances. While a state government might be willing to accept certain kinds of environmental damages and losses in exchange for a set of benefits, Indian tribes cannot be expected to acquiesce readily in trades resulting in the loss of traditional grounds or waters (Zionty, 1980). If a Federal project threatens to adversely affect Indian property or off-reservation usage rights, the Supreme Court has made it clear that congressional consent is needed to validate Federal agency actions and provide appropriate compensation. Compensation for the loss of usage rights can be an extremely complex problem, especially if the spiritual aspects of a tribe's heritage are involved. Judicial review would follow any infringement of Indian rights or any compensation agreement.

In the absence of a Federal constitutional right to a "decent environment," a number of states have incorporated such rights and concerns into their state constitutions. As yet, few court cases have been brought on the basis of these state constitutional rights, and it is therefore impossible to predict the outcome of future law suits on these grounds against an HLW repository. Without doubt, however, such suits could serve to stir public opposition to a site within its designated state which would lead to new rounds of legal obstacles.

Common law rights can be asserted in attempts to halt undesired land uses, most prominently through actions against public or private nuisance. While such rights can be invoked only after the alleged nuisance (for example, environmental damage) occurs, they can be used to challenge a repository once construction is underway and real and/or perceived nuisance actions are occurring.

CONCLUSION

High-level radioactive waste disposal will inevitably encounter legal obstacles. Unless an effort is made to anticipate, comprehensively examine, and resolve many of these potential obstacles before they become issues, delays will seem to be never ending. A philosophy of defensive reaction rather than positive action will result in frequent lengthy delays and an increase in the opportunities for delay. Although all legal obstacles cannot be resolved beforehand, advance legal and political preparation can reduce court time. Some suits will be based on new or minority opinions of existing laws in the hope of creating a delay which will perhaps lead to success in defeating a repository site. On occasion, state and local laws which have been forgotten will be resurrected and used to oppose a repository.

Of course, any legal decisions which are unfavorable to the repository siting can most likely be overruled by new congressional legislation unless congressional action is prohibited by constitutional constraints. But congressional legislation takes time and requires great political effort. Preemptive legislation by Congress should take effect prior to the forecasted onslaught of judicial action, conclusively deciding the siting issue and foreclosing future judicial intervention. This will eliminate the need for numerous legislative remands. As an example, one complaint against the Trans-Alaska Pipeline Authorization Act is that Congress waited too long to remove from the courts an issue of such national and international significance. Since the Authorization Act "overruled all that the courts had taken a necessarily long time to decide, much time and expense could have been saved had Congress acted earlier" (Taylor, 1978: 387).

NOTES

1. In addition, as a result of a Federal agreement concluded between the Carter Administration and the State of Louisiana in 1978 and concurred to by the Reagan Administration, exploration activities have been restricted.

5
Intricacies of
the Nuclear Waste Problem

Steve H. Murdock
Rita R. Hamm
F. Larry Leistritz

Nuclear waste management and repository siting are, as noted in the preceding chapters, complex, multifaceted phenomena involving dimensions that become inextricably interrelated in the public mind and in public debate. It is, in fact, the interrelationships and interactions between the numerous dimensions of the problem that will likely determine the course of action finally pursued in addressing the nuclear waste problem (Cluett et al., 1979). Although it is impossible to describe all of the complex intricacies that make up the image and issues surrounding nuclear waste management and repository siting, it is essential at this point to also provide some indication of the interrelations among key dimensions, and of the characteristics of the total context in which nuclear waste management and repository siting issues must be addressed.

The purpose of this chapter is to provide an overview of the interrelationships among the dimensions and, thus, of the total complex that is the nuclear waste problem. The concerns discussed reflect both technically plausible and technically implausible events which are perceived as plausible by significant numbers of persons and which are thus real in their consequences for affecting human attitudes and behaviors. In fact, the lack of congruence between the real and the perceived forms a significant dimension of the waste issue, and as a result, the perceived effects of repositories may be as important as the technically feasible effects in determining our management of nuclear wastes. The discussion which follows does not attempt to evaluate the technical adequacy of concerns but rather examines those that appear to have significance for nuclear waste management and repository siting regardless of their technical merit. That this overview must be selective and can only partially address the range of interrelated concerns that should be examined is itself an indication of the complexity of the issues surrounding the nuclear waste problem.

In attempting to provide an overview of the

interrelationships between dimensions of nuclear waste management and repository siting, it is useful to have a framework for organizing the discussion of the dimensions. Such a framework, however, must be one which is multidisciplinary in scope with the ability to interrelate technical, biological, physical, and social science dimensions. Few such frameworks exist.

One framework that is at least heuristically useful in this regard is that of human ecology. This perspective is based in Malthusian and Darwinian conceptions of man's close relationship to his environment and about the intricate web of life that connects man with his environment and with other species. The framework has received extensive development in the social sciences (Park, 1950; Hawley, 1944; 1950; Duncan and Schnore, 1959; Duncan, 1964), particularly in relation to environmental concerns and society-environment relationships (Catton and Dunlap, 1978; Murdock, 1979). Basic to the human ecological conception are the premises that: (1) the basic aspects of human existence can be seen as involving a constant struggle to adapt to environmental circumstances and changes in such circumstances; (2) adaptation is generally an aggregate, population-wide process; (3) adaptation is made possible only through man's creation of interdependent collective organizations and enhanced by the applicaton of man's cultural and technical innovations; and (4) man tends to expand his life to the fullest extent permitted by his environment (Hawley, 1950, 1968, 1971; Murdock, 1979; Murdock and Sutton, 1974). These premises have been combined into four heuristically useful concepts--population, organization, environment, and technology--often referred to as the **POET** variables (Duncan and Schnore, 1959; Duncan, 1964).

The concept of Population refers to the unit of persons adapting (or reacting) to a set of environmental (or other) circumstances. Environment refers to both the physical environment (climate, topography and resource base of an area) and the socioeconomic environment (for example, prevailing levels of wealth, values, attitudes and perceptions, and standards of living in an area) that create the basic conditions to which mankind must react. Technology refers to both the mechanical and scientific and the cultural developments of man that increase his capabilities to adapt to the environment. Organization, the key ecological concept, refers to the system of relations among interdependent parts (Boland, 1966) aimed at performing necessary functions for the population (or individuals in it) and involving a distribution of power (system of differentiation and dominance) and a set of dominating functions (key functions).

When examined in light of the above (POET) framework, nuclear wastes can be seen as the undesired by-product of man's application of technology to increase the efficiency and productivity of his use of (adaptation to) environmental resource bases. In addition, if population is broadly seen as a delineating scheme or means of categorizing entities or interests, groupings of people who are affected by or affect waste management and repository siting, then examining such groupings in light of organizational, technological and environmental factors may be a useful means for organizing a discussion of the interrelationships among the dimensions of waste management and repository siting.

The remainder of this chapter, then, is organized around a discussion of each of the population, organizational, environmental, and technology-based interrelations that form the complex of factors affecting nuclear waste management and repository siting. In this discussion, we proceed by examining each one of the four POET factors in relation to all others, then briefly discuss examples of multiple factor patterns of interaction. Although this form of presentation may give the appearance of causal influences for each factor, this is not the intent of the presentation. Rather, the form of presentation merely provides a useful means for beginning and proceeding with the discussion.

POPULATION DIMENSIONS

It is evident that among the major dimensions of critical concern in waste management and repository siting are those related to individual, group and society needs, rights, and responsibilities (Cluett et al., 1979). Although interactively linked with all of the other dimensions, it is clear that some of the areas of controversy relate to which level of government (Federal, state or local) should be responsible for various stages of repository siting and waste management, whose needs should be protected (society's or the individual's) and who should pay (public or private concerns) for the costs of repository siting and operation (Peelle, 1980; LaPorte, 1978). Such issues are complex (see chapter 3) and may involve widely varying perspectives on man and on society (see chapter 2). Thus, how society should attempt to manage a problem, such as waste isolation, that requires that one area of the nation bear the risks for the good of the entire nation often leads to major conflicts between those who see the needs of the society as paramount versus those who see the rights of individuals as of ultimate importance (Peters, 1981). In like manner, the conflicts that evolve around the locus of control over repository development may be based on fundamental sociopolitical differences between those that stress the need for centralized control and coordination versus those championing local control (Hebert et al., 1978).

Yet an additional set of questions relates to who should pay for waste management costs, Federal concerns or private utility waste generators (Clark and Cole, 1982; Halstead et al., 1982). This involves issues such as whether such costs should be born by only those customers of particular utilities that use nuclear generators or whether there is a society-wide obligation to bear such costs and whether private support will lead to market vulnerability and hence potential instability in repository support and maintenance.

In sum, many of the basic issues that surround nuclear waste involve interrelations between levels and types of individual and group concerns that are based on deeply held and basically conflicting perspectives on man and society. Clearly, such issues are unlikely to be definitively resolved by those involved in waste management. However, such issues remain at the base of much of the nuclear debate, and awareness of their potential effects on nuclear waste issues must be maintained.

ENVIRONMENTAL DIMENSIONS

Clearly, some of the deepest concerns in regard to waste siting are due to the environmental dangers posed by nuclear materials. These concerns have, in fact, been the major basis for the extensive technical efforts (see chapter 1) to develop environmentally safe means to isolate waste materials from the environment through containerization, geologic media, and repository design selection procedures (U.S. Department of Energy, 1980b). The issues surrounding such dimensions involve numerous concerns. Some of these concerns relate to the danger of direct exposure to radiation as a result of accidents in waste transportation or storage procedures, while others result from a concern that other environmental resources such as alternative uses of land, ground water quality, or even surface water uses could be endangered by repository development.

Thus, there is concern that a sufficient level of controls cannot be established to prevent the numerous forms of human errors that might lead to radiation exposure for residents along transportation routes (Schilling et al., 1979) and for siting area residents and workers during processing and storage (Hebert et al., 1978).

The nuclear waste storage problem is also largely a product of a new and ever changing social environment. Until the turn of the century (Rodgers, 1976), there was relatively little concern for the need to preserve and protect the environment, and only since the activism of the 1970s has the need for man to live in harmony rather than to exploit the environment become a common belief

(Catton and Dunlap, 1978). The increasing concern with man's ability to irrevocably alter his environment and the belief that society must reverse decades of abuse of the environment form the context in which nuclear waste-- perhaps perceived to be a troubling symbol of man's excessive and unthoughtful exploitation of the environment--management must occur.

The social and historical environment of nuclear power and nuclear arms developments also have a bearing on the nuclear waste problem. The early attempts to site a repository in Kansas with the seeming sudden reversal of technical certainty, and the failure to effectively coordinate siting efforts with state and local officials (Bradshaw and McClain, 1971), the fact that nuclear power in the U.S. grew out of the nuclear weapons program (Cook, 1975), that its history has been marred by several accidents such as those at the Fermi plant in Michigan in 1966, the Browns Ferry Plant in 1975 (Cook, 1982), and the Three Mile Island Plant in Pennsylvania (Walsh, 1982; Kasperson et al., 1979) have produced a climate of distrust and doubt, in which waste management planning must proceed.

For nuclear waste siting, then, the interrelations of physical, resource use, and sociohistorical environmental factors are of critical concern. Knowledge of these factors is essential for understanding the nuclear waste problem.

TECHNOLOGICAL DIMENSIONS

As noted in the Introduction, the technological dimensions of nuclear waste siting have been the focus of the United States' attempt to manage nuclear waste. In fact, technology is both a cause of, and debated cure for, the nuclear waste problem. Thus, nuclear weapons testing and development and nuclear power production are the direct generators of nuclear waste (see chapter 1). In a larger sense, however, the technological issues involved in nuclear waste are part of the larger issue of the effects, both intended and unintended, of technology on human life and human society. Issues such as whether man should develop and utilize technology which has by-products that are dangerous to himself and future generations, the role of careful and concerted technology assessment in the development of advanced technology and man's apparent inability to predict or control the social effects of technology development are issues broader than nuclear waste, but ones which have come to affect the nuclear waste question. Nuclear waste is, in fact, an issue surrounded by questions based on concerns about technology-culture interfaces.

Technology is also seen as a cure for nuclear waste problems by both opponents (Lovins et al., 1980) and

proponents of nuclear power (Glasstone and Jordan, 1980).
To many proponents of nuclear power, belief in existing
storage technology has led to claims that the questions
remaining in waste storage are largely irrelevant ones
related to sociopolitical rather than substantive
concerns. On the other hand, for opponents of nuclear
power there is a nearly equally strong belief that
conservation and alternative energy technologies will
make the need for additional nuclear power and, thus, for
additional nuclear wastes unnecessary. The belief in
technology for the first group is a belief in man's
existing capabilities; for the second group, it is a
belief in man's future creativity.

Finally, the extent to which technology is seen as a
cultural phenomena also affects the context of the
nuclear waste problem. This effect is seen in the
cultural myths that are basic to American society (Rankin
and Nealey, 1978). The belief in the efficacy of
science, the belief in the role of the individual in
changing society, the desire to defend the small against
the large, the defense of free enterprise but also of
government guaranteed security, awe of technology and yet
distrust of its creators, the belief in the basic
principles of public involvement and democracy but also
of the need for the technocrat and for unique
bureaucracies to deal with complex issues--such
conflicting beliefs are often the bases of the
conflicting views on nuclear waste and in many ways
adherence to such views is one of the reasons for the
intransigence of the nuclear waste problem.

Technology, then, in both its engineering-scientific
and in its cultural forms has become a major focus in the
debate over nuclear waste. Its complex interrelations
with societal issues form yet an additional part of the
complex mosaic of nuclear waste management and repository
siting.

ORGANIZATIONAL DIMENSIONS

Organizational dimensions are also playing a major
role in forming the context for waste management and
repository siting. Concern over existing and future
institutional arrangements (Peelle, 1980) and varying
forms of differentiation within the existing system of
institutional arrangements are of utmost importance in
understanding the perceptions as well as the realities of
the nuclear waste problem. Thus, the present Federal
institutional system for waste management is often seen
as a complex, nearly unworkable, collage of Federal
agencies with somewhat conflicting interests and concerns
(Smith, 1979; Office of Technology Assessment, 1982).
The Department of Energy, the Environmental Protection
Agency, the Nuclear Regulatory Commission, and the

Department of Transportation are all involved in the waste management problem and each has different jurisdictional and regulatory responsibilities. In addition, neither the Department of Energy nor any part of the U.S. Congress has established effective working relationships among such Federal agencies and among such agencies and state and local concerns, and state concerns are often poorly coordinated with local interests (Smith, 1979; Curry et al., 1977; Morris et al., 1980). In light of such complexity, there is concern that the present institutional structure may be incapable of siting, constructing, and operating a repository (Peelle, 1980).

Of even greater concern is the question of the possibility of creating an institutional structure that is capable of maintaining and insuring the security of a repository over the several thousands of years essential for repository management (Schuller and Huelshoff, 1981; Office of Technology Assessment, 1982). Given the fluctuations that often occur in the American political structure, the constant reorganization that occurs within Federal and state bureaucracies, and the resultant shifts in emphases within Federal and state budgeting processes, skepticism has arisen about whether any institutional structure created in one social and political era can be maintained through centuries of political, social, and perhaps even environmental change. There is no historical precedent on which to base the belief that any institutional structure can be maintained for the 10,000 or more years that may be necessary to adequately insure the safety and security of nuclear waste storage.

Also, contributing to the organizational concerns over nuclear waste are the conflicting perceptions of power and political efficacy that exist within the present political and social system (Maynard et al., 1976; Rankin and Nealey, 1978). Federal agencies often perceive themselves to be powerless in the face of congressional whims, states believe the Federal government has little concern with their rights and roles, and local siting areas often see neither Federal nor state entities as being concerned with their needs and preferences.

Regionalism has come to play a major role as well. Since the first repository is likely to be sited in the Southern or Western part of the United States, the long-felt perceptions among residents of these regions that their regions are often seen by other areas of the nation as "dumping grounds" for Federal projects (defense, energy, and so forth) that are either undesirable or dangerous have been reinforced (see chapter 13). In like manner, rural residents that have long perceived their more urban neighbors as treating them with condescension and a lack of concern (Murdock and Leistritz, 1979; Dillman and Hobbs, 1982) are raising increasing questions about the repository siting process.

Organizationally, the questions of concern are thus ones of who controls the repository siting process? Who should control the process? How can social, political, geographic, and other forms of equity be insured? How can a structure be created to provide the necessary long-term institutional safeguards necessary to adequately respond to the technical and environmental realities of nuclear waste storage and security? Given the obvious complexity of such questions, it is not surprising that the nuclear waste problem has not been subject to a quick solution.

INTERFACES

As the discussion in previous sections of this chapter indicates, the complexity of the context surrounding waste management and repository siting results, in large part, from the fact that dimensions of the problem have become inextricably linked in ways that make it impossible to separate philosophical, moral, political, social, technical, environmental, economic, and other concerns (Hebert et al., 1978; Kasperson, 1980). Rather, it is the fact that these factors are interrelated in so many complex ways that makes nuclear waste management and repository siting the nuclear waste problem. This section attempts to present a description of some of these many areas of interrelations among dimensions.

It is evident that the population, environmental, technical, and organizational dimensions of waste management and repository siting are closely linked. The potential failure of waste storage technology is problematic because its failure threatens the long-term viability of the environment and such failure is deemed probable because of past sociohistorical events and because of the failure of societal institutions to adequately control for human errors in technology application (Cook, 1982). Technical concerns become linked with environmental and institutional-organizational concerns. Faith in technology comes into conflict with fear of its creators. Concerns over past failures to control technology's effects on environment and to predict such effects become linked with doubts about future efforts to effectively control technology-environment interrelations. Historical events become the basis for judging likely future outcomes and potentials for success and failure in technological applications (Peters, 1981).

In like manner, the history of past failures of the Federal government to acknowledge nuclear contamination (for example, in Utah during the 1950s) and to provide regulations sufficient to prevent human error in technological application (Walsh, 1982) have apparently

led to much of the conflict between Federal and
nonFederal concerns. Failures to adequately involve
local residents in Federal decisions (see chapter 13)
regarding local land use and in facility planning have
led to distrust of present Federal institutions and to
Federal, state and local conflicts (see chapters 14 and
15). The fact that technological failures will be most
significant for local and regional residents has led to a
feeling of regionalism and resentment against Washington
and Eastern-based agencies, to a belief that compensation
is insufficient and that local aid should perhaps include
subtantial incentives for local area risk taking
(Halstead et al., 1982). Distrust of the motives of
private enterprise leads to attempts to disassociate
financial and administrative organizational controls, and
fears of Federal bureaucratic social organizations lead
to Federal-state and Federal-local conflicts (Bishop et
al., 1977). The need for Federal, state, and local
institutions to provide a mechanism for multilevel
governmental cooperation leads to confusion over Federal,
state and local agency jurisdictional, regulatory, and
similar domains and to a need for unprecedented forms of
governmental organizations (Peelle, 1980; Kasperson et
al., 1979).

In sum, the population, environmental,
technological, and organizational dimensions of nuclear
waste management and repository siting become linked in a
multitude of direct and indirect ways. These
interrelations interdependently determine the context as
well as the content of the nuclear waste problem.
Recognition of this interdependence and interaction is
thus essential to understanding nuclear waste management
and repository siting issues and concerns.

CONCLUSION

As the discussion in this chapter has indicated,
nuclear waste management and repository siting is a
multifaceted and complex phenomenon. This volume
emphasizes the socioeconomic dimensions and separately
examines the technical, ethical, legal, and political
organizational dimensions of waste management and
repository siting. Yet, it is the interaction of all of
these factors that forms the bases of the debate over
waste management and repository siting. Although it is
impossible to trace all of these interrelations, this
chapter has attempted to provide the reader with an
appreciation of the complexity of the interactions among
the factors that are involved in, and determine the
nature of, the nuclear waste problem. Unless the
complexity of such interrelations is recognized and at
least partially understood, it is impossible to
effectively examine the socioeconomic dimensions of

nuclear waste management and repository siting.

Although the socioeconomic dimensions examined in the remainder of this work represent only a part of the mosaic of concerns surrounding nuclear waste, they are clearly ones central to the resolution of the nuclear waste problem. Their analysis, though necessarily incomplete, is thus worthy of the attention of scientists and laymen alike and clearly merits the discussion to which we now turn our attention.

Impacts of
Nuclear Waste Storage
and Repository Siting

6
The Socioeconomic Impacts of Repositories

John K. Thomas
Rita R. Hamm
Steve H. Murdock

Many types of impacts are likely to result from the development of a high-level nuclear waste repository, and Federal and state decision makers, community leaders, and residents must know how communities in repository siting areas will be changed. The purpose of this chapter is to briefly identify: factors affecting an assessment of socioeconomic impacts, the types of socioeconomic impacts (for example, economic, demographic, fiscal, community service, and social impacts) likely to occur as a result of a repository development, and the process for assessing socioeconomic impacts. Additional descriptions of socioeconomic impacts and impact assessment techniques can be obtained from Murdock and Leistritz (1979), Leistritz and Murdock (1981), Finsterbusch and Wolf (1981), Chalmers and Anderson (1977), and Denver Research Institute (1979).

FACTORS AFFECTING AN ASSESSMENT OF SOCIOECONOMIC IMPACTS

The factors most likely to affect areas impacted by a repository are numerous and complex. They are similar to the factors that affect nearly all large-scale developments occurring in rural areas; yet, they are unique because of the nuclear characteristics of the project. Leistritz and Murdock (1981) have identified three groups of factors which are most significant: (1) characteristics of a nuclear waste repository project, (2) characteristics of the area where a repository is sited, and (3) characteristics of the inmigrants who will enter the siting area as a result of a repository's development (see also Murdock and Leistritz, 1979). According to these authors, an a priori understanding of such characteristics is instrumental in determining the nature, extent, and interaction of the socioeconomic effects of a repository project.

Project Characteristics

The characteristics of a nuclear waste repository project relevant to socioeconomic impacts can be divided into two categories: (1) its utilization of areal resources and (2) workforce requirements and characteristics (Murdock and Leistritz, 1979). Each of these sets of characteristics is examined below.

Utilization of Areal Resources. The first set of characteristics involves a repository's need for and utilization of resources in a site area. Resource requirements and their linkages with economic factors are key determinants of numerous effects of a repository project. Thus, requirements for land and water are primary determinants of economic effects.

For example, a repository will require land for repository siting, railroads and highways, and water resources for waste processing. These requirements of a repository project may compete in a site area with current water usage needs and land use patterns of the local agricultural industry, which might depend on such land and on aquifers and other water sources for grazing, irrigation and watering of livestock. The repository will also have impacts on land use in the local areas. The repository will require 2,000 acres for the facility and an additional 8,000 acres of controlled buffer zone will be required around the project site. It is unclear how land owners next to the project site will react and how the uses and values of land near the site will be affected. In addition, project characteristics may have other, more subtle effects. For instance, the aesthetic aspects of a facility along with its impacts on the physical environment may affect residents' perceptions and acceptance of the project as well as alter their basic orientations toward land use (Leistritz and Murdock, 1981).

Workforce Requirements and Characteristics. Project characteristics are particularly important in influencing workforce requirements and characteristics. Resource development projects differ in their total workforce requirements, in the timing of those requirements (particularly the relative size of construction and operation workforces), and in the mix of required skill levels. These requirements in turn influence the extent to which a project utilizes local labor and the wage and salary levels of project workers. The nature of the project's technology, coupled with its construction schedule, will determine the size of the peak workforce. Thus, the total demand for labor by a project and secondary business growth are key factors in determining the eventual nature and magnitude of economic, population, public service, and fiscal effects (Leistritz and Murdock, 1981).

Depending on the type of subsurface geological formation and the type of repository (for example, salt, granite, shale, or basalt media and spent fuel or reprocessing facilities), repository facilities will require about 7 years to build and will generally involve (for a spent fuel repository) from 1,700 to 5,000 workers during construction and from about 900 to 1,100 workers during operation (see table 6.1). Furthermore, these facilities are likely to require monitoring for an indefinite period.

The availability and compatibility of labor skills of residents in site areas with those required by the project will determine how many jobs can be taken by residents and how many new employees must inmigrate. Moreover, the existing service industries and community growth preferences will often decrease or accentuate the attractiveness of the communities to new residents and thus alter the number of new residents moving to a community.

Areal Characteristics

Before discussing major types of socioeconomic impacts, it is useful also to discuss areal characteristics which may influence such impacts. This is particularly important for two reasons: (1) differences between the historical, economic, and cultural characteristics of communities in site areas may lead to differences in the effects of such repositories on the communities, and (2) preliminary identification by the U.S. Department of Energy indicates that several potential sites for nuclear repositories will be located in sparsely populated areas.

Historical Factors. A community's history of economic and population growth or decline may influence how a repository development affects it. Despite recent patterns of renewed growth in some rural areas, many areas have shown little renewed growth and, in fact, have shown decades of population and economic decline. For communities in these areas, large resource developments, such as repositories, may bring growth patterns that are difficult to manage and may produce public service demands that burden staffs and fiscal resources of local organizations. For areas that have been experiencing slow or moderate growth, past growth patterns may have provided local leaders and decision makers with a useful base of experience that will allow them to more effectively manage patterns of growth. Finally, in areas with histories of extremely rapid growth, a new development may compound existing problems and further overload existing facilities.

An area's experience with large scale developments

106

Table 6.1

High-Level Nuclear Waste Repository
Employment Requirements

Average Annual Repository Employment

| Repository Medium | Spent Fuel | | Reprocessing Waste | |
	Construction*	Operation	Construction*	Operation
Salt	1,700	870	2,000	1,300
Granite	4,200	1,100	3,000	1,300
Shale	2,200	880	2,100	1,200
Basalt	5,000	1,100	3,800	1,500

*Average of the peak years.

Source: U.S. Department of Energy (1980a).

and developers may also affect its social environment and its desire to support other developments. For example, in many areas of the West, the boom-and-bust cycles of the past have made citizens cautious about growth and its expected benefits (McKee, 1974). In addition, since many areas have experienced large scale developments that have changed the level of community control and autonomy, communities may resist developments that are under the control of decision makers and organizations from outside their local area (Kraenzel, 1955). Thus, the developmental history of an area is an important factor in public acceptance of these developments and other types of social change (Ballard et al., 1981).

Economic Factors. The economic context of an area also affects the residents' perceptions of the development and the availability of goods and services for the project. For example, areas in which agriculture predominates have distinctively different ways of life and different requirements for labor than mining and manufacturing areas. Communities in which tourism and services dominate are different from industrial communities. The economic context and complexity of communities affect how residents' daily social experiences are structured and what types of organizations (for example, granges or union halls) are present.

Further, an area's economic structure may affect firms involved in the development of a repository project in several ways. It may affect their ability to purchase construction supplies and other materials locally and may influence the likelihood of project workers to purchase goods and services locally (Leistritz and Murdock, 1981). Similarly, the number, types, and levels of skills of residents in site areas will affect the availability of workers for certain kinds of jobs necessary in the construction and operation of a repository facility. Thus, if a rural area's economic structure is insufficient to support such a development project, there is a high likelihood that primary and secondary linked businesses and manpower pools will inmigrate (Gilmore et al., 1975). This inmigration, subsequently, will have a substantial influence on settlement patterns, transportation systems, housing, and other public and private services.

Sociocultural Factors. Finally, communities differ in their sociocultural environments. Rural residents may have a smaller range of job opportunities than urban residents, yet historically they have been more self-sufficient and generally less dependent than urban residents on state and Federal welfare programs.

Collectively, people in rural areas have resided in or near communities characterized by informal communication and social relationships (Campbell et al., 1976, Ballard et al., 1981, and Poplin, 1979). Many of their contacts with decision makers in community businesses and organizations are on a first name basis and, despite the geographical distance between them and their neighbors, they either have established friendships with or have knowledge of their neighbors.

Characteristics of Inmigrating Populations

The characteristics of inmigrating workers and their families affect socioeconomic impacts. The magnitude of population change resulting from the project, the rate of that change, the age-sex composition of the new population, and the location of population change within the study area are all affected by these characteristics. These characteristics of project-related populations have substantial implications for public service requirements and can be expected to be a major determinant of the social and fiscal effects of a project.

Population growth associated with a new project, together with the location of that growth, is the key determinant of additional public service and infrastructure requirements. Substantial population growth in a rural community is likely to result not only in increased demands for public services but also to increased formalization of service structures. The composition of new populations will affect the mix of service needs experienced. The composition of these populations (particularly the number of secondary workers in inmigrating households) will also affect the labor supply available to local trade and service firms and public service entities. Likewise, the composition of new populations may affect the propensity to spend locally, with single workers and those with permanent homes outside the area expected to have smaller local expenditures. The residential location of inmigrating populations will in large measure determine the location of secondary economic impacts.

Socioeconomic characteristics of new populations will affect their perceptions of site area communities and the long-term residents' perceptions of them. Origins of inmigrating workers may affect the social acceptance and levels of integration of workers' families into the community. Thus, social acceptance and integration may be less difficult to the extent that inmigrants have a regional and cultural background similar to that of present area residents.

The socioeconomic characteristics of new residents may affect their levels of participation in community activities and organizations. Problems of new resident integration into the community are likely to increase with the magnitude of population growth.

An assessment of the socioeconomic impacts, then,

should include consideration of contextual factors in
regard to the characteristics of the project, the site
area, and inmigrating populations. Such considerations
must include the examination of each factor, its
potential effects, and its interactive relationships with
other predevelopment factors if the socioeconomic impacts
of repositories are to be fully understood.

OVERVIEW OF SOCIOECONOMIC IMPACTS

Many kinds of information and approaches can be used
to assist decision makers in assessing or determining the
socioeconomic impacts associated with a nuclear waste
repository project (Murdock and Leistritz, 1980). To
provide the information that is needed, reseachers
across the country have developed a number of impact
assessment methods (Leistritz and Murdock, 1981;
Finsterbusch and Wolf, 1977; Denver Research Institute,
1979). These consist of a variety of techniques for
assessing a wide range of possible impacts. The types of
socioeconomic impacts assessed vary somewhat from one
analysis to another, but most researchers (Murdock and
Leistritz, 1979; Chalmers and Anderson, 1977) attempt to
describe or project five types of impacts:

Economic--including changes in regional income,
employment and business activity

Demographic--including changes in regional,
county, and community population, population
settlement patterns, and population
characteristics

Fiscal--including the level and distribution by
jurisdiction (county, city, school district) of
public costs and revenues

Community Service--including changes in the
quantity, distribution, and quality of water
and sewer services, educational services,
health care services, police and fire,
transportation, social, and other services

Social--including changes in social or
community organization, community perceptions,
and the effects on specific groups, such as the
elderly, minorities and people on fixed
incomes

Each of these types can be divided into standard and
special impact categories when applied to repository
sites (Hebert et al., 1978). Standard impacts are those
impacts that may typically result from any large-scale

development. **Special impacts** result from the fact that radioactive materials will be handled. Since nuclear waste repositories will produce both standard and special impacts, these impacts must be accurately identified if efforts to moderate or alleviate them are to be successful.

Standard Impacts

Major socioeconomic impacts may occur in local communities because repository developments are large relative to the communities in which they are likely to be located. These impacts are referred to as standard impacts. As mentioned previously, preliminary identification of sites by DOE indicates that repositories are likely to be located in rural areas of the nation (U.S. Department of Energy, 1980b). Such areas can be generally characterized as being sparsely populated, having unique social and cultural environments, and as having limited community services, organizational structures and resources. The siting, construction, and operation of nuclear repositories may involve, then, impacts on local rural communities that are similar to those which have been observed and analyzed for other large developments such as energy projects (Murdock and Leistritz, 1979). Several of the standard impacts are identified in table 6.2. Since these have been discussed elsewhere in much more detail (Murdock and Leistritz, 1979; Leistritz and Murdock, 1981; and Finsterbusch and Wolf, 1981), the discussion here is brief and general.

Although limited information exists on the likely socioeconomic impacts of large-scale developments involving a nuclear waste repository (Cluett et al., 1979), standard socioeconomic impacts resulting from similar large-scale developments in rural areas are likely to include changes in area incomes, employment opportunities and business activity, increases in population size and alterations in population characteristics, increased demands for public services, increased public revenues but also increased public costs, changes in community leadership, alterations of the patterns in which people interact with one another, alterations in the quality of life, and an increased likelihood of confrontations between new and longtime residents (Bowles, 1981).

Equally significant, large-scale developments may alter the way residents view their community and its overall quality of life (Murdock and Schriner, 1978). Although people in rural areas often have very high levels of satisfaction with their communities and community services, and may strongly value environmental conservation and preservation (Murdock and Schriner, 1978; Christenson and Robinson, 1980), they also may

Table 6.2

**Possible Standard Socioeconomic
Impacts of Repository Siting**

Standard Impacts

Economic/Business   Community Services

Increased local employment   Demand for more services
Higher wages   Demand for better service
Increased business sales   quality and accessibility
Higher cost of living   Demand for more and spe-
Competition for labor   cially trained personnel
Development of new business   Improvement of service
Increased competition for   facilities and equipment
  resources   Higher costs for services
Possible economic losses after   Improvement of area road
  the repository closes   and rail systems
Increased land values caused   Increased demand for
  by growth   housing
Changes in uses of land

Demographic   Social

Increased population due to   Perceived changes in the
  new workers and families   quality of life
Changes in the location of   Increased social problems
  population growth   Value conflict between new
Changes in the age, income,   and longtime residents
  and educational character-   More formalized interac-
  istics of the population   tion among residents
                                 Additional sources of
                                   community leadership
Fiscal/Government   More active public
                                   participation in prede-
Additional sales tax   velopment of site
  revenues   Decrease in the proportion
Increased governmental   of informal, primary
  payments to communities   relationships
Increased property taxes
Increased cost of community
  services
Reassessment of property
  values
Jurisdictional inequities
Cost and revenue timing

Source: Adapted from S. H. Murdock and F. L.
Leistritz, 1979.

---

desire development. However, as developments proceed, residents often form less favorable appraisals of the impacts. They may begin to see both positive and negative impacts more clearly.

Special Impacts

In addition to the standard socioeconomic effects of a large development, repositories will have effects that are unique or special because they are "nuclear" repositories and consequently, are subject to the effects of public perceptions and attitudes regarding nuclear power and nuclear waste. Unlike other large-scale developments, nuclear waste facilities must manage and monitor materials with varying levels and durations of radioactivity. Since many unique impacts are likely to result from repository developments, Federal officials, community leaders, and residents must know how communities in site areas may be affected by the transportation, the processing, and the storage of radioactive material.

Although estimates of the risks associated with repositories and the transportation and handling of nuclear materials indicate that these risks are extremely low (U.S. Department of Energy, 1980b), the public may perceive the chance of a major nuclear mishap as much more likely. Regardless of whether these perceptions are based on complete or incomplete information and understanding, public perceptions will influence local residents' receptiveness to the repository, and may determine the significance of other special impacts. Several of these special impacts are listed in table 6.3 and are discussed below.

A major special economic impact is the potential influence of the nuclear repository project on other basic sectors of the local economy (Rice et al., 1980). Because of controls likely to be placed on land use around repositories, changes may occur in the use of public and, possibly, private lands. Also, Federally owned lands constitute a substantial portion of many states' total land bases (for example, Nevada, Utah, and Idaho) and these lands have been used primarily for livestock grazing and timber production, with occasional mining and recreational uses. Thus, such controls may threaten local economies. Decreased agricultural and timber production on public land may require nearby communities to make substantial economic adjustments because of reductions in tax revenues generated by these industries.

Less direct effects of a repository project are also potentially serious in areas where recreation and tourism are important. If the facility is perceived as a threat, many visitors may cease to patronize local recreational facilities and tourist-oriented establishments. The area

Table 6.3

**Possible Special Socioeconomic
Impacts of Repository Siting**

Special Impacts

Economic/Business

Changes in federal land use--
loss of agricultural, forest
or recreational land
Competition for water
resources--agricultural vs.
residential and repository
use
Possible lack of secondary
business growth
Reduction of adjacent land
values
Restricted use of adjacent
land

Demographic

Lack of secondary population
growth
Outmigration of temporary
specialized labor
Possible outmigration of residents caused by perceptions
of changes in the quality of
life

Fiscal/Government

Additional costs associated
with the transportation of
nuclear materials
Federal ownership of repository site, exempting facility
from local property tax
Loss of tax revenues from
agricultural and forest
resources produced on
Federal land
Land value depreciation

Community Services

Special need for emergency
preparedness plans
Need for special health care
personnel and facilities
to treat possible exposure
to nearby radioactive
materials

Social

Perceptions of health and
safety risks from nearby
radioactive materials
Perceptions of lack of equity
in the site selection
process
Increased apprehension of
residents
Concern with security, long-
term safety, and poten-
tial danger to future
generations

Source: Adapted from S. H. Murdock and F. L. Leistritz, 1980.

could become less attractive as a site for residential or second home development with a corresponding decrease in land values (Rice et al., 1980; Cummings et al., 1981; U.S. Department of Energy, 1981a). Finally, the development of a repository could have the effect of forestalling other types of resource or industrial developments such as coal mining or manufacturing facilities.

A potential special demographic impact of a repository development could be a decline in the local population as the repository enters its operational and postoperational phases. That is, if negative perceptions of the repository cause many people to leave the area, local populations may decline rather than grow as a result of the development. A second possible special demographic effect may be a delay in, or lack of, the secondary population growth usually associated with the development of a large facility (Murdock and Leistritz, 1979). Since secondary industry growth often results in higher levels of population increase than basic industry growth, this effect could drastically change the population impacts of a repository.

Special fiscal impacts may be experienced if the unique nature of the repository leads to additional costs for state and local governments beyond those normally associated with large-scale developments. Examples of such costs include those associated with the development of evacuation plans and the provision of special health services for residents.

The assessment of special fiscal impacts also must include consideration of the fact that the facilities will be on Federally-owned property, which is not subject to local and state property taxes. Evaluation of the statutes and administrative precedents governing payments-in-lieu-of-taxes and other forms of Federal assistance to communities affected by such facilities will be important in the fiscal assessment and may be valuable in formulating community impact management strategies.

Among the special effects on public services are the additional demands likely to be placed on community governments as a result of the transportation of nuclear wastes, the need for health and safety maintenance, and the increased need for emergency preparedness services. Many areas do not have personnel trained in the procedures for transporting nuclear wastes and maintaining security at nuclear waste sites. In addition, many areas do not have widely known emergency preparedness plans and personnel trained in evacuation procedures. Finally, health agencies may not have the specialized services that are necessary to diagnose and properly treat cases of radiation exposure and sickness. Clearly, these services will have to be added or expanded. Personnel will need additional training and new personnel will need to be employed to address specialized service needs in the repository communities and along the waste transportation routes. The final set of special or unique effects of nuclear repositories are the social. Although poorly defined, these impacts are often seen as including: (1) fear and anxiety related to present health and safety and the health of future generations, (2) concern over equity in the siting process, (3) concerns about security, short and long-term control, and the transportation and handling of waste materials, and (4) the need for public participation and monitoring (Hebert et al., 1978).

As stated previously, among the major effects of a repository development is the fear it may cause. Because repositories involve the handling and storage of nuclear materials and because of the highly publicized nature of some recent events related to nuclear power, the public may be apprehensive about the siting of nuclear storage facilities near their communities (Kasperson, 1980; Kasperson et al., 1980). Equity is also an important issue because residents in site areas are being asked to accept a facility that may store the nuclear wastes of the entire nation. In addition, the long-term management of repository sites, including security from natural or human-induced events, from terrorism, and from simple human carelessness, is also a major concern. Questions may be raised about the maintenance of even the most carefully designed systems over a period of several centuries (LaPorte, 1978). Finally, local citizens may be concerned that their involvement in the siting process will be minimal. There is apprehension that the major decisions affecting repositories are being made by persons outside their community and that local residents' involvement will occur only in the final stage of the siting process and will involve only a token level of activity.

THE SOCIOECONOMIC ASSESSMENT PROCESS

Given the range of possible standard and special socioeconomic impacts of repositories, it is obvious that their assessment is likely to be a difficult and complex task. In this section, we briefly overview the steps and the procedures used in socioeconomic impact assessment (Leistritz and Murdock, 1981).

Socioeconomic impact assessment generally involves the completion of three research processes: (1) baseline profiling, (2) baseline projections, and (3) impact projections. Baseline profiling consists of the compilation of a comprehensive statistical and verbal description of the characteristics of the siting area prior to development. Secondary and primary data taken from numerous sources are organized to provide

comparisons of the characteristics of the siting area
with those of "standard" regions (such as the state)
outside the siting area and to provide comparisons of the
characteristics of communities and jurisdictions within
the siting areas. This process provides the essential
base against which project-related changes are evaluated.

The baseline projection process consists of
procedures for projecting the future socioeconomic
conditions in the siting area without the proposed
repository. This step is essential because project-
related impacts are future events. It is thus critical
to examine project-related changes not only in comparison
to existing conditions (that is, the baseline profile)
but also in comparison to the future of the area without
the development. Baseline projections usually involve
the use of projection methodologies and techniques common
to the disciplines concerned with each of the impact
dimensions (for example, economics, demography, and so
on). Because of their use as the bases to which impact
projections are compared, baseline projections are
essential.

The impact projection process consists of procedures
for projecting the socioeconomic effects of project
development. It usually involves the use of project-
related economic data such as local project expenditures
and direct employment to project basic economic impacts
such as indirect employment requirements, income, and
business activity. The projections of employment are
then linked to demographically derived projections of
available indigenous labor to determine the number of
inmigrating workers. Then, by the application of certain
assumptions about worker characteristics (for example,
family size), the number of inmigrating persons is
determined. These new populations are then distributed
to potential settlement sites through the use of various
allocation procedures, and projections of community or
jurisdiction-level public service and fiscal impacts are
completed. These procedures are usually completed by
applying population and per capita based rates to the
projections of new inmigrating populations.

The techniques used in completing both the baseline
and the impact projections generally include input-output
or export base techniques for the economic analysis,
population-to-employment ratios or cohort component
techniques for projecting demographic impacts and
weighting, judgemental or gravity models to project
population distribution. Fiscal and public service
projections usually involve the use of per capita or
engineering-based service usage and cost estimates to
determine either project-specific impacts (average
approach) or project-related impacts adjusting for
baseline service levels (marginal approach) (Leistritz
and Murdock, 1981).

Whatever specific methodological technique or

approach is used, the final dimension of the assessment process consists of a comparison of project-induced changes to baseline conditions and baseline projections. By making such comparisons, it is possible to discern the likely magnitude and distribution of project-related impacts. However, given the special characteristics and extensive time frames relevant to repository operation and monitoring, the assessment process for a nuclear repository is likely to require the use of complex and carefully integrated methodological procedures.

CONCLUSION

The magnitude and distribution of the socioeconomic impacts resulting from repository siting are those likely to be affected by a large number of factors related to the characteristics of the project, of the project siting area, and of the new population moving to the siting area as a result of the repository. These impacts include a wide variety of effects related to standard and special economic, demographic, public service, fiscal, and social conditions, and their assessment requires the use of relatively complex procedures. The delineation of these impacts, an examination of their implications, and a description of the modes for assessing them are clearly essential for understanding the repository siting process. It is thus essential that we focus our attention on a more detailed description of the economic, fiscal, demographic, public service, and social impacts of repository siting and on the methods for assessing such impacts in the chapters that follow.

7
Assessing the Economic and Fiscal Effects of Repository Siting

Robert A. Chase
F. Larry Leistritz
John M. Halstead

When sited in areas remote from major population centers, the development of high-level nuclear waste repositories can be expected to produce a substantial stimulus to the local economy. The magnitude of the economic and fiscal effects of such a project and the rapidity with which they occur, however, may pose substantial planning problems for nearby communities. A thorough understanding of the economic and fiscal changes likely to be associated with repository development is essential so that the developer and local officials can plan and initiate measures to alleviate those effects which are viewed as problematic and to enhance those effects which are regarded as beneficial. In this chapter, attention is focused on changes in local employment patterns, the level and distribution of income, community price structures, and revenues and expenditures of local governments likely to occur as a result of repository development.

The chapter is divided into two major sections. First, the major economic and fiscal effects likely to result from repository development are identified, and the current state of knowledge concerning each is reviewed. Second, methods and techniques which can be employed in estimating the magnitude, timing, and distribution of such effects are discussed.

Both standard and special economic and fiscal effects are examined in this chapter. These impacts are discussed under six major categories:

1. effects on employment patterns and characteristics
2. income effects
3. effects on local trade and service firms
4. community price structure changes
5. effects on other basic economic sectors
6. effects on public sector costs and revenues

ECONOMIC AND FISCAL EFFECTS OF REPOSITORY DEVELOPMENT

Employment Effects

The direct employment effects of a nuclear repository, like those at other large development projects, typically occur in two phases: the construction of the facility and its subsequent operation. As the data in table 7.1 indicate, workforce size varies significantly by type of project and by project phase. In like manner, labor force requirements for repositories are expected to differ substantially depending on the geologic medium chosen (for example, salt vs. basalt) and also whether waste reprocessing facilities are included (see chapter 6). In all cases, however, the construction work force requirements are substantially greater than those for the operational phase. In addition, both construction and operational labor requirements are of sufficient magnitude that substantial impacts can be anticipated if such facilities are sited in areas remote from major population centers. These impacts are likely to differ because of differences in the characteristics of construction and operational workers, however. Studies of energy facilities, for example, indicate that construction work forces tend to be dominated by craftsmen with highly specialized skills who are geographically mobile in response to new job opportunities. Wages are high, but employment is temporary; average job tenure for construction workers is about two years (Murdock and Leistritz, 1979). Local workers have been found to make up an average of 40 percent of the total construction work force in some studies, but local workers were most prevalent in the less skilled job categories (Mountain West Research, Inc., 1975). For operational workers at energy facilities, wages are generally higher than those prevalent in other jobs in rural areas, and local workers gain a larger proportion of operational jobs. [In one analysis of 14 energy facilities, local workers made up 62 percent of these work forces, and only two sites had less than 50 percent local workers (see Wieland et al., 1977).]

In addition to the employment created directly in facility construction and operation, repository development can be expected to stimulate increased economic activity and employment in various trade and service sectors of the local economy. This additional employment, created indirectly as a result of the project, is often termed **secondary employment.** (Other commonly used terms are **service, residentiary,** and **indirect** and **induced employment.**) Estimating the amount of secondary employment that will result from a new project is an important facet of any economic and fiscal impact assessment.

Table 7.1

Energy Facility Employment Characteristics[1]

Type of Facility	Size	Construction Period (Years)	Peak Construction Workforce (Number)	Operating Workforce (Number)
Surface coal mine[2]	9 million tons/year	2-3	200	475
Underground coal mine[2]	2 million tons/year	3	325	830
Electric generating plant (includes surface coal mine)[2]	700 megawatts 2,250 megawatts	6 6-8	1,050 3,000	170 650
Synthetic gasification plant (includes surface coal mine)[2]	250 million cubic feet/day	3-4	4,000	1,300
Oil shale processing facility (includes mining)[2]	50,000 barrels/day	3-4	2,400	1,450
Uranium mining and milling[2]	1,000 tons U_3O_8 concentrate/day	1-3	250	250
Nuclear waste repository:[3] in salt in basalt	reference site reference site	3-5 3-5	1,700 5,000	870 1,100

[1]Employment figures are estimates for general planning purposes only. Actual employment for any particular facility will depend on size, type of equipment utilized, mining conditions, construction schedule, and numerous other factors.

[2]Source: Murdock and Leistritz (1979).

[3]Source: U.S. Department of Energy (1980a).

The basic theory underlying efforts to estimate secondary employment is that a new project will inject additional purchasing power into the local economy through purchases of supplies and materials and through expenditures made locally by project employees. These expenditures represent increased business volume for local trade and service firms and will likely require local firms to hire additional employees. In addition, when local firms experience additional demands for their products and services, they require additional inputs, some of which are purchased from other local firms. Thus, the additional expenditures resulting from a new project set in motion a cycle of spending and respending, which has a multiplier effect on local income and employment. The effect of additional project employment on total employment in the impact area is often measured by an employment **multiplier**, which expresses the change in total employment as a multiple of the original change in project employment.

Several factors can influence the magnitude of the employment multiplier associated with a new repository facility. One set of these factors is related to the nature of the project and the characteristics of its direct workers. These factors include: (1) the wage and salary levels of project employees, (2) the propensity of project employees to purchase goods and services locally, and (3) the extent to which the repository facility purchases supplies and services from local firms. The nature of the site area also affects the magnitude of employment multiplier effects. If communities near the project site have poorly developed shopping facilities, project workers may travel to distant trade centers to acquire many goods and services. Similarly, the developer's ability to purchase supplies and services locally will be affected by the degree of development of the local trade and service sectors. If local firms cannot supply needed inputs, the repository will acquire them elsewhere. These factors, which reduce the level of local expenditures resulting from a project, will also tend to reduce its multiplier effects at the local level. During the construction phase of major projects, when many construction workers may commute long distances to the site, the secondary employment effects experienced by small communities nearby may be quite modest. As a result of such factors, employment multipliers may differ widely between project phases and among project sites (Murdock and Leistritz, 1979; Gilmore et al., 1981).

Income Effects

Development of a nuclear repository can be expected to result in substantial changes in income in the affected area. As in the case of employment, both direct and secondary effects are important, and income

multipliers are frequently used to estimate the magnitude
of secondary income effects. However, research aimed at
quantifying the income effects of major resource
development projects has been quite limited.

The direct income effects of a project will depend
primarily on the facility's payroll and on the extent to
which it purchases supplies and materials locally.
Average salaries and wages during the construction phase
of a project typically are quite high, relative to the
wage and salary levels generally prevailing in rural
areas. Leakages of purchasing power from the site area
may also be high during this phase, however, particularly
if a large proportion of the construction workers commute
from outside the area and if local shopping facilities
are limited.

The secondary income effects of a project will
depend on the degree of self-sufficiency of the local
economy, with larger, more diversified economies
generally having larger income multipliers. For example,
Tweeten and Brinkman (1976) report that income
multipliers are frequently of a magnitude of 2.0 for
multicounty districts but often in the range of 1.0 to
1.5 for individual communities (a multiplier of 1.0
indicates no additional net effect beyond the direct
income increase). Chalmers et al. (1977) report similar
findings from a study of counties in the Northern Great
Plains. For regional trade center counties, which
generally had populations in excess of 15,000 and
personal income in their market areas in excess of $100
million (in 1977 dollars), the average income multiplier
was 2.02. For "second order" counties with populations
between 5,000 and 15,000 and market area personal income
exceeding $20 million, the average income multiplier was
1.66. For the remaining counties, with populations less
than 5,000, the average multiplier was 1.23.

A major question with respect to the income effects
of a project relates to their distribution among the
local population. While it appears that local workers
who obtain employment at new energy projects experience
substantial increases in their incomes (Murdock and
Leistritz, 1979) and that the effect of most projects
will be to increase average per capita income levels in
the site area, little is known about the effects of these
projects on income distribution.

In summary, much less attention has been given to
measuring the income effects of new resource developments
than has been the case for employment effects. Further,
very little research has been directed toward the
distribution of these income effects.[1] These topics
would appear to be priority areas for future research.

Effects on Local Trade and Service Firms

While local trade and service firms may expect to

experience increased revenues as a result of repository development, their costs are also likely to increase. Naturally, increased business volume could be expected to result in some added costs for purchased goods, additional labor, and other variable costs. However, costs in some categories may increase disproportionately. Substantial increases may be expected in labor costs and property taxes. Furthermore, some authors suggest that prices of locally purchased goods and services may increase substantially as local businesses attempt to offset rising costs (Gilmore and Duff, 1975).

Some businesspersons in potential development areas are concerned that development will lead to a large influx of new business establishments. It is sometimes hypothesized that the new firms might have better access to capital and/or superior managerial resources, perhaps through affiliation with a national chain (Lonsdale and Seyler, 1979). If such were the case, existing firms might be placed in a disadvantageous position. Recent case studies of rapid growth areas provide little evidence that such changes are widespread (Gilmore et al., 1981; Thompson et al., 1978). However, longitudinal analyses covering a larger number of impacted communities are needed before definite conclusions can be drawn.

Uncertainty as to whether a proposed repository project will actually materialize, when it will begin, and whether it may be developed only to be abandoned later as infeasible, together with uncertainty regarding potential impacts at the community level, can be expected to have substantial effects on business investment decisions. These could include both a reluctance on the part of local merchants to make investments in new or expanded facilities and an unwillingness on the part of financial institutions to make capital available for these purposes. The likely result is that major private sector investments will not occur until the project is a reality and actual dimensions of the resulting impacts can be discerned. Thus, the ability of the local private sector to provide goods and services could lag behind the increase in demand during the early years of a large-scale project (Gilmore, 1976).

Community Price Structure Changes

One of the impacts that often affects rapidly growing resource development areas is the increase in prices resulting from increased demands for many goods and services. Housing costs are particularly susceptible to such effects and have often been found to increase rapidly during periods of energy-related growth (Gilmore and Duff, 1975). Such increases may create price structures that severely limit the range of housing for many residents (Bronder et al., 1977). On the other hand, increases in the cost of new housing units coupled with large increases in demand for housing in rapid growth areas can be expected to result in substantial appreciation in the value of developable land and existing housing units and thus lead to an improved wealth position for some area residents. The increases in prices may pose problems for certain groups. The elderly, those on fixed incomes, and others who are not directly associated with the repository developments may face significantly increased costs, but receive few income benefits. Farm families, for instance, may face increased costs for goods and services--but no income increases.

Because of the nature of the nuclear materials involved and consequent anxieties regarding health and safety risks associated with repository operation, potential decreases in property values may also be a concern. This possible impact would be most significant for owners of property located in close proximity to the repository site or to major waste transportation routes. A recent analysis of the proposed Waste Isolation Pilot Project (WIPP) in New Mexico, however, revealed no conclusive evidence that would suggest that the WIPP will result in adverse effects on property values (Cummings et al., 1981).

Effects on Other Basic Economic Sectors

A potential economic effect of repository development is the project's influence on other basic sectors of the local economy. A repository will require a site area of about 2,000 acres from which other forms of activity will be excluded. In addition, a buffer zone of about 8,000 acres will be established, and certain forms of activity (for example, drilling or mining) will be restricted in this area (U.S. Department of Energy, 1980b). The facility's land requirements will affect the use of such lands for other economic activities. In addition, repository development may lead to changes in private land use, with agricultural, grazing, and forest lands being utilized to meet growing residential or transportation needs.

In areas where recreation and tourism are an important component of the economic base, it is possible that perceptions of repository-related risks could lead to reductions in tourist revenues. Although a recent analysis of the proposed WIPP found no conclusive evidence that this project will result in adverse effects on tourism (Cummings et al., 1981), such potential effects must be carefully examined.

Development of a repository in a given area also could have the effect of forestalling other types of resource or industrial development. Restrictions on mining or drilling in the immediate site area would preclude certain types of development activity. This

effect should be negligible, however, since one of the
site criteria is to avoid areas known to contain valuable
minerals (U.S. Department of Energy, 1979). Of greater
concern from the standpoint of long-term community
development is the possibility that location of a
repository in an area will discourage new plants or other
facilities from locating there, perhaps because of
potential difficulty in recruiting workers. Likewise,
investment in the local trade and service sectors may be
discouraged if the repository is perceived as a negative
influence on the area's long-term growth prospects. On
the other hand, if positively perceived, the development
of a nuclear repository and associated support services
and facilities may enhance the site area's long-term
growth prospects. Improved community infrastructure and
a larger local labor pool, for example, could increase
the area's attractiveness as a site for new industries.

Effects on Public Sector Costs and Revenues

Rapid population growth in communities near
repository development sites can be expected to lead to
increased demands for all forms of public services. Some
forms of services pose particular problems for local
officials because substantial costs are associated with
providing higher levels of these services. A review of
selected studies of the public service impacts of energy
developments indicates that substantial capital costs are
typically associated with expanding schools, water and
sewer systems, and streets and roads (Leholm et al.,
1976a; Gilmore et al., 1976a; Murphy, 1975). These
studies indicate that unless a community initially has
excess capacity in some of its public service
infrastructure, it can expect to experience additional
capital costs from $5,000 to $10,000 per capita and
additional annual operating and maintenance costs of $600
to $900 per capita (in 1980 dollars) for the inmigrating
population. The costs of providing expanded levels of
services may pose severe cash flow problems for local
governments.

The fiscal problems resulting from the increased
service demands and costs created by rapid population
increases lie primarily in the timing of revenue
collection in relation to public service costs and in the
distribution of costs and revenues between jurisdictions.
The problems tend to be greater the larger the population
influx is relative to indigenous population bases and the
larger the differences between the size of the
construction and operational work forces.

Local jurisdictions often experience severe cash
flow problems during the development of a new project
because, although new service demands arise immediately
during construction of the project, many of the revenues
necessary to meet those costs are not available until the

operation of the project begins. This condition arises because local governments tend to be dependent on property taxes; however, construction populations are likely to live in temporary housing with low taxable values, and secondary development of taxable business property occurs relatively slowly. As a result, the revenue-cost squeeze may become critical (Toman et al., 1977; Gilmore et al., 1976a). Local governments must decide whether to invest in local service structures during construction periods when demands are high and be faced with excess capacity to support during operational periods or to muddle through with severely impacted service bases during construction periods and build service structures to meet the lower level of demands expected during operational periods. Equally problematic, local governments must attempt to convince their citizens of the need to increase taxes to pay for services when the uncertainties concerning actual new operational populations, the degree of local dissatisfaction with services and government, fears about tax increases, and concerns regarding closure possibilities all are high.

Jurisdictional distribution problems may be equally severe. The facilities and resources that generate new revenues may be located in one county while the impact-related populations are located in a different county or even a different state. In such cases, the governmental entity receiving the new revenue benefits will experience a tax windfall, while the area with the influx of new population will be faced with especially severe fiscal problems. In addition, the fact that many tax structures distribute a majority of resource-related revenues to state or county governments while the costs often are greatest at the municipal or school district levels may be problematic.

Because repository facilities will be Federally owned and hence exempt from local and state property taxes and also because of the special safety considerations associated with their operation, the fiscal implications of their development will be significantly different from those of many other types of resource and industrial projects. The tax-exempt status of the facility suggests that local governments will be forced to rely heavily on payments-in-lieu-of-taxes (PILOT) or other forms of Federal impact assistance to meet their revenue needs. PILOT payments, however, reflect only the taxes which would have been paid on the undeveloped land on which a facility is sited and hence would generally be inadequate to meet the needs of rapidly growing communities (Bjornstad and Goss, 1981). In addition, jurisdictional mismatches may result in the most seriously impacted units receiving little or no revenue from the PILOT program. Federal programs recently implemented to assist communities affected by major military installations, however, suggest a precedent for a system to more adequately meet the impact needs of repository site areas (see chapters 10 and 12).

Repository development is likely to impose unique service demands and costs on local and/or state governments in the areas where such facilities are sited. Most potential site areas do not have personnel adequately trained in the procedures for transporting and safeguarding nuclear wastes. Such areas also will need to develop emergency evacuation plans, local security personnel will require specialized training, and monitoring equipment may be required for emergency vehicles. Local medical facilities will require additional equipment, and their personnel will need special training. Finally, area roads may require upgrading to meet the standards necessary for waste transportation. The costs associated with these special safety needs could be substantial. For example, a recent analysis of the safety-related expenditures required in connection with the WIPP project concluded that these costs would total $76.8 million over the facility's 30 year life (Cummings et al., 1981). The special fiscal implications of repository development thus demand concerted attention.

METHODS FOR ASSESSING ECONOMIC AND FISCAL EFFECTS

Having reviewed the major economic and fiscal impact dimensions, we now examine the methods by which such effects can be estimated. The conceptual bases and the major methodological alternatives for assessing economic and fiscal impacts are reviewed in the sections which follow.

Economic Effects

Export base theory provides the conceptual foundation for all operational economic impact assessment models. This theory, which has origins in Keynesian national income and growth model analysis, has been thoroughly discussed by Isard (1960), and its applications at the community level are described by Tiebout (1962), among others.

A fundamental concept of the export base theory is that an area's economy can be divided into two general types of economic units. The **basic sector** is defined as those firms which sell goods and services to markets outside the area. The revenue received by basic sector firms for their exports of goods and services is termed basic income. The remainder of the area's economy consists of those firms which supply goods and services to customers within the area. These firms are referred to as the **nonbasic sector** or sometimes as residentiary or local trade and service activities.

A second key concept in export base theory is that the level of nonbasic activity in an area is uniquely determined by the level of basic activity, and a given change in the level of basic activity will bring about a predictable change in the level of nonbasic activity. This relationship is known as the multiplier effect. Thus, export base theory emphasizes external demand for the products of the basic sectors as the principal force determining change in an area's level of economic activity.[2]

The basis for the multiplier effect is the interdependence (or linkages) of the basic and nonbasic sectors of an area's economy. As the basic sector expands, it requires more inputs (for example, labor and supplies). Some of these inputs are purchased from local firms and households. As the firms in the nonbasic sector expand their sales to the basic sector, and workers spend their wages and salaries in the local area, they too must purchase more inputs and goods from local businesses. Again, a portion of these inputs comes from other local firms which in turn must purchase more inputs and so on.

The two major methodological alternatives for economic impact assessment are export base and input-output techniques. The export base (or economic base) model is one of the earliest empirical models to be employed in economic impact studies. Despite the subsequent development of more complex and detailed techniques, export base models are still used in most impact studies. A number of variations of the export base model have been developed.

Export base models can be broadly classified according to the indicator used to measure economic activity (that is, employment or income). Employment is more frequently used because employment data are more readily available for small areas than are measures of income, value added, or other potential indicators. Problems arise, however, because employment may not be a very sensitive indicator of economic activity in sectors which are experiencing technological change. Thus, a sector's output and income may rise relative to employment, especially if the innovations are labor saving. When rates of productivity change are substantially different for the basic and service sectors, the base-service employment ratio may shift substantially. Another problem arises from the fact that basic employment is typically aggregated for multiplier estimation, and the same multiplier is assumed to be applicable to all basic jobs, no matter in what industry they occur. This practice can lead to misleading results if different basic industries have substantially different wage rates and/or local input purchasing patterns. A unit change in employment in a high-wage industry will generate more total employment and income in the local economy than an equal increment in a low-wage industry, but the aggregate employment multiplier masks this effect.

The problems associated with the use of employment as a measure of economic activity can be largely overcome by substituting income for employment in the export base model. The use of income has the distinct advantage of accounting for wage-rate differentials among industries. Businesses are sometimes reluctant to release wage and salary information, however, and it is frequently difficult to obtain reliable estimates of nonwage income. The task of dividing nonwage income into basic and nonbasic components is even more difficult. Finally, income may be quite variable from year to year, and this may complicate the task of multiplier estimation.[3]

Although the export base model has definite limitations as a general theory to explain regional growth, it has found widespread use in impact analysis because of its simplicity and the low costs required for its implementation, which can be done using secondary data exclusively (Pfister, 1976). This model, however, provides very limited impact information. It indicates only the aggregate effect on an area's nonbasic employment or income and analysts who desire more detailed impact projections, including estimates of effects on individual sectors of the local economy, have often turned to input-output models.

Regional input-output models have been utilized extensively in regional impact studies. These models are based on analysis of the interdependence of a region's industries and households as suppliers of inputs and purchasers of products. In developing an input-output model for a given region, the regional economy is divided into sectors (groups of similar economic units), and the transactions among the various sectors are estimated. The quantitative estimates of the interdependencies among the various sectors then provide the basis for tracing the multiplier effects of an exogenous shock to the economy in a more detailed manner than do export base models. In general, a regional input-output model can be viewed as a disaggregation of the export base model which allows for consideration of a large number of local industries with varying proportions of basic activity and for consideration of several sources of exogenous demand for the region's products (Richardson, 1972; Romanoff, 1974).

Input-output models which are used in impact assessments typically include households as a producing sector; these models are said to be **closed** with respect to households. Such models reflect the **induced** effects of the expansion of a given industry (that is, the additional household consumption which results from the

additional income associated with industrial expansion)
as well as the **indirect** effects (arising from additional
requirements for production inputs) and the **direct**
effects (that is, the initial increase in the industry's
output). The income and employment multipliers derived
from the closed I-O model are closely analogous to those
from export base models.[4]
 Whether an export base or an input-output approach
is utilized as the basis for economic impact assessment,
two additional issues demand the analyst's attention.
These are estimating the timing and the geographic
distribution of secondary economic effects (Leistritz and
Murdock, 1981). Both export base and input-output models
indicate only the expected magnitude of secondary
economic effects in an area once complete adjustment has
occurred. A number of different techniques have been
employed to estimate the timing of economic changes,
including the use of different propensities to consume
locally during construction and operation phases
(Mountain West Research, Inc., 1979), the use of smaller
employment multipliers during construction phases
(Briscoe, Maphis, Murray, and Lamont, Inc., 1978; Murphy
and Williams, 1978), and the application of a lag factor
to all changes in nonbasic employment (Denver Research
Institute, 1979). All of these approaches are
acknowledged to be somewhat judgemental, however.
 The geographic distribution of secondary economic
effects has received less attention than their timing.
Techniques which have been utilized to estimate
geographic distribution of secondary economic effects
include hierarchical income multipliers (Chalmers et al.,
1977), gravity models (Leistritz et al., 1979), and
linear programming models (Stenehjem and Metzger, 1976).
Scarcity of data concerning the actual geographic and
temporal distribution of secondary economic effects in
rapid growth areas has severely limited attempts to test
and refine such models.

Fiscal Effects

 The purpose of fiscal impact analysis is to project
the changes in costs and revenues of governmental units
which are likely to occur in response to a development
project. The governmental units of primary interest are
those local jurisdictions which may experience
substantial changes in population and/or service demands
as a result of the project (Muller, 1975). Thus, the
primary objective of fiscal impact studies is to
determine whether new development projects will directly
and indirectly generate enough new local revenues to pay
for the added public services they will require.
 As with other areas of impact assessment, the
projection of fiscal impacts utilizes conceptual bases
which are relatively poorly developed and is an area for

which prevailing practices rather than alternative theoretical perspectives have determined accepted techniques. In addition, it is an area in which the dimensions analyzed are both extensive and complex. The basic concepts of demand, supply, and cost theory provide the basis for fiscal impact analysis. Difficulty in measuring the output of public services, however, usually leads to a number of simplifying assumptions when fiscal impact models are implemented.

The principal methodological alternatives for revenue estimation are either to assume that revenues will be directly proportional to population or to employ more detailed models which involve first estimating the change in the relevant tax base and then applying an appropriate tax rate. Revenue estimation methods tend to differ primarily in their level of detail rather than in their basic form of analysis. It is generally agreed that more detailed analyses which reflect the unique characteristics of the state's tax system will provide more reliable estimates of the magnitude and especially the timing of revenue changes.

Two general approaches may be employed in cost estimation. These are:

1. average cost approaches--which project service demands and associated costs for new population only, utilizing averages per unit of new population and either national, statewide, or local service standards

2. marginal cost approaches--that attempt to take existing services into account and project new service requirements and costs on the basis of marginal demands (that is, requirements above those that can be met by existing service bases)

The average cost approach includes three more specific techniques: per capita expenditures, service standards, and cross-sectional analysis. The marginal cost approach includes case studies, comparable city analysis, and the economic-engineering approach (Leistritz and Murdock, 1981). In general, marginal cost approaches can be expected to be more reliable if the services being analyzed are subject to substantial economies of scale or threshold effects or if excess capacity is likely to exist. Average cost approaches, on the other hand, have the advantage of being quicker and less expensive to employ.

Whatever approach is adopted, care must be taken to insure that the techniques selected allow for adequate analysis of the magnitude and timing of impacts among different types of jurisdictions. Only methods with such characteristics will be of utility to policy and decision makers involved in repository development.

CONCLUSIONS

This chapter describes some of the more important economic and fiscal effects of nuclear repository development and reviews the methods and techniques which can be utilized in assessing such impacts.

Major economic and fiscal impact dimensions include changes in local employment patterns, the level and distribution of income, local business activity and price structures, and the revenues and expenditures of local governments. When a nuclear repository or other large development project is located in a rural area, economic and fiscal changes may be large in magnitude and may occur quite rapidly. Because labor requirements may fluctuate both within and between development phases, impacts are likely to be cyclical with employment and income increasing rapidly during the project construction period and decreasing somewhat once construction is completed. A substantial decrease in the area's economic activity may occur later when the operational life of the project has ended. The rapid rate at which economic and associated fiscal changes may occur and the possibility of substantial differences in these effects among individual jurisdictions indicates a need for economic and fiscal impact assessments to deal with not only the overall magnitude but also the timing and distribution of impacts.

The export base (or economic base) theory is the basis for all economic impact assessments. The principal methodological alternatives include various forms of export base employment or income multiplier models and input-output models. Fiscal impact analysis utilizes conceptual bases which are relatively poorly developed and is an area in which prevailing practices rather than alternative theoretical perspectives have tended to determine accepted techniques. Specific methods for revenue estimation differ primarily in their level of detail rather than the basic form of analysis. Cost estimation methods utilize one of two general approaches--average cost or marginal cost techniques.

The impact assessment techniques which have been employed to date often appear rather simplistic. Given the needs of decision makers in impacted areas, greater attention should be given to assessing the distribution of impacts over time, among jurisdictions, and among population groups. Models which take account of interproject differences in salary levels and input purchasing patterns and which provide disaggregated impact projections probably should be utilized more extensively.

Economic and fiscal impact assessments have been

limited in another important respect as well. The information base concerning the effects of rapid economic and population growth in rural areas is simply insufficient to allow adequate assessment of many impact dimensions. More extensive longitudinal and comparative analyses of areas experiencing such growth are essential if the quality of impact assessments is to be improved.

NOTES

1. A related topic, which has received even less attention, is the effect of resource development on the distribution of wealth. While the potential for substantial increases in property values is generally recognized (Tweeten and Brinkman, 1976; Bradley, 1978), there have been only a few attempts to quantify these effects (Debes, 1973), and no study of which we are aware examines the distributional aspects of these changes.

2. Numerous authors have examined the strengths and limitations of export base models. In particular, see Levan, 1956; Tiebout, 1962; Shaffer, 1979; Richardson, 1978; and Tweeten and Brinkman, 1976.

3. Another approach which can be used to overcome the problems posed by differentials in wage rates and input purchase patterns among basic industries is to estimate separate multipliers for each basic industry (see Weiss and Gooding, 1968; Braschler, 1972; McNulty, 1977; and Bender, 1975).

4. In fact, it has been demonstrated that the export base income multiplier and the consolidated closed I-O multiplier are mathematically identical (Billings, 1969). Both reflect direct, indirect, and induced effects of exogenous changes in demand for a region's output, and both are average rather than marginal multipliers. Further, empirical comparisons of the two multipliers, using similar definitions of basic activity, indicate that their values tend to be similar (Garnick, 1970).

8
Assessing the Demographic and Public Service Impacts of Repository Siting

Steve H. Murdock
Rita R. Hamm

The demographic and public service impacts of a repository are likely to be among the most discussed changes resulting from repository development (Murdock and Leistritz, 1981). The level of employment expected to result from repository construction and operation (see chapter 7) may lead to substantial population growth in rural, siting-area communities. This growth, in turn, will lead to increased demands on nearly all public services (for example, police, fire, water, school, health, education, and so on). In addition, because of potential changes in the distribution and composition of population resulting from rapid growth, both the characteristics of siting area populations and of their service requirements are likely to change dramatically as a result of repository activities. In this regard, repositories are not significantly different than other large-scale projects whose population and service growth have been among the most publicized of the "boomtown" effects of rapid development (Murdock and Leistritz, 1979; Leistritz and Murdock, 1981). The impacts of repository development on population size, distribution and composition and on the level, quality, and distribution of public services, however, may also differ significantly from such impacts in other large-scale projects. Repositories may require new services (for example, radiation treatment), a new mix of services (for example, greater emphasis on emergency preparedness), and new skills among service personnel (for example, training in transportation and plant security). Both the standard and the special demographic and public service impacts of repositories are thus likely to be significant.

It is clearly essential, then, that the potential demographic and public service impacts of repositories be described, methods for their assessment be reviewed, and the unique effects of repositories on such impacts and assessment methods be examined. Because no repository has yet been constructed, we must, as in other chapters in this section, rely heavily on the findings from other large-scale developments (Albrecht, 1978; Chalmers and

Anderson, 1977; Murdock and Leistritz, 1979; Leistritz
and Murdock, 1981; Murdock et al., 1982c) to discern the
likely impacts of repository development.
This chapter is organized into two major sections.
In the first section, the potential demographic and
public service impacts of repositories are delineated and
those likely to be unique to repositories examined. In
the second section, the alternatives for assessing such
impacts are described and the particular difficulties
likely to affect such assessments for repositories are
discussed. The purpose of the chapter is thus to provide
an overview of demographic and public service impacts and
impact assessment techniques and of the unique influences
of repositories on such impacts and on their assessment.

DEMOGRAPHIC AND PUBLIC SERVICE IMPACTS

Demographic Impacts

Demographic impacts are commonly discussed in terms
of three dimensions--changes in population size,
distribution, and composition. These three factors
represent the basic dimensions to be examined in any
demographic analysis and serve as the basis of
organization for this section.
Among the factors that affect demographic impacts in
general are several of those noted in chapter 6--the
characteristics of the project, of the project site area,
and of inmigrating workers. Although the effects of such
characteristics need not be reported in detail here their
interactive effects on demographic impacts must be
recognized.
In general, the larger the number of workers
required by the project, the number of nonlocal workers
employed at the project, the percentage of married
workers and workers with families present in the impact
area, and the larger the size of families present in the
impact area, and the lower the number of other workforce
members in the energy worker's household, the higher the
level of population growth in an area will be. That is,
larger overall projects generally require larger direct
and indirect labor forces and thus have larger
population-creating potential. These labor force
requirements can, in turn, be met by local workers
already included in the population or by nonlocal
(inmigrating) workers. When large numbers of nonlocal
workers must inmigrate, the levels of growth are
increased. Given these basic parameters, the population
resulting from a project will depend on the family
characteristics of inmigrating (nonlocal) workers, with
married workers with larger families bringing larger
population changes. Finally, the presence of other
workers in the energy worker's household will reduce the

inmigration of additional families that would otherwise migrate to the area to fill available employment. Clearly, then, the characteristics of the project, of the local workforces and those of inmigrants determine the overall levels of population growth and changes in population distribution and composition associated with a project such as a repository. These potential impacts as they are likely to affect population size, distribution, and composition are described below.

Size of Repository-Related Populations. Determining the size of the population which will result from a repository development requires consideration of numerous factors. Such populations are a function of the direct and indirect employment created by a repository, which, as noted above, is itself a function of numerous factors (Murdock and Leistritz, 1979; 1981). Although there is little evidence to suggest how much population growth may be associated with repository development, some estimates have been completed (U.S. Department of Energy, 1979). Table 8.1 shows the range of employment and population-related growth projected to occur with various types of repository facilities. An examination of these data clearly reveals that levels of population growth are likely to be significant given the relatively small predevelopment levels of population that exist in such potential siting areas as San Juan County, Utah (1980 population, 12,253), Deaf Smith County, Texas (1980 population, 21,165) and Perry County, Mississippi (1980 population, 9,864).

Determining how extensive project-related population growth is likely to be is difficult, however. Several case studies of energy development areas indicate that such growth is often extensive. Gilmore and his colleagues, for example, estimated that the population of Sweetwater County, Wyoming, increased from 18,000 in 1970 to over 38,000 in 1975, and Thompson, Blevins, and Watts suggested that large population increases occurred in Platte County, Wyoming, and McLean County, North Dakota during the early 1970s (Gilmore et al., 1976b; Thompson et al., 1978). However, Murdock et al. (1982b), in an assessment of the levels of 1970 to 1980 population growth in impacted areas, note that few communities have experienced boomtown levels of growth. Rather, most have experienced moderate and manageable growth.

The question of what various levels of growth may mean is even more difficult to answer. According to a Federal Energy Administration survey of impacted communities, areas with growth rates exceeding 3 percent annually are severely impacted and may experience some problems providing services, but those with rates greater than 6 percent are critically impacted and likely to experience extreme difficulties in providing almost all public services (Federal Energy Administration, 1977).

Gilmore and his colleagues note that annual growth rates
of more than 10 percent are likely to cause severe growth
management problems (Gilmore et al., 1976b). Under these
various criteria, such energy-impacted communities as
Castle Dale and Huntington, Utah; Rock Springs, Green
River, South Superior, and Wamsutter, Wyoming; Page,
Arizona; Hayden, Colorado; and Rosebud County, Montana,
would be considered boom communities. The levels of
projected population growth resulting from repositories
would clearly lead to high levels of nearly boomtown
growth in the smallest of the potential siting areas (for
example, Perry County, Mississippi). Repository
development is thus likely to have significant effects on
population growth in siting areas, but its exact level is
difficult to predict.

Patterns of Population Distribution. The types of
impacts created by a given level of project-related
population growth depend on where new inmigrants choose
to locate. Even relatively large developments may have
little impact if the population increases occur in large
urban centers with surpluses of available housing and
readily accessible public services. In many rural areas,
however, the levels of public services are often already
inadequate, and although the number of vacant housing
units, as recorded in secondary data sources, may appear
high, much of such housing is of low quality. For these
areas, an influx of population may require large private
and public investments. But at what location should such
investments be made? As with the determination of
population size, numerous dimensions appear to affect
settlement decisions and, hence, the determination of
population distributions.

One of the central factors in settlement decisions
appears to be accessibility to the worksite. In general,
workers choose to live in communities close to the
worksite, provided such areas are similar in other
regards to more distant locations. Accessibility,
however, tends to be less important as the length of the
employment period at the site decreases. Thus, workers
who expect to be at a worksite for only a short period
may be willing to live 50 to 75 miles away, whereas
workers working at a site for an extended period may wish
to resettle rather than commute long distances (Leholm et
al., 1976b). Distance from the worksite, then, tends to
be an important factor in determining settlement
decisions, but its effects may be offset by other
factors.

One of the other factors influencing settlement
decisions is the service structure of available
settlement sites. Communities with obvious service
advantages are often attractive locations for new
populations. The availability of a good school system,
paved streets, recreational activities, and other

Table 8.1

**Expected Workforce Requirements and Projected Project-Related
Inmigration for Uranium and Plutonium Recycle Waste Repositories
by Geographic Region and Geologic Media for Selected Years**

Geologic Media Geographic Area	Workforce Requirements/ Inmigration	1985	Year 2000	2015
Salt Formation				
Southwest	Workforce	1,000	1,000	1,000
	Inmigration	5,768	6,871	7,034
Southeast	Workforce	1,000	1,000	1,000
	Inmigration	681	796	821
Midwest	Workforce	1,000	1,000	1,000
	Inmigration	1,571	1,839	1,895
Granite				
Southwest	Workforce	1,200	1,200	1,200
	Inmigration	9,413	11,283	11,533
Southeast	Workforce	1,200	1,200	1,200
	Inmigration	944	1,104	1,141
Midwest	Workforce	1,200	1,200	1,200
	Inmigration	2,186	2,569	2,655
Shale				
Southwest	Workforce	1,000	1,000	1,000
	Inmigration	6,304	7,525	7,699
Southeast	Workforce	1,000	1,000	1,000
	Inmigration	708	828	854
Midwest	Workforce	1,000	1,000	1,000
	Inmigration	1,601	1,875	1,933
Basalt				
Southwest	Workforce	1,170	1,170	1,170
	Inmigration	10,356	12,436	12,706
Southeast	Workforce	1,170	1,170	1,170
	Inmigration	980	1,146	1,185
Midwest	Workforce	1,170	1,170	1,170
	Inmigration	2,270	3,672	2,764

Source: U.S. Department of Energy, **Environmental Aspects of
Commercial Radioactive Waste Management,** Vol. 3, pgs. C.82-C.122.
Springfield, Virginia: NTIS.   1979.

services may increase an area's attractiveness as a settlement location for inmigrants. Such service structures are often a function of the population size of a community. Again, other things being equal, migrants desire to live in larger nonmetropolitan areas where services are more readily available (Fuguitt and Zuiches, 1975).

In addition to distance and service availability, however, numerous and less easily predictable variables may affect settlement patterns. The receptiveness of a community to new residents, the willingness of a contractor to speculate on a new housing subdivision, the decisions of local governments concerning local zoning restrictions, and numerous other factors can alter settlement patterns in ways that are difficult to predict through the use of population, distance and similar factors.

Finally, there may simply be few settlement choices. The sparsity of settlements in many locations, such as in many locations in the Western states, coupled with zoning regulations that restrict housing to established communities, may mean that there will be only one or two viable settlement locations. In summary, then, settlement patterns are likely to be widely diverse and require careful analysis.

Although settlement patterns are difficult to predict, analyses completed to date indicate that workers and population distribution patterns have tended to lead to concentrations of workers living within 30 miles of the project site (Murdock and Leistritz, 1979) and to concentrations of inmigrating populations in places of over 1,000 people (Murdock et al., 1980). The very small towns such as those of only a few hundred persons that dominate many areas in the Western United States are unlikely to attract the new populations resulting from such projects. Thus for repositories, as for many other large-scale developments, the distribution of new populations among settlement sites may be difficult to predict.

Population Composition. In addition to knowledge of population size and distribution, knowledge of population composition is also essential. Planning for community services, the likely levels of acceptance of new persons, and the economic demands of new populations on local businesses are all affected by the characteristics of such populations. The question is what are the characteristics of households and household members who are likely to enter site areas as a result of a repository's development?

Although no evidence regarding the characteristics of repository-related inmigrants is available, evidence from other large-scale developments (Mountain West Research, Inc., 1975; Wieland et al., 1977; Murdock et al., 1980) suggests that such migrants are typical of migrants in general and are thus likely to be younger, better educated, more highly skilled, and to have higher incomes than indigenous residents (Stinner and Toney, 1981). Thus, the characteristics of migrants are likely to markedly alter the composition of community populations near repository sites.

When viewed in total, repository developments are likely to have extensive impacts on the size, distribution and composition of the populations in repository siting areas. As available evidence from other types of developments suggests, however, and the discussion of projection methodologies to follow will reaffirm, the exact nature of such characteristics is difficult to predict.

Public Service Impacts

Of the impacts likely to occur as a result of energy developments and the new populations accompanying them, those affecting community services are likely to be among the most widely discussed. Severe shortages of housing, medical, and water and sewer services have been documented in impact areas (Gilmore et al., 1976a). Simply put, public services serve basic human needs. Consequently, community services and the costs of providing these services have received widespread attention (Gilmore et al., 1976a; Stenehjem and Metzger, 1976; Leistritz and Murdock, 1981) and are of vital concern in impact analyses.

Any examination of community service levels requires the assessment of numerous dimensions of service needs. Such assessments must include an analysis of the levels of services available and required, the quality of those services, and the accessibility of such services to potential service populations. In many rural areas, there are simply too few services available. The numbers of doctors, social workers, and mental health counselors and the levels of law enforcement, fire protection, and other services may be insufficient to meet even current needs (Schriner et al., 1976). Cultural and formal recreational services and facilities may be nonexistent. The range of services available is equally problematic. School systems may offer a limited curriculum; medical specialists, particularly psychiatrists, may be in short supply; and general social services may be limited to the clerical duties of a single social worker.

Insufficient levels of service are often no more problematic than the quality of available services. Levels of professional training in such fields as law enforcement, fire protection, and emergency services are frequently inadequate in rural areas. In addition, for many service areas, those services that do exist may be of poor quality. Personnel at the service agencies, because of advancing age, insufficient financial support, or an overburdened work schedule, are often unable to renew and update their levels of professional knowledge. Physical facilities are often outdated and equipment lacking or too expensive to be merited by the levels of service demands. For many rural areas, such as those likely to house repository sites, then, lack of services is compounded by the poor quality of the services.

Accessibility presents additional problems. Distances to many essential services may simply be too extensive. In many areas, the nearest hospital or other medical facility may be many miles away, involving transport periods that reduce the emergency patient's chances of survival (Gessaman et al., 1978). The nearest law enforcement agency may be available only in the county seat, and fire protection may consist of a volunteer force that is miles away (Murdock and Leistritz, 1979). As a result, even if the general level of services in the region is sufficient, the distribution of such services may not provide the required levels of accessibility.

The levels of service demands accompanying development are not simply a function of baseline service levels or of the number of new persons entering an area as a result of a development. Such demands are also a function of the levels, quality, and availability of services desired by inmigrating groups. In many cases, inmigrating groups may have significantly higher service expectations than indigenous groups. In a survey of residents in impacted areas in Wyoming, for example, Bickert (1974) found that a high percentage of new residents were dissatisfied with medical, housing, educational, and other services. More important, over 60 percent indicated they would leave the area if medical and mental health services did not improve, over 50 percent indicated they would leave if housing did not improve, and over 30 percent indicated intentions to leave if retail, educational, transportation, and sanitation services did not improve. The perceptions of what are adequate levels of public services are thus also likely to affect service demands.

Finally, however, it is essential to note the implications of failing to meet the service demands resulting from a development. Service inadequacies are direct precipitators of high community mobility and high labor turnover rates. The failure to meet new populations' service demands may be costly for the repository developer, as well as for the community. For many communities, an inability to maintain services may mean an end to long-desired renewed population and economic growth. The dimensions and the implications of community service provision in impacted areas is thus an area of clear significance for assessing the impacts of respository development on rural areas, and the community service requirements of a repository site may be extensive. Although few estimates of repository-related service demands have been made, table 8.2 provides one set of estimates of the projected levels of new service demands likely to result from repository development (U.S. Department of Energy, 1979). An examination of the data in this table clearly shows that significant expansion of services may be required in repository siting communities.

Special Demographic and Public Service Impacts

The standard demographic and public service impacts of large-scale developments, such as those described above, are thus also likely to occur at repository sites. However, repositories may also have demographic and public service impacts quite unlike those for other large-scale developments. Although direct project-related population growth may occur, concern about repository safety may also lead to outmigration among nonrepository-related residents and to population redistribution to areas outside the perceived danger area for the repository. In addition, although much of the population growth resulting from other large-scale developments has resulted from secondary population growth (that is, population growth resulting from growth in secondary employment), such employment and its resulting population may be reduced due to apprehension about repository safety.

The service impacts of a repository may also differ from those that often occur as a result of other large-scale developments. Repositories will require both services that have not previously been required in such communities and possibly affect the mix of services and service personnel skills required in the area. Thus, such services as emergency preparedness, increased rail transportation, and police and security services may be required, local medical personnel may be required to obtain advanced training in treating mining-related accidents or radiation exposure, and new public health monitoring systems may be required. In sum, the demographic and public service impacts of large-scale developments often have significant implications for siting areas, but those that may occur as a result of repository siting may be particularly significant.

ASSESSING DEMOGRAPHIC AND PUBLIC SERVICE IMPACTS

Assessment of the demographic and public service impacts of repository developments represents one of the most important steps in the socioeconomic assessment process. Determining the number and the characteristics of people moving to each geographical entity in the

Table 8.2

**Expected Public Service Requirements Associated with Inmigrant
Populations for Uranium and Plutonium Waste Repositories in Salt
Formations by Geographic Region for Selected Years and Services**

Geographic Area	Service Requirements	1985	Year 2000	2015
Southwest	Health			
	# of Physicians	5.5	6.6	6.8
	# of Hospital Beds	19.2	22.8	23.4
	Education			
	# of Teachers K-8	52.7	44.4	37.8
	# of Teachers 9-12	38.5	42.6	34.9
	Sanitation			
	Water Treatment*	3275.0	3901.1	3993.5
	Solid Waste Vehicles	.6	.8	.8
	Fire and Police			
	# of Firemen	3.9	4.6	4.7
	# of Policemen	11.5	13.7	14.1
	Law Enforcement			
	# of Crimes	336.9	401.3	410.8
Southeast	Health			
	# of Physicians	.6	.7	.7
	# of Hospital Beds	2.5	3.0	3.1
	Education			
	# of Teachers K-8	6.5	4.3	4.1
	# of Teachers 9-12	3.8	5.2	3.5
	Sanitation			
	Water Treatment*	386.6	451.7	466.2
	Solid Waste Vehicles	.1	.1	.1
	Fire and Police			
	# of Firemen	.5	.5	.6
	# of Policemen	1.4	1.6	1.6
	Law Enforcement			
	# of Crimes	31.6	36.9	38.1

Table 8.2 (Continued)

Geographic Area	Service Requirements	1985	Year 2000	2015
Midwest	Health			
	# of Physicians	2.1	2.4	2.5
	# of Hospital Beds	9.2	10.8	11.1
	Education			
	# of Teachers K-8	15.2	10.0	9.2
	# of Teachers 9-12	9.1	12.1	8.2
	Sanitation			
	Water Treatment*	892.2	1044.0	1075.7
	Solid Waste Vehicles	.2	.2	.2
	Fire and Police			
	# of Firemen	1.1	1.2	1.3
	# of Policemen	3.1	3.7	3.8
	Law Enforcement			
	# of Crimes	67.6	79.1	81.5

*Cubic meters/day

Source: U.S. Department of Energy, **Environmental Aspects of Commercial Radioactive Waste Management**, Vol. 3., Pgs. C.82-C.122. Springfield, Virginia: NTIS. 1979.

impact area and their service requirements is essential
for assessing other population-related impacts such as
fiscal and social impacts. In fact, to many planners and
decision makers, the magnitude of population and public
service impacts is synonymous with the magnitude of all
impacts. Assessing the size, distribution, and
composition of project-related populations and their
service demands is thus of utmost importance and is the
major topic of concern in this section of the chapter.

Demographic Assessment Techniques

     Demographic assessment techniques are a form of
demographic population projection involving an attempt to
project what an area's population size, distribution and
composition will be, both with and without a repository
or other development. There is, of course, a wealth of
literature on demographic estimation and projection
techniques to guide the assessment analyst (Shryock and
Siegel, 1973; Bogue, 1974; Pittenger, 1976; Morrison,
1971; Irwin, 1977; Lee and Goldsmith, 1982). For the
projection of small area populations, the results of
these efforts (National Academy of Sciences, 1980;
Ascher, 1978), are not encouraging, however. Analyses of
the accuracy of these projections suggest that
projections are generally less accurate for small
population areas, for population components, for longer
time periods, and for areas undergoing rapid change (that
is, the type of projections and conditions likely to be
typical of repository and other rapidly developing sites
in rural areas and likely to be required in their
assessments) than for projections of total populations,
and for larger and more stable areas.
     In addition, the widely varying effects of project,
site area, and inmigrant characteristics on populations
in potential repository siting areas makes the completion
of a demographic impact assessment a formidable one. The
assessment analyst must:

1. project both baseline and impact population
    levels in which standard projection assumptions
    are required

2. project not only the total magnitude and
    characteristics of that growth but also its
    distribution and characteristics at the
    community level

3. make projections that take into account
    a. the characteristics of project labor
        demands and local areas' settlement
        configurations
    b. the workforce as well as the demographic
        characteristics of the indigenous area's

population (that is, availability, skill
levels, and so forth)
c. the fluctuations likely to appear in
various phases of the development project
d. the potential effect of nondemographic
factors, such as development policies,
community growth perceptions, and service
infrastructures
e. the extent of congruence between local
skill levels and the skills required for
the development

4. not only assess the demographic characteristics
of residents in the area but also the likely
characteristics and settlement patterns of
workers and the dependents of workers who will
inmigrate into the area

In sum, the population analyst doing impact
projections must combine the standard, and often
unsubstantiated, assumptions about demographic processes
that must be made in standard population projections,
with the additional assumptions required concerning each
of the impact dimensions. Clearly, an accurate
assessment of demographic impacts can only be
approximated by existing techniques and knowledge bases.
Such an assessment is a process that, because of its
complex nature, requires numerous trade-offs and
simplifying assumptions.

In general, the projection of baseline and impact-
related populations involves a number of key steps.
These steps include:

1. projection of baseline populations for the
impacted region and subregional areas

2. determination of project-related direct and
indirect inmigrating workers including
consideration of
a. characteristics of required employment
b. characteristics of available labor
(unemployment, underemployment, skill
levels and commuting patterns)
c. indirect/direct worker ratios
d. local/nonlocal worker ratios

3. projections of the geographical distribution
(settlement patterns) of inmigrating workers

4. determination of the demographic
characteristics of inmigrating workers and
their dependents to establish project-related
population impacts by site

A description of these steps delineates the nature of the demographic impact assessment process and points out differences in alternative assessment techniques.

Baseline Projections. The projection of baseline populations in impact assessments normally involves two procedures--a projection of total population at the regional or county level and an allocation or distribution of that population to subareas in the region or county. Surveys of prevailing methods (Chalmers and Anderson, 1977; Denver Research Institute, 1979, Leistritz and Murdock, 1981) indicate that several techniques are commonly used to perform these procedures. Projections of populations at the regional level have tended to use either a single population-to-employment ratio or several separate ratios (one for each of several types of employment), a cohort-survival, or a cohort-component method. Population distribution is usually projected on the basis of ratios of local-to-county or regional population or employment or on the basis of ad hoc judgements. Although variations in the frequency of use of alternative techniques are evident in the literature, in general the use of cohort techniques for projecting population size and ratioing techniques to project population distribution are gaining prominence.

Impact Projections. Steps two through four are related to the projection of impact populations. Although impact populations might be determined by projecting a total population figure that includes baseline and impact populations and then subtracting baseline projections from the total population figures, the general pattern is to project impact-related populations separately and to obtain total (project plus baseline) population by adding baseline and impact projections.

The second step, the projection of migrating workers, is the most difficult part of the impact projection process. It involves the completion of several procedures and the use of numerous assumptions. This step, the projection of the number of inmigrating workers, is almost the universally accepted starting point for projecting project-related populations. The reasons for the widespread acceptance of this starting point, rather than a more purely demographic one, are several. First, data on the direct labor requirements of projects are perhaps the most readily accessible of all socioeconomic data on developments. Secondly, although migration patterns as a whole are increasingly motivated by noneconomic factors (Long and Hansen, 1979), the migration related to developments, such as repositories, is likely to be largely employment related. Both of these factors suggest the use of employment-related migration as the key to projecting impact-related population. Finally, there simply are few alternatives to the use of employment. No clear linkages between project characteristics, other than employment, such as type of project, project production capacity, or other characteristics have been established. However desirable the development of alternative means for projecting impact populations might appear to be, few viable alternatives have been developed.

Although simple ratios of indirect-to-direct and local-to-nonlocal workers (see chapter 7) are sometimes used for this projection phase, a somewhat more complex procedure which utilizes more demographic input is receiving increasing use (Stenehjem, 1978; Mountain West Research, Inc., 1975). In this procedure, direct employment and indirect employment are derived from simple ratios, but the application of labor force participation rates to population projections is used as the basis for determining local labor availability.

Even more elaborate techniques have been applied on some, though infrequent, occasions. Among the more elaborate of these are those of Hertsgaard et al. (1978), Cluett et al. (1977), and Murdock et al. (1979a; 1982a). These procedures use separate techniques to project different types of employment and to project labor availability and a separate procedure to match employment demands to labor availability. The results of these matching procedures are then used to project both inmigrating workers and inmigrating populations.

The advantages of these complex procedures are that they simulate most of the major factors known to affect employment-related migration including: (1) types of employment demands that are likely to affect levels of local employment and inmigration; (2) types of labor availability—the different levels of potential (skills) in the local population for taking different types of employment; (3) the effects of age and sex population characteristics on that availability; and (4) the effects of underemployment and unemployment. Conceptually, these procedures are attractive. Their major disadvantages are that such procedures have extensive data requirements, and many of these data requirements cannot be met by available data.

The third step is the projection of the geographical settlement patterns of inmigrating workers. This step may, in fact, be performed with workers or be delayed until after step four and be performed with the total population. It is a procedure that parallels the allocation of populations to communities in baseline projections. Unlike that process, however, the focus in impact projections is the distribution of workers in relation to the project site rather than within a geographically delineated county or region. This distribution involves allocating workers to places that may be located in several separate geographical jurisdictions.

At least three approaches are used with some frequency in the projection of worker distributions in impact assessments (Denver Research Institute, 1979; Chalmers and Anderson, 1977; Leistritz and Murdock, 1981): (1) judgemental weighting models, (2) delphi derived models, and (3) gravity models.

Judgemental weighting models are those models that rely on researchers' or local knowledgeables' qualitative assessments of such factors as available housing and service structures in various communities to differentially weight communities as potential settlement sites (Stenehjem and Metzger, 1976). Weights are assigned to all communities that are expected to receive workers, and then the weight of each community in relation to the sum of weights for all communities is used to proportion workers to each community.

Delphi techniques refer simply to more concerted and definitive efforts using judgemental techniques. In the delphi technique, the sample of persons used to determine community weights is systematically selected to be representative of community groups with different types of knowledge of settlement choices (local leaders, merchants, real estate agents, general residents, and so on). The results of the initial evaluations by these groups are summarized, and these summaries are used for additional rounds of questioning of these groups.

Gravity techniques have a long tradition of use in demography (Carrothers, 1956; Karp and Kelly, 1971) and regional economics (Isard et al., 1972) and are widely used in impact projections (Murdock et al., 1978). The premise underlying their use is that larger communities and those closer to the project site, like particles affected by the physical laws of gravity, will gain more population from the project (will interact more frequently) than smaller and more distant places. This relationship can be specified as follows:

$$W_{ij} = \frac{P_i}{D_{ij}}$$

Where: W_{ij} = workers from project j going to community i

P_i = population of community i

D_{ij} = distance from project j to community i

In addition to these three techniques, increasing use is being made of techniques that utilize either alternatives to population in the gravity formulation or that combine judgemental factors with the gravity formulation (see Hertsgaard et al., 1978; Murdock et al., 1979b; Wieland et al., 1979).

The determination of the demographic characteristics of workers is the last major step in the demographic impact assessment process. In nearly all cases, it involves assuming a standard demographic profile for workers and their families and then applying this profile to the projections of inmigrating or outmigrating workers. The availability of these profiles is increasing rapidly, and useful profiles are now available from a number of sources (Mountain West Research, Inc., 1975, 1979; Leholm et al., 1976b; Wieland et al., 1977; Malhotra and Manninen, 1980). The techniques for applying these profiles can vary from the use of relatively few variables to the use of an elaborate array of variables describing the worker, spouse, children, and their characteristics. The simplest techniques project population by multiplying the average family size per worker by the number of inmigrating workers. More complex techniques use multiple worker-related characteristics including the: (1) percent of workers by age, sex, and marital status, (2) percent of workers with dependents in the area, (3) number of dependents by age and sex, (4) employment status of dependents, and (5) occupational and industrial status of dependents.

The steps delineated above, with some variation, are the major steps generally completed in projecting demographic impacts. It is obvious that these steps involve numerous assumptions about such factors as impact events, baseline conditions, baseline populations, workforce characteristics, and inmigrating population settlement patterns, preferences, and characteristics. As such, it is obvious that the end product of this assessment will be projections that approximate the impacts that will actually occur.

It is essential that two final recommendations be made in relation to demographic projections. The first of these is that series of projections should be made rather than a single set of projections. Series produced should all be projections that are feasible under alternative sets of possible circumstances, and include a high, low, and "best guess" or middle-range projection series.

Second, it may be beneficial to use demographic projections largely as sensitizing mechanisms to assist in understanding the implications of alternative development scenarios. As such, these projections can be useful for both the planner and the decision maker in demonstrating the implications of alternative policies and in examining potential mitigation measures and the effects of such measures. This use of projections may be more realistic than relying on them as the sole base for planning future service requirements.

Assessing Public Service Impacts

The range of dimensions included within public service projections is often broad, including projections of service demands related to:

1. housing
2. education
3. medical and mental health
4. law enforcement
5. fire protection
6. water supplies
7. water treatment
8. solid waste disposal
9. transportation
10. social welfare
11. libraries
12. recreation

The projection of housing services usually includes an examination of both the number and type of units required. Because different types of housing have different effects on local revenues and on long-term community growth, projections of housing without consideration of housing types are generally inadequate. Thus, most projections of housing demands include projections of single-family, multifamily, and mobile home units (Hertsgaard et al., 1978), and some include projections of temporary forms of housing as well (Ford, 1976).

Projections of educational services usually include projections of the number of students and their resultant demands on educational personnel and facilities (Murphy and Williams, 1978; Chalmers and Anderson, 1977). Such projections will usually include estimates of the number of primary and secondary students, the number of teaching, support, and administrative personnel, and the amount of classroom space (square feet) required.

The projection of medical and other health services is particularly difficult because medical services are often centralized in regional clinics and hospitals. Generally, in the projection of medical services, more attention is given to the location of such services than is given in other service areas. Projections in this area may include a wide range of factors, such as patient days and occupancy rates (Murdock et al., 1979a), but projections tend to concentrate on such personnel and facility items as the number of doctors, nurses, psychiatrists, and hospital beds required to serve the inmigrating population.

Law enforcement and fire protection service projections also concentrate on personnel, equipment, and facility requirements although attempts to project the number of offenses and similar occurrences to which such services must respond are sometimes made (Murdock et al., 1979a). In most cases, however, these projections predict the number of law enforcement or fire department personnel required, equipment requirements (number of police cars and fire trucks, etc.), and facility requirements (square feet of floor space per officer, number of jail cells, and so on).

Water supply and treatment service projections usually concentrate on required capacity measured in gallons per capita or per population unit (such as 1000 persons). Such projections seldom consider the size of the functional unit necessary for the efficient operation of such facilities. That is, increments in such services are usually made by adding functional units (for example, a new water treatment facility with a specified gallons per day capacity) rather than as per capita increments. In nearly all cases, however, such projections employ only per capita rates of service demands.

Solid waste disposal is usually considered in terms of landfill area required, and the unit of projection is usually acres. Again, such projections seldom consider the actual functional units required for the effective management of landfill operations. In addition, these projections usually include projections of service personnel and equipment (for example, garbage trucks and bulldozers) required.

Projections of transportation needs are often absent from projections for rural areas because such services are frequently not being used at capacity levels and because the actual level of new demand resulting from new populations is difficult to predict. When such projections are made, miles of new highway or street construction are usually the units of output.

Projections of social services include a wider range of phenomena than any other service area, and there is little agreement on those social services that should be projected in impact assessments. Levels of delinquency, social worker case loads, number of families receiving aid to dependent children, and the number of social workers may be included in such projections. Unlike other public service projection areas, the focus tends to be on service needs rather than on the personnel and facilities required to meet such needs.

Library services are projected less often than other services and are often perceived as being less critical than many of the other services noted above. When such projections are completed, the factors normally projected are the number of volumes and floor space required per unit of population.

Projections of recreational services tend to concentrate on outdoor recreation because of the tendency for indoor recreation to be provided under private auspices. In addition, although extensive analyses have been done to determine outdoor recreational demands for various population units, the levels of demand for indoor recreation services are less well known. When projections of recreational services are made, the items most often projected are acres of open, park, playground, and campground space required per unit of population.

The actual process used in assessing public service impacts, like those used in other assessment procedures, fails to attain many of the characteristics desired for such projections. Few adequately assess service distributions and service delivery systems or provide other detail required to fully characterize the complexity of each service area.

The techniques employed in making public service projections involve the completion of three major assessment processes: (1) the description of baseline services, (2) the selection of a standard for use in projecting service demands, and (3) the projections of service demands.

Description of Baseline Services. As with all assessment processes, the first major step involves a description of baseline service levels. To complete such descriptions, secondary, primary, or a combination of secondary and primary data collection methods can be employed. Whatever data source is used, this description generally consists of a description of the level, distribution and quality of services in the siting area prior to development.

Selection of a Standard. Although the selection of a standard to be used for projecting service demands is largely a decision-making step rather than a procedural step, it is perhaps the most vital step in projecting service demands. It involves the selection of rates of service usage per unit of population and thus, as with other projection methods, the accuracy of these rates (and the assumptions underlying them) will determine the accuracy of the projections. In general, the rates used are derived from one of several alternatives. These alternatives involve the use of: (1) predevelopment local service levels; (2) comparable area service levels; and (3) general usage and engineering standards and estimates. Although each type of standard has clear advantages and disadvantages (Leistritz and Murdock, 1981), the use of general standards (for example, from THK Associates, 1975; Stenehjem and Metzger, 1976; Burchell and Listokin, 1978) has become the most often used procedure.

Projections of Service Impacts. Given an adequate description of baseline conditions and a set of standards for projecting service demands, the projection of service impacts is a relatively simple process. It consists of

procedures for applying the selected standards to
projections of new project-related population. The
population-based standards employed in such projections
may be either per capita or per population unit rates
(for example, rates per 1000 population).
The only variation in the application of these rates
results from the use of average versus marginal
approaches. When an average usage approach is employed,
the projected values are reported in an unadjusted form.
If a marginal approach is used, the values projected are
adjusted (upward or downward) to reflect existing service
deficiencies or excess capacity. Occasional variations
may be made in these procedures to adjust for unique
areal characteristics or to more adequately reflect
service thresholds; that is, to reflect the minimum
facilities required to provide a given level of services.
In nearly all cases, however, the general procedure
outlined above is that employed for service projections.

Repository-Related Considerations

In addition to the considerations noted above, the
special characteristics of repositories are likely to
make accurate demographic and public service assessments
even more difficult. No historical data base exists from
which to predict the probability of, or the rate of,
outmigration likely to occur if levels of fear concerning
repositories become excessive. In like manner,
insufficient data are available on the ability of small
rural communities to respond to potential repository
emergencies, and hence, there is little basis for
developing standards to project such service
requirements. Projections of potential radiation
exposure levels have been made (U.S. Department of
Energy, 1979; 1980b), but projections of special service
personnel and other resource needs under emergency
conditions have been addressed less often. For
transportation services, similar deficiencies are
evident. Few analyses (Gordon et al., 1980) have been
performed on the likely implications of accidents or
other difficulties in the transportation of wastes
(Cummings et al., 1981). There is simply a lack of
sufficient data to use as the basis for projecting the
demographic and public service impacts of repository
development.
Finally, the time frames related to repositories
simply make assessment processes difficult. Repository
construction will likely not begin until the mid to late
1990s, and the operational phase of even the first
repository would span the first quarter of the next
century. Projections for such distant periods of time,
especially for small areas, are unlikely to be accurate.
Even if data become available for projecting the special
demographic and public service impacts of repositories,

the timeframes covered by these projections will require that they be used with extreme care.

CONCLUSIONS

Demographic and public service impacts are likely to be among the most evident of those changes resulting from repository development. These impacts may be particularly acute and difficult to predict in repository siting areas because repositories may have relatively unique impacts on population growth and on service demands. Knowledge of the characteristics of such impacts and of the means to assess them is thus critical to an understanding of nuclear repository development. Although the techniques of projecting such impacts are improving rapidly, such techniques require substantial development, particularly given the time frames and information limitations endemic to repository development. Given the state of development of these techniques and the range of factors that must be considered in making such assessments, it is clear that they should be used with extreme care. They are perhaps, in fact, best used largely as means of sensitizing decision makers to the potential implications of alternative decisions and forms of development for repository siting.

9
Assessing the Social Effects of Repository Siting

John K. Thomas
Don E. Albrecht
Steve H. Murdock

The social impacts resulting from the development of a high-level nuclear waste repository are likely to be extensive. Such impacts often receive widespread coverage in the media and are often the basis of demands by local residents for greater community involvement in the siting process, for mitigation efforts, and for litigation that may delay or stop a development. Social impacts are thus of significance for developers as well as the local residents in impacted areas. It is essential that decision makers be given detailed, accurate and timely information on the social effects of repository development. Such information will be vital to them as they plan for the development and initiate programs for the mitigation of the potentially negative consequences of repository development.

The identification and measurement of social impacts resulting from a repository development represent some very difficult problems since many social impacts are extremely difficult to quantify. Equally serious, there have been no previous repository developments to guide researchers on what the major effects will be and their relative importance. Despite these problems and limitations, the identification and measurement of the social effects of a nuclear repository development represent extremely important aspects of any socio-economic assessment.

In this chapter, we discuss different types of social impacts, describe three types of social assessment methods which can be used to measure such impacts, and present a means of integrating these three research methods in a holistic assessment approach.

SOCIAL EFFECTS OF REPOSITORY SITING

Before delineating the methods appropriate for social impact assessment, it is necessary to more clearly define the term "social impacts." Social impacts can be defined as "impacts that affect the patterns of

interaction, the formal and informal relationships
resulting from such interactions, and the perceptions of
such relationships among various groups in a social
setting" (Leistritz and Murdock, 1981: 156; see also
Popenoe, 1980; and Goodman and Marx, 1978). Based on
this definition, assessment efforts may be best served by
a holistic perspective that emphasizes a wide range of
social, and nonsocial determinants of human behaviors,
perceptions, and attitudes. This perspective is
reflected in the wide range of factors that have been
examined in social impact assessments. Although no
single categorization scheme is adequate for delineating
all of the social impacts likely to result from
repository development, the scheme presented below (see
Murdock and Leistritz, 1979; for an alternative scheme
see Branch et al., 1982) appears to be generally useful
and will serve as a convenient means for organizing the
discussion that follows.

In general, the impacts of large-scale developments,
such as a repository, can be seen as involving either
changes in social organization or changes in values,
attitudes, and perceptions (Murdock and Leistritz, 1979).
Impacts that may occur in each of these major dimensions
are presented below.

Impacts on Social Organization

General analyses of the social impacts of large-
scale developments have noted changes in each of the
major dimensions of social structures: (1) interaction
processes and social relationships, (2) roles and
statuses, (3) social organizations and institutions, (4)
the effects on special groups, and (5) the overall
quality of life and the nature of social structures in
impact areas.

**Effects on Interaction Patterns and Social
Relations.** Forms of interaction and social relationships
between residents in rural areas are often characterized
by informality and based on familial and other forms of
social knowledge about the background and past behavior
of the persons involved. The reputation of one's family
and even the events of one's childhood remain elements in
that interaction process throughout the person's
lifetime. This familiarity between interactants forms a
significant basis for the rural way of life.
Several researchers have noted significant changes
in these patterns during impact conditions (Cortese and
Jones, 1977; Albrecht, 1978; Freudenburg, 1982). The
influx of large numbers of new persons decreases the
number of persons for which the nonimmediate information
bases are available. As a result, interaction is likely
to become more formal and more often based on a person's
official position or employment characteristics than on

historical or other socially relevant roots. This formalization may be especially pronounced in the relationships between newcomers and longtime residents (Massey, 1978) and may lead to increased factionalism in the community and to conflict between newcomer and long-time residents (Cortese and Jones, 1977; Bowles, 1981).

Effects on Roles and Statuses. Several researchers also suggest that the configuration of roles in the community is affected by developments (Murdock and Leistritz, 1979; Freudenburg, 1982). Whereas many rural communities are usually characterized by a concentration of roles and by hierarchies of influence in which agricultural interests are dominant, the initiation of large-scale developments often leads to increased demands for more role specialization (and thus to an increased number of roles), to the professionalization of formal roles, and to an alteration of power structures from those based on agriculture to others based on development-related interests (Gold, 1974).

As a result of such shifts, former status hierarchies and social class patterns may be altered, with longtime residents, especially agricultural groups, becoming less prestigious in the community than before development and with project-related persons taking key leadership roles (Albrecht, 1978; Freudenburg, 1980). On this point, however, there is some contention, and new residents are charged both with not adequately taking part in social affairs in impact communities (Cortese and Jones, 1977) but also with becoming too dominant in local affairs (Little, 1977). This area is clearly one requiring extensive additional analysis.

Effects on Social Organization and Institutions. Rural areas have a relatively large number of formal and informal organizations (Schriner et al., 1976). The structures of these organizations are often threatened by the influx of large numbers of new persons--threatened, that is, in the sense of creating changes in patterns of participation and leadership. In general, a formalization of such organizations is expected to take place (Freudenburg, 1982), but the level of knowledge about changes for such groups is clearly limited.

The effects on social institutions are even less well-known. Although energy developments are believed to increase employment opportunities, some authors charge that little local employment will be created by such developments (Little and Lovejoy, 1977), while some analyses of large-scale development work forces indicate that local employment levels may be quite extensive (Leistritz et al., 1982).

The cohesiveness of families is often felt to suffer as a result of large-scale developments. Higher rates of divorce and increased marital strains have been recorded in some impacted areas (Davenport and Davenport, 1979, 1980; Freudenburg, 1981; Freudenburg et al., 1982; Gartrell et al., 1981), and these strains are felt to be especially experienced by new families because of a lack of familiarity with rural areas and the lack of adequate service structures in rural areas. Governments experience increased specialization and impacts on religion include an increase both in the number of new churches and the membership of established churches (Schriner et al., 1976).

Effects on Specific Groups' Structures. Developments are also believed to have negative effects on groups with particular characteristics such as the elderly, those on fixed incomes, Native Americans, and women. Unfortunately, although it is often assumed that such groups will be negatively impacted, except for a few analyses (Gartrell et al., 1981; Schwartz, 1977; Albrecht, 1977; Freudenburg, 1981), these special groups have received little systematic attention.

Overall Effects On Social Structure and Quality of Life. The factors noted above are widely maintained to lead to a broad range of overall changes in the way of life and the quality of life in impacted rural areas. Destruction of the informal controls typical of rural areas is seen as leading to a wide range of social problems such as increases in crime, drug abuse, mental illness, and child abuse among both new and longtime residents (Freudenburg, 1981; Freudenburg et al., 1982; Gartrell et al., 1981; Davenport and Davenport, 1979, 1980). There are also indications that local persons, particularly elderly persons, come to feel less secure and less integrated into their communities (Albrecht, 1978; Freudenburg, 1982). Increasingly, however, such findings are being questioned and debated (Wilkinson et al., 1982), and most recent analyses (Murdock and Leistritz, 1979; Freudenburg, 1982) have found that the negative impacts of large-scale developments have not been as evident as anticipated.

Impacts on Values, Attitudes, and Perceptions

The effects of large-scale developments, such as a repository, on the values, attitudes, and perceptions of both new and longtime residents in impacted communities have received more empirical attention than the analysis of social organization. Much of this work has focused on the baseline and impact values, attitudes, and perceptions of both new and longtime residents concerning the issues of (1) environmental preservation and conservation (Albrecht and Geersten, 1978), (2) levels of knowledge concerning the impacts of developments (Albrecht, 1978), (3) perceptions of the community prior to development (Mountain West Research, 1975), (4) the desirability of development and social change (Thompson et al., 1978), (5) perceptions of the anticipated (in predevelopment areas) and actual impacts of developments (Mountain West Research, 1975), and (6) overall levels of community satisfaction and community cohesion in impact areas (Lewis and Albrecht, 1977; Freudenburg, 1981).

Available evidence on environmental perceptions reveals a high level of concern for preservation and conservation among persons in rural areas particularly in the Western United States (Murdock and Leistritz, 1979). Definitive evidence concerning residents' levels of knowledge of the likely impacts of large scale development is lacking but available information (Murdock and Leistritz, 1979) generally points to relatively low levels of knowledge of many of the likely dimensions of such developments (Albrecht, 1978; Lopreato and Blisset, 1978; Ludtke, 1978; Murdock and Schriner, 1976).

Available information on community perceptions prior to development seems to point to high levels of satisfaction with the present community and its quality of life, and, in most regards, residents generally see their communities as improving, even in areas where population decline has occurred for some time (Lewis and Albrecht, 1977; Christenson and Robinson, 1980). Evidence on the expected and actual effects of developments shows several emerging generalizations (Murdock and Leistritz, 1979). Residents in predevelopment areas tend to perceive economic opportunities as the major advantages of energy development and the provision of services during impacts, particularly in the areas of housing and recreation, as the major problems for the community. They also seem to be generally aware that social and environmental factors may be threatened by the development, but they evaluate the potential benefits as outweighing the potential costs.

Evidence on the perceptions of the effects in impact areas is less generally available, but the evidence points to less dissatisfaction with developments than sometimes thought. Studies by Lewis and Albrecht (1977), Mountain West Research (1975), Thompson et al. (1978), and Freudenburg (1982) indicate that even after developments have been in operation for some time, they are generally seen as more positive than negative, although those groups least likely to benefit from the development (for example, agriculturalists) are often less satisfied with the development than other groups (for example, business leaders) in development areas.

Information on the overall perceptions residents have toward their communities and the changes in these communities during development is not widely available. Some authors note higher levels of dissatisfaction in impact areas (Gold, 1974) than other authors (Wilkinson et al., 1982). Although levels of satisfaction are likely to be lower for residents in development areas than in nondevelopment areas, the differences found between new and longtime residents' perceptions are often slight (Murdock and Schriner, 1978), and overall levels of satisfaction are often still quite high in impacted areas (Wieland et al., 1977).

SPECIAL SOCIAL EFFECTS OF REPOSITORIES

The social effects of repositories often involve a large number of diverse factors (Hebert et al., 1978). Among the most often discussed effects however are: (1) fear and anxiety related to present health and safety and the health of future generations, (2) concern over equity in the siting process, (3) concerns about security, short-term and long-term control, and the transportation and handling of waste materials, and (4) public participation and monitoring (Hebert et al., 1978).

As stated previously, among the major effects of a repository development is the fear it may cause. Because repositories involve the handling and storage of nuclear materials and because of the highly publicized nature of some recent events related to nuclear power, the public may be apprehensive about the siting of nuclear storage facilities near their homes (Kasperson, 1980; Kasperson et al., 1979). This fear and anxiety reflects both residents' fear for their own health and safety and fear that, although present residents may not be affected, accidents or disturbances at repository sites may lead to health problems for future generations (LaPorte, 1978).

Equity is also an important issue because residents in site areas are being asked to accept a facility that may store the nuclear wastes of the entire nation. Perceptions of inequity may be particularly evident in rural areas where residents have long perceived themselves as being exploited by urban areas (Murdock and Leistritz, 1979).

The long-term management of repository sites, including security from natural or human-induced events, from terrorism, and from simple human carelessness is also a major concern. Control over these facilities must be maintained during the thousands of years for which potential risks will exist. Questions may be raised about the maintenance of even the most carefully designed systems over a period of several centuries. That is, there may be concern that the long-term monitoring of the projects and their socioeconomic impacts may not be adequate or effective, particularly in relation to local risks. For example, many residents may believe that questions about the storage and management of wastes, such as how the funds to support a waste repository can be guaranteed through successive legislative budgetary periods have not been adequately answered.

Finally, another concern of local citizens is that their involvement in the siting process will be minimal. There is apprehension that the major decisions affecting repositories are being made by persons outside their community and that local residents' involvement will occur only in the final stage of the siting process and involve only a token level of activity.

Any analysis of the standard and special social effects of repository siting thus requires consideration of a large number of highly diverse and complex phenomena. Though difficult to identify and less well documented than many other types of impacts, social impacts are widely acknowledged (Office of Technology Assessment, 1982) as being perhaps the key issues in repository siting. The assessment of these impacts, the topic to which we now turn our attention, is thus of vital importance in the repository siting process.

SOCIAL ASSESSMENT METHODS

In selecting an approach to measure the standard and special social effects of a repository development, the options available are as diverse as the measurement methods available in the social sciences generally. In making the selection from this broad range of methods, several factors must be considered. These include: (1) the scope of information required, (2) the availability of data on factors of interest, and (3) the resource requirements entailed in utilizing each approach.

A wide variety of data is needed to adequately assess the social effects of a nuclear repository development. This includes data on the attitudes and values of residents in the impact community, as well as data on the organizational structures and trends therein. Obviously, no single social science method can adequately provide such a broad spectrum of information, so several assessment methods must be used. The methods used in such assessments should reflect those widely used in the social sciences generally, and involve both primary and secondary data collection and analyses. In general, the integrated use of three types of research methods should allow the social and special effects of a repository development to be adequately assessed. These methods include:

1. survey methods, including resident surveys and leadership surveys

2. community structure analyses using secondary data methods

3. participant observation methods

Each of these methods has played an important role in impact assessment efforts. The major aspects of each method, and the advantages and disadvantages of each, are described below.

Survey Methods

Survey methodologies consist of the direct solicitation of information from individuals by personal interview, mail, or telephone-administered questionnaires or some combination of these methods. A survey method is usually selected when data are not available from secondary sources and when individual or household information is essential. Surveys provide an excellent means of assessing such key factors as residents' (used here to refer to the general public) and leaders' attitudes and perceptions concerning: their community and each other; ways that repository development will ameliorate and exacerbate existing community socioeconomic conditions; what social, psychological, and physical problems may result from having high-level nuclear wastes transported, handled and stored near their community; who should be involved in the planning and mitigation of anticipated impacts; what mitigative options or alternatives are most relevant, effective, and efficient for their community to implement; and likely sources of assistance in the mitigation process. The survey is one of the most commonly and effectively used methods in the social sciences for measuring such opinions, attitudes, and perceptions.

Advantages and Disadvantages of Survey Methods. In the selection and use of the survey, or any other method to assess potential social and special effects of repository developments, consideration of the strengths and weaknesses of the method is necessary. A survey of community residents and leaders affected by a repository development has several specific strengths when compared to participant observation and community structure analyses. These include:

1. A well-designed community survey will produce objective information that can be generalized or applied to the community at large.

2. The survey method can be used to quantify a wide variety of attitudinal, perceptual, and behavioral information by providing questions structured in ways to facilitate the classification of responses.

3. Compared to many other (that is, participant observation) methods, a survey permits greater

speed and administrative ease in collecting and reporting impact-related information.

4. Another advantage of a survey is its potential for replication. By using a survey, assessment specialists can acquire comparable data from the repository siting and several other communities and thus identify similarities and differences in the likely impacts on these communities.

The survey method also has several weaknesses which point to the need for selecting additional and complementary methods such as participant observation and community structure analyses and the need for close examination of the community context in which a repository development will occur.

These disadvantages include:

1. A survey obtains information from community respondents at a single point in time. Different types of social and special impacts will occur in a community at different periods during a repository development and these cannot be measured by a single survey conducted at a single point in time.

2. The survey may simply be inappropriate for addressing some types of issues, such as issues that are very controversial and which residents may thus be reluctant to discuss (Warwick and Lininger, 1975).

3. Communities may become over-surveyed. Federal, state and local governments and other entities may be interested in conducting individual assessments for the preparation of environmental impact statements (EIS) or similar reports.

4. Extensive time may be required for governmental approval of questionnaires to be used in a community survey. The Office of Management and Budget in the Federal Government has regulations that control the use of a questionnaire planned for a survey of ten or more individuals.

5. A survey is limited to the assessment of the responses to questions which are addressed. As a result, surveys inevitably (because of time and cost constraints) fail to address some key issues.

Conducting a Survey Analysis. If a survey is selected after considering its strengths and weaknesses, four phases must then be successfully completed. The first phase involves planning the survey. This phase has three basic activities: (1) the design of the survey, which includes consideration of what type of survey should be conducted--mail, telephone, personal interviews, or some combination (Carpenter, 1977; Dillman, 1978; and Heberlein and Baumgarter, 1981); (2) the design of the sample, or decisions about who will be selected to participate in the survey--community residents (Groves and Kahn, 1979; Bailey, 1978; and Dillman, 1978) and community leaders (Hunter, 1953; Bell and Newby, 1972; and Laumann et al., 1977); and (3) the design of the questionnaire, which involves decisions about what types of questions will be asked and how they will be asked (Schuman and Presser, 1981).

The second phase in a community survey is actually conducting the survey. This phase has the two major activities of data collection and quality control of the data. Important parts of data collection are establishing the legitimacy of the study, scheduling the survey, and maintaining the professional demeanor of survey personnel. Quality control must be maintained to prevent the falsification of interviews, introduction of interviewer bias, and administrative error.

The final two phases are data processing and analysis. Data processing involves reviewing completed questionnaires for completeness and accuracy of information, preparing the data for computer processing, and verifying the quality of the prepared data. Emphasis during this phase is placed on the accurate transferral of information from the respondent to the computer. The final phase of a survey is the analysis of the data. In the social sciences, many descriptive and statistical techniques exist that facilitate analysis of survey data. These must be selected with particular care such that the findings are the most meaningful for subsequent users of the information.

In conclusion, if properly done the community survey represents a valuable tool for gathering information on important attitudes and perceptions as they relate to a nuclear repository development. The community survey process, however, clearly reveals the need for meticulous care in the planning, data collection, processing, and analysis of the survey.

Community Structure Analyses

A second approach to the collection of data on the social and special effects of repository development involves the use of secondary data. Secondary data are data already collected by various public agencies and made available to the public in computerized or published form. This approach does not provide information on specific individuals in the community. It does, however, provide data on, and can be used to determine, the overall socioeconomic makeup or structure (set of conditions and relationships) of a community. Thus, such an approach is referred to as a community structure analysis.

Community structure analysis usually consists of multidimensional analyses that attempt to: (1) define the key dimensions of a community's structure, (2) locate indicators of each dimension, and (3) examine the effects of these dimensions on current and expected changes in community conditions.

The roots of community structure analysis can be traced to a wide body of community (Christenson and Robinson, 1980; Warren, 1972; Reiss, 1959; Hollingshead, 1948), social indicators (Beal et al., 1971; Wilcox et al., 1972; Bauer, 1966; Campbell et al., 1976; Land, 1975; Land and Spilerman, 1975; Sheldon and Moore, 1968; McIntosh et al., 1977), and social impact assessment literature (Finsterbusch and Wolf, 1981; Fitzsimmons et al., 1975; Murdock, 1979). This literature suggests that among those factors consistently identified as key dimensions of community are:

1. the location of the community relative to large urban centers and major routes of transportation

2. the natural resource base of the community

3. the demographic characteristics of the community (population size, distribution, and composition)

4. the economic base of the community (that is, agriculture versus manfacturing, services, and so on)

5. the service base (infrastructure) of the community (quality, quantity, and distribution of public services)

6. the socioeconomic characteristics of the community (levels of education, income, poverty, socioeconomic status, and so on)

7. the historical and cultural traditions of the area (for example, its past experience with growth and its ethnic mix)

Advantages and Disadvantages. Like other methods, the community structure approach has relative strengths and weaknesses. These strengths and weaknesses are delineated below. The major advantages of the community structure approach include:

1. Information can be obtained which is not available from other sources. The general public is simply not aware of such things as the ethnic mix in a community, aggregate wealth, the resource base, or hospital occupancy rates.

2. Data collection costs are low and require only minimal involvement of community residents.

3. During data collection, there is need for fewer research staff than those required in a survey effort.

There are also several weaknesses of a community structure analysis which must be considered. These include:

1. It is incapable of providing data on some essential factors such as attitudes, perceptions, and meanings.

2. Since only a few community residents will be contacted, variations in individual perceptions, and the color and richness of community life will not be revealed.

3. Because of the reliance on secondary data, data can only be collected for items on which secondary data are available. Often these data are not totally compatible with the research questions being addressed.

Conducting a Community Structure Analysis. The successful completion of a community structure analysis requires the completion of six major activities. The first and most complex stage is the selection of the structural dimensions to be assessed. Although there is little specific guidance that can be given to indicate the most important dimensions, it is essential that those dimensions that affect major components of the impact be assessed. These factors include ones that provide an understanding of the community's capability to absorb the impacts, to take advantage of the employment and other benefits, and that measure the degree to which a community can control repository development. The dimensions to be examined should thus include:

1. the community's population characteristics

2. the community's physical and sociocultural

environment

3. the technical and other capabilities of the community's population

4. the organizational complexity of the community

5. socioeconomic conditions

6. historic and cultural traditions

7. community service availability

The next stage in a community structure analysis involves the difficult task of selecting indicators to be used to measure each structural dimension of a community. The most critical issues in selecting a set of indicators include concerns of validity (whether the indicators actually measure what they are believed to measure) and reliability (whether they accurately measure these items over time). Although no single list of indicators can adequately characterize all of the important social impact dimensions (see Murdock et al., 1982c: 88-89), table 9.1 presents a list of some of the dimensions and indicators that might be included in such an analysis.

The third step is to locate a source of data for each indicator. Generally, the necessary information can be obtained from three sources: (1) Federal agencies (such as the U.S. Bureau of the Census, the Bureau of Economic Analysis, and the National Center for Health Statistics); (2) state agencies (for example, state health department, welfare department, etc.) which often have important data for more recent periods and for smaller geographical units than Federal agencies; and (3) local service and government agencies (for example, local police and fire departments) which can provide data for smaller units than those obtained from other sources.

The fourth step in a community structure analysis is the actual data collection. If appropriate data sources have been identified, this is one of the least complicated parts of the analysis. The chief difficulties involve insuring that the data collected are for comparable time periods and areal units.

The final steps in a community structure analysis are data processing and data analysis. Data processing involves transferring the collected data to the computer for analysis. The analysis techniques appropriate for a community structure analysis include the most sophisticated analytical and statistical techniques available in the social sciences.

In sum, community structure analysis represents an important vehicle for obtaining information on those community structures likely to be impacted by repository development. Such an analysis must play an important

170

Table 9.1

Dimensions and Indicators of Social Impacts

Individual, Personal Effects		Community, Institutional Effects	
Dimension	Selected Indicators	Dimension	Selected Indicators
Life, Protection, Safety	Persons served Staff size Budget Accessibility of agencies	Demographic	Size Density Ethnicity
Health	Morbidity levels Mortality levels Outpatient facilities Health care personnel	Education	School enrollment Number of personnel and facilities Satisfaction
Family and Individual	Number of families Number of unemployed Family-related services	Government Services	Number and budgets of governments Satisfaction
Attitudes, Beliefs, and Values	Expectations of impacts on local: . environment . economy . community . population . participation . values and customs	Housing & Neighborhood	Substandard housing Number and costs of units
		Law & Justice	Number of violations Number of police officers
		Social Services	Number on welfare Social service personnel Satisfaction
Environmental Conditions	Visual quality Pollution levels Land use patterns	Religion	Church membership Number of clergy
		Culture	Ethnic composition Language Historical sites
		Recreation	Types and costs of facilities Satisfaction
		Information Organizations and Groups	Number, size, and membership in groups
		Community & Institutional Viability	Change in size, type, location, etc., of services

Source: Adapted from Fitzsimmons et al., 1975.

Area Socioeconomic Effects		Aggregate Social Effects	
Dimension	Selected Indicators	Dimension	Selected Indicators
Employment and Income	Workers by type Occupation and industry of workers Persons below poverty level Satisfaction	Change in Quality of Life	Self-development Quality of interpersonal relationships Standard of living Satisfaction
Welfare and Financial Compensation	Number of people receiving assistance Persons below poverty level Satisfaction	Changes in Relative Social Position	Equity of distribution of benefits and costs
Communication	Households with radios and televisions Newspaper circulation Satisfaction	Changes in Social Well-Being	Changes in the quantity and quality of services Changes in income Economic stability
Transportation	Number of vehicles Number and quality of highways Satisfaction		
Economic Base	Persons employed by industry Number and type of establishments Satisfaction		
Planning	Level of local planning		
Construction	Effects of construction on population, housing, and other factors		
Resource Base	Type, form, and quantity		

role in any impact analysis.

Participant Observation Analysis

The final approach for the collection of data on the social and special effects of repository development involves the researcher deliberately involving himself in the community that is being studied in order to gain somewhat of an insider's perspective of what is going on. The general assumption is that no matter how sophisticated the various other social science techniques for data collection and analysis may become, there will always be a possibility that a person actually living in a community will be able to see things that other researchers might have missed.

Participant observation is one of the oldest research methods used in the social sciences. Becker and Geer (1957: 28) have defined participant observation as "the method in which the observer participates in the daily life of the people under study." Wax (1968: 238) has said that the term participant observation "is reserved for those forms of research in which the investigator devotes himself to attaining some kind of membership in or close attachment to . . . (the) group that he wishes to study." In either of these (or dozens of other) definitions, the common theme tends to be that the researcher is in some ways both a participant and an observer. Since most social science techniques are ways of "observing" social facts, it is the "participation" that makes participant observation unusual. "Participant observation is the most personal of all sociological research methods" (Gans, 1968: 316).

Advantages and Disadvantages. Participant observation, like survey research and community structure analysis, has particular strengths and weaknesses. The major strengths include:

1. Participant observation has the distinct advantage of giving the researcher a depth of understanding—he can grasp the native's point of view (Malinowski, 1922; Wax, 1968).

2. One's depth of understanding is increased primarily because the researchers doing participant observation deals with his or her subjects in their world and not in one which is artificially created.

3. Participant observation is very flexible and allows the researcher to be "surprised." By living in a community, a researcher can come to see and comprehend the importance of phenomena that he/she had not even thought to ask about

before the study began.

Just as participant observation as a research tool brings with it important advantages in studying social and special effects within a community, so also does it have important weaknesses that must be considered. Among the most important of these are:

1. By far the most commonly recognized problem of participant observation is the potential for loss of detachment. In the very process of being a "participant" as well as an observer, the researcher runs the risk of losing objectivity.

2. Just as participant observation allows the researcher abundant opportunities for flexibility and for being surprised by new developments, it also fails to provide the researcher with a fixed format and schedule for completing the analyses. It may thus lead to inconsistency in measurement.

3. Participant observation studies involve observations of unique events, usually by a single observer. This creates potentially important reliability and validity problems (Deutscher, 1973).

Conducting a Participant Observation Analysis. Conducting a participant observation analysis requires a great deal of talent and experience. It is beyond the scope of this chapter to provide details on conducting a participant observation analysis. The brief description presented below examines some of the major considerations in doing such a study.

Before a researcher enters a community to conduct a participant observation analysis, preparation efforts must be made. The researcher should decide on the context of the data collection effort and gain some familiarity with the community. This familiarity can be gained by looking at such sources as previous impact studies of the area, local community histories, or newspaper files. This preparation will greatly reduce the time needed in the community and will help insure more valid and reliable results.

After entering the community, there are several important considerations and decisions the researcher must face. A major obstacle which must be overcome is gaining "entry" into the community--or becoming physically and socially a part of the community (Whyte, 1955; Evans-Pritchard, 1964; Wax, 1971). Without entry, the researcher will be treated as an outsider and the chances of gaining an insiders perspective on community

174

residents' orientations will be greatly reduced. An
important step is gaining the permission and cooperation
of community influentials.

After entry into the community, there is a wide
variety of information that can be pursued. Among the
most important of these are: behaviors, meanings,
problems, interactions, discrepancies, and surprises
(Murdock et al., 1982c). It is important for researchers
to ask questions of a wide variety of community
respondents. Every effort possible should be made to
avoid the biases inherent in interacting with only
certain subgroups in the community. Another vital aspect
of participant observation is to take verbatim notes as
promptly and completely as possible.

Data processing and analysis are much different for
a participant observation analysis than for survey and
community structure methods. It is often quite fruitful
to analyze data even as it is being collected. In using
such an approach the researchers will base certain
conclusions on the existing data. These conclusions,
however, will be kept tentative. The results of this
early analysis may then be used to direct further data-
gathering operations. Most likely, the participant
observer researcher will find that many of his initial
conclusions are disproven or modified by subsequent
evidence. With such an approach, researchers often find
that some issues, of which they were previously unaware,
become a central focus of their analyses.

In sum, an effective participant observation
analysis may dramatically increase the perceptiveness as
well as the accuracy of the work that is done. The value
of such analyses in providing information of utility for
repository siting may be substantial.

INTEGRATION OF RESEARCH METHODS

Assessing the social and special impacts of a
repository development is an extremely complex procedure.
Potential impacts are numerous and varied and cannot be
adequately assessed by any single method. We have, as a
result, suggested that three methods be used. These
methods, to a large extent, have different advantages and
disadvantages, and in many cases, the disadvantages of
one method are offset by the advantages of another.
Thus, we believe it is essential to use the three methods
simultaneously in an integrated holistic approach.

In addition to allowing researchers to obtain a
broad range of relevant data, the integrated use, or
triangulation, of the three methods can speed the study
and ease administrative costs. The utility of such an
integrated approach can best be seen by examining the
interrelationships between the three approaches in a five
stage research process. The stages of this process are

used below as a basis for the description of an integrated approach to social assessment and include:

1. background preparation
2. initiation of community contacts
3. research design
4. data collection and processing
5. data analysis and interpretation

The first stage in such an integrated analysis is that of obtaining an adequate background on the study area. This can be initiated by an examination of available secondary data. Thus, data on such factors as the area's population, environmental and resource bases, employment, occupational and industrial skill levels, and local history are commonly collected for a community structure analysis. The data so collected and the general background so obtained are in turn essential background for a participant observation analysis and essential in determining the sampling design (because of the importance of population data) and sampling frame for the survey analysis.

The next stage in a social and special effects analysis consists of the formulation of initial community contacts through frequent visits to the area and with leaders in the community. Such visits are useful steps in all three methods, and will allow the researchers as participant observers to gain familiarity with local organizations, make initial informal contacts, and gain initial entry into the community. For the community structure analysis, this phase will be a period for obtaining public service data and locating potential data sources. For the survey analyst, this phase will provide both a set of contacts with likely participants for a community leader survey and a source of valuable contacts (local utility executives, for example) for obtaining useful sampling frames.

Careful coordination can also be obtained during data collection. Thus, the community leader survey and the collection of community structure data on community organizations and services can usually be combined. In like manner, the collection of agency and organization data can often provide an opportunity for performing an observational analysis, and during personal interviews, both observational and organizational data can be obtained. Finally, the coordination of these activities can be extremely useful in constructing codes for data processing and in cross validating the results of each of the three types of analysis.

During data analysis and interpretation, the counterbalancing strengths and weaknesses of the three approaches and the need for their careful integration is clearly demonstrated. Thus, participant observation analysis provides excellent descriptive data and some comparative data, and an excellent understanding of the meaning of behaviors, actions, and patterns. Community structure analysis provides data appropriate for descriptive, explanatory, and predictive analyses, but its explanations of phenomena and the depth of understanding provided are often less than satisfactory. Surveys provide perhaps the most general form of analysis, allowing all forms of statistical analysis and analytical outcomes to be addressed. However, survey analysis provides neither the depth of understanding of participant observation analyses nor the predictive ability and multivariate sophistication of community structure methods. Clearly all three approaches are essential to an adequate social and special effects analysis.

     In sum, then, if an adequate assessment of repository effects on social factors is to be completed, an integrated approach using survey, community structure, and participant observation analyses must be used. This can be achieved by a careful coordination of different research methods in key phases of the research process. Despite some limitations, such an assessment is essential for public decision making at all levels, including most importantly, the communities near potential repository sites.

Mitigation of the Impacts of Nuclear Waste Storage and Repository Siting

10
Resolving Problems in Repository Siting: A Review of Issues and Mitigation Measures

John M. Halstead
F. Larry Leistritz

The information presented in previous chapters, as well as in other sources (Albrecht, 1978; Dixon, 1978; Gilmore, 1976; Murdock and Leistritz, 1979), strongly suggests that in the absence of substantial advance planning and active intervention measures by communities, project developers, and higher levels of government, nuclear waste repositories are likely to create substantial problems for their host communities. In particular, nuclear repositories, like other large-scale projects, are likely to result in costs which exceed benefits for at least some local interests (for example, fixed income groups) and/or during certain time periods (for example, the facility construction phase). These effects are likely to be perceived by local groups as evidence that repository siting is unfavorable to their interests, which in turn may result in substantial local opposition to the siting decision. The need to examine those measures which can be employed to alter the effects of project development, reducing those effects which are generally viewed as undesirable and enhancing those changes which are deemed beneficial, is thus apparent. Such measures, which have the aim of making the effects of project development more favorable from a local perspective, are often termed **impact mitigation** techniques.

Despite a growing consensus that socioeconomic impacts are important and must be addressed, the processes for effectively coping with such project effects have received very limited attention in the literature to date. Those cursory reviews of impact mitigation (or impact management) which have appeared typically discuss only a few selected types of management measures or review only a few cases where mitigation efforts have been attempted. Such discussions generally fail to take account of the cumulative and interactive effects of multiple impact management measures and provide little basis for evaluating the strengths and limitations of alternative approaches or the conditions under which each may be most effective. Finally, perhaps

the most significant weakness of past attempts to address
impact mitigation issues has been their failure to
develop an adequate conceptual basis for viewing impact
events and their subsequent management.

This chapter and the ones which immediately follow
attempt to address the need for a systematic evaluation
of impact management measures which might be employed in
connection with the development of a nuclear waste
repository. Such an evaluation can be seen as involving
two major dimensions:

1. the identification of problems likely to be
    encountered in siting a nuclear repository and
    the evaluation of impact mitigation measures
    addressing these issues

2. the development of a conceptual basis for
    viewing impact events and their subsequent
    management and thus for designing impact
    management programs

The first of these dimensions is the subject of this
chapter, while the second is addressed in chapter 11.

Finally, there are certain unique issues and impacts
of a repository which fall outside the scope of past
experiences and merit special attention. Some of these
impacts are tangible in nature (such as the lack of tax
revenue accruing to local communities due to the tax-
exempt status of the facility) while others are less
tangible (such as risk aversion, fear and anxiety).
Identifying, and dealing with these issues, as well as a
consideration of the importance of public participation
in the siting process, is the subject of chapter 12.

This chapter examines mitigation measures
implemented at a variety of large-scale projects across
the nation in an attempt to identify the elements that
should be included in a mitigation effort for a nuclear
repository. A case study approach, drawing upon the
experiences of areas where large and/or undesirable
facilities have been sited, is utilized. In selecting
facilities for study, an effort was made to choose
situations which pose impact issues similar to those
likely to be associated with nuclear repository siting.
Some of the more important impact issues expected to be
associated with repository siting together with parallels
drawn from projects with similar characteristics are
listed in table 10.1.

The first section deals with case studies of
individual projects where impact mitigation plans had to
deal with such problems as siting conflicts, the tax-
exempt status of facilities, and plant closures.
Experiences in possible repository candidate states have
shown that a substantial amount of opposition to the

Table 10.1

**Nuclear Waste Repository Impacts
and Parallel Facilities' Impacts**

Impact Issues	Comparable Facility
Fear and Anxiety	Hazardous Waste Facilities
Tax-Exempt Nature of Repository	Trident and Safeguard Military Construction Projects
Funding Sources	Inland Energy Impact Assistance Act; Coastal Zone Management Act; Safeguard-Trident Amendments
Financing Repository Impacts	Severance Taxes
Housing and Service Provision	Company-Provided Infrastructure at Colstrip, Montana and Wright, Wyoming
Monitoring System Needs	Industry Monitoring Programs
Siting Conflicts	Hazardous Waste Facility Siting Conflicts
Closure (Decommissioning)	Jeffrey City, Wyoming and U&I Closure Problems
Planning Needs	Colorado Joint Review Process, Hartsville Coordinating Committee

project can be expected; past successes and failures of other siting attempts for noxious facilities can therefore provide useful information for devising a siting strategy. Other large facilities (especially military sites and bases) have held tax-exempt status and therefore are studied here. Finally, the repository, after its construction-operation phase of fifty-to-sixty years, will ultimately be closed, leaving a workforce only a fraction of the size of the operational workforce. Therefore, case studies of other communities suffering the loss of a major employer are examined. The second section deals with federal legislation designed to provide funds for impact mitigation. Since the repository is a federal project, any funds for mitigation must be approved by Congress; past amendments and legislative precedents for impact assistance provide a useful starting point for the design of repository impact assistance. The third section deals with industry and state participation in providing impact mitigation funding and technical assistance. These methods include interindustry planning programs, monitoring programs, state severance taxes which serve to supply impact funds to local communities, and state and local legislative units designed to facilitate planning. These techniques and processes can form integral components in impact management plan implementation.

DIMENSIONS OF IMPACT MITIGATION

One of the major special impacts that a nuclear waste repository may create is a feeling of fear and anxiety in the local community regarding possible accidents and long-term health effects. Another issue is that of equity--perceptions that the local community is being forced to bear the responsibility for disposing of the entire nation's nuclear refuse (see chapter 8). These same problems are being experienced in other siting efforts. Some developments are perceived as locally noxious or as imposing large environmental, social, or economic costs on a small minority while others (frequently geographically distant) enjoy the benefits. Many of these conflicts occurred in the attempted siting of hazardous waste facilities (for example, Wilsonville, Illinois). However, numerous instances also exist of intense controversies in the case of more standard developments such as power plants (for example, Searsport, Maine) and transmission lines (CU Project). Several cases are documented below where local resistance continued even **after** the facility was sited, taking the form of civil disobedience, quasilegal maneuvers, and even a form of "guerilla warfare."

Problems in Siting

The Case of Searsport, Maine. In 1974, the Central Maine Power Company (CMP) announced Sears Island in Penobscot Bay as the preferred site for its nuclear power plant. This decision came as a result of efforts by Searsport town officials to attract industry to the area in hopes of duplicating the successes of the neighboring town of Wiscasset. Wiscasset, home of the Maine Yankee nuclear plant, had achieved substantial increases in its tax base resulting from the power plant's location there. Although the town officials strongly supported the project, problems arose in CMP's dealings with the public. Inconsistency in information dissemination confused the public as to whether Sears Island was the preferred site or merely one of several sites. CMP denied that Sears Island was the preferred site until "publicly embarassed" into doing so (O'Hare et al., 1982). When this fact was made known, the local public felt deceived by CMP.

In addition, CMP did not make serious efforts to inform state officials of their intentions, and did not discuss its plans with town officials until after the Sears Island site had been chosen. According to O'Hare et al. (1982: 2-10):

> Although CMP played by the rules and violated no regulations, its information policy created confusion, suspicion, and mistrust--conditions that strongly contributed to subsequent opposition and wariness on the part of state officials . . . CMP believed it continually maintained an open policy, but opponents perceived them as deceptive and trusted neither CMP nor town officials.

Although CMP attempted to rectify these problems, the damage was already done. Once public mistrust had been established, the company was unable to undo it. After several years delay and an $8 million investment, CMP scrapped its plans for a nuclear plant on Sears Island.

The Experience of Wes-Con. One of the most difficult siting problems, especially in the wake of such management disasters as Love Canal (New York) and the "Valley of the Drums" (Kentucky), is finding a location for a hazardous waste disposal facility. Numerous towns throughout the country have reacted to the problem by passing ordinances prohibitng hazardous waste facilities within their borders (Morell and Magorian, 1982; O'Hare et al., 1982). The prospects of possible environmental and health damages, noxious odors, and unsightly areas seem to far outweigh any anticipated economic benefits. How then, in 1973 and 1979, did Wes-Con, Inc. site two hazardous waste disposal facilities with very little opposition?

Wes-Con's disposal philosophy involved the use of abandoned missile silos in rural Idaho to store wastes. The first site, ten miles from Grand View, Idaho (1980 population, 260) is two miles from the nearest rancher and surrounded by Bureau of Land Management grazing lands.

During the time Wes-Con was completing its environmental assessment and applying for a site conditional use permit, the company took the initiative to solicit support from the county commissioners

184

(although they had no legal leverage over the site) and the local Cattlemen's Association. Once construction began, Wes-Con hired local residents for the management staff, donated salvage materials to community groups and citizens, and invited visits to the facility. In addition, the company provided free disposal of local hazardous wastes (mostly pesticides), provided area ranchers free use of their heavy equipment, and agreed not to accept any controversial wastes (for example, nuclear wastes and nerve gas). Wes-Con's major site management decisions were deferred to state agencies to maintain political support and public credibility. Finally, the company purchased the first fire truck ever available to local ranchers and farmers.

Wes-Con's second experience near the town of Bruneau (twenty miles away, 1980 population, 100), was located within the same county (Owyhee) as the Grand View site. Again, Wes-Con approached local officials and organizations for support and offered services and benefits to the community. Local politicians and civic leaders saw the Bruneau facility as an extension of the Grand View site and gave their approval. After a public hearing for a conditional use permit and subsequent incorporation of improved operating features into the site, the facility began operating in 1979 with no local opposition (O'Hare et al., 1982).

Conflicts in the Aftermath

The case study of Searsport, Maine documents how failure to identify and address public concerns, in spite of having fulfilled all legal project requirements, may ultimately lead to failure to site a proposed facility (power plant). This case is an illustration of what O'Hare et al. (1982) called the "Lawyer's Fallacy" or viewing the siting process as a series of legal and jurisdictional tests resulting in granting of permits and eventual project completion. As these authors point out, having a legal right to proceed is not necessarily equivalent to having the power to build. This fallacy is aptly illustrated in cases such as the Seabrook, New Hampshire and Montague, Massachusetts proposed nuclear plants, where threats of arrest and imprisonment did not deter opponents from going to enormous lengths to stop these legal projects (for further discussion, see Rose et al., 1979).

Failure to win at least a large measure of local public support for a project can result in delays, increased construction costs, and often cancellation; in some instances, it can lead to demonstrations, closures, and even sabotage **after** the facility has been constructed. Three cases are illustrated.

Wilsonville, Illinois. In 1976 Earthline, Inc. built and began operating a hazardous waste landfill site near Wilsonville, Illinois. Local officials and residents were notified in advance of the company's intent, although in retrospect, it seems that local residents may not have understood the nature of the hazardous waste involved, and may have expected more local economic benefits than later materialized. For the first four months of operation, in spite of some minor problems with odor and traffic, the community was relatively undisturbed by the project.

Then, in April 1977, Wilsonville residents learned that the facility would be receiving PCB contaminated soil from Missouri. Opposition to this undertaking grew until the first trucks carrying the contaminated soil were greeted by an angry armed mob. This touched off a legal battle which lasted sixteen months and eventually led to a decision that the facility was not in the public interest, that it would be closed, and that all wastes stored there would be removed. Although SCA (which succeeded Earthline as manager of the facility) appealed the decision and requested permission to remain open until the appeal was resolved, the village of Wilsonville dug a trench across the access road to the facility, effectively closing it. The roadwork was officially part of culvert repair to control flooding (O'Hare et al., 1982).

Vermont Yankee. The town of Vernon, Vermont is the home of the Vermont Yankee Nuclear Plant, a boiling water reactor which began operation in 1972. Although the plant has been operating for ten years, recent years have shown a marked increase in antinuclear demonstrations at the site. One such civil disobedience action was staged to protest the refueling of the plant on October 8, 1977. The protesters blocked the entrance to the plant and were subsequently charged with criminal trespass (Hadden et al., 1981). The purpose of the action (as stated by the defense) was to: ". . . prevent workers from gaining access to the plant, and thus reasonably attempt to stop the flow of radioactive substances into the environment by preventing its further operation" (**Atlantic Reporter,** 1979). Similar (though much larger) actions have taken place at the site of the proposed Seabrook, New Hampshire nuclear plant where, in 1977, over 1,400 demonstrators were arrested, costing the state $50,000 a day to care for them (Christenson, 1979). The rationale expressed for the demonstration was similar to that at the Vernon Plant.

The CU Project. In 1973 two Upper Midwest utility cooperatives, Cooperative Power Association (CPA) and United Power Association (UPA) of Minnesota, announced plans to build a large electricity generating plant near

Underwood, North Dakota. The project would also entail
building a 430-mile powerline (conducting 800,000 volts)
to Minneapolis. The powerline became known as the CU
project.

The utilities apparently felt they had addressed the
public interest sufficiently in choosing the powerline
right-of-way, which avoided woodlands, lakes, urban
centers, and highways. The final route chosen traversed
mainly agricultural land. Owners of the land were given
what was felt to be generous compensation.

The farmers, however, were not convinced of the
"wisdom of the enterprise, and hence the necessity for
their sacrifice" (Casper and Wellstone, 1981). Although
numerous public hearings and information meetings were
held, the farmers felt that they were fighting a battle
against the state and utility companies, who the farmers
perceived as insensitive to their needs. Litigation gave
way to crowds of angry farmers chasing surveying and
construction crews from their land in 1978, and the
eventual use of state troopers to maintain order.

What is especially interesting in this case,
however, is that opposition did not cease once the
powerline was in place. A kind of "guerilla warfare" was
staged, where mysterious attacks of "bolt weevils"
toppled towers, "insulator disease" shattered glass wire
insulators, and "wire worms" splayed open conducting
wire. Even with the use of state troopers and high-speed
helicopters, the utility experienced extensive losses
(Casper and Wellstone, 1981). Thus, it can be seen that
even legal right **and** project completion are not always
sufficient to achieve the desired siting result.

Problems Associated with Tax-Exempt Developments

Rapid growth in small communities often results in
strains on housing markets, public services, school
systems, and other sectors of the local economy. These
negative impacts are often accepted as the price paid to
receive the project's benefits of new employment
opportunities, expanding local economies, and lower
property taxes (Peelle, 1979; Aronson, 1981; Cortese and
Jones, 1977). However, in the special case of facilities
which happen to be exempt from standard property taxes,
such as military bases and certain public utilities, tax
revenues do not increase to keep pace with the expenses
of providing services for the new population, causing
fiscal strains on the local governments, and possible
shortages of needed facilities and services (President's
Economic Adjustment Committee, 1981). In the absence of
supplemental mitigation activities by the developer or
outside parties, these developments may impose costs on
the local community in excess of perceived benefits,
making the project less attractive (and enhancing the
possibilities of public opposition). Case studies of

several tax-exempt developments where the federal government or public utility supplied impact mitigation assistance provide possible precedents for the case of a repository, which will not be liable for standard property taxes due to its siting on federally-owned land.

The Lanham Acts. During the Second World War, military spending stimulated massive and unprecedented growth in communities affected by the expansion of army and navy facilities across the country. Rural counties like Kitsap County, Washington and Bay County, Florida more than doubled in population in a three-year period. The most serious impact on these communities was an acute housing shortage. This led to the enactment in 1940 of the first Lanham Act (P.L. 76-849) which authorized federal provision of housing in rapid growth areas to avoid ". . . an acute shortage of housing . . . which would impede national defense activities." Impact assistance provided by this act was supplemented in 1941 by the second Lanham Act (P.L. 77-137) which authorized provision of a broader range of services to impacted communities, including schools, sewer and water, hospitals, recreational facilities, and streets (President's Economic Adjustment Committee, 1981). These acts proved to be the forerunner of present-day impact assistance legislation to communities impacted by defense-related activities such as the Trident Submarine Base in Washington and the Safeguard Antiballistic Missile System in North Dakota.

The Safeguard Antiballistic Missile System. In late 1969 the federal government announced that it had chosen northeastern North Dakota as one of the sites for the Safeguard Antiballistic Missile System (ABM). The project was to employ 4,000 workers at the peak of construction activity and cost $468 million. Langdon, North Dakota, which received the bulk of the new population, was not well equipped to deal with the service demands the project brought (Coon et al., 1976).

Langdon's population increased from 2,182 in 1970 to 3,957 in 1973. Shortages in the housing markets caused housing and rental cost increases. Public services and utilities had to be upgraded to provide for the new population, and children of project construction workers caused overcrowding in district school facilities. On the positive side, employment in Cavalier County, where Langdon is located, increased by 47.1 percent over the same period. Total sales by Langdon businesses increased 40.2 percent, while personal income in the county increased by 20.2 percent (Coon et al., 1976).

Recognizing that the local community would be hard pressed to deal with development impacts, Congress enacted legislation providing supplemental Department of the Army Community Impact Assistance. This resulted in passage of Section 610 of the FY1971 Military Construction Authorization Act (P.L. 91-511). A total of $9.7 million Safeguard Section 610 funds were distributed for community projects; in addition, Defense access highway funds and Highway Trust funds provided $8.1 million, while other Federal agencies provided $1.4 million (President's Economic Adjustment Committee, 1981). According to surveys undertaken in the area, most area residents felt that the project was good for the area, and most effects of the development were regarded as favorable. Positive effects were viewed as mainly economic, such as increased employment and income, while negative effects of the project included higher costs of living and overburdened local facilities.

The Trident Submarine Base. The Secretary of the Navy announced in 1973 that the Bangor Navy Annex in Kitsap County, Washington was to be the site of the Trident Submarine Base Support Facility. The project was expected to create an influx of 5,400 military personnel, 2,200 civilian jobs, and 1,200 contractor jobs, leading to a total population increase of more than 27,000 in Kitsap, Mason, and Jefferson counties (President's Economic Adjustment Committee, 1981). Local officials estimated that a private facility comparable to the Trident Base would yield $8.5 million in annual tax revenues (Horsley et al., 1976). Due to the tax-exempt status of the project, however, the potential property taxes were not available to fund impact mitigation.

Passage of Section 608 of the Military Construction Authorization Act (P.L. 93-552) acknowledged the Federal Government's responsibility to assist in alleviating adverse impacts. In this way, an effort was made to supply revenue lost to the local communities due to Trident's tax-exempt status. Aid was channeled through existing Federal programs. Kitsap County was reimbursed for roads ($40 million), schools ($20 million), and planning, law enforcement, water/sewer, and court services (approximately $15 million) (Helgath, 1982).

Dealing with Plant Shutdowns

Another issue which may concern potential repository host communities is coping with the readjustment associated with project closure. When the repository has reached full capacity and backfill operations are completed, 800 operation jobs will terminate. Assuming that the community has not experienced extensive growth in other industries during the project's operation, a major labor surplus could result as well as slack capacity in the housing and service sectors. A recent example of community adjustment to the loss of a major employer is provided by the closure of the U&I sugar beet processing plants, which affected four small western communities.

U&I, Inc. was a major sugar beet processor in the Intermountain West for eighty-seven years. The company had plants at Toppenish and Moses Lake, Washington; Idaho Falls, Idaho; and Garland, Utah. Total employment at these plants was more than 3,000. In 1978 officials at U&I announced the shut-down of all four plants, with closing dates ranging from three to seven months distant. In all four counties, the sugar beet plants were a major employer.

The Utah State University Business and Economic Development Services (USU-BEDS) were involved from the outset in trying to ease community adjustment, as well as building a framework for use in similar situations in the future. The main approach of USU-BEDS was to initiate formation of a community shutdown team (CST) composed of local community, industry, and labor leaders to evaluate and implement community alternatives. In cases where the CST approach was used, shutdown-related unemployment was reduced from 4 to 7 percent compared to communities where the approach was not used. Policy recommendations included:

1.   development of techniques for the organization of a community-based committee or group which can be adapted to community needs to deal with shutdown problems

2.   development of a consulting network, nationwide, of knowledgeable parties to lend assistance to CSTs

3.   an extensive campaign to educate community officials, public agency personnel, and employers and unions about shutdown problems

4.   some form of state or Federal legislation to provide a better framework for implementing the study's recommendations (Hansen and Bentley, 1981)

IMPACT ASSISTANCE LEGISLATION

Various legislative actions have, either directly or indirectly, addressed the problem of socioeconomic impacts (table 10.2). As noted in the previous section, legislation can be a vital tool in resolving problems such as tax-exempt developments. Some of the relevant impact assistance legislation over the past decade is summarized in this section. A summary of Federal legislation designed to mitigate socioeconomic impacts is presented in table 10.2.

190

Table 10.2

Chronology of Federal Legislation Addressing
Resource Development and Socioeconomic Mitigation

Date	Federal Law	Socioeconomic Mitigation
1920	Mineral Leasing Act (41 Stat 449)	Allowed 37.5% of receipts to be returned to local governments.
1969	National Environmental Policy Act	Required human factors be assessed.
1972	Coastal Energy Impact Program	Placed federal government in a secondary role behind state and local governments.
1975	Federal Coal Leasing Amendments Act	Increased percent of revenues for mitigation.
1976	Federal Land Policy and Management Act	Required revenues received by states to go to impacted areas.
1976	Mineral Leasing Act Amendment	Increased the amount of receipts to 50% and broadened categories for expenditures.
1978	Power Plant and Industrial Fuel Use Act	Federal government can pay for planning and land acquisition for community facilities.
1978	Inland Energy Impact Assistance	Most comprehensive S/E act to date. Provides mechanism and funding for active federal role in mitigating impacts. This act did not pass Congress by one vote.
1981	Military Construction Authorization Act	Allows up to $1 million of federal funds per county for impacts of military projects.

Source: Helgath, 1982.

The National Environmental Policy Act (NEPA)

Agencies involved in major development projects are required, by the National Environmental Policy Act of 1969, to prepare environmental impact statements to assess the environmental consequences of their actions. This requirement has been expanded to include assessment of potential socioeconomic impacts.

Several states have also imposed requirements similar to NEPA (Murdock and Leistritz, 1979). Others have mandated requirements for monitoring, assessment, and mitigation that go beyond those of NEPA (Murdock and Leistritz, 1980). For example, Washington's facility siting legislation requires that industries pay socioeconomic impact mitigation and monitoring expenses and costs that exceed anticipated revenues (Helgath, 1982).

The Power Plant and Industrial Fuel Use Act

The Power Plant and Industrial Fuel Use Act of 1978, also called the "Coal Conversion Act," was designed to foster the increased use of coal and alternate fuels as primary energy sources and as fuel for power plants (P. L. 95-988). Section 601 of this act provided for assistance to areas impacted by coal or uranium development ("impacted" being defined as an 8 percent annual growth rate in either coal or uranium mining employment). This assistance takes the form of planning grants and grants for land acquisition and development.

The Inland Energy Impact Assistance Act of 1978

The Inland Energy Impact Assistance Act of 1978 (S 1493), which was defeated by one vote, would have established an Office of Energy Impact Assistance to provide financial and technical assistance to states, Indian tribes, and local governments adversely impacted by energy development. An impact team to be established would have prepared mitigation plans and coordinated Federal assistance programs. The act also would have authorized the Secretary of Commerce to make grants to states and Indian tribes to carry out mitigation plans.

Socioeconomic Impact Amendments

The cases of the Trident Submarine Base and the Safeguard ABM present examples of amendments to existing construction acts to deal with socioeconomic problems arising from military activity. The amendments to the Military Construction and Authorization Act (P.L. 93-552, Sec. 608--Trident; P.L. 91-511, Sec. 610--Safeguard) provided for the Secretary of Defense to assist affected communities near defense installations in meeting the costs of required services and facilities. The key wording of the amendments was that defense activity must create "an unfair and excessive financial burden." Provision was also made for carrying out such assistance through existing Federal programs.

These amendments provide useful precedent, as such amendments may be added to S 1662 (The National Nuclear Waste Policy Act of 1981) to deal with socioeconomic impacts of a repository. However, although this so-called "Safeguard" approach has been largely effective (Coon et al., 1976; President's Economic Adjustment Committee, 1981), problems remain. These include:

1. lag time in obtaining impact funds--up to twelve months

2. problems of small communities in complying with Federal regulations for grant applications

3. problems in matching community needs with existing programs

4. need for provision of maintenance and operation funds for public service agencies

5. need to place more weight on local community recommendations

6. need for early community involvement (Faas, 1982a)

Recommendations for incorporating the strengths and avoiding the problems of these approaches in future legislation are discussed in chapter 12.

STATE AND INDUSTRY MITIGATION

The past decade has seen rapid development in many parts of the West and Southwest, as spiraling energy prices have increased the economic benefits of domestic energy production. Failure to plan for the population increases from such progress led to the "boomtown" syndrome exemplified in Rock Springs and Gillette, Wyoming. Industry and state officials, realizing the role of advanced planning in increasing worker productivity and maintaining quality of life, have both provided direct assistance to energy impacted communities and set up mechanisms for collecting impact mitigation funds and facilitating local planning and monitoring.

Funding Impact Mitigation

Several methods are utilized by states to generate

revenue for mitigation expenditures. Two which will be examined here are the Oil Shale Trust Fund (Colorado) and the severance tax (North Dakota, Wyoming, and Montana).

The Oil Shale Trust Fund is supplied by the state's share of bonuses, royalties, and revenues from the sale or lease of public lands within Colorado. Under the provisions of Section 35 of the Federal Mineral Lands Leasing Act of 1920, 50 percent of the proceeds from the sale or rental of public land is returned to the state. The funds are then distributed to impacted counties for use in planning and in the provision of needed facilities (Quality Development Associates, Inc., 1978).

The second major source of revenue is the severance tax, which is a per unit tax levied on minerals mined within the state, such as gas, coal, and oil. Funds are then distributed back to the impacted counties. Formulas for distribution vary from state to state.

In this way, taxes on the minerals, whose development is causing the socioeconomic impacts, are providing part of the revenues for mitigating those impacts (as well as increasing state revenues for other uses). A similar approach is being applied to repository construction, wherein a one-mill-per-kilowatt-hour fee on electricity generated by civilian nuclear power plants will be levied to cover costs (S 1662, Sec. 603a). This approach differs in that the bulk of revenue generated will be used for construction and operation of the repository; however, whatever impact payments are allocated will likely be drawn from these funds.

Direct Industry Assistance

The rapid growth and boomtown atmosphere of such towns as Rock Springs, Wyoming led to declines in worker productivity and high workforce turnover rates. Metz (1980) has estimated that $50 million of cost overruns at the Jim Bridger power plant in Rock Springs were caused by worker turnover [a 35 percent decline in productivity was also noted (TOSCO Foundation, 1980)]. These lessons have taught industry the value of providing their workers with a stable, high quality living and working environment, and companies have responded by giving impact payments and services to communities, as well as constructing entire towns.

On the community side, local governments have used such leverage as zoning and permitting requirements to obtain funds for impact mitigation payments. Such a situation occurred in the case of the Deserado Mine in Rio Blanco County, Colorado, where the power plant using the mine was located in Utah (paying tax revenues there). An agreement was reached whereby the company, Western Fuels, Inc., made payments to the county for schools, public services, and so forth on a preformulated per-relocating worker basis (Western Fuels, Inc., 1981).

Company Towns

Construction of self-contained communities in rural areas is not a new idea. Such activity was a common occurrence in coal, copper, iron, and lumber development areas of the West, where several thousand towns were constructed between 1850 and 1950 (Metz, 1979). The concept of providing total support facilities for project personnel is also being examined in the case of the proposed MX missile (Holmes and Narver, Inc., 1981).

One such company town is Colstrip, Montana, owned by Montana Power Company, operators of an electrical generating project at the site. Mining and construction activity at the site increased Colstrip's population from several hundred to over 3,000 (Myhra, 1975).

Western Energy Company (a subsidiary of Montana Power) organized the development process, employed contractors, and provided financing and capital as required. Single-family, apartment, and mobile homes were provided, including permanent housing for long-term employees and apartments and mobile homes for temporary personnel. The company financed water and sewer systems (with some help from federal and state programs), recreational facilities, streets, public facility construction and maintenance, and fire protection. Plans for the company town involve its incorporation, self-government, and eventual transfer of ownership to its residents. Montana Power has benefited through high worker productivity and low worker turnover and plans to recoup some of its initial investment in the town by sale of its properties to the occupants (Myhra, 1976).

A more recent example of the company town is that of Wright, Wyoming. The developer of Wright is Housing Services, Inc., a wholly-owned subsidiary of Atlantic Richfield Company. The town is expected to accommodate population growth stimulated by the area's twenty (producing or proposed) coal mining operations. Atlantic Richfield's Black Thunder Mine (operating) and Coal Creek Mine (developing) are expected to account for about 16 percent of Campbell County's projected mining employment of about 5,000 through 1985.

Atlantic Richfield is providing considerable front-end financing for development in Wright in the form of building lots (with sewers, utilities, and streets), a school site, and park lands. All housing is constructed and sold by private home builders on sites purchased from Housing Services. The development will ultimately accommodate 1,800 to 2,000 housing units of all types for an eventual 1987-1988 population of about 6,500. Ultimately, a framework for urbanization will be sought which will culminate in an incorporated town directed by resident-elected officials (Housing Services, Inc., 1979).

The company town represents the highest degree of

impact mitigation commitment. Most levels of developer-provided services embody a lesser degree of financial commitment; however, the repository developer may be faced with many of the infrastructure deficiencies which result in company town construction (depending on the final site chosen for the repository).

The risk element in major service provision should be emphasized in the event of project reduction or cancellation. Exxon Corporation's recent decision to table its Colony Oil Shale Development project left 1,600 workers unemployed and the company lost a $900 million investment. In addition, the fate of partially constructed Battlement Mesa, a 7,000 dwelling model company town designed to accommodate the population generated by an oil shale project, is uncertain (**Minneapolis Star and Tribune,** 1982). In addition, the "bust" in the uranium industry resulted in uncertainty for the future of Jeffrey City, Wyoming, which is owned by Western Nuclear, Inc. The decline in the uranium industry led to a population decrease in Jeffrey City from 4,000 in 1980 to about 1,000 in 1982. The county school district has just completed a $1.5 million recreational complex (financed by bond issue). This debt may have to be assimilated by the state (Ebringham, 1982; Peck, 1982).

Monitoring and Arbitration Programs

One of the key elements in an efficient impact mitigation program is that of developing a flexible, comprehensive system for monitoring impacts as they occur. Designing and maintaining an effective monitoring program is usually in a community's best interest; however, industry often initiates this phase of the planning process for the sake of complying with permitting regulations and maintaining an orderly growth process. Three monitoring systems are examined below.

The Campbell County Monitoring Program. Campbell County, Wyoming has been the center of extensive coal mining and petroleum drilling activities in recent years. Gillette, the county seat and largest city, was especially impacted by the energy development; in addition, Atlantic Richfield Company constructed a new town, Wright, to accommodate population growth (see previous section).

State regulations required that county industries maintain data on development impacts. Rather than each participating firm conducting its own monitoring assessment, the Campbell County Socioeconomic Monitoring Association (a subgroup of the Campbell County Chamber of Commerce Industry Committee) commissioned a private consultant to develop annual monitoring reports for the county. In this way, the process was centralized, facilitating the monitoring effort. Variables monitored include:

1. population characteristics

2. economic characteristics

3. housing

4. community facilities and services

5. public sector fiscal conditions

6. socioeconomic characteristics of the workforces of the Campbell County Chamber of Commerce industry committee companies

7. future economic conditions in Campbell County

The primary goal of the monitoring program is to provide government officials, industry decision makers, and community leaders with a single, comprehensive source of socioeconomic data (Browne, Bortz, and Coddington, Inc., 1982).

The Deserado Mine Agreement. The Deserado Mine, in Rio Blanco County, Colorado poses an interesting situation. The mine and much of the inmigrating population are in Colorado. The power plant fueled by the mine (and hence, much of the project's tax revenue) is in Utah. Since Rio Blanco County was receiving many of the adverse impacts of development and little of the tax revenue, an agreement was negotiated whereby Western Fuels, Inc. (owner of the facilities) made impact payments to Rio Blanco County and associated service districts.

Monitoring in this case was important both to the community and the company. Western Fuels had committed itself to make up any operating deficit incurred by Rio Blanco institutions from project-related population. Specific formulas were calculated to determine the number of relocating project workers, secondary employment, and students resulting from the mine. Lump-sum payments were provided for various service districts in Rio Blanco County and the town of Rangeley. Provisions were also made for revision of payments (either additional payments to the county or credits to the firm) on a per capita basis; the importance of accurate monitoring data is therefore obvious.

The Ontario Hydro Monitoring System. In 1976-1977 Ontario Hydro entered into agreements with the towns of Newcastle, Atikokan, Hope, and Bruce to compensate the communities for impacts of its proposed electric

generating facilities. The agreements set funds aside
into two accounts: one to pay costs of "hard" services
such as sewers and roads, and one to pay the costs of
planning, legal fees, and administration.
Ontario Hydro bore the responsibility for proposing
a monitoring program, which was to be carried out by the
municipality with the assistance of the company. The
approach used was the "rolling target" approach where an
initial target (based on policy or objectives) is set and
modified as new information becomes available. This
approach benefits the company by providing both a data
base to reply to impact claims and a planning process
needed for impact mitigation. The municipality benefits
by having both a basis for making claims and a planning
system capable of responding to changing conditions.
Differences between Ontario Hydro and the municipality
are settled by a board of arbitration with members
appointed by each party (Baril, 1981).

Arbitration Procedures

    A useful component in a siting agreement is a process
for resolving disputes over impacts which occur after
construction has started. Since initial impact
assessments may prove inaccurate, and negotiations may
not yield a mutually acceptable solution, an arbitrator
may be needed to resolve grievances.
    As previously mentioned, Ontario Hydro has set up an
arbitration board to deal with disputes which may arise
between the company and the community over interpretation
or application of the terms of agreement. The board is
composed of members appointed by both the company and the
community, and all board decisions are final (Baril,
1981).
    Another example of arbitration is that used in the
Northern Flood Agreements between the Province of
Manitoba, the Northern Indian Tribes, and Manitoba Hydro.
In this procedure, each party submitted a list of five
individuals to the other parties; any individual
unanimously selected was appointed arbitrator. The
agreement provides that:

> The arbitrator shall have broad authority and
> power to make awards capable of implementation
> and to fashion an appropriate and just remedy
> in respect of any and all adverse effects of
> the project on any person and that such remedy
> shall at a minimum place that person in no
> worse position . . . than he would have been in
> the absence of the adverse effect . . . (pp.
> 59-60).

The arbitrator is further empowered to mandate terms and
amount of compensation for afffected individuals

(**Northern Flood Agreement**, 1977).
The fact that impacts often vary substantially from those anticipated or that problems occur which are entirely unexpected points up the need for flexibility and adaptability in the planning process. This re-emphasizes the need for effective monitoring and arbitration plans. Existence of an arbitration or "grievance" procedure also assures the community that a legally-based mechanism to assess negative impacts and obtain fair compensation exists.

Government Planning Assistance

One source of community assistance in planning is government--local, regional, state, and Federal. State staff are often needed to design areawide planning organizations (APO). These APOs can produce policies and growth management objectives to include considerations of costs, revenues, bonding positions, and service levels of alternative growth options (Houstoun, 1977). Organization and utilization of the APO method can greatly assist small rural communities having to cope with the complexities and problems of rapid growth. Two of these organizations, which could serve as models for the repository case, are described in the following sections.

The Colorado Joint Review Process. The Colorado Joint Review Process (JRP) is designed to coordinate regulatory and administrative reviews by the Federal, state, and local governments concerning major energy and mineral resource development projects (TOSCO Foundation, 1980). Government and industry voluntarily enter the JRP; this encourages increased public and industry involvement in the review process. Basically a management system, the JRP involves all parties in the decision-making process, and its success is highly dependent on communication, cooperation, and compromise.

The Hartsville Project Coordinating Committee. The Hartsville Project Coordinating Committee (HPCC), created by the Tennessee Valley Authority (TVA), was designed to help mitigate the socioeconomic impacts of TVA's Hartsville Nuclear Plant. More of a regional committee than the JRP, this type of planning organization may be more effective when impacts are localized. The committee is composed of twenty-one mayors and county officials in a five-county impact area. It meets quarterly to discuss, evaluate, and recommend actions to TVA concerning socioeconomic impacts (Peelle, 1979). TVA contributes up to $50,000 per year to support a local office and staff for the HPCC. TVA's community coordinator is the principal contact and intermediary for citizens and local officials. Final decisions on money and allocations by TVA are based on the coordinator's recommendations.

Although the APO method can be an effective planning tool, there may be drawbacks to the process. It has been noted that the "outsiders'" tendency to desire formation of joint boards, commissions, and advisory groups to simplify the planning process may be counterproductive. In addition, local officials may feel their power and influence have been diminished by the establishment of a "super board" (Rogers, 1982).

SUMMARY

This chapter briefly outlines the role that past experiences might play in dealing with the socioeconomic impacts created by a high level nuclear waste repository. Review of the models of negotiation and arbitration procedures as well as the planning programs, monitoring agreements, and impact assistance legislation described here may help provide a basis for dealing with repository impacts. It appears clear from available analyses that a combination of past strategies with site-specific information is the strongest approach to impact mitigation. Emphasis should be on a comprehensive approach to mitigation, accounting for construction, operation, closure, and monitoring phases, along with early and effective involvement of all potentially affected parties.

11
Planning for Impact Management: A Systems Perspective

F. Larry Leistritz
John M. Halstead
Robert A. Chase
Steve H. Murdock

As noted in chapter 10, the issues surrounding mitigation have received only limited attention in the academic literature. Although individual case studies discussed in the previous chapter provide valuable insight into important dimensions of the mitigation process, they do not provide an adequate conceptual or organizational scheme for suggesting an integrated approach to impact management.

In fact, one of the major weaknesses of such attempts has been their failure to develop an adequate conceptual basis for viewing impact events and their subsequent management. Impacts occur within an ongoing set of interrelated systems; local, regional, and even national systems affect such impacts. If impacts are to be understood and effectively managed, we maintain that they must be seen as occurring within a set of interdependent systems and therefore that economic and social systems theory can be usefully applied to increase our understanding of the essential elements of an impact management system.

Existing system theories clearly point out that exogenous events, such as the project-related impacts of major resource developments, are likely to disturb the basic equilibrium of a local socioeconomic system and of larger area systems (Parsons, 1951; Buckley, 1967). Such theories thus point to the need to view impact management in terms of both its local and national implications.

Systems theory also suggests that the key to understanding and managing a system lies in seeing such systems as an integrated complex in which the inputs, relationships within, and outputs must be assessed and measured. The need to integrate the impact management process and to use a comprehensive approach which measures expected impacts (the impact assessment process), the effects of such impacts on key parts of, and actors in the system (impact management), and system outputs (through monitoring programs) is clarified through the use of a systems approach. In addition, such an approach suggests that impact mitigation can best be effected by altering the magnitude of the exogenous variables affecting the system (the impacts), by strengthening selected parts of the system (enhancing local capabilities), and by initiating programs aimed at retaining or restoring the equilibrium of the system (compensation and incentives). Finally, the use of such an approach suggests a continuous need to perform the key systems analysis processes of identifying the systems of interest, the essential parts of those systems, and the interrelationships within those systems throughout the impact management process.

A systems approach thus appears to be applicable to the impact management process. Although such a general systems framework cannot supply specific guidelines for impact management, we believe it offers a valuable perspective for ensuring that impact management activities are seen in an integrated and inclusive manner.

This chapter addresses impact management from a systems perspective. First, the pragmatic rationales for an impact management program for large-scale projects-- such as a nuclear waste repository--are briefly examined. Second, the interrelated nature of impact events that clarify the need for an integrated systems-oriented socioeconomic impact management framework is discussed. Third, the key components of such a management system are presented. Fourth, the implementation of an impact management program within a systems context is discussed, with emphasis on the relationship between impact management activities and project development (system) phases. Finally, conclusions are presented and implications for future research are discussed.

RATIONALE FOR IMPACT MANAGEMENT PROGRAMS

The rationale for devoting scarce resources to impact management activities can be examined from the perspectives of three interdependent parts of the system, those of: (1) the communities affected by a project, (2) the firm or agency responsible for project development, and (3) society as a whole. While each of these entities has somewhat different stakes in the outcome of the development process, it can be shown that each stands to benefit from an effective impact management effort.

From the viewpoint of the affected communities, impact management efforts are essential in order to avoid the potentially disruptive effects of development (see chapters 6 through 9). Community leaders are frequently aware of the potential problems and thus place a high priority on avoiding them. In addition, an impact management program can be viewed in a more positive light as an opportunity to utilize development-induced change to further community goals (for example, improve facilities and services). Finally, local planners and decision makers often realize that an effective impact management and planning process is essential not only as a means of meeting immediate needs and solving short-term problems but also to ensure the community's long-run viability. Thus, sound physical and financial planning during the period of rapid growth is necessary in order to avoid a legacy of future service problems and fiscal difficulties (Murray, 1980).

The firm or agency responsible for project development in the case of repositories is the Federal Government. It can anticipate both short-term and long-term benefits from an effective impact management program. First, such efforts should serve to build local support for the project, thus enhancing its prospects for approval by regulatory bodies and reducing the potential for litigation and associated delays (Luke, 1980; O'Hare et al., 1982). Second, a well designed impact management plan can help to ensure adequate housing and services for the project workforce, which can be expected to enhance recruitment and retention and improve worker morale and productivity (Metz, 1980; Myhra, 1980; Holmes and Narver, Inc., 1981). A final factor which may encourage the Federal Government to implement impact management programs is their desire to avoid adverse community impacts (and associated publicity) which might affect their future projects. Thus, publicity of the type associated with rapid growth impacts in the Rock Springs, Wyoming area could have negative effects on the developer's prospects for obtaining siting approval for a subsequent project (Myhra, 1980). Similarly, adverse publicity associated with the development of an initial nuclear repository could hamper future efforts to site such facilities.

From the societal viewpoint, at least three justifications exist for support of efforts to require developers to mitigate, or compensate for, the adverse impacts of their projects. First, and probably most important, is the fact that in the absence of mitigation or compensation measures desirable projects (from a societal viewpoint) may be stymied because of local opposition. Thus, if local groups feel that a proposed project is detrimental to their interests, they are likely to organize in opposition to its development; and such opposition is frequently effective in either stopping an essential project or causing it to be inappropriately located (O'Hare et al., 1982).

A second reason why impact alleviation measures may be encouraged is that by requiring developers to internalize the external costs associated with their facilities (through specific measures to prevent or compensate for adverse impacts), such costs are made more visible; and society can be better assured that the project meets the "net benefits" criterion (that is, total benefits to society exceed total costs).

The third major consideration which may lead to public (that is, societal) support for impact management measures is that of equity. It has been noted that the equity argument for compensation is weaker than the efficiency arguments (O'Hare et al., 1982). This is because of conflicting interpretations of what is meant by equity or fairness. No matter how equity is defined, however, there appears to be a general reluctance to impose large losses on small and identifiable segments of society (Morell and Magorian, 1982). Overall, equity as well as efficiency considerations tend to encourage public support for impact management efforts.

AN IMPACT MANAGEMENT FRAMEWORK

While "impact mitigation" and related concepts have been discussed more frequently in recent years, precedents for activities of this type go back several decades (see chapter 10). The term "impact mitigation" came into widespread usage, however, following its inclusion in NEPA. There has been a common tendency to view impact mitigation in a narrow context and as involving merely "reductions or eliminations of negative impacts" (O'Hare et al., 1982; Urban Systems Research and Engineering, Inc., 1980; Metz, 1979; Myhra, 1980; Faas, 1982a).

A broader and more comprehensive approach encompassing measures that enhance the project's local benefits and approaches through providing various forms of compensation (for example, monetary, in-kind) to local interests, as well as actions to reduce or eliminate negative effects, is needed. Hence, we, as well as others (Gilmore et al., 1981; Berkey et al., 1977), believe that the term "impact management" is a more appropriate description.

A systems approach to impact management suggests that the major aspects of such an approach should involve attempts to anticipate and alleviate those project effects that upset the equilibrium of the system and are thus generally perceived as undesirable and to enhance effects that lend stability to the system and are deemed beneficial. In designing an impact management program, then, the use of a systems perspective stresses the need for an integrated approach. There are four elements to such a process:

1. the need for a comprehensive approach

2. the need to integrate the impact management activities with the overall project development schedule

3. the need to appropriately involve all key interests and groups

4. the need to deal realistically with the uncertainties inherent in the development process and the impacts thereof

Each of these major design considerations is discussed below.

In designing an impact management program, it is important that the full range of project management and community growth management options that may be relevant be considered, given the characteristics of the particular project and the community system. Thus, not only should measures to increase local housing and infrastructure capacity (system resilience) be examined; actions which can reduce the exogenous demands imposed on local community systems (for example, worker transportation programs and construction camps) should be evaluated as well. It is also important to consider potential interactions among various components of the management systems being contemplated and to evaluate trade-offs between alternative approaches.

In integrating impact management considerations into the overall project planning and development process, the need for adequate lead time should be kept in mind. It is thus desirable for a preliminary reconnaissance-level impact evaluation/issue identification to be performed while the project is still in the feasibility analysis phase. Conducting an initial evaluation early in the project planning process provides a basis for scoping future impact assessment and management activities, allows adequate time for subsequent management efforts to be incorporated into the overall project schedule, and enables explicit incorporation of impact management costs into the project budget (Luke, 1980). As the project planning process moves forward, it is essential that appropriate lead time be programmed to allow completion of a detailed impact assessment and preparation of community growth management plans.

A third major consideration in designing an impact management program is the need to involve all key interest groups or actors in the system. While public participation in resource development decisions is mandated by NEPA and most state facility siting legislation and while much has been written concerning the most appropriate structuring of such participation programs (Creighton, 1980; Myhra, 1980 and chapters 13-15), past public involvement efforts have often been viewed as too little, too late by concerned environmental, civic, and neighborhood groups (Luke, 1980; Abrams and Primack, 1980; Centaur Associates, 1979). An approach which has been relatively effective in several energy development areas in the Western United

States has been the formation of impact management teams or task forces. These bodies have typically included representatives of a broad spectrum of local interests and, in some cases, state and Federal agency representatives. Such groups have reviewed impact assessments and mitigation plans and in several cases have been able to reach an effective consensus concerning acceptable impact management procedures (Myhra, 1980).[2]

A final, and very important, consideration in designing an impact management program is the need to deal adequately with the uncertainties inherent in the development process. Uncertainty concerning both the future of the project and the magnitude and distribution of its socioeconomic effects invariably complicates the impact management process (Gilmore et al., 1981). It must be recognized that such uncertainty cannot be entirely eliminated. It is therefore essential that the impact management plan be sufficiently flexible to allow for modification as the project progresses and that a system for monitoring both the nature and magnitude of project effects and the effectiveness of management responses be incorporated into the overall framework (Leistritz and Chase, 1982; DePape, 1982).

IMPACT MANAGEMENT--A SYSTEMS FRAMEWORK

An overall impact management system can be seen as requiring the measurement and management of system inputs, system interrelationships, and system outputs. Thus, such an approach suggests the need to focus on three basic elements. These are: (1) an impact assessment system, (2) an impact management plan, and (3) an impact monitoring system.

Impact Assessment System

The purpose of the impact assessment system is to forecast project-induced changes in local economic, demographic, public service, fiscal, and social characteristics and thereby provide a basis for anticipating areas in which problems are likely to arise and where impact management efforts will be needed. The system can also be useful in identifying opportunities for enhancement of project-related benefits. The impact assessment system thus plays a primary role in guiding impact management efforts. Though the elements of such a system have been discussed in earlier chapters, two points must be emphasized. The system must be **user-oriented** and **flexible**, providing the data required for decision making and allowing easy alteration of key parameters for rapid analysis of alternative scenarios.

Impact Management Plan

The impact management plan presents the sets of actions which will be taken to minimize the costs imposed by the project on local residents and other actors in the system, to maximize local project-related benefits, to compensate individuals or groups which are adversely affected by the project, and/or to provide incentives for community acceptance of the facility. A systems perspective would suggest that impact management could be affected by altering the exogenous factors affecting the system, the elements of the system itself, or by measures to restore system equilibrium. The types of measures which may be considered for inclusion in an impact management plan thus typically fall into four general categories. These are:

1. measures to minimize demands on local systems (economic, governmental, and social)

2. measures to enhance the capacity of local systems to cope with change

3. measures to compensate individuals or groups (components of the system)

4. measures to provide incentives to local interests

The extent to which these various types of impact management actions may be applicable to a specific energy development project will depend in large measure on the nature of the project and of the site area as well as the institutional setting within which development occurs. Specific measures within each of these categories are discussed below.

Minimizing Demands on Local Systems. Local socioeconomic impacts of resource development projects tend to be closely associated with the relocation (inmigration) of project workers and their families to the site area. Measures to lessen demands on local systems thus tend to focus on reducing the number of relocating workers and dependents associated with project development by: (1) effecting alterations in facility design or construction schedules, and (2) development of workforce policies geared to reducing the proportion of the project workforce which will inmigrate to the site area (table 11.1).

Alterations in facility design or construction schedules which could be considered as means of reducing the demands imposed on the site area include three major options. The first possibility relates to the choice of the site for the project. By choosing a site within commuting distance of a major metropolitan area, the developer can substantially reduce both the number of relocating workers and the need for increased community infrastructure capacity. However, geologic and other technical requirements are likely to supersede these socioeconomic considerations.

A second strategy would be to lengthen the construction schedule, thereby leading to a reduction in peak employment requirements. This alternative may be unattractive, however, since lengthening the construction schedule usually leads to increased project costs.

A third option is to have some of the facility components fabricated off-site and assembled in the field. Shop fabrication generally tends to be more efficient than field assembly, and can possibly ease potential shortages of construction craftsmen and engineers. However, it has not been widely practiced, presents problems in transportation, and may be limited by union-employer contractual agreements.

Once the project site and construction parameters have been established, the principal method for lessening local impacts is to reduce the proportion of the project workers who inmigrate to the site area.

This strategy has two major options. The first is to increase the number of workers hired locally. This is one means of enhancing economic benefits which the site area receives, thereby increasing community acceptance of the project. In addition, increased local hiring will tend to reduce the number of workers inmigrating into the area. Such programs are looked upon favorably by local communities, as they enhance the positive benefits accruing to the community, and may tend to promote the future stability of the workforce. Problems with this procedure may arise in: (1) union-labor agreements that constrain local hiring of nonunion workers, (2) questions of discrimination against nonlocals, and (3) competition with local businesses for the area's labor resources, forcing local employers to raise their compensation levels. A final limitation concerns the source of the locally hired workers. If these workers were previously unemployed, their employment at the project will serve to reduce the inmigrating population. However, if they were lured away from previous local employment, additional workers may still need to inmigrate to fill the newly vacated (nonproject) jobs.

Another method of increasing local hiring is to implement job training programs for local residents. Such programs are usually popular with local residents and can help to reduce the project's competition with other local employers. Limitations of job training programs stem from: (1) problems with labor agreements, which may limit locals from acquiring jobs in spite of their training, (2) consideration of sufficient lead time for the program to be effectively initiated, and (3) the

Table 11.1

Measures to Reduce Inmigration

Option	Method	Advantages	Disadvantages/Limitations
Alterations in facility design or construction schedule	Site selection close to metropolitan area	-reduction of inmigrants -reduced need for new infrastructure	-may not be applicable to nuclear repositories because of stringent geologic criteria for sites
	Lengthening construction period	-reduction in peak work force requirements -reduction in number of relocating workers	-increases project cost
	Off-site component fabrication	-greater construction efficiency -eases needs for craftsmen and engineers on-site	-limited by union-employer contractual agreements and/or capability to transport large components
Reducing the percentage of inmigrating project workers and families	Increasing local hiring a) local hiring preferences	-increases percentage of economic benefits accruing to local residents -enhances stability of workforce	-may violate union-labor agreements -may be viewed as discriminatory -increases competition for local labor with area businesses -success depends on current employment situation in area
	b) training programs	-may reduce project's competition with local employers -popular with local residents -increase number of workers hired locally	-may not increase local hiring due to union-labor contractual agreements -requires careful initiation and lead-time consideration
	Increasing commuting a) measures to reduce travel costs b) provision of temporary housing	-increased ease of labor force recruitment -increased productivity -reduction in number of relocating workers	-may aggravate local traffic problems -induces payroll leakages from local community -may lead to higher turnover

potential duration of demand for these skills in the area after the project ends.

The second major alternative for reducing the proportion of the project's workers who inmigrate to the area are measures to encourage commuting. These are generally aimed at either reducing workers' travel costs or providing convenient workweek accommodations for those who commute weekly.

The first of these measures, reducing workers' travel costs, may include provision of bus or vanpool transportation, or provision of travel allowances. Benefits of the bus and vanpool strategy, in addition to reducing the number of inmigrants, include: (1) increased ease of labor force recruitment, (2) reduced worker turnover and absenteeism, (3) increased worker punctuality and productivity, (4) reduced traffic congestion on roads leading to the site, and (5) reduced costs for providing parking for workers (Metz, 1981).

A second measure to increase commuting is providing temporary single-status housing on-site (when the project is far removed from major population centers). This may encourage workers to commute from their permanent homes on a weekly basis.

Increasing commuting may generate additional problems, however. First, traffic problems on local roads may be aggravated. An increase in multiple ridership, perhaps through increased use of buses and vans, is a means of alleviating this problem. Second, increased commuting may be seen by locals as causing project benefits to leave the area. Finally, high levels of commuting may lead to higher worker turnover rates (Holmes and Narver, Inc., 1981).

Enhancing the Capacity of Local Systems. Even though measures may be implemented to reduce the level of inmigration associated with project development, a large-scale facility will generally lead to significant population growth with resultant increases in the demands imposed on local systems. It will usually be necessary, therefore, to consider implementing impact management measures aimed at enhancing the capability of local systems to cope with change. Existing literature suggests that such measures can be seen as falling into five general categories (Aronson, 1981; Briscoe, Maphis, Murray, and Lamont, Inc., 1978; Faas, 1982a; Metz, 1980; Myhra, 1980). These are:

1. local planning assistance

2. provision by the developer of housing and support infrastructure

3. stimulation of housing development and business expansion by the local private sector

4. financial assistance to the local public
    sector, often in the form of front-end
    financing

5. enhancement of local public safety and medical
    capabilities

Each of these measures is described in more detail below.
One of the most important activities in developing
an impact management program is initiating advanced
planning at the local level. This is frequently a
problem for small communities, which seldom have the
capabilities to manage growth resulting from large-scale
development (Greene and Curry, 1977). The local planning
phase of the growth impact management task (although a
continual process) is of greatest value during the
predevelopment stage, and should begin as soon as the
community learns of the project. Timing is an important
factor, since more planning lead time generally results
in more successful mitigation efforts. The developer can
facilitate these planning efforts by providing technical
assistance and funding. (For examples of such efforts,
see Metz, 1978, and Quality Development Associates,
1978.)
The first and most obvious problem often encountered
by energy-impacted communities is a lack of adequate
housing for the new population. The relocation of a
large portion of the project workforce into a small
community will increase area housing demands. In the
absence of adequate planning, this increase may result in
inflated housing prices, rental fees, property values,
and property taxes. The commensurate decline in
availability and quality of housing may also cause higher
worker turnover rates.
Since it is in the best interest of the developer to
assure an adequate supply of housing within commuting
distance of the project (and local contractors may be
unable to accommodate the increased demand), measures may
be taken to increase the housing stock. Such actions
could include construction of a self-contained community
(company town), development of permanent housing
(subdivisions) or mobile home parks, revitalization of
existing housing, or provision of temporary housing
facilities (mancamps). While energy development firms
have often provided housing and related infrastructure
directly (Aronson, 1981; Metz, 1979), most efforts by
developers have been aimed at stimulating private housing
developers by assembling land, subsidizing mortgage
rates, or guaranteeing occupancy rather than through
direct investments.
When rapid development occurs, local governments
typically face a cost-revenue squeeze. Substantial
capital costs often must be incurred to provide for

necessary expansion of service capacity at a time well before significant development-related revenues are received. In such cases, it may be necessary for local governments to rely on grants, prepayment of taxes, borrowing, or other front-end financing mechanisms (see table 11.2).

Grants from the developer or from Federal or state governments transfer resources to local entities without an obligation to repay. With the use of grants, the risk of underexpenditure or expansion of services with insufficient demand is borne by the local government units, especially if the grantor has no further obligation to assist.

Some communities have also required the developer to prepay property or sales taxes. These prepayments, which are credited against future tax liabilities, can be an important source of resources to support initial service expansion. Prepayment of taxes would have limited applicability to repository development, however, since Federal property is exempt from local property taxes.

A third means for local governments to acquire resources is through borrowing. This relies on future revenue to repay the debt, placing some of the cost on inmigrants. There are, however, both legal and practical limits to the amount of debt that a community can and should incur. Most states limit the amount of bonds a local government can issue; the local debt servicing capacity and the willingness of investors to purchase bonds also limit local borrowing (Briscoe, Maphis, Murray, and Lamont, Inc., 1978).

A final source of revenue for rapid growth communities is user charges. Services, such as water and sewer, which facilitate charging actual users often can be made largely self-supporting through the assessment of regular service fees (covering operation and maintenance costs) and initial hookup charges (sometimes called tap fees). In addition, progressive rate schedules can be used to impose costs for such services on those who use them most heavily; differential rate structures (business versus residential users) can be used to concentrate costs on those who are perceived to be receiving large segments of the development-related benefits.

When the potential hazards to health and safety associated with a facility are a significant local issue (as is certainly the case for nuclear repositories), various protective measures may be in order. For example, the developer could fund special emergency preparedness training for local public safety and medical personnel. Likewise, environmental monitoring systems could be instituted. Monitoring activities could be conducted by the developer, by state or federal agencies, or by a local group (with some or all of the costs borne

Table 11.2

Methods of Financing Impact Mitigation

Type of Financing	Source	Advantages/Disadvantages
Grant: -Direct cash -In-kind	Federal or state government or developer	-Meets front-end costs -Little risk to community -Does not assure efficient allocation of resources -Community may not retain decision-making authority
Prepayment of Taxes	Developer	-Meets front-end costs -May or may not remove risk from community -Problem with agreeing on type and amount of credit and prepayment -Jurisdictional mismatch problems may not be addressed

Borrowing:
-Bond issues
  1) general obligation
  2) special assessment
  3) revenue
-Loans
	Third parties with possible guarantees from developer	-Meets front-end costs
		-New development may not bear its full service costs
		-Community bears risk
		-Possible problems with retiring mature bonds

User Charges	Service recipients	-Users pay for services -A flexible tool which is under the control of local decision makers

by the developer).

Compensation Measures (for system components).
Development of any large-scale facility will almost
invariably lead to some adverse effects on local groups
and communities. Compensation, which can be defined as
including those mechanisms which provide monetary
payments or other forms of benefits to local interests as
a form of recompense for project-induced costs or losses,
may thus be necessary. Compensation seeks to make
affected parties as well off as they were prior to
development, in contrast to incentives, which provide
benefits above and beyond the costs incurred (Urban
Systems Research and Engineering, Inc., 1980).

Compensation measures can take one of four basic
forms: (1) monetary, (2) conditional, (3) in-kind, and
(4) offsetting. Direct monetary payments are the form
most frequently employed. This is the mechanism used to
compensate landowners whose property is taken in the
course of development. Likewise, direct payments by
developers to local governments have been used in a
number of cases as a means of compensating for fiscal
deficits during the construction phase (Faas, 1982b).

Conditional compensation mechanisms are implemented
only if a particular adverse circumstance occurs. For
example, the developer might post a surety bond or
acquire liability insurance to guarantee that repository
closure and cleanup costs will be covered or to provide
for compensation in case of a facility-related accident.
Likewise, the developer could offer property value
guarantees (for example, an offer to purchase at
presiting value) to nearby landowners.

In-kind compensation typically involves replacement
of lost amenities. For example, a developer might
dedicate lands to the community for park and recreation
purposes or contribute funds for wildlife habitat
preservation as a form of compensation for recreational
opportunities or habitats foreclosed by development
(O'Hare et al., 1982).

A final form of compensation could be termed
"offsetting" measures. This concept recognizes that some
adverse effects of development are virtually impossible
to prevent (for example, loss of small town atmosphere)
but that creation or enhancement of benefits in other
areas (for example, attractive job opportunities,
enhanced local business participation in development
activities, improved community facilities) may in some
sense offset the negative effects. This concept is being
employed increasingly as an overt strategy of impact
management in connection with some Canadian resource
communities (DePape, 1982).

An effective compensation plan is composed of
several steps. First, impacts must be identified during
the assessment phase. Second, the impacted groups

entitled to receive compensation must be determined. This step involves identifying each individual or group that desires compensation, evaluating the basis and validity of the claim, and determining the level of compensation to be paid. Third, a method of payment must be chosen (grants, guaranteed loans, etc.). Finally, the terms of payment must be specified.

The literature suggests that at least five types of local groups may claim to be entitled to some form of compensation (Halstead et al., 1982; Metz, 1980; Myhra, 1980; Morell and Magorian, 1982; O'Hare et al., 1982). These include (see table 11.3):

1. local landowners whose property is taken for facility development

2. nearby landowners whose property may be diminished in value

3. local governments which experience significant fiscal deficits

4. low income and fixed income groups affected by local inflationary effects of development

5. environmental groups

The precedents for compensation differ substantially among these types of claimants and appear to be strongest with respect to the first and third categories (Rice et al., 1980; Faas, 1982a; O'Hare et al., 1982). In most cases, negotiation between the developer and the affected parties will be vital in reaching a mutually agreeable settlement.

Incentives (for system components). In order to obtain substantial local support for the siting of new energy facilities, many consider it essential that local residents be able to feel that "they have gained something" (Morell and Magorian, 1982). Thus an impact management program may need to incorporate positive incentives in order to elicit local support.

Incentives, which have the goal of making local interests better off than prior to facility siting, can take a variety of forms. In essence, any of the mechanisms discussed previously with respect to compensation can also serve as vehicles for incentives. The major distinction between compensation and incentives is whether the measures employed are seen as only serving to make local interests as well off as before or better off. This distinction is clearer in concept than in practice, however, because what may appear to some observers to be an incentive may be regarded by others as merely compensation for various intangible costs (such as risk bearing) associated with development and to others as "bribery" (Morell and Magorian, 1982).

In summarizing considerations in impact management planning, several other considerations also should be mentioned. First, the plan should be specified in sufficient detail to provide measureable goals or targets against which the progress of the management effort can be evaluated. Thus, it may be useful to specify target values (by time period if relevant) for such factors as local hire rates and number of housing units to be developed. Likewise, payment mechanisms and formulas should be specified in detail. Second, the plan should explicitly identify the responsibilities of the major parties-at-interest (for example, the developer, various local governments). Finally, the plan should provide a mechanism for periodic review and revision in light of changing conditions, a monitoring system for establishing these changes, and a means for resolving disputes which may arise.

Impact Monitoring System

The primary purpose of a monitoring system is to provide accurate and timely socioeconomic information concerning both the state of the system and the effects of exogenous factors on the system. Such information enables project officials and community leaders to periodically reassess community needs and revise associated mitigation plans and also serves as the basis for developing revised impact projections. Thus, at any given time throughout the development period, the monitoring system allows policy personnel to evaluate the effectiveness of impact management activities and provides them with information necessary for future mitigation efforts.

In response to the need for impact management programs developed on the basis of accurate information, several socioeconomic impact monitoring systems have been implemented. These systems all provide for the periodic review of economic and social changes as they actually occur, but differ substantially in the indicators evaluated, the mechanisms for and the frequency of data collection, the selection of communities to be monitored, and the frequency of reporting, as well as in other respects (Leistritz and Chase, 1981, 1982).[3]

Data Collection Scope and Procedures. A socioeconomic impact monitoring system is essentially a standardized process for the periodic collection and analysis of data reflecting key indicators of economic and social change. Generally, the indicators monitored should correspond to those for which projections were made in the anticipatory impact assessment. The indicators included in a monitoring system are generally

Table 11.3

Major Compensation Mechanisms

Impact	Validation of Claim	Means of Compensation
Condemnation of Private Land for Facility Use	Eminent domain	Cash payment based on fair market value plus moving expenses
Property Value Diminution	Historical survey Econometric modeling	Payment of difference between preproject and postproject value
		Assurance of reimbursement if devaluation occurs
Infrastructure Overburdening		
• Schools	Cost estimates from impact assessment	Payments to school districts
• Municipal	Cost estimates from impact assessment	Payments to municipalities; construction of new facilities
• Roads	Road use/capacity estimates	Road construction and maintenance payments
Low Income Groups and Elderly, Affected by Local Inflation	Local welfare programs Local surveys	Rent subsidies
		Payments to enhance local welfare programs
Environmental and Wildlife Groups	Environmental and wildlife analysis from the impact assessment	In-kind mitigation (e.g., to provide replacement habitats)

categorized as: (1) those reflecting characteristics of the project and its work forces and (2) those reflecting changes in the communities affected by the project. Key project characteristics generally considered for inclusion in a monitoring system include the number of workers, worker characteristics (for example, local vs. nonlocal origin, place of residence, number and ages of dependents, and so forth), and percent of project completion. Community characteristics generally included in monitoring efforts are those indicators of the demands placed on local facilities and services and of the capacity of local systems. Examples of such indicators include population, school enrollments, housing units available or under construction, capacity of sewer and water systems, capacity (space and personnel) of local schools, law enforcement activity (number of calls and arrests) and capacity (staff and equipment), revenues and expenditures of local governments, and various social impact indicators.

The choice of the specific indicators to be monitored can be difficult because a wide range of variables are relevant to various aspects of impact management. In determining the variables to be included in a monitoring system, it is important to remember that the primary purpose of the system is to supply current information that will be useful in guiding impact management decisions. The types of data to be collected should be closely linked to expected impacts and priority issues. A monitoring system cannot be "all things to all people," and an overly inclusive approach to system design should be avoided (Leistritz and Chase, 1982). A major goal must be to arrive at a relatively small set of impact indicators that both developer and community representatives consider important and that are sufficiently comprehensive to achieve their purposes. Trade-offs are thus inherent in determining variables to be included.

Another major system design decision with obvious trade-offs relates to the frequency of monitoring. Frequent monitoring is desirable as it offers rapid feedback regarding changing conditions and emerging problems. The more frequent the monitoring, however, the higher the costs.

Mechanisms for data collection also require careful consideration. Generally, the greater the degree to which the system can rely on information produced through the standard recordkeeping/reporting processes of the developer's organization, local governments, and state agencies, the less will be the overall cost of the monitoring effort. In some cases, however, existing data sources are not adequate to provide information in the required form or with sufficient rapidity to meet the needs of impact management. In these situations, special data collection efforts will be required.

Procedures for Updating Impact Projections. A second general requirement for an adequate monitoring program is the capability to use monitored information to develop updated impact projections. As noted earlier, a number of factors can cause actual impacts to differ substantially from those projected. The monitoring system should, therefore, include an impact projection capability as an integral component. The system should be designed to rapidly detect departures of project schedules, work force levels, worker characteristics, and other key impact parameters from assumed levels and to reflect these changes in revised projections. Thus, it is important to view impact assessment techniques not merely as mechanisms for developing one time anticipatory projections, but rather as impact management tools to be used throughout the project development process (Leistritz and Murdock, 1981).

Reporting Procedures and Formats. A final, very important element to be considered in designing and evaluating monitoring systems concerns the reporting of monitoring results. If a monitoring system is to be an effective part of the impact management process, data and analyses must be translated into a series of concise, decision-oriented reports that reflect changes at the level of individual jurisdictions, are in a format facilitating comparisons of present and projected service demands with existing and projected facility capacity, and that are compatible with the existing administrative procedures (such as requirements for grant applications) of the affected entities.

PROGRAM IMPLEMENTATION

Implementing a successful impact management system for a sensitive facility, such as a nuclear repository, can be a very complex undertaking. As such, this task deserves concerted attention by the developer. In order to ensure that impact management efforts receive appropriate attention on a continuing basis, it has been suggested that an individual or group within the developer's organization should be assigned specific responsibility for implementing the impact management program (Luke, 1980).

Management of socioeconomic impacts and related community acceptance risks should be a major concern in predevelopment planning. Impact management efforts should thus be integrated with engineering and regulatory schedules in the developer's critical path charts and budgets. A suggested schedule of major impact management activities in relationship to the stages of project development is presented in table 11.4.

Table 11.4

Chronological Sequence of Key Impact Management Activities

Project Phase	Impact Management Activity
Feasibility Analysis and Site Selection	• Preliminary reconnaissance level impact evaluation/issue identification
	Public involvement at macro level
	Information dissemination
Site Evaluation and Permitting	• Formation of local impact committee (planning grant)
	Conduct anticipatory impact assessment
	Prepare impact management plan
Postpermit Preparations	• Obtain final funding commitment
	More detailed design of mitigation measures
	Initiate implementation of selected measures (training programs, housing and infrastructure development)
	Initiate monitoring of community indicators
Construction	• Complete implementation of impact management plan (with periodic evaluation)
	Complete implementation of monitoring system (with periodic reassessments)
	Coordination of information exchange with public
Operation	• Implementation of impact management plan continues with shift of measures to accommodate more permanent population
	Continue monitoring
	Ongoing public participation
Closure	• Interaction with community regarding economic readjustment
	Monitoring for several years following closure to assure successful economic readjustment

CONCLUSIONS AND IMPLICATIONS

While the effective management of project effects is the end toward which all impact research and assessment efforts are directed, an integrated concept of and approach to impact management has been notably lacking. The purpose of this chapter was to suggest a systems framework for meeting this need. This was done by presenting a conceptual framework for, and key components of, such a program and suggesting an approach for implementing such a system as an integral part of the project development process. Although difficult to implement and complex in design, unless a concerted impact management program similar to that entailed here is developed, we believe it will be extremely difficult to complete the repository siting process.

NOTES

1. While the concept of procedural justice would always appear to support impact mitigation/compensation actions, allocative justice may or may not favor such an approach depending on the distributional outcomes of such actions (that is, are the "poor" being asked to compensate the "rich").

2. While the general concept of an impact management task force appears desirable, key issues remain concerning the structure of the entity (which groups should be represented) and the timing of its formation relative to the overall project development schedule.

3. For example, see Cross, 1981; DeVeney, 1981; Harnisch et al., 1980; McGinnis, 1981; Missouri Basin Power Project, 1980; Pace Quality Development Associates, Inc., 1980; Pearson, 1981; Rafferty, 1981; Tennessee Valley Authority, 1980; Washington Public Power Supply System, 1980.

12
Additional Considerations for Repository Impact Mitigation

John M. Halstead
F. Larry Leistritz

The two previous chapters illustrated past experiences with socioeconomic impact management and a framework for a comprehensive, systematic approach to mitigation planning. Past case studies (as illustrated in chapter 10) give useful insight into many of the problems likely to be experienced in repository siting; these insights were incorporated into the impact management framework in chapter 11. However, many of the special impacts and issues raised in other parts of this book are important and unique enough to bear further amplification and discussion. These issues are the subject of this chapter.

In planning for impact management for a nuclear waste repository, two issues immediately stand out. First, the fact that the facility will be sited on Federal land with the Federal Government as developer means that, under present legal conditions, very little (impact mitigating) tax revenue will accrue to the host community. Second, many of the impacts will stem from the noxious nature of the facility and will thus pose unique problems in mitigation and compensation.

The first problem can be dealt with through the use of special legislation to provide impact assistance. Strengths and weaknesses of previous programs (for example, Safeguard ABM, Trident Submarine Base) should be considered in designing the components of this ideal legislation, as well as incorporating the recommendations of several states with regards to mitigation procedures. This includes not only funding the impact management program, but also a framework for structuring the planning, negotiation, arbitration, and compensation procedures of the program.

The second problem is two-fold. The first step is to identify the special impacts which may occur. This has been a major focus of previous chapters in this volume (chapters 6 through 9). As noted in these chapters, this identification can involve the use of concerns voiced by residents of potential host candidate states, past experiences with similar noxious facilities, and development of survey techniques to be used in host communities. The second step involves developing methods to compensate individuals for these unique impacts.

The final section of this chapter reiterates the need for effective public participation. Although dealt with elsewhere in this book (see chapters 13 through 15), it bears mentioning here as both a means to facilitate repository siting and a channel through which to identify special impacts.

ADDRESSING FISCAL REALITIES

Special Legislation Needed for Mitigation

A high level nuclear waste repository, which will be owned and operated by the Federal Government on Federally-owned land, will not be liable for standard property taxes.[1] Therefore, alternative means will need to be found to finance expansions and improvements in public services and facilities.

In the past, various methods have been used to supply impact management funds to offset the lack of community revenue generated by tax-exempt facilities. For instance, the Tennessee Valley Authority, a public utility, makes direct payments to impacted communities in the area of its Hartsville, Tennessee nuclear plant. The Federal Government also makes aid available for schools, recreational facilities, and roads through a variety of programs. In addition, amendments have been added to military construction bills to provide funds for impact alleviation (see chapter 10). The impact assistance programs which were implemented in connection with the Safeguard and Trident projects in particular appear to offer a useful point of departure in designing legislation for repository impact assistance.

The Safeguard funding approach has been largely successful in the past. Serious problems were encountered, however, which could be avoided through several modifications of these past programs. With the strengths and weaknesses of these mitigation approaches in mind, a format for impact assistance legislation is outlined.

The proposed impact assistance approach, which could be implemented through special provisions in the legislation authorizing repository construction, would differ from the Safeguard approach in three major respects. These are:

1. The repository impact assistance program would be viewed as a **primary** source of funds (in contrast to the more supplemental philosophy of the Trident and Safeguard programs).

2. Impact assistance funds would be appropriated
    by Congress and placed in a **trust fund** to be
    administered by an interagency **mitigation task
    force.**

3. An arbitration process would be established to
    resolve disputes which might arise during the
    development period.

These recommended features of the repository mitigation
program could overcome many of the problems experienced
by the Safeguard and Trident mitigation efforts.
   The identification of the repository impact
assistance program as a primary source of funding could
substantially reduce the time required to obtain impact
funds and could also lessen the problems involved in
matching community needs with existing Federal programs.
Authorization of a substantial trust fund for impact
assistance should also provide greater assurance to local
governments that adequate resources will be available to
meet their needs.

   The Mitigation Task Force. A major consideration in
designing an impact assistance plan is to determine how
it is to be administered. The Kitsap County area
organized several local groups to deal with project
impacts; the Secretary of Defense was required to consult
with heads of related departments or agencies to
determine funding levels. This task may be better
allocated to one interagency team.
   One means of developing this "mitigation task force"
would be to borrow personnel from various domestic
agencies with related goals: Department of Housing and
Urban Development, Farmer's Home Administration, Federal
Highway Administration, etc. (Luke, 1982). Local
community representatives could be added to this group to
assure identification of local concerns and problems and
liaison with community groups. This task force would be
entrusted with allocating impact mitigation funds.
   The three major advantages this approach would
embody are:

1. Responsiveness--Community leaders know who is
    responsible for mitigation, and can focus their
    requests. The task force, being closely
    involved with local concerns, is in a good
    position to respond quickly and effectively.

2. Timeliness--Once funding has been allocated,
    the task force can dispense it to address the
    sources of impact as needed. This eliminates
    the lag time in obtaining funds through
    existing Federal programs.

3. Credibility--Since the task force is highly visible within the community, and local citizens are represented in the group, residents can be more assured that the developer is taking an active and involved role in dealing with community problems.[2]

   Resolving Disputes. A final feature which should be incorporated in the impact assistance legislation is a mechanism for resolving disputes. It is unreasonable to assume that the impacted communities will be issued a "blank check" to deal with mitigation expenses. Similarly, it is unlikely that all disagreements between the community and the dispensing agency could be settled through negotiation and discussion. Therefore, a mutually agreed upon arbitration process should be designed. Some possibilities for designing this process are provided by the agreements utilized by Ontario Hydro and in the Northern Flood Agreement (see chapter 10).
   The fact that impacts often vary substantially from those anticipated or problems occur which are entirely unexpected points to the need for flexibility and adaptability in the planning process and for effective monitoring and arbitration plans. Creation of an arbitration or "grievance" procedure also assures the community that a legally-based mechanism exists to assess negative impacts and obtain fair compensation. This could be accomplished by the appointment of an arbitration board consisting of candidates chosen by both the local community and the developer (and possibly the state) which would have final authority to resolve disputes.

   Timing and Distribution. A final feature of this legislation is that it allows adequate lead time for initiating and implementing recommendations from the planning process. Time must be allotted for: (1) organization of local citizens to form an impact committee, (2) formulation of a comprehensive impact management plan to deal with anticipated problems, and (3) consideration and provision of new infrastructure to deal with project impacts.

ADDRESSING THE UNIQUE EFFECTS OF REPOSITORY SITING

Special Problems in Compensation

The repository, because of its radioactive contents and the fact that such radioactivity will exist for an extended period of time, will generate impacts unlike those of more standard developments (see chapter 6). Some of these impacts will pose difficult and unusual mitigation problems, possibly generating a need for new techniques and ideas for compensating the affected parties. Residents living in and around the host community may be concerned over risks to health and safety, possible consequences to future generations (that is, the intergenerational issue), the question of equity (that is, why their county should have to be the storage area for an entire nation), and possible loss of property value.

Compensation for Risk. It has been argued by economists that the risk generated by such a facility, however small, constitutes an externality[3] if it goes uncompensated (Schulze et al., 1981). In order for the repository to reflect its true social costs, these risks will have to be internalized by the developer. Unfortunately, the Price-Anderson Act of 1957 (which limits liability for a nuclear accident to $560 million) may act to relieve the risk-causing facility of liability for possible accidents, which in turn leaves accident risks to the community uncompensated.

In order to address local concerns of health and safety, new mechanisms to deal with possible accidents need to be devised. These might include:

1. Increasing the liability provisions of the Price-Anderson Act--A best estimate of the cost of a worst case accident could be devised and used as a liability ceiling. A recent version of proposed bill, HR 3809, recommended that Price-Anderson coverage be increased to $5 billion. Problems with this would arise in that the whole nuclear industry would be affected; the original intent of the Act was to limit individual liability to defray risk costs to the industry (Burness, 1981).[4]

2. Posting of a performance bond--to cover the estimated costs of a necessary cleanup.

3. Institution of a cleanup "Superfund"--P.L. 96-510, the Comprehensive Environmental Response, Compensation, and Liability Act of 1980, calls for vessels carrying hazardous waste to establish and maintain liability coverage for their contents; this can take the form of insurance, surety bond, guarantee, or self-insurance. A similar approach could be used for radioactive waste.

Approaches such as those which remove liability ceilings for accidents have several advantages. They assure the local community that they will be compensated in the event of a major accident, as opposed to the case where the legal framework removes the developer from bearing the consequences of such an event. Also, by being forced to internalize the costs of a possible accident, the developer is given the incentive to reduce the possibilities of an accident a priori (Faas, 1982b). In conclusion, providing for the developer to bear the risk of an accident yields three major benefits. It:

1. provides the developer with the incentive to reduce accident probabilities through design and operation safeguards

2. assures the local population that they are being compensated for risk-taking, and that the developer will be making every effort to minimize risks

3. assures that the project reflects its true social costs

Property Value Guarantees

Landowners in the repository area may be affected in three ways:

1. outright acquisition of the owner's land for the repository site

2. possible loss of property value

3. aversion to the facility so great that the owner is "forced" to move away

Since the first group presents no theoretical difficulties in compensation, the second and third groups will be addressed here.

Several methods of compensation are possible. Guarantees can be issued so that landowners are reimbursed for the difference between prefacility and postfacility value of their land. This could be done by preagreed formulas for estimating property value changes. Residents moving in after the facility is sited would be ineligible for these payments, since their compensation would take the form of a discounted property price. Residents moving away when the facility is sited would be eligible for a compensation payment, if it is later determined that postsiting property values have declined as a result of the project.

A second compensation measure might be to use a form of "inverse condemnation," whereby the developer purchases the owner's property at fair market value. Luke (1982) has expanded on this philosophy by recommending that property owners within a specified "impact zone" be eligible for payment of 125 percent of fair market value, the extra 25 percent being compensation for moving and inconvenience. If the landowner resettled within the impact zone, he or she would be ineligible for the additional 25 percent payment.[5]

Burden of Proof. A final consideration is to assure local communities that they may obtain timely and appropriate redress of negative project impacts. In many cases, contractual costs in proving damages can be high, if not prohibitively expensive. The Washington State Energy Facility Site Evaluation Council (EFSEC), for example, provides that the energy developer pay "any valid claims against it . . . arising out of any actually incurred or clearly anticipated net financial burden . . ." but that the burden of validating "any such claim shall be upon the claimant" (EFSEC, 1976).

One possible means of lessening the burden of proof might be for the developer to post a bond or create an impact mitigation trust fund, whereby the developer must prove claims against it invalid. This would shift the transactions cost back on the developer to prove that there would be no adverse impacts (Faas, 1980).

CONCLUSIONS AND IMPLICATIONS

This chapter and the two that precede it have attempted to develop a framework for an impact management plan for a high level nuclear waste repository. The approach has examined past experiences in impact mitigation to draw insight into possible problems in repository development. In addition, methods for development of an impact management plan including assessment, management, and monitoring have been discussed. Finally, several of the repository's unique features which may pose problems in mitigation planning have been elaborated.

In addition to the issues discussed in this chapter, the importance of public participation in the siting process bears re-emphasis. Although local involvement is a necessity in any attempt at mitigation planning, it is especially important in the case of the nuclear waste repository. Constructive involvement of state and local officials, as well as local citizens, not only helps in identifying social and economic impacts--it can be a mitigation measure in itself (see chapter 15).

It is also important that the sponsoring agency pay special attention to the local political and social climate of any area chosen for study. Questions of participation techniques and public perceptions must be answered on a site-specific basis. There is no reason why local reaction to the siting procedure in Utah or Texas would be the same as in Wisconsin or Mississippi. Therefore, each location should be dealt with individually. Before any formal studies are undertaken in an area, care must be taken to identify key public figures, groups, and issues, and to establish communication with these groups so that information can be disseminated and participation encouraged.

In conclusion, we feel that drawing from the strengths and experiences of past mitigation efforts--and combining this knowledge with careful review and analysis of both the unique features of the repository and the characteristics of the final site chosen--an effective socioeconomic impact mitigation plan for repository siting can be developed. The key to the success of the planning effort is that the process consider all aspects of repository development, from initial siting considerations to closure and monitoring.

NOTES

1. They will, however, be eligible for payments-in-lieu-of-taxes (PILOT), in the amount of the tax that would have been paid on the repository land in its undeveloped state (see chapter 10).

2. These attributes are a synthesis of recommendations of the President's Economic Adjustment Committee's **Community Impact Assistance Study** (1981).

3. An externality is an external benefit or cost of an activity for which no compensation is made (also called a spillover).

4. Increasing Price-Anderson coverage alone would not necessarily enhance risk internalizing; this would depend on whether the additional insurance coverage was assumed by private industry or by the Federal Government.

5. A consideration that should be made here is that the agency purchasing the property look at **relocation cost** as well as fair market value, that is, if property values in the host community are already relatively low, the displaced landowner may not be able to purchase new property in the surrounding region.

Local Community
Response and Participation
in Nuclear Waste
Repository Siting

13
Community Response to Large-Scale Federal Projects: The Case of the MX

Stan L. Albrecht

One of the most difficult aspects in evaluating the potential community response to nuclear waste repository siting lies in the fact that no repository has ever been constructed and thus there is simply no historical base from which to judge the potential response to such a facility. In addition, because repositories are to be Federal projects which address a national concern but which require that only a few rural areas bear the impacts and potential risks of the project, many of the findings from impact analysis of large-scale private or even of regionally oriented public projects that dominate the impact literature (Murdock and Leistritz, 1979) are of limited applicability to understanding community response to repository sitings.

Large-scale defense projects, particularly if they hold potential risks for the siting area, may be more applicable. One such project that may be particularly applicable to the community response issues related to repositories is the MX missile system. The recent response of communities in Utah and Nevada to the MX has several direct and important parallels with those community participation and response issues likely to surround repository siting. An analysis of community response to the MX system may thus provide one means of identifying those factors likely to be important in determining community response to repository siting.

This chapter thus provides a description of community response to the early proposals for MX siting in Utah and Nevada, delineates those factors which appear to have affected the nature of that response, and suggests how such factors are likely to be paralleled in nuclear repository siting. Specifically the chapter provides: (1) a brief overview of the MX system's characteristics and the potential impacts it would have had on the rural areas in Utah and Nevada where it was to be located, (2) a description of the patterns of community mobilization that occurred in Utah and Nevada in response to the MX system, and (3) describes the parallels between patterns of community response to the

234

MX and those likely to be important in repository siting. The intent, then, is to use the experience gained from a large-scale project that is similar in many respects to respositories[1] to identify community concerns that are likely to affect respository siting.

THE MX SYSTEM

As originally proposed, MX would be a new missile, more than twice the size of the Minuteman III which is currently the most modern U.S. missile aimed at the Soviet Union. It would be 71 feet long, 92 inches in diameter, and would weigh 192,000 pounds. It would be equipped with 10 separate nuclear warheads, each independently targetable. Each of these 10 high-powered warheads would be about twice as accurate as the Minuteman which carries a maximum payload of 3 nuclear warheads (U.S. Department of the Air Force, 1981; Utah Consortium for Energy Research and Education, 1981).

As originally proposed, the system would deploy 200 of these new missiles among 4600 multiple protective structures (MPS). That is, each of the 200 missiles would have 23 separate protective structures from which it could be launched. The MPS sites would be of sufficient hardness and spacing that no Soviet warhead could destroy more than one site. Since the locations of the missiles among the 23 potential launch sites would be unknown to the attacker, he would have to destroy substantially all of them to ensure that he had eliminated the United States' land-based missile force (U.S. Department of the Air Force, 1981; Utah Consortium for Energy Research and Education, 1981).

The construction of this system has been described quite simply as the largest public works project ever undertaken in the history of this country. It is estimated that the construction effort would be at least two and one-half times that required to build the Alaskan pipeline (U.S. Department of the Air Force, 1981; Utah Consortium for Energy Research and Education, 1981). As proposed, the MX would require the construction of 12,000 miles of road, and would use twice the amount of concrete used in Hoover Dam. It would also use 1.6 million tons of steel, 86 million tons of gravel, and 5.6 million tons of sand. The proposed site itself in the Great Basin area of Utah and Nevada is equal in size to the combined area of 5 Eastern Seaboard states of Vermont, New Hampshire, Rhode Island, Massachusetts, and Connecticut (U.S. Department of the Air Force, 1981; Utah Consortium for Energy Research and Education, 1981).

The communities to be impacted by the project, as originally sited, are very small communities relative to the projected impacts of the project. In Utah, communities nearest the sites include Minersville,

Milford, Beryl, Delta, and Hinkley. In Nevada, they are Pioche, Tonopah, McGill, Ruth, and Ely. These relatively tiny communities are located in a sea of Federally-owned land. In fact, more than 90 percent of the 31,000 square-mile area where the Air Force would build the MX system is owned by the Federal government (U.S. Department of the Air Force, 1981; Utah Consortium for Energy Research and Education, 1981).

The area is sparsely populated and none of the communities are well prepared to inherit a large population influx. Delta is the largest community on the Utah side that is near one of the proposed bases and its population is only about 2,000. Nevada impact areas are likewise characterized by small, rural communities (the one exception to this is Las Vegas which would have absorbed much of the impact that would have been associated with a construction base in the Coyote Spring Valley area). In addition to smallness, the population of the area exhibits other characteristics that imply even more significant impacts than would be the case in an area having rather different characteristics.

The present population of the area, particularly on the Utah side of the border, is remarkably homogeneous and stable. For example, more than half of the residents of Millard County in Utah have lived there for 40 years or more. In a society that has been characterized by high levels of population mobility, this is a rather unusual statistic. The high level of social and cultural homogeneity of the area is reflected in the fact that over 90 percent of all residents in the four impact counties are members of the Mormon Church (Architect/Planners Alliance, 1980). Nevada communities are more diverse religiously but are quite homogeneous in other ways.

The project itself was originally projected to require 28,000 construction workers and lead to an influx of 105,000 new residents. Over 10,000 housing units, 780 new school classrooms and 1,800 new school personnel would be required in the two-state impact area. Medical and human services, water and sewer services, police, fire and nearly all other services would require substantial and costly upgrading (U.S. Department of the Air Force, 1981; Utah Consortium for Energy Research and Education, 1981). The Federal lands in the area on which the project would be located are presently used for grazing and many ranch-related activities would thus be displaced by the project. The rural and recreational activities that residents cherish would also be altered. In conjunction with the substantial impacts of energy development expected in the area, the MX system would thus thoroughly alter the socioeconomic structure of the areas in which the system was to be sited.[2]

In many ways, however, the site area was one that might be expected to be receptive to a national defense growth inducing project. As will be noted, residents of the area could generally be characterized as progrowth and pronational defense. By the height of the MX debate, however, residents in the area were nearly uniformly opposed to the MX (see table 13.1) with a majority of those of both sexes, different ages, political parties, educational levels, and religious orientations in both states opposing the siting of the MX system. Given the area's history of strong support for growth and for defense, why did many local residents mobilize in opposition to the MX system? Although the magnitude of the project clearly played a role in leading to local negative responses, several other factors, described below, also played a major role in creating local opposition.

COMMUNITY MOBILIZATION

In recent years there has developed a growing literature concerning factors that are important in community mobilization. The question has usually been: "Under what conditions do communities become mobilized in response to particular issues or needs?" Bridgeland and Sofranko (1975: 186-187) have noted that two different explanatory frameworks have been offered to account for differences in community mobilization:

> The first, for which there is a considerable amount of research data, emphasizes elements of community structure: communities mobilize, and move quickly, because of certain sociodemographic, organization, or cultural features of the resident population.

> The other explanatory perspective has focused more on issue-specific factors: communities become mobilized in relation to the centrality of an issue for the community; when community leaders become aware of a problem; when a problem becomes serious; or when a 'precipitating' event occurs which focuses attention on or sensitizes the public to an issue.

Much of the research on these issues has been conducted in large urban communities. And a large proportion of the research has been designed to test the first explanatory framework; that is, that community structural characteristics are critical in determining community response to issues. For example, Crain and Rosenthal (Crain and Rosenthal, 1967; Rosenthal and Crain, 1968) observed that the particular **form** of city government was important in determining the success of

Table 13.1

**Attitudes Toward Deploying MX in Utah
and Nevada by Respondent Categories[1]**

Respondent Categories	(N)	Strongly Favor	Somewhat Favor	Somewhat Oppose	Stongly Oppose	No Opinion
TOTAL	(400)	11.2	17.2	19.2	46.2	6.0
Sex						
Male	(194)	14.4	17.0	19.1	44.3	5.2
Female	(206)	8.3	17.5	19.4	48.1	6.8
Age						
18-34	(127)	15.0	14.2	22.8	43.3	4.7
35-49	(106)	7.5	19.8	14.2	49.1	9.4
50+	(167)	10.8	18.0	19.8	46.7	4.8
Political Party						
Republican	(131)	10.7	15.3	22.9	45.0	6.1
Democrat	(168)	13.1	15.5	18.5	47.0	6.0
Independent	(93)	9.7	23.7	15.1	46.2	5.4
Other	(4)	0.0	25.0	0.0	50.0	25.0
Education						
Less than H.S.	(57)	15.8	15.8	21.1	38.6	8.8
High School	(150)	8.7	19.3	20.7	46.0	5.3
Some Col./Bus.	(134)	11.9	15.7	18.7	47.8	6.0
College Grad.	(58)	12.1	17.2	15.5	50.0	5.2
Religion						
Catholic	(44)	18.2	2.3	18.2	52.3	9.1
Protestant	(69)	4.3	13.0	14.5	59.4	8.7
LDS	(229)	10.0	21.4	21.8	41.9	4.8
Other	(27)	14.8	18.5	29.6	33.3	3.7
None	(29)	24.1	17.2	3.4	48.3	6.9
Area						
Southern Utah	(200)	11.0	22.0	22.0	41.0	4.0
Nevada	(200)	11.5	12.5	16.5	51.5	8.0

[1]Question: From what you know or have heard, do you favor or oppose the Air Force plan for deployment of the MX Missile Project in the desert area of Utah and Nevada?

Source: Dan Jones and Associates Poll conducted for the **Deseret News**, March, 1980.

referenda on fluoridation of city water supplies.
Similarly, Aiken and Alford (1968, 1970), in studying the
success of communities in mobilizing to receive Federal
funds and to participate in other Federally-sponsored
programs, found that such structural characteristics as
population diversity, income level, political culture,
political structure, organizational density, level of
integration, bureaucratization, and occupational
structure were important in predicting response to the
war on poverty, public housing, urban renewal, and other
such programs.

Bridgeland and Sofranko (1975) argue, however, that
community mobilization can only be understood by looking
both at structural characteristics of communities and at
issue-specific variables. They define community
mobilization as a combination of three factors: (1)
public awareness of the issue, (2) public involvement in
efforts to change some current or projected event (or, in
some instances, prevent its happening at all), and (3)
public commitment of resources to accomplish the goal.
These authors concluded in their analysis of community
response to environmental issues that there is no
adequate single indicator of mobilization across all
communities. That is, in some cases structural
characteristics were more predictive of outcomes while in
others, issue-specific factors were more important.
However, they do support Downs' (1972) thesis that
dramatic events and incidents play an important role in
community mobilization on environmental issues in that
presence or absence of an environmental incident was the
single most important explanatory variable in their
analysis.

While data are not available to test either the
community structure model or the issue centrality model
in explaining the mobilization of local residents in
response to the MX proposal, observational data indicate
that both are important. In terms of the former,
leadership for the movement emerged primarily from the
larger communities and from among the more highly
educated, professionally trained segments of these
communities. However, the "dramatic event" of the
proposed construction of the MX in Utah and Nevada may be
an even more critical factor in the mobilization of local
community response. It is generally true that the closer
to the area where the missile would be based, the higher
the level of opposition that was expressed. A clear
majority of the large number of rural Nevada and Utah
residents who attended the several scoping meetings that
were held by the Air Force to present the plans for the
construction of the MX were from the communities nearest
where the missiles were to be sited and a large
percentage of these attendees expressed clear opposition
to the project.

In attempting to assess the emergence of this high

level of local opposition to the project, we will focus
primarily on the community of Delta in Millard County in
Utah which is near where one of the Air Force bases would
have been located and is in the midst of the area where
many of the 4,600 MX shelters were proposed to be
constructed. What happened in Delta may not be identical
to what happened throughout the area. Nevertheless, the
Delta experience parallels what happened in many other
communities. In addition, the process through which an
anti-MX movement emerged in Delta makes this an
interesting focus for study.

In studying the emergence of anti-MX movement in the
Delta area, it is important to again stress the general
attitude and value patterns of local residents as these
relate to the abstract issues of growth, patriotism, and
national defense. Three issues need to be emphasized:

(1) Residents of this entire area tend to be
strongly progrowth. For many decades they have
experienced a stagnating local economy. A high
percentage of young people have been forced to migrate
from the area following high school in order to obtain
employment. Many local residents are farmers and
ranchers and a majority of these operations have been
very marginal for a number of years. Accordingly, the
children of the ranching and farming families have been
encouraged to leave the area, even though many of them
would prefer to live locally. Because of this history,
local residents have tended to favor practically any sort
of industry or other development of the area. This
attitude has not been unlike that which Molotch (1976)
attributes to most American communities. He argues that
"the political and economic essence of virtually any
given locality, in the present American context, is
growth." In fact, Molotch argues that localities are
constantly competing with each other to gain the
preconditions of growth. On the surface, then, MX with
its huge infusion of job and income opportunities should
have been viewed favorably by local residents.

(2) Residents of the area are highly patriotic.
This is an area of the country where there was virtually
no opposition to American involvement in Vietnam.
Residents viewed it as their duty to support their
government and were proud to do so. Most of them found
it difficult to understand what they were seeing happen
in other areas of the country. Being an American and
supporting one's government are highly valued.

(3) Finally, local residents are very hawkish in
their military posture. They are concerned about a
potential Soviet threat to their country. As a result,
they favor a strong military and support the expenditure
of large sums for national defense.

Given this set of attitudes, it is difficult to understand why strong opposition emerged to a system which would promote local growth with attendant job and income opportunities, that was presented as something local residents should favor as a patriotic duty, and that would appear to promote the development of a strong national defense.

There are two critical issues that help us understand what happened. One of these contributed to the emergence of the anti-MX group; the other contributed to its continued viability. In terms of the first, one cannot underestimate the anger that was created in the local communities by the Air Force in the scoping meetings. The behavior of the Air Force spokespersons is generally described as "patronizing" and "antagonistic." The following are some quotes obtained from members of the anti-MX group describing their impressions of the actions of the Air Force:

They came in like we were a bunch of local hicks. It was clear that they had no appreciation or concern for our local values or lifestyles. 'You are expendable' was the clear message that we received.

We were being defined as expendable, inconsequential. We are not a commodity to be expended. We have been looking around the area for an endangered fish or an endangered species of some sort so that we could get someone to listen to us. Obviously, they don't care about people.

Some of the people they have sent in to talk with us are so obnoxious the Russians would almost be a welcome change.

They acted like we knew nothing. We surprised them because we were informed and interested and were not going off half-cocked.

The tragedy is that they have made the average citizen feel inconsequential. This is what makes us angry.

They expected us to do anything they wanted us to do under the assumption that the Air Force knows best.

The public relations failure of the MX spokespersons is well summarized by a recent editorial in the **Salt Lake Tribune** in response to new proposals for siting nuclear waste repositories in Southeastern Utah:

Utah officials, the news report said, are
hoping the state won't be in the same position
with the Federal Government as it now is with
the MX when it comes to developing repositories
for nuclear wastes. And small wonder.

MX is being imposed on Utah and neighboring
Nevada despite widespread objection from
residents of the two states. It is being
pushed to frightening reality despite well
identified possible alternatives, doubts as to
its ultimate usefulness, and fears that it's
deployment will inflict economic and social
hardship on the state during construction and
force the Soviet Union to more threatening
countermeasures.

Despite these and other objections, the
steamroller is lumbering along toward the
fragile deserts of Utah and Nevada where some
4,600 shelters will be constructed to house 200
of the new intercontinental ballistic missiles
called MX.

If that kind of disdain for contrary opinion
and local feeling is repeated in the nuclear
wastes disposal program, Utah officials and
residents have cause for concern . . .

If underground disposal of nuclear wastes is
found to be the best all around method and it
can be demonstrated that a Utah site is
preferable to all others, it should not be too
difficult to convince Utahns to accept the
"honor" proferred them. But Federal officials
charged with finding the best disposal site
must show greater political savvy and make a
more solid case for their project than the MX
merchants have done (**Salt Lake Tribune,**
November 17, 1980: A-10).

Following the first local scoping meeting on MX,
then, many area residents found themselves expressing
feelings of anger and frustration. Several of them
decided that they should become more informed on the
issue and so a number of experts of various types were
invited to speak in the area to discuss the potential
impacts of MX on ranching, mining, area water supplies,
and so on. The initial group engaged in an information
gathering and dissemination action. Their message to the
Air Force was that they refused simply to be run over
roughshod.
Many of the initial actions of the anti-MX group in

Delta were designed to gain legitimacy throughout the
community. Farmers and ranchers, local housewives,
church leaders, and others who would represent a general
cross-section of the community were invited to
participate with the group. This was a conscious effort
to diversify and to involve as many community leaders and
influentials as possible. The success of this effort can
be found in the degree of unanimity in the opposition one
finds toward MX in the Delta area.

While the initial movement grew out of anger
generated in part by the treatment that many local
residents felt they were receiving from the Air Force, it
retained its viability largely because of the doubts that
residents felt about the whole concept of basing the MX
in a large number of shelters in the deserts of Utah and
Nevada. Several group members indicated that they
strongly favored the deployment of an MX but became
convinced by the debates on the issue that the proposed
Air Force basing mode would become obsolete before it was
ever completed. Their concern was that their chosen
lifestyle would be destroyed for nought.

The vitality of the anti-MX group came largely from
its diversity. Many of the leaders of the group were
those one would expect from the literature to emerge as
leaders of voluntary organizations. They were better
educated and more likely to hold professional positions
than is true for the general populace. For example, the
leaders include a local newspaper editor, an M.D.,
several professionals working for the community office of
the state mental health and social services
organizations, and so on. Several of these leaders were
also fairly recent inmigrants to the area. They could be
characterized, on the surface, as exhibiting what has
come to be called the "last settler syndrome." That is,
they have lived in urban America, haven't liked it and so
have moved to a rural community to find a lifestyle that
is more pleasing to them. Having found this lifestyle,
they want to close the door behind them so that it is not
disrupted by others who will follow. The basic problem
with this thesis in Delta is that most of these people
were progrowth. Many were working actively for the
Intermountain Power Project. However, they did not want
to see the complete and total destruction of all that is
local and all that is valued. Many have made the point
that they have consciously chosen a particular way of
life. They could live elsewhere and they could probably
make more money elsewhere. However, they have chosen to
trade-off such economic benefits for other things they
find of value in small rural communities. They felt that
MX would destroy this unnecessarily.

Anti-MX activists have not taken these actions
without some cost. Local opinion was not entirely
unanimous, and so the opponents to MX were called
subversive and communistic by others who felt that to be

patriotic would mean accepting at any cost the program
proposed by the government. These pro-MX groups
basically argued that if the government felt the basing
of the MX in Utah and Nevada was needed for national
defense purposes, then the local residents should support
this decision whatever the consequences.

We can summarize the primary reasons for local
opposition to the MX as follows:

(1) Residents felt that the system was being
imposed on them by the Federal government with little
concern for or interest in local views and feelings.
This concern was compounded by the attitude that was
taken by many of the Air Force spokespersons during local
scoping meetings. The basic question asked was that of
whether or not local communities have any right to avoid
unpopular changes.

(2) Many local residents felt that a particular
basing mode was being imposed on them without adequate
consideration being given to possible alternatives.
These alternatives include the possiblity of split-
basing, which would put part of the system in another
area such as New Mexico and Texas or a totally different
basing mode such as hardened Minuteman silos or shallow
underwater submarine basing. Local support for the MX
increased considerably when residents were presented the
option of basing half the system in another area.

(3) Closely related to the above point, a good deal
of local concern was expressed as to the ultimate
usefulness of the proposed system. For example, many
experts felt that the system would be obsolete before it
was ever completed and that less costly alternatives are
available that would offer an adequate degree of
deterrent effect.

(4) Finally, it was felt that the system would
inflict economic and social hardships on the area that
are of far greater magnitude than has been true of any
other project in the past. Many local residents felt
that they would be simply unable to deal with impacts of
this magnitude.

PARALLELS WITH NUCLEAR REPOSITORY SITING

To this point, particular emphasis has been given to
a discussion of community mobilization in response to the
proposals made by the Air Force to locate the missile
system near relatively isolated, sparsely populated rural
communities in Utah and Nevada. This discussion
demonstrates types of problems that have emerged and will
emerge in response to proposals to locate other

controversial programs like nuclear waste storage facilities. Some of these directly parallel problems of siting the MX missile and siting nuclear waste storage facilities are identified below.

The parallels between the two problems of nuclear repository siting and the MX missile project make an understanding of what has happened with MX relevant to the question of repository siting. Among the most important of these are the following:

The Issue of Public Involvement

Both the problem of nuclear waste repository siting and that of the construction of a highly sophisticated, very costly military weapons system raise the question of public involvement. For example, to what extent should the public be involved in policy decisions regarding something like nuclear waste or the development of a weapons system? Brenner (1979: 4) has recently noted:

> The impacts of governmental policies relating to the deployment of controversial technologies are often powerful and pervasive. There is now a heightened public awareness that decisions relating to issues such as the siting of energy facilities give rise to major social, economic, and environmental changes. These issues have become politically volatile after a long period of relative insulation from public scrutiny.

In a recent public policy conference concerned with the nuclear waste siting issue, it was argued that the decision-making process should be open and fair and that it should provide the opportunity for feedback from the public at all levels (Hebert et al., 1978). Similar arguments have been made quite clear in both cases that because of critical national security issues, states and local areas may not be granted veto power over siting decisions. However, because both cases involve the siting of a Federally-desired but highly controversial technology in a local area, local and state governments appear to want to have a major input into siting decisions. Any attempt on the part of the Federal Government to ignore local input will lead to cries against "Federal imperialism" (Brenner, 1979: 2a).

Because of a perceived lack of attention to local concerns, many people ask the question of whether we should bother with public involvement at all. Assuming that our society still values public input into important policy decisions, the critical question seems to be one of how that process can be made more meaningful and relevant.

245

The Issue of Confidence

Public involvement might not be such an important question if the public had more confidence in the Federal and nuclear industry decision makers (Hebert et al., 1978: 11), or in those individuals who are responsible for defense policy. In both cases, there is a good deal of ambiguity among the general public as to whether or not they can place much confidence in what they are being told.

Brenner (1979: 6) argues that policymakers must legitimize their claim that a particular technology or program is necessary by creating both public confidence in a program and at least some degree of consensus for it--particularly among the groups which will be most heavily impacted. Otherwise, he notes, the tendencies of a fragmented political system to permit dissenting groups to distort or even gut a policy or proposal will prevail.

He also argues (Brenner 1979: 10) that siting of nuclear waste repositories cannot be viewed solely as a technical process. The same thing can be said about the siting of a controversial military weapons system. Decision makers must recognize that political problems are at least as critical as technical problems. This is particularly true if they hope to obtain state and local approval for a particular proposal. In both instances far more time and resources have been spent on dealing with technical problems and project feasibility issues, and political and social concerns have only been considered after the fact. This is a critical mistake. Decision makers must search out and respond to the concerns of a variety of groups relatively early in the decision-making process. In fact, Green and Hunter (1978) argue that political opposition or concern, whether by community residents or special interest groups, will be one of the most significant impacts associated with the siting of nuclear waste repositories. Accordingly, it must be taken very seriously.

Uncertainty About Expert Testimony

Closely related to the above point is what appears to be a growing public uncertainty about whose statements can really be believed. In both the cases of repository siting and the MX missile there are highly reputable scientists testifying on almost every side of the issue. In the case of nuclear waste storage, three questions seem central (Hebert et al., 1978: 11): (a) uncertainty regarding just what the effects of low levels of radiation received in low doses over long periods of time will be, (b) uncertainty about whether the wastes can be kept out of the biosphere for long enough periods, and (c) uncertainty regarding human fallibility and malevolence.

With the MX missile system, uncertainty also revolves around a series of points: (a) the need for a new missile to serve as a counterforce to increased Soviet ability to destroy our land-based Minuteman system, (b) the strategic necessity of maintaining the land-based leg of the military triad, (c) whether the proposed basing mode is the most effective and viable, (d) whether the two key ingredients of concealment and mobility can be maintained, (e) whether or not the system will become obsolete even before it is completed because of new advances in Soviet technology and weapons development, and (f) whether the land-based MX is either the least expensive or the most survivable alternative.

Both the MX missile and nuclear waste repository siting are examples of highly controversial technologies. The lack of consensus among experts regarding these technologies greatly complicates the situation for the lay public.

Risk and Equity Issues

In response to the nuclear waste storage question, Hebert et al. (1978: 14-15) asked some important equity questions:

> Another important risk issue related to radioactive waste disposal is the distribution of risk due to the geographic location of a waste repository. Should a person who possibly does not benefit from nuclear power be put at risk because of the proximity of a waste repository? Should residents of a state having a waste repository be put at risk from radioactive wastes generated in other states?

They also note that:

> There is no mechanism in place for compensating a person who lives near a waste repository for being involuntarily placed at risk and none for compensating the person if he or she actually suffers genetic or health damage either now or in the future.

Locating the MX in the Great Basin would seriously impact local communities. Area residents would suffer the most deleterious socioeconomic impacts from MX construction because the large influx of outsiders would dramatically and permanently change current lifestyle patterns. On the other hand, the benefits from a military defense system or from a nuclear waste repository are much more widespread--they theoretically benefit the entire country. Brenner (1979) notes that controversial technologies tend to almost always produce an inequitable distribution of costs and benefits. Costs tend to focus on small, more highly localized groups while the benefits are more widely dispersed. Is this an equitable decision? Some have argued that the Great Basin has been selected as the prime site for the MX because of the low population density of the area and the consequent lack of political clout. Questions of equity will remain of critical importance to the future of both efforts.

Questions of equity almost inevitably lead to questions of compensation. Do individuals and communities have any right to expect compensation when unpopular change is forced upon them by an outside governmental entity? If so, what should be the nature of that compensation? The question of compensation for those most negatively impacted by the siting of a nuclear waste facility is discussed at some length in a recent paper by Cole and Smith (1979). They argue that some equitable method of compensation must be developed in the case of nuclear repository siting. In the case of a military installation, a precedent has already been set for compensating local communities as evidenced by what happened when the Navy built the Trident submarine base in the state of Washington. (Further discussion of mitigation efforts is found in the preceding section of this book.)

The Problem of Security

Both the MX and the nuclear waste issues are enmeshed in important security questions. Since the MX is dependent upon concealment, it is critical that no one develops the capability to determine which of the twenty-three potential launch sites really contains the missile. The Air Force claims that point security can be used whereby only the immediate site is fenced. If true, this will only require about 25 square miles to be closed to the public. However, if it is later determined that area security is required, then the amount of land closed to the public would be much larger--approximately 1600 square miles--and would have very dramatic impacts on local residents. Ranchers would lose grazing rights in the area; miners would no longer be able to explore for and mine important mineral deposits; hunters, fishers, backpackers, and campers would be kept out of an area that is used extensively for all of these purposes now. The nuclear waste issue is also characterized by important security concerns. What would happen, for example, if reprocessible materials are stolen by terrorist groups? How can it be guaranteed that a system of secure transportation to the repository can be developed? Some have expressed the fear that adequate security against such threats will be obtained only at the price of gradual infringements of personal freedom

248

(Flowers, 1976).

The Question of Alternatives

It has been argued that how one perceives the ability of resource conservation and nonnuclear power production to meet power needs will greatly affect perceptions of nuclear waste issues (Hebert et al., 1978). For example, if one believes that alternative policies will result in superior means of meeting energy needs, then one would be less inclined to support policies that will produce nuclear wastes. There are also important alternatives that can affect attitudes toward the MX. These include alternative basing modes, more emphasis on international arms control treaties, the selection of entirely different weapons systems, and so on. The presence of what some see as viable alternatives in both cases makes the debate more lively.

Cost

Finally there is the question of cost. Both the development of the MX and the development of waste storage facilities will entail very significant costs.

CONCLUSIONS

The problems associated with the introduction of major projects like the MX missile system or nuclear waste repositories into what are basically rural or semi-rural areas of the country are significant and demand continued attention. In the past, the deployment of highly controversial technologies such as these received relatively limited public scrutiny. However, the growth of a much more environmentally conscious citizenry, combined with numerous new Federal and state regulations that require a very careful consideration of important environmental, economic, and social consequences of projects such as these, has dramatically changed the picture. Siting decisions have now become highly volatile and have moved us toward the point where technical problems often become almost secondary to political problems.

Of particular interest from the point of view of social impacts is the fact that siting decisions, when these are applied to things like nuclear waste storage and, to a lesser extent, military installations, raise important equity concerns at the local community level. It has been noted that the costs associated with such projects often tend to be highly localized while the benefits are much more widely dispersed. Yet, there are some important benefits that can accrue to the local community. For example, as was noted earlier, many of the areas that are potential sites for operating or construction bases for the MX missile system or where nuclear waste repositories might be located are areas that have gone through periods of economic stagnation and decline. Projects such as these, properly managed, can reverse trends of population outmigration and can provide an important infusion of jobs and economic opportunities for current and future inhabitants. However, to have more positive impacts will require different approaches than have often been used in the past.

Based on the experience with the MX missile system, several important lessons can be learned. Briefly, these can be noted as follows:

(1) Local residents are often being asked to accept a disproportionate share of the potential negative impacts of projects like the MX missile system and nuclear waste repository sites. Therefore it is not fair to ask them to assume these costs simply on an appeal to their patriotism. Residents in the Great Basin area of Utah and Nevada are highly patriotic, but this message has come to wear rather thin. Because they will be most heavily impacted, local citizens should be involved in the siting process at an early stage.

(2) Closely related to this is the suggestion that care be taken to approach and interact with locals on an "equals" basis, and not on the basis of one-way information dissemination. The quotes from the residents of Delta, Utah in response to public presentations made by the Air Force indicate how people react when treated as second class citizens. If local residents are treated as if they really matter, then the message that "you are inconsequential" or that "you are expendable" will never come through.

(3) It is evident from the MX experience that local residents are likely to be extremely sensitive to the feeling that there has not been a full assessment of alternatives or that other alternatives have been ruled out because of what appear to be unfair or unreasonable criteria. The proposed MX missile system and nuclear waste repository siting are, almost by definition, highly controversial. Because of this, many options have been and continue to be examined. While the lay public cannot be expected to understand all of the technical details of these various options, they need to be able to see how a particular decision has been reached. If a particular choice is best, then this should be communicated to an audience in a manner that they can understand. One can virtually guarantee local anger and opposition if it appears that a siting decision has been made on the basis of what is politically expedient rather than on some set of more clearly defendable criteria. Many times these decisions come down to political expediency, and if this

is the case, perhaps greater emphasis should be placed on questions of compensating those communities and individuals who must experience the most negative impacts.

NOTES

1. There are of course numerous differences in the two projects. Assuming location in a salt deposit, repository work forces are not expected to exceed 2,000, and the land area covered by a repository is unlikely to exceed 10,000 acres. The similarity between the two types of projects must thus be seen as lying more in the social and psychological response they elicit in siting areas' residents than in their specific project characteristics.

2. Although the Air Force later scaled down its projected workforce, the impacts remained large compared to the populations of the local areas.

3. These major objections have been summarized in more detail in a Congressional Research Service Issue Brief, entitled "MX Intercontinental Ballistic Missile Program." Issue Brief Number IB77080, The Library of Congress, Congressional Research Service, Washington, D.C.

14
Community Development in Nuclear Waste Isolation

Donald E. Voth
Billy E. Herrington

Community development and the community development process are well established aspects of the social science literature and of the applied social sciences. Although community development has a wide variety of connotations, it can generally be defined as:

(1) a group of people (2) in a community (3) reaching a decision (4) to initiate a social action process (i.e., planned intervention) (5) to change (6) their economic, social, cultural, or environmental situations (Christenson and Robinson, 1980: 12).

The similarity of community development processes and issues to the policy and management issues faced in siting nuclear waste repositories are evident. The Federal repository siting process is, in fact, a concerted community development program (see chapter 3). The levels of intergovernmental cooperation, the discussion of alternative forms of mitigation, the development of intracommunity and intercommunity information systems, and assessments basic to the repository siting process are also basic to any community development process. The long history of community development projects and the literature derived from them can thus be used to describe both the phases through which the community development aspects of the siting process might proceed and to suggest specific approaches that might be used in the process of working with potential siting communities.

The purpose of this chapter is thus twofold: (1) to delineate basic approaches and steps in the community development process that may be applicable to repository siting and (2) to outline and evaluate several alternative specific approaches for community development in repository siting areas. The intent then is to show both the general and specific relevance of community development to nuclear repository siting.

ALTERNATIVE ROLES FOR COMMUNITY DEVELOPMENT

Community developers have identified several
different general strategies that can be followed
(Christenson, 1980; Warren, 1977: 119-157; Rothman,
1979). We shall focus upon these different strategies in
describing community development since they provide
alternative approaches that should be considered in the
nuclear waste repository siting process. Both Rothman
(1979) and Christenson (1980) identify three strategies.
Although the two authors use different labels, the
strategy types each developed are almost identical (see
table 14.1).

Table 14.1

Community Development Approaches

Strategy	Rothman	Christenson
A	Locality development	Self-help approach
B	Social planning	Technical assistance approach
C	Social action	Conflict approach

The three strategies are discussed in detail by
Rothman (1979) and, in the Christenson and Robinson book
(1980), by Gamm and Fisher, Littrell, and Robinson. The
detailed discussions cannot be repeated here. However,
in the following sections, we discuss each of the three
strategies briefly.

Strategy A

In this strategy, the community is regarded as
viable or potentially viable and as having no
irreconcilable internal conflicts of interest. The
community makes its own decisions and achieves its own
goals. The task of the development agent is to assist
the community but not to make decisions for it. Thus,
the development agent is a catalyst and enabler. The
objective of this strategy is to improve community
capability rather than to complete specific tasks.

The locality development strategy was very popular
in rural development in the United States in the 1950s,
and was also adopted by many international agencies at

that time. Step-by-step procedures following the locality development strategy have been presented by Beal and Hobbs (1964), Poston (1953, 1976), the U.S. Chamber of Commerce (1968), and Strauss and Stowe (1974). It depends heavily upon voluntary participation in study and action committees, upon the use of community-wide meetings or some similar organizational structure, and emphasizes the development of public and private sector cooperation and partnerships.

Strategy B

In this strategy, the community as such is less important. Community members are seen as consumers served by local decision makers and administrators. The task of the development agent is to provide technical assistance to administrators and decision makers to improve the quality of their decisions and of the services they deliver to and for community members. Gamm and Fisher identify three types of technical assistance which may be provided: (1) assistance in decision making, (2) assistance in developing community resources, and (3) assistance in the performing of specific tasks (1980: 53). Christenson characterizes this approach aptly as follows:

> The role of the technical intervenor or the planner is to assess the situation in a community, a county, or region, and, based on the best technical information (such as cost-benefit analysis), to suggest the most economically feasible and socially responsible approaches for improving the situation. Usually some sort of physical intervention is involved, for example, building a convention center, establishing a comprehensive plan, or developing zoning ordinances. Technical assistants and planners are primarily technicians who use professional skills in designing and developing physical projects (Christenson, 1980: 46).

The emphasis in this strategy is upon a rational process, whereas the emphasis in the locality development strategy is involvement. Due, no doubt, to the increased complexity of the issues confronting communities in contemporary society, this strategy of community development has become more popular recently.

Strategy C

The conflict strategy focuses upon power, its use, and its redistribution. Those who use it emphasize building power bases through organization, the building of coalitions, and so on. Its objectives may be building the community's capabilities on the one hand, or much more specific tasks on the other. In either case power and influence, and ways that power and influence can be seized, are paramount. Saul Alinsky (1946) was one of the first protagonists of this strategy, and ACORN (Association of Community Organizations for Reform Now) is one of the most prominent organizations using it currently (Arkansas Institute for Social Justice, 1977). Evidently, a version was used by local residents in a conflict with the Corps of Engineers at the North Bonneville power generating project (**Christian Science Monitor**, 1978). Finally, Strategy C was widely adopted, sometimes with disruptive results, in the War on Poverty of the 1960s (Weissman, 1969; Kahn, 1970; Rubin, 1969).

The three approaches thus represent different roles and serve somewhat different functions. Only the first two seem viable within the context of nuclear repository siting, and only these are examined in detail below.

STEPS IN THE COMMUNITY DEVELOPMENT PROCESS

Whatever approach is used in community development, certain processes must nearly always be addressed. The causal schema shown in figure 14.1, though not inclusive of all possible development processes, provides a useful characterization of some of the most critical processes that must be performed.

In figure 14.1, the community development process is expressed in terms of inputs, throughputs and outputs. The inputs are the techniques applied by community development practitioners and others operating in specific agencies or organizations. The throughputs are the actual changes that happen to the communities and their behavior. The outputs are the objectives of community development. The latter are divided into process and content objectives, with the process objectives potentially being affected by all of the various community processes. Thus, for example, a community development practitioner might be called upon to assist in carrying out a community self-study, which could increase citizen involvement in community affairs. This, in turn, might improve the community's decision making capability. It might also contribute to the development of specific community improvement projects which create better community services. The various throughputs may be causally related to each other. Leadership development may contribute to community organization and vice-versa. Especially important in this regard is the contribution that experience with actual community projects and community planning and decision making makes toward leadership and organizational development in the community.

Inputs (Intervention Techniques)	Throughputs (Change in Community Behavior)	Outputs (Ultimate Objective of CD)
• Help in organizing, holding meetings, etc. Help with communications Overt community organization work	The development of networks and organizations within the community that can act for the community	Process Objectives: Improve problem solving capability of the community
• Help in surveys and self-study Help in use of mass media Training of citizens Public affairs programs	Mobilization, involvement, and education of community citizens	
• Provide technical information Help in planning, decision making, and implementation Help in obtaining resources	Carrying out projects and activities to improve the community A. Needs assessment and priority setting B. Planning and decision making C. Action and implementation	Content Objectives: Improve the quality of life of the community through improved services, etc.
• Help with leader identification and mobilization Leadership training	Emergence, development, and exercise of community leadership	

Figure 14.1

Causal Schema for Community Development

The inputs shown in figure 14.1 imply many of the concrete tasks that a community development practitioner might engage in during the community development process. These tasks would, typically, be followed in a logical, step-by-step fashion and might include, as a preliminary step, determination and delineation of the actual affected community. As these tasks make evident, then, the community development process involves a complex set of interrelated processes and procedures. How such procedures might be used to address the specific needs of repository siting is described below.

COMMUNITY DEVELOPMENT ALTERNATIVES
FOR NUCLEAR REPOSITORY SITING

Although a variety of development strategies might be employed in repository siting, the discussion here will focus on several strategies that represent a wide range of administrative and participatory alternatives. The intent is to describe a set of alternatives in detail and by so doing demonstrate the implications of the development process for repository siting.

The relevance of community development to nuclear waste isolation is to be considered in the context of some assumptions about the repository siting situation, some alternative decision-making scenarios, and some of the community development tasks that must be performed. These issues are taken up in turn in this chapter.

Assumptions

The nuclear waste isolation siting decision-making process is discussed in numerous publications prepared for or by DOE (U.S. Department of Energy, 1980b; Jakimo and Bupp, 1980; Greene and Hunter, 1978). Based upon these discussions, we make several assumptions about what would occur in the siting process.

First, we assume that since mined geologial disposal is the preferred method, waste disposal repositories would be located within the continental United States (Jakimo and Bupp, 1978). We also assume that heavily populated areas would be avoided to the extent possible, and that, as a consequence, repositories would be located in isolated areas or near small, rural communities.

Second, we assume that the building and maintenance of a nuclear waste repository would usually involve a small community within a reasonable distance of the repository to serve as the residence for repository facility personnel and to provide the day-to-day services required by these personnel and their families. While, if repositories were located in very remote sites, it might be necessary to literally create new communities to serve this function, we assume that this would not be the preferred method and that, in fact, it might not even be possible.

Finally, we make several assumptions about the decision process itself. We assume that numerous technically feasible potential sites will be located--or at least can be located. We assume that some form of mitigation and/or compensation assistance will or can be provided to affected communities by public or private concerns. We assume that the public's acceptance or rejection of nuclear waste repositories will be affected by (1) the behavior of the siting agency and by (2) the nature and extent of mitigation or compensation made available.

With this background, we can now consider several possible alternatives for the siting decision-making process and the several different community strategies that are implied.

We examine the potential implications of three alternatives:

Alternative 1--The siting agency (most likely DOE) makes the decision using both geological information and detailed socioeconomic information about the community and the potential impacts of the nuclear repository upon the community.

Alternative 2--The siting agency makes the decision as in Alternative 1, but provides the community with an intervenor or advocate to argue the community's case within the agency's decision-making environment. Presumably, the community would argue against selection, or the intervenor might be assigned specifically to argue the case for special segments within the community, such as the poor or elderly.

Alternative 3--The siting agency invites communities to engage in an auctioning process, with mitigation or compensation being the price paid by the siting agency to "purchase" acceptance. In this case, all potential communities would be informed that they were eligible. They would be advised of the forms of compensation available. Then they would be asked to present "bids" consisting of compensation packages that would make the repository acceptable to them. DOE would then select the least-cost site.

In Alternative 1, the siting decision and decisions about types or levels of compensation rest solely with the siting agency. Of course, information on economic, physical, and social impacts, as well as extensive input from the community may be used. However, the siting agency makes the decisions. This corresponds to the social planning strategy of community development. Although not identified as such, this is clearly the perspective of Greene and Hunter (1978).

Alternative 3, on the other hand, goes to the extreme of respecting the rights of the community as a unit. Although the same amount--perhaps even more-- of technical information may be used, the community itself decides whether or not it wants a nuclear repository and what it wants as compensation. Obviously, this makes very bold assumptions about the community's capacity, both to decide rationally and to treat all of its members with respect and fairness. Alternative 2 forms a logical intermediate step between Alternative 1 and 3 in terms of local control and participation.

When looked at in detail, the differences and implications of each approach become even more apparent. The third alternative involves potential communities engaging in an auctioning process in order to make the decision about siting, and at the same time, to set a price on mitigation and impact assistance. This process has been advocated for the siting of large-scale facilities by O'Hare, and he discusses the logic of the process in some detail (O'Hare, 1977; Susskind and O'Hare, 1977). O'Hare's proposal does differ from that presented here in that he rejects compensation to the community as a unit in favor of compensation to individuals, even though the decision about the compensation package would be a collective decision (O'Hare and Sanderson, 1977).

In the proposed bidding process, a number of potential sites would be identified by the siting agency, and all informed that they may be selected. The siting agency then: (1) indicates to the community the forms of compensation that can be made available, (2) supports a community organization process in which each of the communities decides whether or not they want to bid, and if they do, what kind of compensation package they will require as a bid, and (3) provides technical information and assistance to this community organization and decision-making process in each of the communities. Of special importance is the provision of information on impact assessment for use by the community in preparing a compensation package. When all bids are available, the siting agency selects the least-cost alternative as the community to receive the nuclear repository. At this point, the selected community enters into the implementation phase.

Realistically, there is a possibility that none of the potential communities will bid. Consequently, our proposal would include the possibility of falling back on Alternative 2 if this occurs. Of course, all communities must be informed of this possibility when the process begins. Alternative 2 requires that the siting agency provide an advocate or intervenor who can argue the point of view of the community in the siting agency's decision-making process itself. To be effective this will require close liaison with the community and community populations and, hence, will require substantial community organization.

For the social planning alternative (Alternative 1), the primary decision-making authority for site selection rests with the siting agency and is based upon agency-managed impact assessment and public involvement. It might have three phases. In the first phase, information would be collected, impact assessment performed, and a parallel public involvement program carried out to provide information from the public (feedback) to facilitate the decision-making process.

After site selection by the siting agency, the second phase would begin for the selected community. In this phase, the community would work with the siting agency in developing a detailed mitigation or compensation package. In Phase 2, emphasis would be placed on maximum community involvement in this process. This is consistent with the ideology of community development and with the discussion of the relevance of citizen participation to nuclear waste isolation by Howell and Olsen (1981). As such, the proposed Phase 2 would be as nearly parallel to Phase 2 of the bidding process as possible. The siting agency does have alternatives here, however. It could employ a more directly-managed citizen participation process allowing less autonomy to the community in the preparation and selection of a mitigation or compensation package than is implied by Phase 2. In the third and final phase, a full mitigation plan would be formulated through community-based organizations.

It is extremely important, in this approach, that several basic principles of such administratively-induced public participation be observed. These include the following:

1. The role that the public is to play in the decision-making process must be clearly defined and well known.

2. The points at which public input is desired must be clearly identified, well known, and announced well in advance.

3. The public must be informed about decisions that are made and, as much as possible, must be given the reasons for these decisions.

Whichever of the two approaches is used, the final

development step is that of implementation. Three issues related to implementation require concerted attention: (1) the selection of the agency that should be responsible for implementation, (2) the development of specific programs to address community needs, and (3) the selection of the personnel required to implement the development plan. Several alternatives have been proposed for selecting an implementation agency including using the siting agency itself, creating a regional or community task force, or even hiring independent contractors (Greene and Hunter, 1978). Whatever method is selected, it is essential that the agency have the ability to operate in an open-ended "process" environment; that is, be able to deal with conflict while protecting the community development practitioner's authority, that it be thoroughly committed to the community development process, and that it have credibility in the community. Such characteristics usually make the selection of a third (neither the community nor the siting agency) party desirable.

The type of feasible compensation or assistance programs may vary widely, but planning assistance as well as financial assistance is essential. In addition, a unified compensation program rather than one that involves numerous agencies is probably optimal for small communities with limited management resources. Finally, implementation will usually require the use of professional staff who have generalistic orientations, who are committed to and trained in public participation techniques, effective in small group interaction, and skilled in resource identification. In sum, programs specifically designed to meet the particular needs of a given community managed by professional community development specialists under the auspices of credible agencies are essential to effectively implement any development program.

The three approaches thus proposed, and the procedures necessary to implement them, represent a continuum of development scenarios from one that involves only negotiations over compensation after the siting agency has made its siting decision (Alternative 1) to one (Alternative 3) in which the community is a full participant in all selection and siting phases. These alternatives all require careful implementation. The approaches offer quite different advantages and disadvantages, however, and the examination of these advantages and disadvantages further demonstrates the need for, and the potential role of, community development in the siting process.

COMPARISON OF THE TWO ALTERNATIVES

The following discussion focuses upon the advantages

and disadvantages of Alternative 3, the auctioning process, and thus avoids repetition since most of its advantages imply parallel disadvantages of Alternative 1, the planning process and vice-versa. As an intermediate alternative, Alternative 2, shares some of the advantages and disadvantages of both Alternatives 1 and 3.

Advantages of Auctioning

The general objective of the auctioning process is to create a partnership between DOE, the implementing agency, and the local community. Such a partnership cannot be created through coercion but only through following a genuine community development and community decision-making process. Crucial to this process are a quasimarket approach and community involvement.

Quasimarket Approach. It is frequently taken for granted that detailed studies of the impacts of nuclear waste repository siting and their relative weights for different members of the community will have to be done in order to design equitable mitigation or compensation programs, and that these must then be applied by administrative fiat. Since, in the auctioning process, the public is required to come up with an overall price acceptable to at least a majority, much of this detailed analysis is unnecessary. This is especially true of that part of such impact analysis that is the most intractable to technical solution, the application of values or weights to the respective impacts.[1] In fact, it needs to be emphasized that the agency must still assist the public in the sense that the agency--or someone--must be able to provide concrete information on impacts such as the number of employees expected, the effects on school enrollments, and so on. What the agency does not have to do is to try to put dollar values on perceived disamenities associated with safety, rapid growth, and so forth. One of the costs associated with the disposal of nuclear wastes that is the most difficult to deal with is the potential impact on succeeding generations, since those generations cannot be consulted. As a result, the current generation must make a judgement concerning these values.

Community Involvement. While this expresses an important ideological commitment of community development, it would be naive to overlook its practical implications. In the case of repositories, the gainers (for example, users of electricity generated by nuclear power) are highly diffused, whereas the losers (residents of the affected communities) are concentrated. This, plus the recent history of hazardous waste disposal and extreme sensitivity about nuclear safety in general, may lead to strong opposition in employing the social action strategy. In fact, the spate of state laws prohibiting or severely restricting nuclear waste disposal is evidence of such resistance (see chapter 4). It seems clear that political resistance to nuclear waste repository siting poses the greatest threat to its resolution (Greene and Hunter, 1978: 2.3.1).

What is required in these circumstances is a mechanism whereby specific populations who may be affected in specific ways have the opportunity to examine those effects and decide, for themselves, what price they attach to them. This must be done in an environment of realism, in which all requisite technical information is made available. More importantly, it must be a genuine decision-making environment. That is, the outcome must not be predetermined. Under these circumstances, it should be possible to devise decision rules for a community to follow that would lead to its setting a mitigation or compensation price that makes the siting agency and the community partners in the task of building and operating a nuclear waste repository and greatly reduces the probability and force of opposition. Obviously, not all opposition will be prevented, even with the auctioning approach. However, the various cross-cutting ties of associations within the community (Coleman, 1957) will reduce the degree of conflict and facilitate compromise. Herein, of course, lies one of the greatest potential contributions of the techniques and ideology of community development to this issue. Finally, this involvement of the community in the preparation of a bid will prepare the community as a whole, and individuals and groups in the community, for participation in more detailed planning and in the actual implementation process.

Disadvantages of Auctioning

No Bid or Unrealistic Bid. Perhaps the most obvious disadvantage is the possibility that all potential communities would regard the disamenities of a nuclear waste repository as too great and simply would not bid at all. Or bids would be made unrealistically high, resulting in an unreasonable burden upon the utilities and their consuming public, and, consequently, a suboptimal allocation of resources.

The possibility of no bid or an unrealistic bid has been anticipated in the procedure outlined above. If that occurs, it is suggested that Scenario 2 be adopted; that is, the communities obtain intervenor assistance, but the siting agency makes the decision. Obviously, if the possibility of reverting to Scenario 2 exists, this fact must be known by the potential communities at the outset. This knowledge, while it should stimulate communities to bid, would have a negative effect upon the auctioning environment. The only way to eliminate this problem would be to allow the possibility that all communities approached in the initial phase could, in fact, reject the repository if they chose not to bid. The implications of this for the entire process are probably unacceptable.

Collective Bidding. Collective or community bidding has a number of advantages, as identified above. However, it also has disadvantages--or at least some elements that create both practical and theoretical problems. Generally, individual utilities of living in a community with a nuclear waste repository could not be aggregated in a simple linear fashion to derive a set of community utilities. There are problems of minority rights, of differential impact, and of determining the degree of acceptance of a mitigation proposal, as well as the distribution of acceptance among the population that is necessary to both effectively eliminate organized resistance and to motivate partnership with the siting agency. In theory, these issues are not unresolvable, but they do suggest the need for a very carefully designed decision process which is enforced by the siting agency. This may require both extraordinarily detailed check-off procedures such as hearings to protect the rights of minorities and to allow resistance to be heard.

Unrepresented Constituencies. One of the most serious problems of all approaches to resolution of the nuclear waste siting decision-making process is the inability to represent certain affected populations. Although the auctioning process emphasizes representation of current community residents, it does not solve this problem entirely. Future generations are still unrepresented, as are persons who may move to the community in the near future (for example, future employees of the nuclear waste repository).

Ethical Objections. Perhaps one of the most severe criticisms of the auctioning process is ethical. The argument is that poor communities will be more likely to bid than affluent communities, and that, consequently, the auctioning process will result in these communities accepting risks and negative effects they should not have to accept. The response to this objection is that whether or not the auctioning process is used, low-income communities may be more likely to be selected, at least if the repository is seen as a serious disamenity, since they do not have the power to resist whereas affluent communities do. Thus, it may become a question of whether technicians or the members of poor rural communities should set the price of compensation for the disamenitity they will experience.

In summary, the auctioning process assumes that the local community is capable of rational, democratic decision making and that such a decision-making process will be basically equitable as regards all populations within the community. It also assumes that such a decision-making process can be carried out in what may be a newly constructed community that includes several pre-existing jurisdictions, but which are all likely to be impacted by the nuclear waste repository. This would require, of course, collaboration of formal and informal leadership and the citizenry of the affected jurisdictions in the creation of a new decision-making entity. To the extent these assumptions cannot be met, the siting agency's alternative is to use a technical planning process which, while it uses community input, depends primarily upon analytic judgments made by technicians.

Strong arguments can be made on both theoretical and empirical grounds for both Alternatives 1 and 3. It is easy to find evidence of irrationality in local community decision making (Martin, 1964; Crain et al., 1969), especially when emotional issues are at stake. The criticisms of the outcomes of such decision making, on the one hand, tend to focus on the tendency of powerful local interests to take advantage of those with less influence, and the finding that emotional issues bring out actors who, because they are not normally active in local affairs, are uninformed and incapable of rational decision making. On the other hand, it has frequently been argued that technical planners and professional administrators also represent the limited perspective of the middle class and consequently are no more capable of making decisions that are equitable than are community people themselves.

In reality, of course, whichever alternative the siting agency chooses, the issues are not entirely black and white. If it chooses the auctioning alternative, it would be possible to impose a decision-making process that at least maximizes rationality and consideration for those likely to be overlooked by local power elites. On the other hand, if it chooses the planning perspective, it has considerable flexibility in the amount and type of community input it obtains.

SUMMARY

Community development and the processes associated with it provide a general set of guidelines applicable to the siting of nuclear waste repositories. On the basis of the basic premises of community development, a variety of community development approaches for completing the siting process can be suggested. The intent of this chapter has been to point out the importance and feasibility of a carefully designed, professionally administered, community development program in nuclear repository siting. Basic to any such process is open and concerted debate of key issues by siting agency and community residents and the display of mutual respect and consideration between residents and agency officials. The community development process and the successful siting of a large-scale public project, such as a repository, can only succeed if these elements form a foundation for such efforts. If these elements exist, a community development program may form an essential and integral part of the nuclear repository siting process.

NOTES

1. See Finsterbusch (1977: 22-26) for a discussion of several similar "political" methods of assessing impacts and Becker (1980) for a discussion of the use of incentives and compensation to overcome opposition to hazardous waste facilities.

15

Citizen Participation in Nuclear Waste Repository Siting

Robert E. Howell
Marvin E. Olsen
Darryll Olsen
Georgia Yuan

Given the importance of socioeconomic considerations
during the process of siting a nuclear waste repository,
it is evident that citizen participation aimed at
addressing major public concerns must form a central part
of that process. Citizen participation has been viewed
as a necessary component of federal decision making for
several years. Both legal requirements and Federal
policy mandate a variety of citizen participation
programs. In particular, regulations outlined by the
Resource Conservation and Recovery Act (Public Law 94-
580) demand strict control of the management of hazardous
wastes and require that public hearings, meetings, and
other opportunities for citizen involvement be held by
responsible Federal and state agencies before any final
siting or construction decisions are made. Furthermore,
the National Environmental Policy Act of 1969 dictates
that before a waste management facility can be
constructed on a prospective site, an impact statement
must be prepared which assesses environmental and social
impacts and discusses why other sites and other
approaches are less appropriate. Environmental impact
statements must be presented to the public for review and
comment in a series of public hearings (Bishop et al.,
1977: 88; Nealey and Redford, 1978: 60; U.S. Community
Services Administration, 1978: 64-65; U.S. Environmental
Protection Agency, 1980: 8).

Citizen participation is more than a legal concern,
however. It reflects principles basic to American
society. Among the many social benefits that can result
from this process--whether it is conducted by
governmental agencies or private industry--the following
are fundamental (Howell and Olsen, 1981):

1. Democracy: Citizen participation programs
    provide input which contributes to the
    "democratization" of the American political
    processes (Andrews, 1980; Burch, 1976; Carroll,
    1971). The programs increase public access to
    decision making, and are consistent with

collaborative planning strategies which emphasize the formulation of public policy by the consent of the governed.

2. Communication: A properly conducted citizen participation program can enhance understanding of an issue and communication among the various participants. Citizens become knowledgeable about the environmental, economic, and social costs and benefits of specific actions; in return, citizen recommendations can help decision makers to better understand local attitudes and values and to identify particularly sensitive issues within the community (Lucas, 1976; Langton, 1978; Van Es, 1976). Mutual understanding and two-way information exchange increase the likelihood that all relevant information will be reviewed and carefully evaluated (Krawetz, 1979; Duberg et al., 1980; Bishop et al., 1977; Voth and Jackson, 1980; Davis, 1976).

3. Legitimacy: Direct involvement in the decisions affecting them tends to provide citizens with greater faith in the decision and in the decision makers. Because of its stress on information exchange and democratization, a citizen participation program creates legitimacy and credibility.

4. Parity and Mitigation: Citizen participation programs can help to ensure "rational" decision making. Communities directly affected—and society at large—can benefit if extreme positions are balanced in a "reasoned policy debate" which thoroughly explores various options and alternatives (Langton, 1978; Abrams and Primack, 1980; Susskind and Cassella, 1980; Meier, 1981). Citizen participation programs also aid in the identification of needed mitigation measures, particularly if the implementation of a proposed decision includes adequate compensation for adverse impacts.

The past failures of participation efforts dealing with nuclear waste management indicate a pressing need to design more viable citizen participation programs in this area, however. Nuclear waste management controversy began in the early 1970s with the provisional proposal to site a repository in Lyons, Kansas. Project Salt Vault was a series of experiments conducted in a salt mine near Lyons by the Atomic Energy Commission (AEC). The goal of Project Salt Vault was to "establish the feasibility, safety, and techniques for disposing of high-level power reactor wastes in natural salt formations" (Bradshaw and McClain, 1971: 317). After eight years of experimentation with both heaters and actual radioactive waste, the AEC announced in June, 1970, that a site near Lyons, Kansas, had been tentatively selected for an initial salt mine repository for long-term storage of solid high-level radioactive wastes (Bradshaw and McClain, 1971: 356). However, in October 1971, the AEC decided that it might have to cancel its planned repository at the Lyons site because of the "unexpected discovery that water could flood parts of the mine" (U.S. Senate, 1971: 36452).

Although the AEC considered this change in plans to be the result of a technical flaw, it was viewed by many elected officials as evidence of a cover-up of significant safety problems at the project site. United States Congressional Representative Joe Kubitz of Kansas felt that he had been misled and asserted that the AEC had known for months that there were problems with the Lyons site. He urged a denial of the AEC's permission to establish a repository in Kansas (U.S. Senate, 1971: 36453). In addition, the Sierra Club threatened a lawsuit (U.S. Senate, 1971), which was followed by then-Governor Docking asking the AEC to look elsewhere for a nuclear waste repository site.

The Lyons controversy was not the only case in which a potential repository site was abandoned because of political pressure. In 1975, the AEC's successor, the Energy Research and Development Administration (ERDA), began a geological investigation in Michigan, hoping to find a suitable site for a nuclear waste repository. Continuing to view this problem as primarily a technical issue, the ERDA asked the Michigan Department of Natural Resources to provide relevant geologic information, but failed to notify elected officials and local citizens of its investigation until several months later. In May, 1976, United States Representative Phillip E. Ruppe, who represented the rural counties in Michigan under investigation, wrote to the ERDA expressing his frustration with the agency's failure to carry out a public debate on its repository siting activities (U.S. House of Representatives, 1976: 170; Abbotts, 1979: 12). Ruppe was joined by Michigan's Governor Milliken, who requested from the ERDA the formal authority to veto, if necesary, any potential repository site in Michigan. Milliken sought assurance that the ERDA would not proceed without the consent of the state and its citizens. Because many Michigan residents had already developed a mistrust of the ERDA, it was unable to convince the public and its elected officials that it had not yet selected a site in Michigan and was, in fact, only in the very early stages of site investigation. In 1977, following a referendum to ban nuclear waste disposal in parts of Michigan, Governor Milliken formally requested the removal of Michigan from further consideration as a nuclear waste disposal site.

These highly publicized and precedent-setting cases marked the beginning of the "not-in-my-backyard" syndrome that plagues nuclear waste repository siting today. In both situations, the failure to inform and discuss plans and decisions with the public seems to have been the major source of contention between local and federal officials. Elected representatives viewed citizen participation as being an essential element in the agency's siting decisions. Thus, the framework for citizen participation in the repository siting process has developed not only from legal and moral mandates, but more significantly, from an outcry by the public for involvement in the decisions which affect them.

As these examples indicate, despite the legal, moral and experiential factors that point to a need for effective public participation programs when making decisions concerning the siting of major development projects, such programs have generally not been implemented. This situation must be changed. As stated by William Christensen, former Lieutenant Governor of Montana and chairperson of the Montana Energy Council:

> Recent national events should have taught us that excluding the public and their elected representatives from the decision-making process can lead to disaster. If nothing else, these events have taught citizens to be even more suspicious and cynical [about their government]. . . In order to achieve vital public input and cooperation, the federal government and the national leaders must open the analytic planning and decision-making process to pubic scrutiny . . . They must seek the suggestions of the public . . . and use them in reaching decisions (Christensen and Clack, 1976: 583-584).

Given the lessons of the past and the moral and ethical considerations that mandate citizen participation in public issues, it is clear that unless effective participation programs are conducted, the nuclear waste repository siting process is unlikely to be completed anywhere.

Two critical factors that have severely limited the success of past public participation programs have been the failure of program designers to: (1) effectively utilize information on public participation programs available from other large-scale projects and (2) ground such programs in principles derived from theories of individual and group behavior. As a result, such programs have tended to be uninformed and atheoretical.

Clearly, both knowledge of past participation efforts and the best of social science theory should be brought to bear on the issues surrounding public participation in repository siting.

The purpose of this chapter is threefold. In the first section, we briefly review public involvement efforts at selected large-scale projects throughout the U.S. and suggest basic considerations for designing a citizen participation program that can be drawn from these efforts. In the second section, we describe a theoretical basis for designing an effective public participation program. In the third section, we draw on both the experiences of past public involvement efforts and on social theory to describe the dimensions and forms of a public participation program that we believe could be effectively applied to repository siting. Our intent, then, is to describe the general dimensions essential for establishing an effective experientially and theoretically grounded citizen participation model for use in repository siting.

PUBLIC PARTICIPATION IN LARGE-SCALE DEVELOPMENTS

The citizen participation programs reviewed in this section illustrate the significance of key public involvement program actions. These programs--generally documented by social scientists--cover a wide range of natural resource and energy development projects, and reflect the success which various agencies have achieved in promoting citizen participation. Some programs relied primarily on traditional public input techniques such as public hearings, while others stressed innovative approaches to citizen participation in the planning and decision-making arena. These contrasting approaches to citizen participation demonstrate how different program actions, or the lack of specific actions, result in desirable or undesirable outcomes.

Hazardous Waste Disposal Siting

In 1975, the Environmental Protection Agency (EPA) awarded a grant to the Minnesota Pollution Control Agency (MPCA) to develop a demonstration chemical waste land-fill (U.S. Environmental Protection Agency, 1978: 190-206). The development of this facility was viewed by the EPA as a means of collecting information for future land-fill programs which are authorized under the Resource Conservation and Recovery Act. Because the MPCA is a regulatory agency, it subcontracted the site acquisition and operation responsibilities to the Metropolitan Waste Control Commission (MWCC), as authorized by Minnesota state law. This commission, in turn, contracted with a local consulting and engineering firm to prepare siting criteria and to identify four counties as potential sites for landfill locations. The firm performed all legally required analyses and selected four sites without public input, except for one formal hearing.

Public response to the proposed sites was uniformly negative. In particular, local officials and residents rebuked the MWCC and MPCA for not having contacted the communities which were involved prior to preliminary site selection. Moreover, citizen discontent over potential site selection was heightened when local newspapers published information about the proposed waste facilities which had not been presented at the public hearing. As a result of severe public criticism, the MPCA held three more public meetings near the proposed sites. Instead of reducing public discontent, the additional public meetings led to further public opposition, and the MWCC decided to postpone site selection until site criteria and public opinion could be reviewed. Although MPCA and MWCC subsequently experienced several administrative changes and attempted to initiate a new citizen participation program, all proposed land-fill sites were eventually rejected by the general public, local officials, and nearby industries. As a result, EPA, in concurrence with MPCA, terminated the Minnesota Land-Fill Grant.

Waste Isolation Pilot Plant (WIPP)

The WIPP project was an example of an attempt by the U.S. Department of Energy (DOE) to implement the consultation and concurrence process in New Mexico at a site being investigated for a Waste Isolation Pilot Project (WIPP) (U.S. Department of Energy, 1981a: III.29). The Waste Isolation Pilot Plant was a proposed repository for radioactive wastes being generated by defense activities and was not subject to the same regulatory requirements as a commercial radioactive waste disposal facility. It was to include a 100-acre mined repository for the disposal of military waste, and a twenty-acre underground area for research on high-level waste (U.S. Department of Energy, 1981a). Located in Southeastern New Mexico, twenty-five miles east of Carlsbad, the proposed repository was to have been approximately 2,100 feet beneath the surface in salt formations. Studies of the geological suitability of the region and the site selection process identifying this specific location for the WIPP project were begun in 1973.

The public participation program implemented by the DOE is difficult to characterize because the WIPP project spanned two major reorganizations of the DOE (from the Atomic Energy Commission to the Energy Research and Development Administration in 1974, and from the ERDA to the U.S. Department of Energy in 1978). DOE has emphasized independent technical reviews of its site investigation activities as one form of public participation, but not until 1978 did it provide $2.6 million to the state of New Mexico so that the state could form its own review staff. This staff, called the Environmental Evaluation Group, helped the state to analyze and raise questions regarding the adequacy of the WIPP site in protecting the citizens of New Mexico from exposure to radiation and undue health risks should radioactive wastes be buried at the WIPP site (see Yuan, 1981). In addition, the National Academy of Sciences established a panel to review the scientific and technical basis for radioactive waste disposal at the proposed WIPP site.

The Department of Energy attempted to provide information to everyone concerned, following a "consultation and coordination" design. As evidenced in DOE's monthly reports on the WIPP site, Federal officials and contractors met, upon request, with groups such as the Carlsbad Chamber of Commerce, the American Nuclear Society, and the local Lions' Club (see, for example, U.S. Department of Energy, 1981a). In preparing its environmental impact statement (EIS) on the WIPP site, the DOE also held discussions with "key informants" and the general public in the area immediately surrounding the WIPP site. Key informants were identified as people active in political, civic, business, or environmental affairs, while the general public was selected randomly from the local telephone listings of the Carlsbad area (U.S. Department of Energy, 1981a: 9.55-9.56). These discussions revealed that local citizens were seriously concerned about population growth and adequate public services. In addition, the need for sufficient housing for temporary construction workers and newcomers proved to be a major issue. Over half of the people who participated in the discussions believed that there were more suitable locations elsewhere for radioactive waste disposal (U.S. Department of Energy, 1981a: 9.55-9.56). The EIS did not, however, attempt to respond to these concerns after having identified them. It included neither proposals nor procedures for resolving the problems identified by local citizens. As a result, the WIPP project has become a major point of contention in the nuclear waste management process.

Resource Management Planning

In 1969, the governments of Canada and the province of British Columbia agreed to develop a comprehensive plan for land-use and natural resource management in the Okanogan Valley (O'Riordan, 1976). Until the mid-1960s, the Okanogan Valley's economic base consisted primarily of forestry, mining, and agriculture. However, economic incentives to manufacturing, along with a boom in the tourist trade, expanded the valley's economic base and attracted many new residents. Hence, concern for the diversification of economic activity and the protection of natural resources sparked new interest in the formation of a comprehensive land use and natural resource management plan. The comprehensive plan preparation focused on a management program for water quality, air quality, water-based recreation, and sport-fishing resources to the year 2020.

Citizen participation became the cornerstone of the comprehensive plan's foundation because the plan's coordinators, who had been provided by the government of British Columbia, relied upon an "interest-based planning model" to involve the public and address major issues.

Simply stated, the interest-based planning model consisted of several public involvement techniques which served to enhance two-way information exchange and widespread citizen input, recognized affected interest groups, and prevent any single special interest group from dominating the planning process. The model utilized a system of citizen task forces--regionally based, incorporating major environmental and economic concerns--composed of: organized public groups, select special interest groups, and local politicians. Only one representative of any particular interest group was allowed to sit on each of the task forces. Each task force met once a month, for a six-month period, to evaluate the five major components of the comprehensive plan: economic growth projections, water quality management, air quality management, municipal and industrial waste management, and water-based recreational planning.

In addition to the task forces, facilitators extensively used all public media during the citizen participation process to inform the public of various plan options. Techniques such as specific-issue news conferences and call-in question shows were employed. Near the end of the information exchange process, three multimedia seminars were held. These seminars utilized television, radio, and press coverage, and provided an "open-line" system for citizens throughout the valley to call in their views.

After the multimedia seminars, an executive task force was formed, consisting of representative members of the original task forces, to draw up a "white paper" summarizing the recommendations which had been presented during the citizen participation process. Time was also allocated for public forums in which citizens could respond to the formal white paper. After reviewing citizen responses from the public meetings and summarizing citizen recommendations, government officials prepared the Okanogan Basin Comprehensive Plan. The Plan incorporated several of the recommendations derived from the citizen participation process.

Middle Fork Dam

During the early 1970s, the Seattle District Army
Corps of Engineers explored a new approach to citizen
participation. It has been described as an open
planning, or "fishbowl" planning, program (Mazmanian and
Nienaber, 1979: 132-180; Folkman, 1973: 1-29). The Corps
first utilized the fish-bowl planning technique when
controversy arose over its proposal to build a dam on the
Middle Fork of the Snoqualmie River in Washington State
to provide flood control. Opponents of the proposal
stressed that the dam would eliminate the natural quality
of the Snoqualmie River Basin, an agricultural green
belt. Opposition to the Corps' proposal became so
intense that Governor Daniel Evans of Washington
requested the Corps to postpone construction of the dam
and join with several Washington State agencies in an
intensive study to evaluate all possible project
alternatives.

Immediately prior to Governor Evans' decision,
Colonel Howard L. Sargent became district engineer of the
Seattle area. He readily accepted Governor Evans'
request and viewed the study as an opportunity to employ
a new kind of public involvement program. The resulting
fish-bowl planning process engaged many citizens in
numerous workshops, citizen committees, public forums,
and an alternative-option selection process similar to
the Policy Delphi Technique (Sargent, 1972). In fish-
bowl planning, alternatives to a course of action--
generated from citizen/agency workshops and information
forums--are described in a series of public information
brochures. Citizens can express their views in a space
designated for this purpose on the brochures, and then
mail the brochures back to the distributing source.
Citizen comments are reported and analyzed in successive
issues of the brochure, adding new information and
comments at each step. The brochure may be cycled back
and forth between the agency and the public as many times
as necessary.

In the new Middle Fork Dam study, community
leaders--aided by Corps facilitators--sponsored and
conducted a series of community-wide delphi processes.
The outcome of the study was a compromise decision
between the Army Corps of Engineers and the citizens,
whereby the Corps proposed a much smaller multipurpose
dam on the North Fork of the Snoqualmie River instead of
on the original Middle Fork. Washington State citizens
and Governor Evans viewed the new alternative as
compatible with the goal of preserving the Snoqualmie
River Basin green belt, and the Corps found the project
to be environmentally and economically justifiable.[1]

The projects reviewed in this section span a wide
range of approaches and levels of success in citizen
participation, and together they provide substantial

insight into basic factors that must be taken into consideration when designing citizen participation programs. The "lessons learned" from these past projects include the following:

1. Citizen involvement must occur early in the development cycle.

2. The citizen participation program should be led by an objective professional organizer/facilitator.

3. The citizen participation process must be legitimized among community residents as well as government and industry leaders.

4. The local community, sponsoring government agencies and industrial firms, and the organizer/facilitator must make written agreements regarding the overall design of the citizen participation program and the expectations of all major groups involved in the action.

5. A realistic time-line and an acceptable plan for involving technical assistance personnel, volunteers, and agency/industry representatives must be adopted.

6. The responsibilities of government agencies and private industry involved in the siting process must be made explicit.

7. Social and political factors must be considered along with geological and economic factors when deciding what locations seem feasible for a project.

8. The local setting must be fully understood by the organizer/facilitator before designing the specific elements of the citizen participation process and deciding who should be involved in lead roles.

9. The motivations of citizens must be considered when selecting persons to serve on a deliberative body which is intended to represent the local public interest.

10. A local information dissemination process and education program must be conducted to ensure intelligent and rational citizen participation.

11. Citizens must have a central role in all planning and decision making.

12. Citizens must understand their rights and powers vis-a-vis other actors in the siting process.

A THEORETICAL BASIS FOR CITIZEN PARTICIPATION

The above case studies, as well as the historical experience of community development specialists (Christenson and Robinson, 1980), suggest the need for a theoretically grounded community development approach when designing a citizen participation program for repository siting. A recent study of citizen involvement in political party activities (Olsen, 1976) discovered several paths which people are likely to follow in becoming politically active. Two of these are that: (1) people can be mobilized for political activity as the result of a prior involvement in community affairs and in organizations which have specific interests and (2) people can be attracted to political activity as a result of having been contacted by a party or a candidate and shown how involvement can benefit them in some way.

Since both paths can lead a person toward greater involvement in political parties, we assume that they also apply to citizen participation in other public decision-making settings. Two basic social theories can be used to explain why people become more involved in public affairs through one or both of these routes. The following subsections briefly describe each theory.

Social Mobilization Theory

Social mobilization theory, most recently applied by Olsen (1982) as an explanation of political involvement, is an outgrowth of sociopolitical pluralism. It argues that people are mobilized for political involvement through membership and participation in all types of community activities and special interest associations. Although some of these activities and organizations might be politically oriented, others might not be; nor is it necessary that the citizens have ever taken any political action. Groups which can provide the basis for involvement might be fraternal or service organizations, business or professional associations, labor unions, charitable or welfare associations, PTAs and other educational groups, neighborhood clubs, sports or recreational groups, or any other type of local organization. As people join and participate in such activities, they tend to become: (1) more aware of and informed about public issues, (2) skilled in discussion and decision-making techniques, and (3) concerned about influencing the decisions which affect them. In short, they become socially mobilized for involvement in collective activities. Once mobilized, individuals are then quite likely to turn their attention to public affairs and participate in many different kinds of political endeavors.

A considerable amount of empirical research (Verba and Nie, 1972; Olsen, 1982) has demonstrated that the mobilization process can be very effective in bringing citizens into the political arena. Moreover, this process operates among people from all socioeconomic levels, of all ages, of both sexes, and regardless of previous political socialization or experience with political affairs.

Social Exchange Theory

Social exchange theory, most thoroughly elaborated upon by Blau (1964), Homans (1961), and Thibaut and Kelley (1959), contends that, much of the time, people engage in social activities to satisfy needs or to acquire benefits. However, these activities also incur various costs to the participants, including resources expended, time committed, and other activities foregone. Consequently, individuals treat social interactions as being exchange transactions in which they seek to minimize their costs and maximize their benefits. Over time, if a particular social activity is not perceived by the individual as being beneficial, he or she will likely cease to engage in it--unless that person is coerced or chooses to continue because of an overriding commitment stemming from group loyalty or altruism.

Although some social exchanges are straightforward economic transactions, the majority are not. In noneconomic situations, the cost-and-benefit "accounts" may be rather imprecise and unspecified, so that, in the short run, a social exchange may become somewhat unbalanced, with some people contributing more than their fair share and others receiving more than they have contributed. Because an unbalanced exchange relationship invites coercion, however, people generally attempt to keep their relationships balanced as evenly as possible. Another critical aspect of on-going exchange relationships is the presence of a climate of trust. If the participants trust one another to repay social debts in a satisfactory and timely manner, they will be likely to work toward a lasting relationship. If trust is lost, the relationship will quickly die.

Applying social exchange theory to citizen participation in public decision making suggests that people will become actively involved in such activities only if they perceive that the rewards from such involvement will be equal to or greater than the costs, and if they feel certain that those rewards will be realized (MacNair, 1981: 1-17). Thus, three things must be done in order to stimulate and sustain citizen participation: (1) maintain a situation in which the costs of involvement are minimized, (2) maximize the rewards which are associated with involvement, and (3) establish a climate of trust among the citizens that the perceived rewards will be delivered.

The theories of social mobilization and social exchange outlined above can be used to design an approach to community development which incorporates the lessons learned from past citizen participation efforts and which is generalizable to all large development projects. In the following section, those theoretical principles and experiential lessons are combined to formulate a more effective program for citizen participation in nuclear waste repository siting.

A CITIZEN PARTICIPATION PROGRAM FOR REPOSITORY SITING

The model citizen participation program described in this section is both theoretically grounded and shaped by the lessons learned from previous participation efforts. It is specifically designed for nuclear waste repository siting cases, with minor modifications it should be applicable to a wide variety of public issues.[2] The model should be viewed as a set of guidelines for conducting a successful citizen participation program, with the understanding that those guidelines must be adapted to each particular situation.

The proposed model is divided into five phases, each of which contains several activities. The first phase includes several essential steps which develop a sound foundation for a citizen participation program. The second phase covers the preliminary research and organizational activities which occur prior to launching the citizen-led aspects of the program. In the third phase, a committee of local citizens, with the assistance of a community development professional, carries out the citizen action part of the program. Following the presentation of the committee's report to the responsibile public agency, the fourth phase of decision making occurs, in which appropriate public officials review the report and reach a decision on the proposed project. The fifth phase covers post-decision actions under conditions of either project approval or disapproval.

Phase I. Developing a Foundation for Citizen Participation

Conduct a Social and Political Feasibility Study. In addition to economic feasibility studies, the social and political feasibility of carrying out the proposed project in the selected areas is studied by the sponsoring agency prior to entering into discussions with leaders of that area.

Contact Key Area Leaders. Agency or industry representatives contact key area public and private sector leaders to discuss with them both the proposed project and the possibility of conducting a citizen participation program. The citizen participation program must receive strong support from local leaders.

Appoint a Community Development Professional. Key area leaders agree upon and secure the appointment of an objective community development professional who will organize and facilitate the citizen participation program. This person will be responsible to the citizen participation program's Steering Committee, and will play a central role in carrying out the entire program.[3]

Establish a Written Agreement. The community development professional prepares a written statement of the principle features of the citizen participation program and the responsibilities for carrying it out. This statement is agreed to and signed by agency or industry representatives, public officials legally responsible for the siting decision, other key area leaders, and the community development professional. Specified in this agreement are the: (1) responsibilities of the agency or industry, (2) responsibilities of key area leaders, (3) prerogatives of the legal decision-making body, (4) primary duties of the community development professional, (5) responsibilities of the Citizen Task Force and its Steering Committee in carrying out the citizen participation program, (6) responsibilities for financially supporting the program, and (7) criteria for ultimately deciding what conditions will be taken as constituting citizen agreement on the proposed project.

Inventory Major Area Organizations. The community development professional compiles a list of all major organizations in the area, including civic and professional organizations, community service clubs, political organizations, environmental groups, business associations, ethnic organizations, and important special interest associations. Discussions are conducted with their leaders in order to identify potential problem issues regarding the proposed project and the citizen participation program, as well as likely points of consensus and conflict.

Attend Organizational Meetings. The community development professional attends meetings of as many of the major area organizations as possible in order to explain the citizen participation program and its relationship to the proposed project. A request is made for: (1) organizational support of the program, and (2) each organization to select a representative to serve on the Citizen Task Force (see Phase II below) for the program.

Evaluate Phase I. The community development professional prepares a written report describing the actions taken during Phase I and evaluating the effectiveness of those actions. Corrective actions, if necessary, are taken by the professional before proceeding further.

Phase II. Preliminary Organizing

Organize the Citizen Task Force. The community development professional organizes the Citizen Task Force, whose responsibility will be to oversee and guide the entire citizen participation program. The Citizen Task Force will be composed of: (1) representatives of all interested organizations in the area, (2) representatives of organizations from outside the area with an interest in the proposed project, (3) relevant and interested public officials, and (4) individual citizens who may be asked to represent groups of area residents not otherwise represented.

Conduct Special Educational Programs for Citizen Task Force Members. Conduct one or more workshops for all Citizen Task Force members on topics such as roles, responsibilities, and expectations of members; problem-solving; conflict resolution; volunteer recruitment and management; listening; leadership styles; team skills; and organizational development, including program planning. In order to maintain a high level of participant interest, the workshops should focus upon issues that are necessary for effectively completing the committee's task. It is expected that, during these training programs, Citizen Task Force members will develop a better understanding of member skills and qualities, and will become sufficiently acquainted with one another so that they will be able to decide upon the best possible people to perform leadership roles.

Select the Steering Committee. The Citizen Task Force meets and selects from among its members a Steering Committee of eight to ten persons who will act as its executive body and direct its activities. The Steering Committee, in turn, elects its own officers.

Collect Technical Information. A committee of the Citizen Task Force, with the assistance of the community development professional, collects all presently available technical reports and data about the proposed project, including information regarding its: (1) design, (2) projected costs, (3) construction schedule, (4) construction and operational workforce requirements, (5) expected benefits for the local area, and (6) expected negative consequences for the local area.

Conduct Background Study. A committee of the Citizen Task Force, with the assistance of the community development professional, conducts a background study of the economic, social, and political structures of the area and its sociodemographic characteristics. An assessment of the resources in the area that might be utilized in carrying out the citizen participation program is also made.

Carry Out Baseline Survey. A committee of the Citizen Task Force, with the assistance of the community development professional, carries out a telephone or mail survey of a random sample of area residents. The survey should obtain baseline information on such items as: (1) public knowledge about the proposed project, (2) prevailing public attitudes toward and opinions about the project, and (3) attitudes and interests of area residents regarding citizen participation in public policy formation concerning the project. With this information, an assessment of the knowledge and attitudes of the general public regarding the proposed project is made.

Plan Citizen Task Force Activities. A committee of the Citizen Task Force, with the assistance of the community development professional, identifies critical issues and problems to be investigated by the Citizen Task Force, and outlines the kinds of information that will be needed by the Citizen Task Force in addressing those issues and problems.

Design a Draft Participation Program. A committee of the Citizen Task Force, with the assistance of the community development professional, designs a draft outline of the activities to be included in the citizen participation program and the procedures for conducting that program. This involves both: (1) adapting this general citizen participation model to the specific proposed project and local conditions, and (2) specifying as precisely as possible all details of the program.

Finalize the Citizen Participation Program Design. The above committee presents the draft citizen participation program design to the full Citizen Task Force, elicits suggestions for modifications, and obtains Citizen Task Force approval of the final design.

Publicize the Citizen Participation Program. A committee of the Citizen Task Force, with the assistance of the citizen participation professional, uses all available media to inform area residents about the design for the citizen participation program, how and when it will be carried out, the role of the Citizen Task Force and the Steering Committee in conducting the program, how citizens can become involved in it, and the public forum described below.

Hold a Public Forum. The Citizen Task Force, with the assistance of the community development professional, organizes and conducts a public forum to which all area residents are invited. At this forum, agency/industry representatives describe the proposed project, and representatives of the Citizen Task Force: (1) summarize the main findings of the background study and the baseline survey, (2) outline the citizen participation program, including specific subcommittees which will carry out the work, and give citizens an opportunity to ask questions about it, (3) request public support for and involvement in subcommittees and in the overall program, and (4) invite organizations or groups of citizens not already represented on the Citizen Task Force to select their representatives to be included on it.

Organize Working Groups. The Citizen Task Force creates a set of working groups to investigate each of the critical issues and problems identified during the background research phase of the process. These working groups might deal with: (1) possible socioeconomic impacts of the proposed project, (2) potential environmental impacts of the project, (3) procedures for preventing or mitigating those socio-economic and environmental impacts, (4) problems that the project might create for particular groups of people, such as the poor or elderly, (5) special interests of area businesses, (6) publicity for the activities of the citizen participation program, and (7) any other relevant issue. Each working group will be composed of several members of the Citizen Task Force, plus other interested individuals who volunteer to serve on that group. The community development professional examines the composition of each working group to ensure that it contains at least some individuals whose interests and concerns are directly relevant to the task of the group, and, if necessary, asks such individuals to become members of the working group. Technical and professional experts might also be appointed as consultants to the various working groups.

Evaluate Phase II. The community development professional prepares a written report describing the actions taken during Phase II and evaluating the effectiveness of those actions. Corrective actions, if necessary, are taken by the professional before proceeding further.

Phase III. Conducting the Program

Conduct Public Information/Educational Activities. A committee of the Citizen Task Force conducts an extensive series of information and educational activities in order to inform the public about the proposed project. These activities utilize a wide variety of communication techniques, including: (1) the mass media, (2) written materials, (3) public information meetings, (4) presentations at meetings of local organizations, (5) discussions with neighborhood groups, and (6) audio-visual materials.

Investigate Issues and Problems. Each working group: (1) prepares a written statement of its scope of work, (2) assigns its members to specified tasks, and (3) requests information relevant to its area of responsibility from all available sources.

Hold Public Workshops. Each working group holds one or more open workshops for interested citizens at which the findings of the working group are presented and discussed. Views and opinions regarding issues and problems being investigated are expressed, and ideas for coping with those issues and problems are proposed.

Prepare Working Group Reports. Each working group analyzes all information that it has collected, including workshop outcomes, and with the assistance of the community development professional and other technical specialists, prepares a written report containing that information, an analysis of the data, findings, and conclusions. Each working group report is presented to the full Citizen Task Force.

Conduct a Second Survey. A committee of the Citizen Task Force, with the assistance of the community development professional, conducts a second survey among a random sample of area residents. The purpose of this survey is to obtain public views and opinions concerning the desirability of the proposed project and the issues and problems associated with it in light of data obtained during the public information/educational campaign and public workshops. Data from this survey could also be compared with the results of the baseline survey in order to determine what changes, if any, have occurred in public opinion about the proposed project as a result of the information/educational campaign and public workshops.

Encourage Other Public Input. The Citizen Task Force encourages and facilitates all other possible forms of public input concerning the proposed projects. This might involve such techniques as: (1) letters to newspaper editors, (2) radio call-in talk shows, (3) opinion ballots printed in local newspapers, (4) a telephone hotline that people can use to express their views, (5) letters to the Citizen Task Force, and (6) statements by organizations giving their position on the project or associated issues and problems.

Prepare Draft of Final Report. A committee of the Citizen Task Force compiles and integrates all relevant information obtained from working group reports, the second survey, and other forms of public input, and with the assistance of the community development professional and other technical specialists, prepares a draft final report. This report should present a complete description of the attitudes and concerns of area residents about the proposed project. It should also contain analyses of all potential impacts of the project upon the area, both desirable and undesirable, together with any mitigation procedures that citizens feel to be absolutely necessary to deal with those impacts, costs, and benefits of the project that will fall upon particular groups of people, and all other relevant information. Because the Citizen Task Force is not a decision-making body, it should only express "the sense of the community" toward the project as completely and unequivocally as is warranted by the results of the citizen participation program. It should not explicitly recommend approval or disapproval of the proposed project.

Hold a Second Public Forum. The Citizen Task Force holds a second public forum at which it presents its draft final report, encourages discussion of the report, and invites written comments from all interested organizations and individuals.

Prepare a Final Report. The Citizen Task Force, with the assistance of the community development professional and other technical specialists, prepares its final report to incorporate appropriate comments that have been offered at the public forum and in written statements. All written statements about the report that have been submitted by organizations and individuals should be included as attachments to the final report.

Give the Final Report to the Proposing Agency/Industry. The Citizen Task Force gives a copy of its final report to the agency or industry proposing the project so that it can revise its original proposal, if necessary, to take into account any new information.

Evaluate Phase III. The community development professional prepares a written report describing the actions taken during Phase III and evaluating the effectiveness of those actions. Corrective actions, if necessary, are taken by the professional before proceeding further.

Phase IV. Decision Making

Conduct a Formal Hearing. The public body with legal authority to make a final decision concerning siting of the proposed project holds a formal public hearing at which (1) the agency or industry presents its revised final proposal, (2) the Citizen Task Force presents it final report, (3) other individuals or groups present further testimony, and (4) the decision-making body questions agency/industry representatives and Citizen Task Force representatives about their final documents, as well as questioning other individuals about their testimony.

Make the Final Siting Decision. The decision-making body makes a final decision to approve or disapprove siting the proposed project in the area. Alternatively, if the residents of the area are fairly sharply divided in their stands toward the project, and if permitted by state land use legislation, the decision-making body could submit the question to a binding public referendum.

Phase V. Postdecision Activities

If Siting of the Project is Approved: The Citizen Task Force reviews, modifies if necessary, and approves impact mitigation procedures which have been proposed by the agency or industry. The Citizen Task Force then selects a Citizen Review Board that will monitor the impacts of the project as it progresses and the effectiveness of the mitigation procedures. The Citizen Review Board should keep the public informed about these developments on a periodic basis. The Citizen Task Force is then dissolved.

If the Siting of the Project is Disapproved: The Citizen Task Force designs a set of procedures which will assist residents of the area in resolving any conflicts, cleavages, or other problems that may have been created as a result of the citizen participation process. The plan is presented to the appropriate public body for adoption and implementation. The Citizen Task Force is then dissolved.

Evaluate the Overall Program. With a special sub-committee of the former Citizen Task Force, the community development professional evaluates the overall effectiveness of the citizen participation program, and prepares a report consisting of major program features and the lessons learned as a result of having conducted the program.

CONCLUSION

Citizen participation must be an essential part of the repository siting process. Such participation is both legally and morally mandated, and the experience obtained from the siting of other large-scale development projects, as well as that obtained from the exploratory phases of nuclear waste repository siting, suggests that a repository is unlikely to be sited without an effective citizen participation program. For such a program to be successful, its design features must be based upon the lessons learned from past experience and principles derived from appropriate social science theory. That program must be based on open and mutually respectful communication between repository developers and local citizens and be guided by a trained and experienced community development professional. If founded on such bases, we believe that an effective citizen participation program can be designed and successfully applied to the repository siting process.

NOTES

1. Just as the Corps' economic study was being completed, a new governor was elected in Washington State who asked to review the new mediated plan. "In July, 1977, Governor Dixy Lee Ray endorsed the plan, and encouraged the Corps to proceed with its feasibility study. However, she also virtually re-opened the entire issue by asking that the future of the Cedar River Basin (adjoining the Snohomish Basin to the south and west) and the long-range water supply needs of Seattle be incorporated into the planning effort. This expanded study, initiated by the Corps and the state of Washington, is scheduled for completion in late 1981. Clearly, the controversy is far from over" (Mazmanian and Nienaber, 1979: 156).
2. For a discussion of different citizen participation techniques as applied to the assessment of the citizens' needs, see Butler and Howell (1980). See also U.S. Department of Transportation (1976).
3. Given the importance of a neutral professional community development specialist to the success of the citizen participation program, we recommend that the agency or industry initiating the siting proposal be required to place in escrow sufficient financial support for carrying out the citizen participation program

outlined in this chapter. This would include financial
support for a full-time community development specialist,
an administrative assistant and facilitator, and other
program-related expenses.

Summary and Conclusions

Socioeconomic Factors Affecting the Future of Nuclear Waste Management and Repository Siting

Steve H. Murdock
F. Larry Leistritz
Rita R. Hamm

The discussion in the preceding chapters clearly indicates that high-level nuclear waste management and repository siting are likely to involve numerous socioeconomic issues. Social, economic, political, ethical, and numerous other socioeconomic dimensions must be addressed, and it is apparent that unless such issues are addressed, the nuclear waste problem is unlikely to be adequately and equitably resolved. The socioeconomic dimensions of nuclear waste examined in this book are thus of critical importance to resolving the nuclear waste problem.

The goal of this book has been to identify many of the socioeconomic dimensions of nuclear waste management, the socioeconomic impacts, and the mitigation, community development, and citizen participation strategies related to repository siting. The purpose of this concluding chapter is twofold. In the first section of the chapter, we briefly summarize the major sections of the book attempting to highlight the major points of each section. In the second section of the chapter, we attempt to draw conclusions concerning future issues, policy, and research needs in nuclear waste management and repository siting. Specifically, in the second section, we examine research needs and issues and policy dimensions of the nuclear waste problem as they bear on concerns at the Federal (societal), state, and local levels, and as they relate to the major periods of repository development-- siting, construction, operation, closure, and long-term monitoring. Although some issues must obviously be omitted from the discussion, the research needs, issues, and policy concerns addressed are some of those that we believe are essential to increasing our understanding of the nuclear waste problem and to resolving the nuclear waste issue.

SUMMARY

High-level nuclear waste management and repository

siting requires the careful examination and analysis of numerous technical, ethical, legal, and management dimensions, and of their interactions with major socioeconomic dimensions. Section I of this book briefly examined each of these dimensions. Among the critical points highlighted in this section were the facts that, although many of the technical problems of nuclear waste (such as the most likely media and repository form to be used) have been resolved, other questions remain. In particular, Hoskins and Russell note that technical questions have yet to be fully resolved concerning the best combination of processes to be placed at a repository facility and about stability of geologic formations over the very long periods required for repository storage.

Peters (chapter 2) clearly delineated that equity both to present and future generations in siting areas requires that the siting process be as carefully and as completely planned and as equitably implemented as possible but that attempts to otherwise address intergenerational concerns may be problematic.

The Federal structure in place to insure repository safety and equity in repository siting was the focus of chapter 3, by James Finley. This chapter described the programs presently being pursued by the Department of Energy to insure repository safety and citizen involvement, the likely courses of action for such programs in the future, and the Federal intentions regarding information disclosure, public participation, and state and local consultation.

The fourth chapter, by William Metz, examined the legal constraints likely to be used to delay or stop the siting of a nuclear waste repository. The findings in this chapter clearly point out that the Federal legislative mandate for siting a high-level nuclear repository has been firmly established but that the Congress will have to take a firmer stand if such siting is to occur over state, local, and/or special interest groups' objections.

The final chapter in this section, by Murdock, Hamm, and Leistritz, examined some of the complex interrelations that exist between technical, ethical, institutional, organizational, and socioeconomic dimensions of waste management and repository siting. Perhaps the major point of this chapter is that socioeconomic, as well as technical, institutional, ethical, and other issues, become inextricably linked in the repository siting and waste management process. Paradoxically, then, although mastery of the complex issues and interrelations among issues affecting nuclear waste management and repository siting is essential to adequately address the nuclear waste problem, such knowledge is not yet available. It is critical that areas where levels of knowledge are insufficient, as well as those areas where substantial progress has been made, be recognized.

Overall, the chapters in Section I point to a complex set of issues that form the basis of the nuclear waste problem. For nearly all dimensions, unanswered questions remain, and, in nearly all cases, additional analyses are essential to identify the complex of factors that must be addressed by policy makers wishing to resolve the nuclear waste issue. Although the chapters in this section provide few definitive solutions to the issues in nuclear waste, the identification of these issues represents an important step in the initiation of a solution to the nuclear waste problem.

Section II presented an attempt to delineate the standard and special economic, demographic, public service, fiscal, and social impacts of repository siting, construction, operation, and long-term monitoring. Chapter 6, by Thomas, Hamm, and Murdock, clearly indicated that there is a broad range of potential impacts that may affect repository siting communities and that their assessment requires an extensive and complex effort involving numerous assumptions and suppositions.

Chapter 7, by Chase, Leistritz, and Halstead highlighted the fact that large-scale projects generally have positive economic impacts on the host communities and that when fiscal difficulties arise, it is usually not because of the lack of sufficient public revenues to offset public costs, but because of the timing and jurisdictional problems that often occur with such projects. These authors also point out, however, that special characteristics of repositories, such as their potentially negative impacts on land values and the fact that they will be federally-owned, tax-exempt facilities, may lead to unique economic and fiscal effects for repositories and make the assessment of their impacts quite difficult.

Chapter 8, by Murdock and Hamm, provides a description similiar to that in chapter 7. However, it examines the demographic and public service impacts of repository development. The authors of this chapter highlight the fact that although demographic and public service impacts have often been the focus of public and media attention in other large-scale developments, definitive information on the actual magnitude and distribution of such impacts as rapid population growth, changes in population characteristics, and new service demands is not available. These authors note that the assumptions underlying demographic and public service projections, in general, and for repository sites, in particular, may be problematic if such techniques are used in making projections for the small towns that abound in many of the potential siting areas.

In chapter 9, Thomas, Albrecht, and Murdock examined the broadest and least easy to quantify type of impacts, social impacts. The authors of this chapter suggest that given the range of such impacts and the difficulties entailed in their measurement, an integrated research approach using survey, participant observation, and community structure analysis is to be recommended. These authors also note, however, that although difficult to assess, the social impacts of repository development are likely to be among the most critical of those factors affecting the success of repository siting actions.

The purpose of Section II was thus to delineate the wide range of socioeconomic impacts that might occur as a result of repository development and to briefly overview the methods that may be applied to assess such impacts for repository siting areas. The chapters in this section point to the need to consider a wide range of factors when assessing the socioeconomic impacts of repository development and the need to understand both the strengths and the limitations of the information that can be provided by prevailing assessment techniques.

The third section of the book examines strategies and means for mitigating the local impacts of repository siting. The three chapters in this section by Leistritz and his colleagues form an integrated section which delineates the lessons learned from mitigation efforts at other large-scale developments (chapter 10), outlines the dimensions of a systems-based approach to the mitigation or management of the impacts of large-scale developments (chapter 11), and points out those dimensions of impact management that are likely to require special consideration in the impact management of high-level nuclear waste repositories (chapter 12).

The case studies in chapter 10 point out that many of the difficulties in past mitigation efforts have resulted from the fact that these efforts were initiated too late in the development cycle or without proper citizen involvement. This chapter also provides an excellent indication of the extensive range of strategies, financing mechanisms, and management alternatives available for mitigating the impacts of large-scale developments.

Chapter 11 draws on the lessons learned from the case studies described in chapter 10 to delineate a systems-based approach to impact management. This chapter emphasizes the need to see mitigation in a broad perspective as an impact management process in which not only negative, but also positive project-related impacts are examined and as one in which a comprehensive, integrated (that is, systems-based) approach should be used to coordinate management events during all phases of the development cycle. A systems-based perspective is used to point to the need to examine the interrelated parts of the impact management system (particularly its inputs, interrelationships within, and outputs) and the impacted area's socioeconomic system. In addition, the utility of using such a perspective to delineate the aspects of a development that can be addressed and the means to address them in the impact management process is a major focus of this chapter. The impact management steps and phases outlined in this chapter are ones likely to be of utility for impact management throughout the development cycle of nearly any large-scale development.

Chapter 12, the final chapter in this section, points out that impact management at repositories will likely differ substantially from that at other large-scale developments. The major point of this chapter is that impact management and mitigation at repositories will require a comprehensive, delicately-balanced, carefully designed, and long-term effort involving Federal, state, local, and private concerns.

Section III of the book thus provides an overview of the need and alternative means and systems for mitigating the socioeconomic impacts of repository siting. Its chapters point out that, as with impact assessments, the task of impact management and the mitigation of repository impacts is a large and complex one. At the same time, the range of options to address mitigation requirements is substantial. The key to successful impact management, then, lies largely in the selection of techniques that will insure that the needs of all parties, at all levels, are addressed in an equitable and effective manner. Impact management is thus as much a sociopolitical art as a scientifically imbued process.

The final section of the book, Section IV, pointed to the need for, and potential difficulties entailed in ignoring the need for, careful community development and citizen participation in repository development. Chapter 13, by Albrecht, examined the recent failure of the Federal system in addressing local concerns related to the MX project. The major point of this chapter was that even in a relatively favorable development climate, failure to involve residents of the siting area early in the development cycle, to insure that complete and accurate information is provided to local residents thoughout the development process, to sincerely solicit and utilize the input of these residents in project design, and to show sensitivity to local social and cultural traditions and concerns will lead to siting difficulties and generate local opposition to a project.

Chapters 14 and 15 in this section attempt to specify the dimensions of community development (chapter 14) and citizen participation (chapter 15) plans that might be used to avoid difficulties (such as those encountered in MX) in the repository siting process. Chapter 14, by Voth and Herrington, points out that a variety of alternatives might be used to allow communities to obtain greater participation in the siting process, including a potential bidding process among communities. Among the major conclusions of this chapter is a clear delineation of the need for repository developers to provide potentially impacted communities with full information on project plans and to candidly specify points where communities will and will not be allowed to have inputs to the decision-making process.

Chapter 15, by Howell, Olsen, Olsen, and Yuan, in large part reiterates the lessons of the two preceding chapters through case study examples, but at the same time specifies a step-by-step procedure for insuring adequate citizen involvement in the siting process. Among the key conclusions of chapter 15 is the need for professional community development and public participation specialists to play a central role in the citizen participation process, for local citizens to become systematically self-organized to participate in the development process and for sufficient time to be provided in the development process to allow for meaningful citizen involvment. This chapter vividly describes the potential problems entailed for developers who have failed to provide for such involvement.

The chapters in Section IV provide lessons that are, in some ways, quite simple, yet critical for repository developers. These lessons are: (1) that the local residents of siting areas should be involved early in the development process and (2) that the involvement of local residents should be as complete as possible and based on open and complete communication among all parties with interests in the development process. As with the mitigation process, however, insuring that such principles are implemented and adhered to in the politically-charged environment in which repository development is occurring requires a careful and complex effort.

The volume as a whole attempted to provide a broad delineation of many of the general dimensions of nuclear waste management and repository siting and to provide a more detailed discussion of a range of impact, mitigation, and community development and public participation dimensions of repository development. Although it has not resolved many of the issues it has raised, it has described procedures for assessing impacts, management systems for mitigating impacts, and community development and citizen involvement strategies that, if carefully followed, seem likely to lead to better informed, more equitable, and effective solutions to many of the most difficult nuclear waste concerns. Finally, as noted below, its chapters have suggested issues that must receive further empirical and policy analysis if the nuclear waste problem is to be resolved.

CONCLUSIONS

The dimensions of the nuclear waste problem outlined

in this book are clearly complex ones, and, although several chapters have outlined processes that might be pursued to help resolve these issues, many dimensions have yet to be resolved. In a book such as this, which has attempted to describe a wide range of factors bearing on the nuclear waste problem, it is thus appropriate that it conclude with a discussion that attempts to delineate socioeconomic issues that have not been adequately addressed in its pages nor in similar works. The policy and research questions that will likely require additional attention before nuclear waste management and repository siting issues are resolved, should also be examined. In this section, we attempt to outline some of the critical research needs and policy issues and questions that must be addressed in the coming years if the nuclear waste problem is to be resolved. No attempt is made to address all of the relevant issues, questions, and research needs that might be addressed, but only to delineate those that clearly have socioeconomic dimensions and that appear likely to be the most critical to the resolution of the nuclear waste problem.

Areas Requiring Additional Research

As the discussion in the preceding chapters indicates, many factors critical to waste siting have not been adequately examined empirically. Although many of the key dimensions may have been sufficiently identified to merit attention by policy makers, given the pressing needs for a resolution of the nuclear waste issue (see section below), basic and applied scientific questions remain. In this section, we examine some of those questions that require attention in future research efforts. General and specific research needs related to impact assessment, impact mitigation, and public participation and community development for repository siting are examined.

Clearly, many of the research needs related to repository developments reflect the often discussed research needs of socioeconomic impact assessment, mitigation, and community development research in general (Murdock and Leistritz, 1979; Finsterbusch and Wolf, 1981; Leistritz and Murdock, 1981, Christenson and Robinson, 1980). That is, the need for more longitudinal and comparative analyses of community events over time; careful assessments of the accuracy and utility of past impact assessments, mitigation efforts and community development processes (Murdock et al., 1982c); the need to develop more systematic, theoretical frameworks for use in such assessments; and for the best social scientists and social science methodologies to be used in assessing the impacts and in designing mitigation and community development strategies for large-scale developments are as applicable to repository developments as they are to other types of developments. On the other hand, repository developments display numerous, relatively unique, research needs in each of the major areas examined in this volume.

Numerous research needs are evident in relation to economic concerns. Thus, additional attention must be given to the effect of repository development on local land values and uses, on recreational opportunities and investments, and to the effects such developments may have on the potential for nonnuclear industrial development in repository siting areas. Greater attention must also be given to defining the likely characteristics of the repository workforce and the potential for rural residents to obtain employment in such workforces. Finally, greater attention must be given to establishing the detailed estimates of local and nonlocal expenditures for repositories for each year during repository construction and operation, and more definitive procedures must be developed to assess the impacts of the repository shutdown and monitoring phases. Extensive additional economic research is clearly required.

Equally evident is the need to examine several important fiscal concerns. Foremost among these is the need to systematically assess the implications of alternative schemes for meeting public costs in the absence (because of the tax-exempt status of the facility) of generally available tax revenues. Analysis is required to establish the costs for the special services (such as emergency preparedness) likely to be required in repository siting communities and of the potential costs of low probability, large-magnitude events, such as various types of accident-related incidents. Finally, further attention should be focused on establishing the fiscal liability of repositories and the range of events and areas over which such liability might extend. Although several of these factors have received some attention (see chapter 7), many have not been subjected to rigorous empirical analyses and should thus receive further examination.

Numerous dimensions of demographic impacts also require careful attention. Although the potential population decline that might result from repository development and the potential population growth that might be foregone by areas with nuclear waste facilities have been discussed (see chapter 8), few attempts have been made to examine such factors for localities receiving other types of noxious facilities. In addition, little attention has been given to establishing the likely demographic characteristics of repository-related workers or their likely settlement preferences and patterns. Relatively few analyses have been performed of the likely long-term demographic implications of various types of potential incidents, and as with economic factors, virtually no analysis of the demographic declines likely to accompany the closure and monitoring phases of repository development have been completed.

In the area of public service impacts, although some research efforts have been completed (U.S. Department of Energy, 1981a), substantial additional efforts are required to more clearly specify the exact types of new services that would be required as a result of repository development, what types of skills and expertise will be needed by local public service personnel and the actual levels of such expertise presently available in potential siting areas. Additional attention must also be given to establishing the jurisdictional responsibilities for various types of services and to evaluating the relative utility of various alternatives for coordinating such responsibilities across jurisdictions. Finally, additional research efforts are critical for establishing the utility of numerous means for enhancing service management skills in potential siting areas.

The social and social-psychological impacts of repository development require especially concerted research efforts. Not only do we know relatively little about such impacts in general (Murdock and Leistritz, 1979), but we have virtually no knowledge of the utility of alternative means of alleviating societal-wide levels of fear and anxiety and for establishing perceptions of equity and long-term institutional stability (Hebert et al., 1978). We know little about the effects of rapid growth on social structures, but even less about the effects of calamitous changes (such as might result from a potential nuclear incident) on such structures. In sum, in the area of the social impacts of repository developments, as for other large-scale developments, the need for additional systematic research is critical.

In regard to impact management and mitigation, the research needs are no less evident (Halstead et al., 1982). Past research in this area has consisted largely of descriptions of single case studies, and rigorous systematic comparative analyses have seldom been performed. Thus, substantial additional research efforts seem merited in a variety of areas. For example, evaluation of the usefulness and cost effectiveness of alternative impact management measures in various developmental contexts appears to be a very fruitful area for additional research. Thus, additional analysis is needed concerning such topics as:

1. the effectiveness of various recruitment and training programs in stimulating local employment at project sites

2. the usefulness of measures to encourage long distance commuting as an alternative to

workforce relocation

3. considerations affecting decisions to directly provide housing and associated infrastructure as opposed to undertaking measures to stimulate the local private sector

4. advantages and disadvantages associated with alternative mechanisms for providing front-end financing to local governments

5. efficiency and equity characteristics of alternative compensation and incentive approaches

In addition, numerous areas for research concerning institutional and policy aspects of impact management can be suggested including:

1. determination of the most appropriate roles for various interests to play in the management process

2. evaluation of alternative approaches to public involvement and information dissemination

3. further evaluation of the applicability of alternative models for the facility siting process (for example, Federal or state preemption, local veto power, negotiation)

Greater attention should be given to the long-term implications of nuclear repository development and especially to the ultimate closure of repository facilities.

Finally, additional empirical analyses are required concerning community development and public participation issues. As Howell and Olsen (1981) note, additional research is required on how the public wishes to be involved in decision making and concerning the most effective processes for insuring that participation. Attention must be given to establishing the public's perceptions and levels of support for alternative forms of disposal. Equally important, the relative importance of the factors affecting such perceptions must be established, and the importance of such perceptions in the determination of public behaviors more clearly established. Assessments must be made of the best means of communicating technical knowledge to various types of publics, of the advantages and disadvantages of various types of citizen participation strategies and program characteristics, and of the best role for development specialists to play in the participation process. Comparative, quasi-experimental research designs have been suggested as means of addressing these needs (Howell and Olsen, 1981). However examined, it is clear that the completion of such research is critical to the successful resolution of the nuclear waste problem.

It is evident that the research needs related to nuclear waste management and repository siting are extensive. Ideally, these research endeavors might be completed and the issues resolved prior to the initiation of repository siting activities. However, as noted in the following section, many of the issues addressed by such research efforts will, and perhaps should, be addressed by policy makers before their resolution through empirical analyses. At best, given the pressing state of the nuclear waste problem, one can only hope that such research can be completed in sufficient time to be of utility in guiding public decision making regarding nuclear waste management and repository siting. The research needs outlined above though similar in many regards to the research needs in other resource, energy, and community research areas, are different in one critical regard. This research must be pursued with an immediacy and completed using a complexity of research designs that exceed in timeliness and rigor those pursued in many research activities but which are reflective of the immediate need to resolve the nuclear waste problem.

Remaining Issues

A major premise of this book has been that a wide range of issues and research needs must be addressed before an adequate understanding of the nuclear waste problem can be obtained. Although questions remain, it is evident that many of these issues can be addressed by policy makers. It is critical, then, to evaluate the degree to which selected issues can and should be addressed by policy actions. This task is the focus of this final section of the chapter.

The Unresolvable Issues. Perhaps the starting point for any evaluation of the issues affecting the nuclear waste problem is to recognize that some of the issues that remain unresolved may not be directly resolvable on the basis of scientific or even political actions. Although steps can be taken to obtain knowledge and to implement processes to alleviate the concerns surrounding such issues, direct solutions may not be possible.

Thus, it appears that many of the public's fears and anxieties concerning the handling and storage of nuclear materials cannot be fully resolved given the past history of nuclear incidents. Even the most technically safe storage and handling systems or the most elaborate waste management system are unlikely to alter the public's perception of the potential risks and uncertainty underlying nuclear waste management. Only a perceived historical record of accident-free nuclear storage and management[1] will resolve this issue, and only the future can provide such a record.

Equally difficult to resolve is the concern over the design of an institutional management structure that can be maintained over the centuries for which nuclear wastes must be monitored. Because the past provides a history of uncertainty and even contemporary periods show wide fluctuations in political stability and in the continuity of policy-makers' concerns regarding single issues, the public's concerns about institutional stability are unlikely to be resolved by present actors in the nuclear management structure.

In like manner, many of the issues surrounding intergenerational responsibilities appear to be difficult to resolve. Despite an array of philosophical perspectives on such responsibilities (see chapter 2), it appears unclear whether this generation is responsible for retaining the quality of life it inherited for future generations, or whether it should seek to provide a better quality of life than it inherited. Since it is often unclear what epoch or generation in history is responsible for a given set of socioenvironmental factors, it is also difficult to establish existing levels of responsibility and even more difficult to project future responsibilities.

These and similar issues are not likely to be resolved by technical, political or socioeconomic factors. They clearly can be mitigated by many of the processes described in this volume (see chapters 10 through 15), may be resolved by presently unforeseen events, and clearly will be altered by history, but within the foreseeable future, it is perhaps best to approach such issues as conditions that cannot be totally altered, but which must be addressed. It should be recognized that knowledge of the limitations of our ability to change certain conditions may be an essential first step in resolving the nuclear waste problem.

Neglected Issues. Yet additional issues have simply not received sufficient attention by researchers or policy makers. For example, although a significant amount of attention has been given to Federal and state relationships in repository siting, little attention has been given to the relationship between state and local areas. Federal agencies are largely limited by regulation and protocol to dealing with state-level agencies rather than local residents, but state agencies cannot be assumed to have, nor can it be assumed that they will develop, adequate relationships with local areas. Particularly in large states, state bureaucracies may be nearly as alien to local residents as the Federal bureaucracy. Additional attention is thus essential to delineate the issues in state-local relations on nuclear waste management, to outline relative state and local rights and responsibilities, and to insure that local involvement, not just state involvement, becomes the norm in Federal, state, and local relations in nuclear waste management.

The development of a substantive plan for deciding which of the less tangible concerns related to repository siting should be given concerted attention and which should be addressed by mitigation and compensation measures has also been neglected. Are the fears and anxieties, the concerns for future generations (though unlikely to be resolved, as noted in the preceding section) to be taken as sufficiently serious to merit compensation? Such factors must either be directly addressed in the nuclear waste management system or relegated to an important, but unaddressable, category of concerns. The latter course of action is apparently the one being pursued (intentionally or unintentionally), but a more open discussion of these factors in the policy arena by decision makers is merited.

Issues Nearing the Decision Point. It may seem presumptive to assert, given the present state of uncertainty concerning many nuclear waste issues, that some issue areas appear to merit the formulation of policy decisions, but the imminence and magnitude of the nuclear waste problem clearly require that actions be taken toward the resolution of at least some issue areas. Although some scholars will clearly disagree that the areas described below have reached the decision-making point, those listed are among the most widely examined nuclear waste management issues, and an evaluation of their policy status is merited.

Among the issues apparently nearly resolved, at least from the standpoint of Federal siting agencies, are those related to the technical feasibility of alternative storage and repository systems. It is clear, however, that policy makers must also formulate a stand on the relative safety of existing systems, if repository development is to be initiated. Given the consequences of failing to act, the point in time is approaching when Federal, state, and local decision makers must make a decision and take a public stance supporting selected systems.

Another issue area where policy decisions may be possible is that regarding Federal, state, and local rights, responsibilities, and levels of participation in nuclear waste management and repository siting. Although precedents have apparently been set which establish Federal preeminence in regard to such issues (Metz, 1981), court interpretations have given considerable discretion to states in interpreting existing laws, Congress has attempted to sidestep the most difficult to address issues, and Federal agencies with nuclear responsibilities have attempted to avoid confrontations with states. It appears likely that no solution equitable to all parties involved, and without political costs, can be found. However, the relative roles of various levels of government have been extensively examined, and it thus appears that policy formulation may be possible, and soon essential, in this area.

Decisions concerning mitigation must also soon be made. Who should be mitigated for what, over what period of time, and who should pay for the costs of such mitigation are being examined (see chapters 10 through 12), but many of the decision points may fast be approaching. Additional analyses (as outlined previously) are necessary to establish the best processes for effecting such mitigation, but basic decisions appear possible and essential.

In like manner, decisions must be formulated concerning the institutional mechanisms that must be put in place to manage and monitor nuclear repositories. Such decisions as those concerning the public-private nature of these institutional systems, alternative mechanisms for insuring their continued funding and maintenance, the role of local, state, and Federal interests in these systems must be established and have received extensive discussion. As with many of the other factors described above, the ultimate resolution of the concerns regarding these factors may be difficult to address, but decisions are necessary to initiate the resolution of key issues.

Overall, then, many of the issues surrounding nuclear waste management and repository siting may be unresolvable, others have received insufficient attention, and still others have reached a point where at least cautious action and policy formulations seem possible. Premature issue resolution must be resisted, but it is clear that it is essential to take stock of where we are in terms of issue resolution. Although the attempt presented here to evaluate the progress toward resolution of key issues may be considered by some to be faulty in its judgement and by others to have neglected key issues, we would argue that such an evaluation process is long overdue. If existing nuclear wastes are to be safely managed, we must begin to at least evaluate which issues are important and which we can and cannot directly, equitably, and effectively address. In this regard, we hope this section has served a useful purpose.

This volume has attempted to delineate many of the dimensions of the nuclear waste problem, of nuclear waste management, and of repository siting. It has also attempted, in this final chapter, to suggest additional research needs that must be pursued and issue areas that both can and perhaps cannot be resolved in addressing these dimensions. The intent has thus been to provide a broad introduction to the factors that bear on the nuclear waste problem. It is our hope that this effort provides the reader with a better appreciation of the importance and the complexity of the socioeconomic dimensions of nuclear waste. Even more important, we hope that it has, by describing the socioeconomic dimensions of nuclear waste, served in some small way to expedite the resolution of the nuclear waste problem.

NOTES

1. It can, of course, be argued that the history of nuclear materials handling is largely an accident-free and exemplary one (Glasstone and Jordan, 1980). However, the public remains skeptical (Hebert et al., 1978), and it is the public's perception, not the objective reality, that is the issue of concern.

References

Abbotts, J. "Radioactive Waste: A Technical Solution." **The Bulletin of the Atomic Scientists** 35, 1979.

Abrams, Nancy E. and Joel R. Primack. "Helping the Public Decide--The Case of Radioactive Waste Management." **Environment** 22, 1980.

Aiken, Michael and Robert Alford. "Community Structure and Innovation: The Case of Public Housing." **American Political Science Review** 64, 1970.

Aiken, Michael and Robert Alford. **Community Structure and Mobilization: The Case of the War on Poverty.** Madison, Wisconsin: Institute for Research on Poverty, 1968.

Albrecht, Stan L. "Energy Development and Native Americans." Paper Presented at the Symposium--State of the Art Survey of Socioeconomic Impacts Associated with Construction/Operation of Energy Facilities. St. Louis, Missouri, 1977.

Albrecht, Stan L. "Socio-cultural Factors and Energy Resource Development in Rural Areas in the West." **Journal of Environmental Management** 8, 1978.

Albrecht, Stan L. and Bruce Chadwick. **Sociocultural Analysis for the Proposed Waste Isolation Pilot Plant.** Las Cruces, New Mexico: Adcock and Associates, 1980.

Albrecht, Stan L. and H.R. Geersten. "Land Use Planning: Attitudes and Behavior of Elected Officials and Their Constituents." **Social Science Quarterly** 59, 1978.

Alinsky, Saul. **Reveille for Radicals.** New York, New York: Vintage Books, 1946.

Andrews, Richard N.L. "Class Politics or Democratic Reform: Environmentalism and American Political Institutions." **Natural Resources Journal** 20, 1980.

Architect/Planners Alliance. **Intermountain Power Project Draft Socioeconomic Impact Report.** Salt Lake City, Utah: Architect/Planners Alliance, 1980.

Arkansas Institute for Social Justice. **Community Organizing: Handbook 2.** Little Rock, Arkansas: Arkansas Institute for Social Justice, 1977.

307

308

Aronson, Craig. **Energy Development in Rural Areas: Corporate Provision of Community Infrastructure.** Seattle, Washington: Battelle Human Affairs Research Center, 1981.

Ascher, William. **Forecasting: An Appraisal for Policy Makers and Planners.** Baltimore, Maryland: Johns Hopkins University Press, 1978.

Atlantic Reporter. Second Series. **State of Vermont vs. Warshow** 410, 1979.

Bailey, Kenneth D. **Methods of Social Research.** New York, New York: The Free Press, 1978.

Ballard, Chester C., Myrna S. Hoskins, and James H. Copp. **Local Leadership Control of Small Community Growth.** College Station, Texas: Texas Agricultural Experiment Station, Technical Report 81-3, Department of Rural Sociology, 1981.

Baril, R.G. "Community Impact Agreements and Monitoring." Paper presented at Second International Forum on the Human Side of Energy. Edmonton, Alberta, Canada, August 1981.

Bauer, Raymond A. **Social Indicators.** Cambridge, Massachusetts: The Massachusetts Institute of Technology Press, 1966.

Bauman, Judith C. and John Platt. "Casenote: May a State Say 'No' to Nuclear Power? Pacific Legal Foundation Gives a Disappointing Answer." **Environmental Law** 10, 1979.

Beal, George M. and Daryl Hobbs. **The Process of Social Action in Community and Area Development.** Ames, Iowa: Cooperative Extension Service, Iowa State University, 1964.

Beal, George M., Ralph M. Brooks, Leslie D. Wilcox, and Gerald E. Klonglan. **Social Indicators: Bibliography I.** Sociology Report No. 92. Ames, Iowa: Department of Sociology and Anthropology, Iowa State University, 1971.

Becker, Howard S. and Blanche Geer. "Participant Observation and Interviewing: Comparison." **Human Organization** 16, 1957.

Becker, Jeanne Felbeck. "The Use of Incentives and Compensation to Overcome Public Opposition to the Siting of Hazardous Waste Landfills." Unpublished M.A. thesis. Milwaukee, Wisconsin: The School of Architecture and Urban Planning, 1980.

Bell, Colin and Howard Newby. **Community Studies: An Introduction to the Sociology of the Local Community.** New York, New York: Praeger, 1972.

Bender, Lloyd D. **Predicting Employment in Four Regions of the Western United States.** Washington, D.C.: Economic Research Service, U.S. Department of Agriculture, in Cooperation with Agricultural Experiment Station, Montana State University, 1975.

Bentham, Jeremy. **An Introduction to the Principles of Morals and Legislation.** London, England: T. Payne, 1789.

Berkey, Edgar, N.G. Carpenter, W.C. Metz, D.W. Meyers, D.R. Portes, J.E. Singley, and R.K. Travis. **Social Impact Assessment, Monitoring, and Management by the Electric Energy Industry.** Pittsburgh, Pennsylvania: Energy Impact Associates, Inc., 1977.

Bickert, Carl von E. **The Residents of Sweetwater County, Wyoming: A Needs Assessment Survey.** Denver, Colorado: Denver Research Institute, 1974.

Billings, R.B. "The Mathematical Identity of the Multipliers Derived From the Economic Base and the Input-Output Model." **Journal of Regional Science** 9, 1969.

Bishop, A. Bruce, Mac McKee, and Roger D. Hansen. **Public Consultation in Public Policy Information: A State-of-the-Art Report.** Prepared by Intermountain Consultants and Planners, Inc. for the Office of Waste Isolation, Energy Research and Development Administration, 1977.

Bjornstad, David J. and E. Goss. **Measuring the Impacts of Using Payments-in-Lieu-of-Taxes to Compensate Communities when Siting High-Level Nuclear Waste Isolation Facilities.** Oak Ridge, Tennessee: Oak Ridge National Laboratory, 1981.

Blau, Peter M. **Exchange and Power in Social Life.** New York, New York: John Wiley and Sons, 1964.

Bogue, Donald J. **Techniques for Making Population Projections: How to Make Age-Sex Projections by Electronic Computer.** Chicago, Illinois: University of Chicago Community Family Study Center, 1974.

Boland, Walter. "American Institutions of Higher Education: A Study of Size and Complexity." Unpublished Ph.D. dissertation. Ann Arbor, Michigan, 1966.

Boulding, Kenneth. "The Economics of the Coming Spaceship Earth," pgs. 235-43 in **The Futurists.** Alvin Toffler, Ed. New York, New York: Random House, 1972.

Bowles, Roy T. **Social Impact Assessment in Small Communities: An Integrative Review of Selected Literature.** Toronto, Canada: Butterworths, 1981.

Bradley, Edward B. "Problems and Opportunities Affecting Local Landowners' Attitudes Toward Coal Development and Federal Coal Leasing: A Case Study of Wyoming's Powder River Basin." Paper Presented at 1978 Annual Meeting of Western Agricultural Economics Association. Bozeman, Montana. July 23-25, 1978.

Bradshaw, R.L. and W.C. McClain, Eds. **Project Salt Vault: A Demonstration of the Disposal of High-Activity Solidified Wastes in Underground Salt Mines.** Oak Ridge, Tennessee: Oak Ridge National Laboratory, Union Carbide Corporation, Nuclear Division, 1971.

310

Branch, Kristi, James Thompson, James Creighton, and Douglas Hooper. **Guide to Social Assessment.** Denver, Colorado: Bureau of Land Management, 1982.

Braschler, Curtis. "A Comparison of Least Squares Estimates of Regional Employment Multipliers with Other Methods." **Journal of Regional Science** 12, 1972.

Brenner, Robert D. **The Social, Economic, and Political Impacts of Nuclear Waste Terminal Storage Repositories.** Princeton, New Jersey: Center for International Studies, Princeton University, 1979.

Bridgeland, William M. and Andrew J. Sofranko. "Community Structure and Issue-Specific Influences: Community Mobilization over Environmental Quality." **Urban Affairs Quarterly** 11, 1975.

Briscoe, Maphis, Murray, and Lamont, Inc. **Action Handbook: Managing Growth in the Small Community.** A Report for the U.S. Environmental Protection Agency. Washington, D.C.: U.S. Government Printing Office, 1978.

Bronder, L.D., N. Carlisle, and M. Savage. **Financial Strategies for Alleviation of Socioeconomic Impacts in Seven Western States.** Denver, Colorado: Western Governors' Regional Energy Policy Office, 1977.

Browne, Bortz, and Coddington, Inc. **The Campbell County Monitoring Program.** Denver, Colorado: Browne, Bortz, and Coddington, Inc., 1982.

Buckley, Walter. **Sociology and Modern Systems Theory.** Englewood Cliffs, New Jersey: Prentice Hall, Inc., 1967.

Burch, William R., Jr. "Who Participates: A Sociological Interpretation of Natural Resource Decisions." **Natural Resources Journal** 16, 1976.

Burchell, R.W. and D. Listokin. **The Fiscal Impact Handbook.** New Brunswick, New Jersey: Rutgers Center for Urban Policy Research, 1978.

Burness, H. Stuart. "Risk: Accounting for an Uncertain Future." **Natural Resources Journal** 21, 1981.

Butler, Lorna Michael and Robert E. Howell. **Coping with Growth: Community Needs Assessment Techniques.** Pullman, Washington: Cooperative Extension Service, Washington State University, 1979.

Butler, Lorna Michael and Robert E. Howell. **Coping with Growth: Community Needs Assessment Techniques.** Corvallis, Oregon: Western Rural Development Center, Oregon State University, 1980.

Campbell, Angus, Philip E. Converse, and Willard L. Rodgers. **The Quality of American Life: Perceptions, Evaluations, Satisfactions.** New York, New York: Russell Sage Foundation, 1976.

Carnes, S.E., E.D. Copenhaver, J. Reed, E. Soderstrom, J. Sorenson, E. Peelle, and D. Bjornstad. **Incentives and the Siting of Radioactive Waste Facilities.** Oak Ridge, Tennessee: Oak Ridge National Laboratory, 1981.

311

Carpenter, Edwin H. "Evaluation of Mail Questionnaires for Obtaining Data for More Than One Respondent in a Household." **Rural Sociology** 42, 1977.

Carroll, James D. "Participatory Technology." **Science** 171, 1971.

Carrothers, Gerald P. "An Historical Review of the Gravity and Potential Concepts of Human Interaction." **Journal of the American Institute of Planners** 22, 1956.

Carter, J.E., President, U.S. "Comprehensive Radioactive Waste Program: Presidential Message to Congress, 12 February, 1980." **Weekly Compilation of Presidential Documents** 16. Washington, D.C., 1980.

Casper, Barry M. and Paul Wellstone. **Powerline: The First Battle of America's Energy War.** Amherst, Massachusetts: University of Massachusetts Press, 1981.

Catton, William. R., Jr. and Riley E. Dunlap. "Environmental Sociology: A New Paradigm." **The American Sociologist** 13, 1978.

Centaur Associates. **Siting of Hazardous Waste Management Facilities and Public Opposition.** Washington, D.C.: Centaur Associates, 1979.

Chalmers, J.A. and E.J. Anderson. **Economic-Demographic Assessment Manual: Current Practices, Procedural Recommendations, and a Test Case.** Denver, Colorado: U.S. Bureau of Reclamation, 1977.

Chalmers, J.A., E.J. Anderson, T. Beckhelm, and W. Hannigan. "An Empirical Model of Spatial Interaction in Sparsely Populated Regions." Paper Presented at 24th Annual Meeting of the Regional Science Association. Philadelphia, Pennsylvania. November 11-13, 1977.

Christensen, Steven. "Analysis of Public Intervention in the Siting Process in France and the United States." **Journal of International Law and Policy** 8, 1979.

Christensen, William and Theodore H. Clack, Jr. "A Western Perspective on Energy: A Plea for Rational Energy Planning." **Science** 194, 1976.

Christenson, James A. "Three Themes of Community Development," pp. 38-47 in **Community Development in America.** James A. Christenson and Jerry W. Robinson, Jr., Eds. Ames, Iowa: Iowa State University Press, 1980.

Christenson, James A. and Jerry W. Robinson, Jr., Eds. **Community Development in America.** Ames, Iowa: Iowa State University Press, 1980.

Christian Science Monitor. "A Nation of Neighborhoods: A Christian Science Monitor Reprint." Boston, Massachusetts: The Christian Science Publishing Society, 1978.

Citizens to Preserve Overton Park, Inc. v. Volpe. 401 U.S. 402, 416, 1971.

312

Clark, L.L. and B.M. Cole. **An Analysis of the Cost of Mined Geologic Repositories in Alternative Media.** Washington, D.C.: U.S. Department of Energy, 1982.

Cluett, C., M.T. Mertaugh, and M. Micklin. "A Demographic Model for Assessing the Socioeconomic Impacts of Large-Scale Industrial Development Projects." Paper Presented at 1977 Annual Meeting of the Southern Regional Demographic Group, Virginia Beach, Virginia. October 21-22, 1977.

Cluett, Christopher, Charles Sawyer, Marvin Olsen, and Diane Manninen. **Social and Economic Aspects of Nuclear Waste Management Activities: Impacts and Analytic Approaches.** Seattle, Washington: Battelle Human Affairs Research Center, 1979.

Cole, Roland J. and Tracy A. Smith. **Compensation for the Adverse Impacts of Nuclear Waste Management Facilities: Application of an Analytical Framework to Consideration of Eleven Potential Impacts.** Seattle, Washington: Battelle Human Affairs Research Center, 1979.

Coleman, James. **Community Conflict.** New York, New York: The Free Press, 1957.

Cook, Earl. "Ionizing Radiation," pgs. 297-323 in **Environment.** W. W. Murdoch, Ed. Sunderland, Massachusetts: Sinauer, 1975.

Cook, Earl. "The Role of History in the Acceptance of Nuclear Power." **Social Science Quaterly** 63, 1982.

Coon, C., N.L. Dalsted, A.G. Leholm, and F.L. Leistritz. **The Impact of the Safeguard Antiballistic Missile Construction on Northeastern North Dakota.** Fargo, North Dakota: North Dakota State University, 1976.

Cortese, Charles and Bernie Jones. "The Sociological Analysis of Boom Towns." **Western Sociological Review** 8, 1977.

Council of Energy Resource Tribes. "Impact of Nuclear Waste Legislation." Washington, D.C.; n.d.

Council of State Governments. **1972 Suggested State Legislation.** Denver, Colorado: Council of State Governments, 1972.

Crain, Robert L., Elihu Katz, and Donald B. Rosenthal. **The Politics of Community Conflict.** Indianapolis, Indiana: Bobbs-Merrill, 1969.

Crain, R. and D. Rosenthal. "Community Status as a Dimension of Local Decision Making." **American Sociological Review** 32, 1967.

Creighton, James L. **Public Involvement Manual: Involving the Public in Water and Power Resource Decisions.** Denver, Colorado: Water and Power Resources Services, 1980.

Cross, Marilyn. Socioeconomic consultant. Personal communication. Denver, Colorado: Pace Quality Development Associates, Inc., 1981.

Cummings, Ronald, Stuart H. Burness, and Roger G. Norton. **The Proposed Waste Isolation Pilot Project (WIPP) and Impacts in the State of New Mexico: A Socioeconomic Analysis.** Albuquerque, New Mexico: University of New Mexico, 1981.

Curry, M.G., J.A. Goodnight, M.R. Greene, D.J. Merwin, and R.F. Smith. **State and Local Planning Procedures Dealing with Social and Economic Impacts for Nuclear Power Plants.** Washington, D.C.: Nuclear Regulatory Commission, 1977.

Davenport, Judith A. and Joseph Davenport, III, Eds. **Boom Towns and Human Services.** Laramie, Wyoming: University of Wyoming Department of Social Work, 1979.

Davenport, Joseph, III and Judith Ann Davenport, Eds. **The Boom Town: Problems and Promises in the Energy Vortex.** Laramie, Wyoming: University of Wyoming Department of Social Work, 1980.

Davis, Thomas P. "Citizens' Guide to Intervention in Nuclear Power Plant Siting: A Blueprint for Alice in Nuclear Wonderland." **Environmental Law** 6, 1976.

Debes, Leroy. "The Impact of Industrialization on Property Values in Parsons, Kansas, 1960-1970." Unpublished M.S. thesis. Manhattan, Kansas: Kansas State University, 1973.

Denver Research Institute. **Socioeconomic Impact of Western Energy Resource Development.** Washington, D.C.: Council on Environmental Quality, 1979.

DePape, Denis. "Government/Industry Agreements for Resource Development: Socioeconomic Considerations." Presentation to CIM Annual General Meeting. Quebec City, Quebec. April 27, 1982.

Deutscher, Irwin. **What We Say/What We Do.** Glenview, Illinois: Scott, Foresman and Company, 1973.

DeVeney, G.R. Personal communication. Knoxville, Tennessee: Tennessee Valley Authority, 1981.

Dillman, Don A. **Mail and Telephone Surveys: The Total Design Method.** New York, New York: Wiley Interscience, 1978.

Dillman, Don A. and Daryl J. Hobbs, Eds. **Rural Society in the U.S.: Issues for the 1980s.** Boulder, Colorado: Westview Press, 1982.

Dixon, Mim. **What Happened to Fairbanks? The Effects of the Trans-Alaska Oil Pipeline on the Community of Fairbanks, Alaska.** Boulder, Colorado: Westview Press, 1978.

Downs, Anthony. "Up and Down With Ecology--The Issue-Attention Cycle." **Public Interest** 28, 1972.

Duberg, John A., Michael L. Frankel, and Christopher M. Niemczewski. "Siting of Hazardous Waste Management Facilities and Public Opposition." **Environmental Impact Assessment Review** 1, 1980.

314

Duncan, Otis D. "Social Organization and the Ecosystem," pgs. 36-82 in **Handbook of Modern Sociology.** Robert Faris, Ed. Chicago, Illinois: Rand McNally and Co., 1964.

Duncan, Otis D. and Leo Schnore. "Cultural, Behavioral, and Ecological Perspectives in the Study of Social Organization." **American Journal of Sociology** 65, 1959.

Ebringham, Jim. Superintendent of Schools. Telephone interview. Jeffrey City, Wyoming, 1982.

Edwards, Allan D. and Dorothy G. Jones. **Community and Community Development.** The Hague, Netherlands: Mouton, 1976.

E.I. **Dupont de Nemours and Co. v. Train** 541 F. 2d 1018 (4th Cir.), 1976.

Energy Facility Site Evaluation Council. **Site Certification Agreement Between the State of Washington and the Washington Public Power Supply System, WPPSS Nos. 3 and 5.** Olympia, Washington: Energy Facility Site Evaluation Council, 1976.

Environmental Defense Fund v. Ruckelshaus, 439 F. 2d 584, 597-98.

Ethyl Corp. v. EPA, 541 F. 2d 1, 68-69 (D.C. Dir.), 1976.

Evans-Pritchard, E.E. **Social Anthropology and Other Essays.** New York, New York: The Free Press, 1964.

Faas, Ronald C. **Mitigation of Local Community Fiscal Impacts Related to Nuclear Waste Repository Siting: A Background Paper.** Corvallis, Oregon: Western Rural Development Center, Oregon State University, 1980.

Faas, Ronald C. **Evaluation of Impact Mitigation Strategies: Case Studies of Four Tax-Exempt Facilities.** Pullman, Washington: Washington State University, 1982a.

Faas, Ronald C. Personal communication. Pullman, Washington: Washington State University, 1982b.

Farhar, Barbara C., Patricia Weis, Charles T. Unseld, and Barbara Burrs. **Public Opinion About Energy: A Literature Review.** Golden, Colorado: Solar Energy Research Institute, 1979.

Federal Energy Administration. **Regional Profile of Energy Impacted Communities.** Denver, Colorado: Federal Energy Administration, 1977.

Finsterbusch, Kurt. **Methods for Evaluating Non-Market Impacts in Policy Decisions with Special Reference to Water Resources Development Projects.** Fort Belvoir, Virginia: U.S. Army Corps of Engineers Institute for Water Resources, 1977.

Finsterbusch, K. and C.P. Wolf, Eds. **Methodology of Social Impact Assessment.** Stroudsburg, Pennsylvania: Dowden, Hutchinson, and Ross, Inc., 1977 and 1981.

315

Fitzsimmons, S.J., L.I. Stuart, and P.C. Wolff. **Social Assessment Manual: A Guide to the Preparation of the Social Well-Being Account.** Washington, D.C.: U.S. Bureau of Reclamation, 1975.

Flowers, Sir Brian. **Nuclear Power and the Environment.** Sixth Report of the Royal Commission on Environmental Pollution, London, United Kingdom: Her Majesty's Stationery Office, 1976.

Folkman, William S. **Public Involvement in the Decision-Making Process of Natural Resource Management Agencies with Special Reference to the Pacific Northwest.** Seattle, Washington: Institute of Government Research, 1973.

Ford, Andrew. **User's Guide to the BOOM 1 Model.** Los Alamos, New Mexico: Los Alamos Scientific Laboratory, 1976.

Frankena, W.K. "The Naturalistic Fallacy," pgs. 50-63 in **Theories of Ethics.** Philippa Foot, Ed. New York, New York: Oxford University Press, 1967.

Freudenburg, William R. "Balance and Bias in Boomtown Research." **Pacific Sociological Review** 25, 1982.

Freudenburg, William R. "The Effects of Rapid Population Growth on the Social and Personal Well-Being of Boomtown Residents." Paper Presented at the Western Rural Development Center Conference, Coping with the Impacts of Rapid Growth. Scottsdale, Arizona, 1980.

Freudenburg, William R. "Women and Men in an Energy Boomtown: Adjustment, Alienation, and Adaptation." **Rural Sociology** 46, 1981.

Freudenburg, W.R., L.M. Bacigalupi, and C. Landoll Young. "Mental Health Consequences of Rapid Community Growth: A Report from the Longitudinal Study of Boomtown Mental Health Impacts." **Journal of Health and Human Resources** 4, 1982.

Fuguitt, Glenn V. and James J. Zuiches. "Residential Preferences and Population Distribution." **Demography** 12, 1975.

Gamm, Larry and Frederick Fisher. "The Technical Assistance Approach," pgs. 48-63 in **Community Development in America.** James A. Christenson and Jerry W. Robinson, Jr., Eds. Ames, Iowa: Iowa State University Press, 1980.

Gans, Herbert J. "The Participant-Observations on the Personal Aspects of Field Work," pp. 300-317 in **Institutions and the Person: Papers Presented to Everett C. Hughes.** H.S. Becker, B. Geer, D. Riesman, and R.S. Weiss, Eds. Chicago, Illinois: Aldine, 1968.

Gardner, Jim. "Discrimination Against Future Generations: The Possibility of Constitutional Limitation." **Environmental Law** 9, 1978.

Garnick, D.H. "Differential Regional Multiplier Models." **Journal of Regional Science** 10, 1970.

Gartrell, J.W., H. Krahn, and F.D. Sunahara. "A Study of Human Adjustment in Fort McMurray." Prepared for Alberta Oil Sands Environmental Research Program. Edmonton, Alberta: Thames Group Research, Ltd., 1981.

Garvey, Gerald. **NWTS Policy and Public Choice.** Princeton, New Jersey: Center For International Studies, Princeton University, 1979.

Gessaman, Paul H., Lonnie L. Jones, William E. Kamps, and William C. Nelson. **Consumer Perceptions of Selected Community Services in the Great Plains.** Lincoln, Nebraska: Nebraska Agricultural Experiment Station, 1978.

Gilmore, J.S. "Boom Towns May Hinder Energy Resource Development." **Science** 191, 1976.

Gilmore, J.S. and M.K. Duff. **Boom Town Growth Management: A Case Study of Rock Springs--Green River, Wyoming.** Boulder, Colorado: Westview Press, 1975.

Gilmore, J.S., R.E. Giltner, D.C. Coddington, and M.K. Duff. **Factors Influencing an Area's Ability to Absorb a Large-Scale Commercial Coal-Processing Complex.** Washington, D.C.: Energy Research and Development Administration, 1975.

Gilmore, J.S., D. M. Hammond, K.D. Moore, J. Johnson, and D.C. Coddington. **Socioeconomic Impacts of Power Plants.** Denver, Colorado: Denver Research Institute, 1981.

Gilmore, J.S., K.D. Moore, D.M. Hammond, and D.C. Coddington. **Analysis of Financing Problems in Coal and Oil Shale Boom Towns.** Washington, D.C.: Federal Energy Administration, 1976a.

Gilmore, J.S., K.D. Moore, and D.M. Hammond. **Synthesis and Evaluation of Initial Methodologies For Assessing Socioeconomic and Secondary Environmental Impacts of Western Energy Resource Development.** Working Paper No. 2. Denver, Colorado: Denver Research Institute, 1976b.

Glasstone, Samuel and Walter H. Jordan. **Nuclear Power and its Environmental Effects.** La Grange Park, Illinois: American Nuclear Society, 1980.

Gold, Raymond L. **A Comparative Case Study of the Impacts of Coal Development on the Way of Life of People in the Coal Areas of Eastern Montana and Northeastern Wyoming.** Denver, Colorado: Northern Great Plains Resources Program, 1974.

Goodman, N. and G.T. Marx. **Society Today.** Third Edition. New York, New York: Random House, 1978.

Gordon, D., T.F. Gessell, H. Prichard, and C. Anderson. Review and Integration of Existing Literature Concerning Potential Social Impacts of Transportation of Radioactive Materials in Urban Areas. A Report for the U.S. Nuclear Regulatory Commission. Washington, D.C.: U.S. Government Printing Office, 1980.

Greene, Marjorie and Martha G. Curry. The Management of Social and Economic Impacts Associated with the Construction of Large-Scale Projects: Experiences from the Western Coal Development Communities. Seattle, Washington: Battelle Human Affairs Research Center, 1977.

Greene, Marjorie R. and Ted Hunter. The Management of Social and Economic Impacts Anticipated with a Nuclear Waste Repository: A Preliminary Discussion, (Draft). Seattle, Washington: Battelle Human Affairs Research Center, 1978.

Groves, R.M. and R.L. Kahn. Surveys by Telephone: A National Comparison with Personal Interviews. New York, New York: Academic Press, 1979.

Hadden, Susan, James Chiles, Paul Anaejionu, and Karl Cerny. High Level Nuclear Waste Disposal: Information Exchange and Conflict Resolution. Austin, Texas: Texas Energy and Natural Resources Advisory Council and U.S. Department of Energy, 1981.

Halstead, John M., F. Larry Leistritz, David G. Rice, David M. Saxowsky, and Robert A. Chase. Mitigating Socioeconomic Impacts of Nuclear Waste Repository Siting. Draft Report to the Office of Nuclear Waste Isolation. Fargo, North Dakota: North Dakota State University, 1982.

Harnisch, Arthur A., W.R. Burton, K.G. Larssow, and M.A. Hadaway. Chief Joseph Dam, Columbia River, Washington Community Impact Reports. Seattle District Reports. Fort Belvoir, Virginia: U.S. Army Corps of Engineers Institute of Water Resources, 1980.

Hawley, Amos H. "Ecology and Human Ecology." Social Forces 22, 1944.

Hawley, Amos H. "Human Ecology." International Encyclopedia of the Social Sciences, Vol. 4. New York, New York: Macmillan, 1968.

Hawley, Amos H. Human Ecology: A Theory of Community Structure. New York, New York: Ronald Press, 1950.

Hawley, Amos H. Urban Society: An Ecological Approach. New York, New York: Ronald Press, 1971.

Heberlein, Thomas and Robert Baumgartner. "Is a Questionnaire Necessary in a Record Mailing?" Public Opinion Quarterly 45, 1981.

318

Hebert, J.A., W.L. Rankin, P.C. Brown, C.R. Schuller, R.F. Smith, J.A. Goodnight, and H.E. Lippek. **Nontechnical Issues in Waste Management: Ethical, Institutional, and Political Concerns.** Seattle, Washington: Battelle Human Affairs Research Centers, 1978.

Helgath, Sheila F. **Legislative Policy and Impact Mitigation Trends in Large Energy and Construction Projects.** Fairbanks, Alaska: Office of the Federal Inspector. Alaska Natural Gas Transportation System, 1982.

Hertsgaard, T., S. Murdock, N. Toman, M. Henry, and R. Ludtke. **REAP Economic-Demographic Model: Technical Description.** Bismarck, North Dakota: North Dakota Regional Environmental Assessment Program, 1978.

Hirsch, W.Z. "Fiscal Impact of Industrialization on Local Schools." **Review of Economics and Statistics** 46, 1964.

Hollingshead, August B. "Community Research: Development and Present Condition." **American Sociological Review** 13, 1948.

Holmes and Narver, Inc. **Life Support Facility Planning and Evaluation Concept Study for Construction and Deployment Personnel, MX Weapons Systems.** San Francisco, California: U.S. Army Corps of Engineers, 1981.

Homans, George C. **Social Behavior: It's Elementary Forms.** New York, New York: Harcourt, Brace and World, 1961.

Horsley, John C., Paul Isaki, and Kenneth Jensen. "The Trident Submarine Comes to Kitsap Co.--An Analysis of Secondary Community Impacts." Paper Presented at the 10th Annual Pacific Northwestern Regional Economic Council. Victoria, British Columbia. May 7, 1976.

Housing Services, Inc. **Wright, Wyoming: A Planned Community Development Final Environmental Impact Statement.** Denver, Colorado: Department of Housing and Urban Development, 1979.

Houstoun, Lawrence. "Here's What Should Be Done About Energy Boom Towns." **Planning,** March 1977.

Howell, Robert E. and Darryll Olsen. **Citizen Participation in the Socio-Economic Analysis of Nuclear Waste Repository Siting.** Pullman, Washington: Department of Rural Sociology, Washington State University, 1981.

Hunter, Floyd. **Community Power Structure.** Chapel Hill, North Carolina: University of North Carolina Press, 1953.

Hutcheson, Francis. **An Inquiry Concerning Moral Good and Evil.** London, England: J. Darby, 1725.

319

Irwin, Richard. **Guide for Local Area Population Projections.** U.S. Bureau of the Census. Washington, D.C.: U.S. Government Printing Office, 1977.

Isard, W. **Methods of Regional Analysis: An Introduction to Regional Science.** Cambridge, Massachusetts: The MIT Press, 1960.

Isard, W., C. Choguill, J. Kissin, R. Seyfarth, and R. Tatlock. **Ecologic-Economic Analysis for Regional Development.** New York, New York: The Free Press, 1972.

Jakimo, Alan and Irvin C. Bupp. "Nuclear Waste Disposal: Not in My Backyard." **Technology Review** 80, 1978.

Jaksetic, Emilio. "Legal Aspects of Radioactive High-Level Waste Management." **Environmental Law** 9, 1979.

Johansson, Thomas B. and Peter Steen. **Radioactive Waste from Nuclear Power Plants.** Berkeley, California: University of California Press, 1981.

Johnstone, J.K. and K. Wolfsberg, Eds. **Evaluation of Tuff as a Medium for a Nuclear Waste Repository: Interim Status Report on the Properties of Tuff.** Albuquerque, New Mexico: Sandia National Laboratories, 1980.

Kahn, Sy. **How Poor People Get Power: Organizing Oppressed Communities for Action.** New York, New York: McGraw-Hill, 1970.

Kahneman, D. and A. Tversky. "Prospect Theory: An Analysis of Decision Under Risk." **Econometrica** 48, 1979.

Karp, H. and D. Kelly. **Towards an Ecological Analysis of Intermetropolitan Migration.** Chicago, Illinois: Markham, 1971.

Kasperson, J.X., R.E. Kasperson, C. Hohenemser, and R.W. Kates. "Institutional Responses to Three Mile Island." **The Bulletin of Atomic Scientists** 35, 1979.

Kasperson, Roger E. "Anticipating for the Socioeconomic Impacts of Nuclear Waste Facilities Upon Rural Communities." Testimony before the U.S. Senate Subcommittee on Rural Development of the Committee on Agriculture, Nutrition, and Forestry. Washington, D.C., August 26, 1980.

Kasperson, Roger E., Gerald Berk, David Pyawka, Alan B. Sharaf, and James Wood. "Public Opposition to Nuclear Energy: Retrospect and Prospect." **Science Technology, and Human Values.** August, 1980.

Kelly, John E. **In the Matter of Proposed Rulemaking on the Storage and Disposal of Nuclear Waste.** Washington, D.C.: Testimony before the Nuclear Regulatory Commission, Docket No. PR 50-51, April 15, 1980.

Klingsberg C. and J. Duguid. **Status of Technology for Isolating High-Level Radioactive Wastes in Geologic Repositories.** Washington, D.C.: U.S. Department of Energy/Technical Information Center, 1980.

Kraenzel, Carl Frederick. **The Great Plains in Transition.** Norman, Oklahoma: University of Oklahoma Press, 1955.

Krawetz, Natalia M. **Hazardous Waste Management: A Review of Social Concerns and Aspects of Public Involvement.** Prepared for the Research Secretariat, Department of the Environment. Edmonton, Alberta, Canada, 1979.

Land, Kenneth C. "Social Indicator Models: An Overview," pp. 5-36 in **Social Indicator Models.** K.C. Land and S. Spilerman, Eds. New York, New York: Russell Sage Foundation, 1975.

Land, Kenneth C. and Seymour Spilerman, Eds. **Social Indicator Models.** New York, New York: Russell Sage Foundation, 1975.

Langton, Stuart. "What Is Citizen Participation," in **Citizen Participation in America.** Stuart Langton, Ed. Lexington, Massachusetts: D.C. Heath, 1978.

LaPorte, Todd R. "Nuclear Waste: Increasing Scale and Sociopolitical Impacts." **Science** 201, 1978.

Laumann, Edward O., Peter V. Marsden, and Joseph Galaskiewiez. "Community-Elite Influence Structure: Extension of a Network Approach." **American Journal of Sociology** 83, 1977.

League of Women Voters. **A Nuclear Waste Primer.** Washington, D.C.: League of Women Voters Education Fund, 1980.

Lee, Everett S. and Harold F. Goldsmith. **Population Estimates: Methods for Small Area Analysis.** Beverly Hills, California: Sage Publications, 1982.

Leholm, A.G., F.L. Leistritz, and T.A. Hertsgaard. "Fiscal Impact of a New Industry in a Rural Area: A Coal Gasification Plant in Western North Dakota." **Regional Science Perspectives** 60, 1976a.

Leholm, A.G., F.L. Leistritz, and J.S. Wieland. **Profile of North Dakota's Electric Power Plant Construction Work Force.** Statistical Series No. 22. Fargo, North Dakota: North Dakota Agricultural Experiment Station, 1976b.

Leistritz, F.L. and R.A. Chase. "Socioeconomic Impact Monitoring Systems: A Review and Evaluation." **Journal of Environmental Management** 12, 1982.

Leistritz, F.L. and R.A. Chase. "Socioeconomic Impact Monitoring Systems: Review and Recommendations." Paper presented at Second International Forum on the Human Side of Energy. Edmonton, Alberta, Canada. August 16-19, 1981.

321

Leistritz, F. Larry, and Steve H. Murdock. **Socioeconomic Impact of Resource Development: Methods for Assessment.** Boulder, Colorado: Westview Press, 1981.
Leistritz, F. Larry, Steve H. Murdock, and Arlen G. Leholm. "Local Economic Changes Associated with Rapid Growth," pgs. 25-62 in **Coping with Rapid Growth in Rural Communities.** Bruce A. Weber and Robert E. Howell, Eds. Boulder, Colorado: Westview Press, 1982.
Leistritz, F.L., S.H. Murdock, N.E. Toman, and T.A. Hertsgaard. "A Model For Projecting Economic, Demographic, and Fiscal Impacts of Large-Scale Projects." **Western Journal of Agricultural Economics** 4, 1979.
Levan, C.L. "Measuring the Economic Base." **Papers of the Regional Science Association** 2, 1956.
Lewis, C. and S. Albrecht. "Attitudes Toward Accelerated Urban Development in Low Population Areas." **Growth and Change** 8, 1977.
Lindell, M.K., T.C. Earle, J.A. Hebert, and R.W. Perry. **Radioactive Wastes: Public Attitudes Toward Disposal Facilities.** Seattle, Washington: Battelle Human Affairs Research Center, 1978.
Little, R.L. "Some Social Consequences of Boom Towns." **North Dakota Law Review** 53, 1977.
Little, R.L. and S.B. Lovejoy. **Employment Benefits from Rural Industrialization.** Los Angeles, California: Lake Powell Research Project, 1977.
Littrell, Donald W. "The Self-Help Approach," pgs. 64-72 in **Community Development in America,** James A. Christenson and Jerry W. Robinson, Jr., Eds. Ames, Iowa: Iowa State University Press, 1980.
Long, L.H. and K.A. Hansen. **Reasons for Interstate Migration.** Current Population Reports. No. P-23, 81. Washington, D.C.: U.S. Government Printing Office, 1979.
Lonsdale, Richard E. and H.L. Seyler, Eds. **Nonmetropolitan Industrialization.** New York, New York: John Wiley and Sons, 1979.
Lopreato, S.C. and M. Blisset. **An Attitudinal Survey of Citizens in a Potential Gulf Coast Geopressured Geothermal Test-Well Locality.** Washington, D.C.: Energy Research and Development Administration, 1978.
Lovins, A.B., L.H. Lovins, and L. Ross. "Nuclear Power and Nuclear Bombs." **Foreign Affairs** 58, 1980.
Lovins, Amory and John H. Price. **Non-Nuclear Futures: The Case for an Ethical Energy Strategy.** New York, New York: Harper, 1975.
Lucas, Alastair R. "Legal Foundations for Public Participation in Environmental Decision-Making." **Natural Resources Journal** 16, 1976.

322

Ludtke, Richard L. **Social Impacts of Energy Development: A Combined Report of Content Analysis and Survey Data for Southwestern North Dakota.** Grand Forks, North Dakota: University of North Dakota, 1978.

Luke, Ronald T. "Managing Community Acceptance of Major Industrial Projects." **Coastal Zone Management Journal** 7, 1980.

Luke, Ronald T. President, RPC, Inc. Personal communication. Austin, Texas: RPC, Inc., May 1982.

McClain, W.C. and J.D. Russell. "Radioactive Waste Isolation." **Proceedings of Fifth International Symposium on Salt.** Cleveland, Ohio: Northern Ohio Geological Society, 1980.

McGinnis, K.A. Environmental economist. Personal communication. Richland, Washington: Washington Public Power Supply System, 1981.

McIntosh, William Alex, Gerald E. Klonglan, and Leslie Wilcox. "Theoretical Issues and Social Indicators: A Societal Process Approach." **Policy Sciences** 8, 1977.

McKee, Russell. **The Last West: A History of the Great Plains of North America.** Toronto, Canada: Fitzhenry and Whiteside, 1974.

MacNair, Ray H. "Citizen Participation as a Balanced Exchange: Analysis and Strategy." **Journal of the Community Development Society of America** 12, 1981.

McNulty, James E. "A Test of the Time Dimension in Economic Base Analysis." **Land Economics** 53, 1977.

Malhotra, Suresh and Diane Manninen. **Migration and Residential Location of Workers at Nuclear Power Plant Construction Sites.** Vol. 1: **Forecasting Methodology** and Vol. 2: **Profile Analysis of Worker Surveys.** Seattle, Washington: Battelle Human Affairs Research Center, 1980.

Malinowski, Bronislaw. **Argonauts of the Western Pacific.** New York, New York: E.P. Dutton and Co., 1922.

Martin, Roscoe. **Grass Roots: Rural Democracy in America** (2nd Edition). New York, New York: Harper & Row, 1964.

Massey, Garth. **Building a Power Plant: Newcomers and Social Impact.** Prepared for the Metro Center, National Institute of Mental Health. Rockville, Maryland, 1978.

Maxey, Margaret N. **Bioethical Perspective on Acceptable Risk Criteria for Nuclear Waste Management.** Livermore, California: Lawrence Livermore Laboratory, 1977.

Maxey, Margaret N. "Radwastes and Public Ethics: Issues and Imperatives." **Health Physics** 34, 1978.

Maynard, W.S., S.M. Nealey, J.A. Hebert, and M.K. Lindell. **Public Values Associated with Nuclear Waste Disposal.** Richland, Washington: Battelle Northwest Laboratories, 1976.

323

Mazmanian, Daniel A. and Jeanne Nienaber. **Can Organizations Change?: Environmental Protection, Citizen Participation, and the Corps of Engineers.** Washington, D.C.: Brookings Institution, 1979.
Meek, Daniel W. "Nuclear Power and State Radiation Measures: The Importance of Preemption." **Environmental Law** 10, 1979.
Meier, Kenneth J. "Micropolitical Economy: The Biases of Cost-Benefit Analysis." Paper Presented at the Annual Meetings of the Midwest Political Science Association. Cincinnati, Ohio, 1981.
Melbar, Barbara D., Stanley M. Nealey, Joy Hammersla, and William J. Rankin. **Nuclear Power and the Public: Analysis of Collected Survey Research.** Richland, Washington: Battelle Northwest Laboratories, 1977.
Metz, William C. **Construction Work Force Management: Worker Transportation and Temporary Housing Techniques.** Report Prepared for Western Rural Development Center. Corvallis, Oregon, 1981.
Metz, William C. "Energy Industry Uses of Socioeconomic Impact Management." Paper Presented at International Congress for Energy and the Ecosystem. Grand Forks, North Dakota. June 12-16, 1978.
Metz, William C. **Socioeconomic Impact Management in the Western Energy Industry.** Upton, New York: Brookhaven National Laboratories, 1979.
Metz, William C. "The Mitigation of Socioeconomic Impacts by Electric Utilities." **Public Utilities Fortnightly** 106, 1980.
Minneapolis Star and Tribune. "Exxon to Close Oil-Shale Project." May 3, 1982.
Missouri Basin Power Project. **Socioeconomic Impact Monitoring Program.** Monitoring Report #42. Wheatland, Wyoming: Missouri Basin Power Project, 1980.
Mitchell, Robert Cameron. **The Public Response to Three Mile Island: A Compilation of Public Opinion Data about Nuclear Energy.** Washington, D.C.: Resources for the Future, Inc., 1979.
Molotch, Harvey. "The City as a Growth Machine: Toward a Political Economy of Place." **American Journal of Sociology** 82, 1976.
Moore, G.E. **Principia Ethica.** London, England: Cambridge University Press, 1903 and 1968.
Morell, David and Christopher Magorian. **Siting Hazardous Waste Facilities: Local Opposition and the Myth of Preemption.** Princeton, New Jersey: Center for Energy and Environmental Studies. Princeton University, 1982.
Morris, F.A., D. Keller, and A.H. Schilling. **Statutory Constraints on High Level Waste Disposal in Selected States.** Seattle, Washington: Battelle Human Affairs Research Center, 1980.

Morrison, P.A. **Demographic Information for Cities: A Manual for Estimating and Projecting Local Population Characteristics.** Rand Report. Santa Monica, California: Rand Corporation, 1971.

Mountain West Research, Inc. **Construction Worker Profile.** Washington, D.C.: Old West Regional Commission, 1975.

Mountain West Research, Inc. **A Guide to Methods for Impact Assessment of Western Coal/Energy Development.** Omaha, Nebraska: Missouri River Basin Commission, 1979.

Muller, T. **Fiscal Impacts of Land Development: A Critique of Methods and Review of Issues.** URI 98000. Washington, D.C.: The Urban Institute, 1975.

Murdock, Steve H. "The Potential Role of the Ecological Framework in Impact Analysis." **Rural Sociology** 44, 1979.

Murdock, Steve H. and F. Larry Leistritz. **Energy Development in the Western United States: Impact on Rural Areas.** New York, New York: Praeger Publishers, 1979.

Murdock, Steve H. and F. Larry Leistritz. **Methods for Assessing the Socioeconomic Impacts of Large-Scale Resource Developments: Implications for Nuclear Repository Siting.** Report to the Office of Nuclear Waste Isolation and the Department of Energy. Draft Report for the Socioeconomic Analysis of Repository Siting Project for Fiscal Year 1980. College Station, Texas: Texas Agricultural Experiment Station, 1980.

Murdock, Steve H. and F. Larry Leistritz. **Methods for Assessing the Socioeconomic Impacts of Large-Scale Resource Developments: Implications for Nuclear Repository Siting.** A Report to the Office of Nuclear Waste Isolation. College Station, Texas: Texas Agricultural Experiment Station, 1981.

Murdock S.H. and E.C. Schriner. **Findings from the North Dakota 100 Survey, Total State Area Report No. 1.** Prepared by the Center for Social Research, North Dakota State University. Bismarck, North Dakota: North Dakota State Planning Department, 1976.

Murdock, Steve H. and Eldon C. Schriner. "Structural and Distributional Factors in Community Development." **Rural Sociology** 43, 1978.

Murdock, Steve H. and Willis A. Sutton, Jr. "The New Ecology and Community Theory: Similarities, Differences, and Convergencies." **Rural Sociology** 39, 1974.

Murdock, Steve H., F. Larry Leistritz, and Eldon Schriner. "Local Demographic Changes Associated with Rapid Growth," pp. 63-96 in **Coping with Rapid Growth in Rural Communities.** Bruce A. Weber and Robert E. Howell, Eds. Boulder, Colorado: Westview Press, 1982b.

Murdock, S.H., F.L. Leistritz, and E.C. Schriner. "Migration and Energy Developments: Implications for Rural Areas in the Great Plains" in **New Directions in Urban-Rural Migration.** D. Brown and J. Wardwell, Eds. New York, New York: Academic Press, 1980.

Murdock, Steve H., John K. Thomas, and Don E. Albrecht. **Handbook for Assessing the Social and Special Effects of Nuclear Repository Siting.** A Report to the Office of Nuclear Waste Isolation. College Station, Texas: Texas Agricultural Experiment Station, 1982c.

Murdock, S.H., J.S. Wieland, and F.L. Leistritz. "An Assessment of the Validity of the Gravity Model for Predicting Community Settlement Patterns in Rural Energy-Impacted Areas in the West." **Land Economics** 54, 1978.

Murdock, Steve H., F. Larry Leistritz, Rita R. Hamm, Robert A. Chase, and Barbara Kiel. **The SocioEconomic Analysis of Repository Siting (SEARS): Technical Description.** A Report to the Office of Nuclear Waste Isolation. College Station, Texas: Texas Agricultural Experiment Station, 1982a.

Murdock, S.H., F.L. Lesitritz, L.L. Jones, D. Andrews, B. Wilson, D. Fannin, and J. de Montel. **The Texas Assessment Modeling System: Technical Description.** College Station, Texas: Texas Agricultural Experiment Station, 1979a.

Murdock, S.H., F.L. Leistritz, L.L. Jones, D. Fannin, D. Andrews, B. Wilson, and J. de Montel. **The Texas Assessment Modeling System: User Manual.** College Station, Texas: Texas Agricultural Experiment Station, 1979b.

Murphy, J.K. "Socioeconomic Impact Assistance for Synthetic Fuels Commercial Demonstration Program," pgs. 112-118 in **Financing Energy Development: Proceedings of the First National Conference on Financial Requirements For Energy Development in the Western States Region.** H. Hughes and R. Zee, Eds. Sante Fe, New Mexico: New Mexico Energy Resources Board, 1975.

Murphy and Williams, Consultants. **Socioeconomic Impact Assessment: A Methodology Applied to Synthetic Fuels.** Washington, D.C.: U.S. Department of Energy, 1978.

326

Murray, James A. "The Effects of Rapid Population Growth on the Provision and Financing of Local Public Services." Paper Presented at Seminar on Social and Economic Impacts of Rapid Growth, Western Rural Development Center. Scottsdale, Arizona. February 26-27, 1980.

Myhra, David. "Colstrip, Montana . . . The Modern Company Town." **Coal Age,** May 1975.

Myhra, David. "Energy Development: Dealing With the Social and Economic Impacts Is the Hard Job Often Left to Rural or County Planners and Officials." **Practicing Planner,** September 1976.

Myhra, David. **Energy Plant Sites: Community Planning for Large Projects.** Atlanta, Georgia: Conway Publications, Inc., 1980.

National Academy of Sciences. **Estimating Population and Income of Small Areas.** Washington, D.C.: National Academy Press, 1980.

National Academy of Sciences, National Research Council. **The Disposal of Radioactive Waste on Land.** Washington, D.C.: National Academy of Sciences, 1957.

National Aeronautics and Space Administration. **Feasibility of Space Disposal of Radioactive Nuclear Waste.** Cleveland, Ohio: National Aeronautics and Space Administration, 1974.

National Waste Terminal Storage (NWTS) Program. **Proceedings of the 1981 National Waste Terminal Storage Program Information Meeting.** Columbus, Ohio: U.S. Department of Energy Battelle Project Management Division, 1981.

Nealey, Stanley M. and Linda M. Radford. **Public Policy Issues in Nuclear Waste Management.** Seattle, Washington: Battelle Human Affairs Research Center, 1978.

Northern Flood Agreement. Agreement among Her Majesty the Queen in Right of the Province of Manitoba, the Manitoba Hydro Electric Board, the Northern Flood Committee, Inc., and Her Majesty the Queen in Right of Canada. Manitoba, Canada. December 16, 1977.

Office of Nuclear Waste Isolation. **Framework for Community Planning Associated with Nuclear Waste Repository Siting.** Columbus, Ohio: Battelle Memorial Institute, October 1981.

Office of Nuclear Waste Isolation. **NWTS Program Criteria for Mined Geologic Disposal of Nuclear Waste: Site Performance Criteria.** Columbus, Ohio: Battelle Memorial Institute, February 1981a.

Office of Technology Assessment. **Summary: Managing Commercial High-Level Radioactive Waste.** Washington, D.C.: U.S. Congress, April 1982.

O'Hare, Michael. "'Not on My Block You Don't' Facility Siting and the Strategic Importance of Compensation." **Public Policy** 24, 1977.

O'Hare, Michael, Lawrence Bacow, and Judah Rosc. **Facility Siting and Public Opposition.** New York, New York: Van Nostrand-Reinhold, 1982.

O'Hare, Michael and Debra R. Sanderson. "Fair Compensation and the Boomtown Problem." **Urban Law Annual** 14, 1977.

Olsen, Marvin E. "Three Routes to Political Party Participation." **Western Political Quarterly** 29, 1976.

Olsen, Marvin E. **Participatory Pluralism: Political Participation and Influence in the United States and Sweden.** Chicago, Illinois: Nelson-Hall, 1982.

O'Riordan, Jon. "The Public Involvement Program in the Okanogan Basin Study." **Natural Resources Journal** 16, 1976.

Pace Quality Development Associates, Inc. **Cathedral Bluffs Shale Oil Project Socioeconomic Monitoring Report.** Denver, Colorado: Pace Quality Development Associates, Inc., 1980.

Pahner, P.D. **A Psychological Perspective on the Nuclear Energy Controversy.** Research Memorandum. Laxenburg, Austria: International Institute for Applied Systems Analysis, 1976.

Park, Robert E. **Race and Culture.** Glencoe, Illinois: The Free Press, 1950.

Parsons, Brinckerhoff, Quade, and Douglas, Inc. **Waste Isolation Facility Description: Bedded Salt.** Oak Ridge, Tennessee: Nuclear Division, Office of Waste Isolation, 1976.

Parsons, Talcott. **The Social System.** New York, New York: The Free Press, 1951.

Pearson, C. Personal communication. Bismarck, North Dakota: Basin Electric Power Cooperative, 1981.

Peck, Roy. State Senator. Telephone interview. Riverton, Wyoming, May 1982.

Peelle, Elizabeth. **Community Impacts of Energy Production.** Oak Ridge, Tennessee: Oak Ridge National Laboratory, 1979.

Peelle, Elizabeth. "Social Impact Mitigation and Nuclear Waste Repository Siting." Testimony before the Senate Subcommittee on Rural Development of the Committee on Agriculture, Nutrition and Forestry. August 26, 1980.

Percival, Donald E. "State and Local Control of Energy Development on Federal Lands." **Stanford Law Review** 32, 1980.

Peters, Ted. "Ethical Considerations Surrounding Nuclear Waste Repository Siting and Mitigation: A Background Paper." A Paper Prepared for the Office of Nuclear Waste Isolation, Battelle-Columbus. July 1981.

Pfister, R. "On Improving Export Base Studies." **Regional Science Perspectives** 6, 1976.

328

Pittenger, Donald. **Projecting State and Local Populations.** Cambridge, Massachusetts: Ballinger Publishing Company, 1976.

Popenoe, David. **Sociology.** Fourth Edition. Englewood Cliffs, New Jersey: Prentice-Hall, 1980.

Poplin, Dennis E. **Communities: A Survey of Theories and Methods of Research.** Second Edition. New York, New York: MacMillan Publishing Co., 1979.

Poston, Richard W. **Democracy is You.** New York, New York: Harper & Row, 1953.

Poston, Richard W. **Action Now! A Citizen's Guide to Better Communities.** Carbondale, Illinois: Southern Illinois University Press, 1976.

President's Economic Adjustment Committee. **Community Impact Assistance Study.** Washington, D.C.: Intergovernmental/Interagency Task Force on Community Assistance, 1981.

Quality Development Associates, Inc. **Oil Shale Development: A Description of Socioeconomic Mitigation Strategies at the Community and County Level.** Denver, Colorado: Quality Development Associates, 1978.

Rafferty, T. Socioeconomic coordinator. Personal communication Spokane, Washington: Washington Water Power Company, 1981.

Rankin, William J., Barbara D. Melbar, Thomas Overcast, and Stanley M. Nealey. **Nuclear Power and the Public: Recent Survey Research.** Seattle, Washington: Battelle Human Affairs Research Center, 1982.

Rankin, W.L. and S.M. Nealey. **Public Concerns and Choices Regarding Nuclear Waste Repositories.** Seattle, Washington: Battelle Human Affairs Research Center, June 1981.

Rankin, W.L. and S.M. Nealey. **The Relationship of Human Values and Energy Beliefs to Nuclear Power Attitudes.** Seattle, Washington: Battelle Human Affairs Research Center, 1978.

Ratigan, J.L. and G.D. Callahan. **Evaluation of the Predictive Capability of the Finite Element Method: II, Project Salt Vault-Thermo/Visoelastic Simulation.** Washington, D.C.: Office of Waste Isolation, 1978.

Rawls, John. **A Theory of Justice.** Cambridge, Massachusetts: Harvard University Press, Belknap Edition, 1971.

Ray v. **Atlantic Richfield Co.** 435 U.S. 151, 173 n. 25, 1978.

Reiss, Albert J., Jr. "The Sociological Study of Communities." **Rural Sociology** 24, 1959.

Resources for the Future, Inc. **Public Opinion on Environmental Issues.** Washington, D.C.: Council on Environmental Quality, 1980.

Rice, David G., David M. Saxowsky, and F. Larry Leistritz. **Probable Effects of Nuclear Repository Study Site Designation on Local Land Values and Precedents/Procedures for Indemnification of Affected Parties.** Report Prepared for the Office of Nuclear Waste Isolation/Department of Energy. Fargo, North Dakota: North Dakota State University, 1980.

Richardson, H.W. **Input-Output and Regional Economics.** New York, New York: Halstead Press, 1972.

Richardson, H.W. **Regional and Urban Economics.** New York, New York: Penguin Books, 1978.

Robinson, Jerry W., Jr. "The Conflict Approach," pgs. 73-95 in **Community Development in America.** James A. Christenson and Jerry W. Robinson, Jr., Eds. Ames, Iowa: Iowa State University Press, 1980.

Rodgers, Joseph Lee. **Environmental Impact Assessment, Growth Management and the Comprehensive Plan.** Cambridge, Massachusetts: Ballinger Publishing Co., 1976.

Rodgers, William. "A Hard Look at Vermont Yankee: Environmental Law Under Close Scrutiny." **Georgetown Law Journal** 67, 1979.

Rogers, John. Beulah city planner. Personal communication. Beulah, North Dakota, April 1982.

Romanoff, E. "The Economic Base Model: A Very Special Case of Input-Output Analysis." **Journal of Regional Science** 14, 1974.

Rose, Judah, Alan Weinstein, and Julia Wondolleck. **Nuclear Energy Facilities and Public Conflict: Three Case Studies.** Cambridge, Massachusetts: Massachusetts Institute of Technology, Energy Impacts Project, 1979.

Rosenthal, Donald B. and Robert L. Crain. "Structure and Values in Local Political Systems: The Case of Fluoridation Decisions," pgs. 215-242 in **Community Structure and Decision Making: Comparative Analyses.** Terry N. Clark, Ed. Scranton, Pennsylvania: Chandler Publishing Co., 1968.

Rothman, Jack. "Three Models of Community Organization Practice," pgs. 25-44 in **Strategies of Community Organization: A Book of Readings** (Third Edition). Fred M. Cox, John L. Erlich, Jack Rothman, and John E. Tropman, Eds. Itasca, Illinois: F.E. Peacock, 1979.

Rubin, Lillian B. "Maximum Feasible Participation: The Origins, Implications, and Present Status." **The Annals of the American Academy of Political and Social Science** 385, 1969.

Russell, J.E. **Areal Thermal Loading Recommendations for Nuclear Waste Repositories in Salt.** Washington, D.C.: Department of Energy, Office of Waste Isolation, Union Carbide Corporation, Nuclear Division, 1979.

Russell, J.E. "Underground Storage of Nuclear Waste," **Underground Space** 2, 1977.

Sahakian, William S. **Ethics: An Introduction to Theories and Problems.** New York, New York: Barnes and Noble, 1974.

Salt Lake Tribune. Editorial. November 17, 1980, pg. A-10.

Sargent, H.L., Jr. "Fish-Bowl Planning Immerses Pacific Northwest Citizens in Corps Projects," **Civil Engineering** 42, 1972.

Schilling, A.H., A. Harris, M. Lindell, A. Marcus, R. Perry, and M. Selvin. **Emergency Response in Transportation of Radioactive Materials: An Evaluation Methodology.** Seattle, Washington: Battelle Human Affairs Research Center, 1979.

Schriner, E.C., J.N. Query, T.D. McDonald, F. Keogh, and T. Gallagher. **An Assessment of the Social Impacts Associated with a Coal Gasification Complex Proposed for Dunn County, North Dakota.** Fargo, North Dakota: North Dakota State University, 1976.

Schuller, C.R. and M. Huelshoff. **Long Term Nuclear Waste Management: The Problem of Retaining Information and Maintaining Surveillance for 100 Years.** Seattle, Washington: Battelle Human Affairs Research Center, 1981.

Schulze, William, David Brookshire, and Todd Sandler. "The Social Rate of Discount for Nuclear Waste Storage: Economics or Ethics?" **Natural Resources Journal** 21, 1981.

Schuman, Howard and Stanley Presser. **Questions and Answers in Attitude Surveys: Experiments on Question Form, Wording, and Context.** New York, New York: Academic Press, 1981.

Schwartz, D.F. **Reservation Manpower Survey.** Bismarck, North Dakota: United Tribes Educational Technical Center, 1977.

Shaffer, R.E. "Estimating Local Income Multipliers: A Review and Evaluation of the Techniques for Ex Ante use." Paper Presented to North Central Interest Network on Ex Ante Growth Impact Models. Columbus, Ohio, March 6-7, 1979.

Shaffer, R.E. and L.G. Tweeten. **Economic Changes from Industrial Development in Eastern Oklahoma.** Stillwater, Oklahoma: Oklahoma Agricultural Experiment Station, 1975.

Sheldon, E.B. and W.E. Moore, Eds. **Indicators of Social Change: Concepts and Measurement.** New York, New York: Russell Sage Foundation, 1968.

Shryock, H.S. and J.S. Siegel. **The Methods and Materials of Demography.** Washington, D.C.: U.S. Bureau of the Census. U.S. Government Printing Office, 1973.

Smart, J.J.C. "Extreme and Restricted Utilitarianism," pgs. 171-183 in **Theories of Ethics**. Philippa Foot, Ed. New York, New York: Oxford University Press, 1967.

Smith, R.F. **Federal-State Relationships in Nuclear Waste Repository Siting**. Seattle, Washington: Battelle Human Affairs Research Center, 1979.

State ex rel. Andrus v. Click. 97 Idaho 791, 554 p. 2d at 979, 1976.

Stenehjem, Erik J. **Summary Description of SEAM: The Social and Economic Assessment Model.** Argonne, Illinois: Argonne National Laboratory, 1978.

Stenehjem, Erik J. and J.E. Metzger. **A Framework for Projecting Employment and Population Changes Accompanying Energy Development.** Argonne, Illinois: Argonne National Laboratory, 1976.

Stinner, William F. and Michael B. Toney. **Energy Resource Development and Migrant-Native Differences.** Logan, Utah: Utah Agricultural Experiment Station, 1981.

Strauss, Bert and Mary E. Stowe. **How to Get Things Changed.** New York, New York: Doubleday and Company, 1974.

Susskind, Lawrence E. and Stephen R. Cassella. "The Danger of Preemptive Legislation: The Case of LNG Facility Siting in California." **Environmental Impact Assessment Review** 1, 1980.

Susskind, Lawrence E. and M. O'Hare. **Managing the Social and Economic Impacts of Energy Development.** Summary Report of Phase I of the Energy Impacts Project. Cambridge, Massachusetts: Laboratory of Architecture and Planning, Massachusetts Institute of Technology, 1977.

Taylor, Randall L. "NEPA Pre-emption Legislation: Decisionmaking Alternative for Crucial Federal Projects." **Environmental Affairs** 6, 1978.

Tennessee Valley Authority. **Hartsville Nuclear Plants Socioeconomic Monitoring and Mitigation Reports.** Knoxville, Tennessee: Tennessee Valley Authority, 1980.

Thibaut, J.W. and H.H. Kelley. **The Social Psychology of Groups.** New York, New York: John Wiley and Sons, 1959.

THK Associates. **Factors Influencing an Area's Ability to Absorb a Large-Scale Commercial Coal-Processing Complex.** J.S. Gilmore, R.E. Giltner, D.C. Coddington, and M.K. Duff, Eds. Washington, D.C.: Energy Research and Development Administration, 1975.

Thompson, J.G., A.L. Blevins, and G.L. Watts. **Socioeconomic Longitudinal Monitoring Report.** Washington, D.C.: Old West Regional Commission, 1978.

332

Tiebout, C.M. **The Community Economic Base Study.**
Supplementary Paper No. 16. New York, New York:
Committee for Economic Development, 1962.
Toman, N.E., A.G. Leholm, N.L. Dalsted, and F.L.
Leistritz. "A Fiscal Impact Model For Rural
Industrialization." **Western Journal of Agricultural
Economics** 1, 1977.
TOSCO Foundation. **Socioeconomic Impact Mitigation
Program, NOSR-1.** Boulder, Colorado: TOSCO
Foundation, 1980.
Tweeten, L. and G.L. Brinkman. **Micropolitan Development.**
Ames, Iowa: Iowa State University Press, 1976.
U.S. Chamber of Commerce. **Forward Thrust: Guidelines
for Mobilizing Total Community Resources.**
Washington, D.C.: Chamber of Commerce of the United
States, 1968.
U.S. Community Services Administration. **Citizen
Participation.** Washington, D.C.: U.S. Government
Printing Office, 1978.
U.S. Department of Air Force. **Environmental Impact
Assessment Analysis Process: Deployment Area
Selection and Land Withdrawal/Aquisition Draft EIS.**
Washington, D.C.: U.S. Department of the Air Force,
1981.
U.S. Department of Energy. **Answers to your Questions
about High-Level Nuclear Waste Isolation.**
Washington, D.C.: Department of Energy, 1982.
U.S. Department of Energy. **Environmental Aspects of
Commercial Radioactive Waste Management,** Vol. 3.
Springfield, Virginia: NTIS, 1979.
U.S. Department of Energy. **Final Environmental Impact
Statement: Waste Isolation Pilot Project,** Volume 1.
Washington, D.C.: U.S. Department of Energy, 1981a.
U.S. Department of Energy. **Management of Commercially
Generated Radioactive Waste, Final Environmental
Impact Statement.** Washington, D.C.: U.S.
Department of Energy, 1980a.
U.S. Department of Energy. **National Plan for Siting
Radioactive Waste Repositories and Environmental
Assessment.** Columbus, Ohio: Battelle Memorial
Institute, February 1982a.
U.S. Department of Energy. "Program of Research and
Development for Management and Disposal of
Commercially Generated Wastes: Record of Decision
(to adopt a strategy to develop mined geologic
repositories . . .)." **Federal Register** 46, May
1981c.
U.S. Department of Energy. **Spent Fuel and Radioactive
Waste Inventories and Projections as of December 31,
1980.** Washington, D.C.: U.S. Department of Energy,
1981b.

333

U.S. Department of Energy. **Statement of Position of the
United States Department of Energy: Proposed Rule-
making on the Storage and Disposal of Nuclear Waste.**
Washington, D.C.: U.S. Department of Energy, 1980b.
U.S. Department of Transportation. **Effective Citizen
Participation in Transportation Planning.** 2 Vols.
Washington, D.C.: Socioeconomic Studies Division,
Federal Highway Administation, 1976.
U.S. Environmental Protection Agency. **Environmental
Protection Agency Action Handbook: Managing Growth
in the Small Community, Part One: Getting a Picture
of What's Ahead.** Washington, D.C.: U.S. Government
Printing Office, 1978.
U.S. Environmental Protection Agency. **Everybody's
Problem: Hazardous Waste.** Washington, D.C.:
Office of Water and Waste Management, 1980.
U.S. House of Representatives. **Nuclear Waste Disposal in
Michigan, July 6.** Washington, D.C.: Sub-committee
on Energy and the Environment, Committee on Interim
and Insular Affairs, United States House of
Representatives, 1976.
U.S. Senate. **Congressional Record, October 15.**
Washington, D.C.: United States Senate, 1971.
Urban Systems Research and Engineering, Inc. **A Handbook
for the States on the Use of Compensation and
Incentives in the Siting of Hazardous Waste
Management Facilities.** Prepared for U.S.
Environmental Protection Agency. Cambridge,
Massachusetts: Urban Systems Research and
Engineering, Inc., 1980.
Utah Consortium for Energy Research and Education.
**Review of the U.S. Air Force Draft EIS on Deployment
Area Selection and Land Withdrawal/Acquisition for
the MX Missile System: A Report to Governor Scott
M. Matheson.** Salt Lake City, Utah: Utah State MX
Coordination Office, 1981.
Van Es, John. "Citizen Participation in the Planning
Process," in **Aspects of Planning for Public Services
in Rural Areas.** David L. Rogers and Larry R.
Whiting, Eds. Ames, Iowa: North Central Regional
Center for Rural Development, Iowa State University,
1976.
Verba, Sidney and Norman H. Nie. **Participation in
America: Political and Social Equality.** New York,
New York: Harper and Row, 1972.
Voth, Donald E. and Virginia M. Jackson. "Citizen
Participation in Rural Development: An Analysis of
Research Literature With a Focus Upon Evaluation."
Paper Presented at the Symposium on Evaluation of
Citizen Participation. Washington, D.C., 1980.

334

Wahi, K.K., D.E. Maxwell, and R. Hofmann. **A Simulation of the Thermomechanical Response of Project Salt Vault.** Washington, D.C.: Office of Waste Isolation, Energy Research and Development Administration, 1977.

Walsh, Edward J. "Resource Mobilization, Three Mile Island Protest, and Nuclear Waste Repository Siting." A Paper Prepared for the Office of Nuclear Waste Isolation, Battelle-Columbus. University Park, Pennsylvania: Pennsylvania State University, January 1982.

Warren, Roland. **The Community in America.** Chicago, Illinois: Rand McNally, 1972.

Warren, Roland. "The Good Community: What Would it Be?" pgs. 535-545 in **New Perspectives on the American Community** (Third Edition). Roland L. Warren, Ed. Chicago, Illinois: Rand McNally, 1977.

Warwick, Donald P. and Charles A. Lininger. **The Sample Survey: Theory and Practice.** New York, New York: McGraw-Hill, 1975.

Washington Public Power Supply System. **Quarterly Socioeconomic Report of WNP-3/5, Satsop Construction Project, July 1, 1980 to September 30, 1980.** Vol. 4, Report No. 3. Richland, Washington: Washington Public Power Supply System, 1980.

Wax, Rosalie H. **Doing Fieldwork: Warnings and Advice.** Chicago, Illinois: University of Chicago Press, 1971.

Wax, Rosalie H. "Participant Observation," pp. 238-241 in Vol. 11 of **International Encyclopedia of the Social Sciences.** David L. Sills, Ed. New York, New York: Macmillan and the Free Press, 1968.

Weiss, S.J. and E.C. Gooding. "Estimation of Differential Employment Multipliers in a Small Regional Economy." **Land Economics** 44, 1968: 235-244.

Weissman, Harold. **Community Development in the Mobilization for Youth Experience.** New York, New York: Association Press, 1969.

Western Fuels, Inc. **Deserado Mine Socioeconomic Impact Agreement.** Washington, D.C.: Western Fuels, Inc., 1981.

Whyte, William Foote. **Street Corner Society: The Social Structure of an Italian Slum.** Chicago, Illinois: The University of Chicago Press, 1955.

Wieland, J.S., F.L. Leistritz, and S.H. Murdock. "Characteristics and Residential Patterns of Energy-Related Work Forces in the Northern Great Plains." **Western Journal of Agricultural Economics** 4, 1979.

Wieland, J.S., F.L. Leistritz, and S.H. Murdock. **Characteristics and Settlement Patterns of Energy-Related Operational Workers in the Northern Great Plains.** Fargo, North Dakota: North Dakota Agricultural Experiment Station, 1977.

Wilcox, Leslie D., Ralph M. Brooks, George M. Beal, and Gerald E. Klongan. **Social Indicators and Societal Monitoring: An Annotated Bibliography.** Amsterdam, Holland: Elsevier Scientific Publishing Co., 1972.

Wilkinson, Kenneth P., James G. Thompson, Robert Reynolds, Jr., and Lawrence M. Ostresh. "Local Social Disruption and Western Energy Development: A Critical Review." **Pacific Sociological Review** 25, 1982.

Yuan, Georgia. "The Geologist and Radioactive Waste Disposal, or, Can Geologists Agree?" Paper Presented at the Symposium on Uncertainties Associated With the Regulation of Geologic Disposal of High-Level Radioactive Waste. Gatlinburg, Tennessee, 1981.

Zionty, Alvin J. Letter to Congressman Morris K. Udall. Seattle, Washington: Zionty, Pirtle, Morisset, Ernstoff, and Chestnut, Attorneys at Law. August 15, 1980.

Index

Arbitration.
See Mitigation
Atomic Energy Act, 74-75
Administrative Proce-
dures Act, 80-81

Battlement Mesa, Colorado,
195
British Columbia, Canada,
273-274
Bruneau, Idaho, 184

Campbell County Monitoring
Program, 195-196
Central Maine Power
Company (CMP), 182-183
Citizen involvement.
See Public involvement
Citizen participation.
See Public involvement
Cohort. See Demographic
Colony Oil Shale Project,
195
Colorado Joint Review
Process, 198
Colstrip, Montana, 194
Community Development,
231-288
auctioning process in,
257, 260-264
bidding process in, 257,
260-264
conflict approach, 253-
254
evaluation of, 281, 283-
284, 286-287
mobilization theory in,
277-278

past failures in, 271-
276
principles in, 276-277
process of, 251-254,
279-288
professionals in, 251-
254
self-help approach, 252-
253
social exchange in,
278-279
steps in, 254-256
technical assistance
approach, 253
theories of, 251-254,
277-279
Community services.
See Service
Community Shutdown Team
(CST), 188-189
Company towns, 194-195
Concurrence.
See Consultation and
Concurrence Program
Consultation and Concur-
rence Program, 68-69,
272-273
Cooperative Power Asso-
ciation (CPA), 185-186
CU Project, 185-186

Deaf Smith County, Texas,
137
Delta, Utah, 235, 239-243
Demographic assessment,
baseline projections
in, 148
cohort methods in, 146

gravity models in, 148-149
impact projections in, 148-151
methods for, 146-151
population-to-employment ratios in, 146
research needs in, 298-299
Demographic impacts, 132-143
effects on migration, 138-140
effects on population composition, 140-141
effects on population distribution, 136-140
effects on population size, 137-138
forms of, 135-136
special forms of. See Special impacts
Deserado Mine Agreement, 196

Earthline, Inc., 185
Ecological theory, 92-93
Economic, 119-134
export base theory, 128-130
input/output theory, 130-131
multiplier, 120-122
secondary, 120
Economic assessment, 128-131
baseline projections in, 131
export base methods in, 128-130
impact projections in, 131
input/output methods in, 130-131
location quotients in, 131
methods for, 128-131
research needs in, 298
Economic impacts, 120-128
effects on business sectors, 125-126
effects on employment, 120-122

effects on income, 122-123
effects on prices, 124-125
effects on property taxes, 126-127
effects on property values, 127, 228-229
effects on public costs and revenues, 126-128
effects on trade and services, 123-124
effects on wages, 120-123
forms of, 120-128
special forms of. See Special impacts
Education. See Service impacts
Elderly. See Social impacts
Employment, 120-122
construction, 103-104, 106, 120-122
direct, 106
impacts, 120-122
indirect, 120-121
induced, 120-121
operation, 103-104, 106, 120-122
repository, 103-104, 106
secondary, 120-121
tertiary, 120-121
See also Economic impacts
Energy Impact Assistance Act of 1978, 190-191
Energy Facility Site Evaluation Council (EFSEC), 229
Energy Reorganization Act, 74-75
Environmental, 57-60, 80, 94-95
concerns, 57-60, 80, 94-95
impact statements, 57-60, 80, 94-95
Equity, 41-56
intergenerational, 50-53
geographical, 46-50

Ethical, 41-56
  approaches, 41-46
  dimensions, 41-56
  implementation ethics
    in, 53-54
Federal Mineral Lands Act
    of 1920, 190
Fire. See Service
  impacts
Fiscal, 119-134
  front-end financing,
    126-128, 224-225
  jurisdictional disputes,
    126-128
  jursidictional mis-
    matches, 126-128
  payment-in-lieu-of
    taxes (PILOT), 69,
    114, 126-128, 224-226
  tax-exempt status, 114,
    126-128, 224-226
Fiscal assessment, 128-134
  average cost approaches
    to, 132-133
  baseline projections in,
    132-133
  impact projections in,
    132-133
  marginal cost approaches
    to, 132-133
  methods for, 131-133
  per capita methods in,
    132
Fiscal impacts, 111, 126-
    128
  effects on costs, 126-
    128
  effects on revenues,
    126-128
  forms of, 126-128
  special forms of. See
    Special impacts

Garland, Utah, 189
Gillette, Wyoming, 192
Grand View, Idaho, 183-184
Gravity model, 148-149

Hartsville Project Coor-
    dinating Committee,
    198-199, 224
High-level wastes (HLW),
    6, 19-22

Housing. See Service
  impacts

Idaho Falls, Idaho, 189
Impact assessment, 101-176
  demographic, 143-156
  economic, 128-133
  fiscal, 128-133
  services, 143-156
  social, 163-174
  special. See Special
    impacts
Impacts, 101-176
  demographic, 135-143
  ecological, 91-99
  economic, 119-128
  ethical, 41-56
  factors affecting, 103-
    105
  fiscal, 119-128
  inmigrant effects on,
    108-109
  legal, 73-89
  local area effects, 105-
    108
  project effects on, 103-
    105
  service, 135-143
  social, 157-163
  special forms of, 112-
    115
  standard forms of, 110-
    112
  types of, 110-115
Impact management. See
  Mitigation

Jeffrey City, Wyoming,
    181, 195
Jim Bridger Power Plant,
    193
Joint Review Process
    (JRP), 198
Jurisdictions. See Fiscal

Kitsap County, Washington,
    188

Langdon, North Dakota,
    187-188
Lanham Acts, 187
Law Enforcement. See
  Service impacts

Legislation, 73-89, 189-
192
alternatives for, 73-89
impact assistance, 189-
192
siting, 83-89
Libraries. See
Service impacts
Location quotient, 131
Love Canal, 183
Lyons, Kansas, 33-34, 268-
269

Medical and mental health.
See Service impacts
Mercer County, North
Dakota, 186
Middle Fork Dam, 275
Migration. See
Demographic impacts
Military Construction
Authorization Act,
187-188, 190
Minnesota Pollution
Control Agency, 271-
272
Minnesota Waste Control
Agency, 271-272
Mitigation, 192-199, 201-
230
arbitration in, 197
compensation in, 64-66,
68-71, 214-216
company towns approaches
in, 194-195
finances for, 192-199,
211-212
framework for, 201-202,
204-207
forms of, 207-216
incentives in, 64-66,
68-71, 214-216
industry role in, 193-
195
legislation for, 224-225
reasons for, 202-204
systems theory in, 204-
206
task forces in, 225-226
Monitoring, 216-219
data collection in, 216-
217
reasons for, 179-182,
216

systems in, 216-219
Moses Lake, Washington,
189
MX missile, 233-250

National Environmental
Policy Act (NEPA), 60,
66-68, 80, 190-191
National Nuclear Waste
Policy Act of 1981, 192
Nuclear waste
containers for, 6, 24-27
demographic dimensions,
135-156
ecological dimensions,
91-95
economic dimensions,
119-134
environmental dimen-
sions, 94-95
ethical dimensions, 41-
56
fiscal dimensions, 119-
134
geologic dimensions, 19-
39
institutional dimen-
sions, 8, 97-98
intricacies of, 91-100
legal dimensions, 73-89
media for, 6, 32-34
management dimensions,
57-71
organizational dimen-
sions, 96-98
philosophical dimen-
sions, 41-56
quantity of, 20-22
repositories for. See
Repository
risk from, 19-22, 43-44
service dimensions, 135-
156
social dimensions, 157-
176
special dimensions. See
Special impacts
storage system for, 22-
32
technical dimensions,
19-39
transportation of, 114-
115, 128, 143
uncertainty in, 37-39,

42-43
National Waste Terminal
Storage (NWTS)
Program, 58-60
Northern Flood Agreement,
197-198

Office of Nuclear Waste
Isolation (ONWI), 58-
60
Oil Shale Trust Fund,
192-193
Ontario Hydro Monitoring
System, 196-197

Participant observation.
See Social assessment
Participation. See
Public involvement
Payment-in-lieu-of-taxes,
(PILOT). See Fiscal
Perry County, Mississippi,
137
Police. See Service
impacts
Population. See
Demographic
Power Plant and Indus-
trial Fuel Use Act,
190-191
Public involvement
(public participation),
11-12, 64-66, 68-70,
96-97, 115, 231-288
Public services. See
Service (community)
Price-Anderson Act, 227-
229

Quality of life. See
Social impacts

Radionuclides, 19-22
Recreation. See
Service impacts
Regulation,
See Legislation
Repository, 34-38
characteristics of, 34-
38
impacts of. See
Impacts
resource needs of, 34-38
types of, 34-38

Rio Blanco County,
Colorado, 193-194
Risk. See Nuclear
waste
Rock Springs, Wyoming,
136, 193

Safeguard Antiballistic
Missile System, 187-
188
Safeguard approach, 224-
225
San Juan County, Utah, 137
Searsport, Maine, 182-183
Service (community), 109,
111, 114, 135-156
accessibility of, 141-
143
characteristics of, 141-
143
costs of, 126-127, 131-
133
distribution of, 141-143
quality of, 141-143
quantity of, 141-143
standards for, 154
Service assessment, 152-
156
baseline projections
in, 152-154
impact projections in,
154-156
methods for, 152-156
per capita approaches
in, 132-133, 154-155
marginal approaches in,
132-133, 154-155
standards used in, 156
Service impacts, 141-143
effects on education,
152
effects on fire, 152-153
effects on housing, 152
effects on law
enforcement, 152-153
effects on libraries,
153
effects on medical and
mental health, 152
effects on recreation,
153-154
effects on social
welfare, 153

effects on solid waste
disposal, 153
effects on transpor-
tation, 153
effects on water
supplies, 153
effects on water
treatment, 153
special forms of. See
Special impacts
Settlement patterns. See
Demographic impacts
Severance taxes, 181, 193
Siting
concerns in, 1-16
dimensions of, 1-16
legislation for, 83-87,
182-184, 189-192
Social, 157-176
action, 253-254
exchange theory, 278-279
mobilization, 236-239,
277-278
planning, 253
Social assessment, 163-176
baseline projections
in, 163-174
community structure
analysis in, 166-172
impact projections in,
163-174
integrated methods for,
174-176
methods for, 163-176
participant observation
analysis in, 172-174
research needs in, 299
steps in, 174-176
survey analysis in, 164-
168
Social impacts, 157-163
effects on attitudes,
perceptions, and
values, 160-162
effects on elderly, 160
effects on inter-
action patterns and
social relations, 158-
159
effects on groups, 160
effects on quality
of life, 160
effects on roles and
statuses, 159

effects on social
organization and
institutions, 159-160
effects on social
structure, 160
forms of, 158-162
special forms of. See
Special impacts
Special impacts, 112-115
effects on demographic
factors, 143
effects on economic
factors, 122, 124-127
effects on fiscal
factors, 122, 124-127
effects on service
factors, 143
effects on social
factors, 162-163
forms of, 112-115
methods for assess-
ment, 112-115
research needs in, 297-
301
Social welfare. See
Service impacts
Solid waste disposal.
See Service impacts
Standard impacts. See
Impacts
Sweetwater County,
Wyoming, 193-194

Taxation. See Fiscal
Tennessee Valley
Authority (TVA), 198-
199
Three-Mile Island, 95, 98-
99
Toppenish, Washington, 189
Transportation. See
Service impacts
Transuranic wastes, 19-20
Trident Submarine Base,
188

United Power Association
(UPA), 185-186
U.S. Army Corps of
Engineers, 275-276
U.S. Department of
Energy, 57-62, 73-83

U.S. Environmental
    Protection Agency, 57-
    62, 73-83, 271-272
U.S. Nuclear Regulatory
    Commission, 57-62, 73-
    83

Vermont Yankee Nuclear
    Plant, 185
Vernon, Vermont, 185

Waste Isolation Pilot

Project (WIPP), 58,
    125, 272-273
Water supplies. See
    Service impacts
Water treatment. See
    Service impacts
Wes-Con, Inc., 183-184
Wilsonville, Illinois, 185
Wiscasset Yankee Nuclear
    Plant, 182-183
Workforce. See
    Employment
Wright, Wyoming, 194